P9-APN-782

PRENTICE HALL

SCIENCE EXPLORER

Human Biology and Health

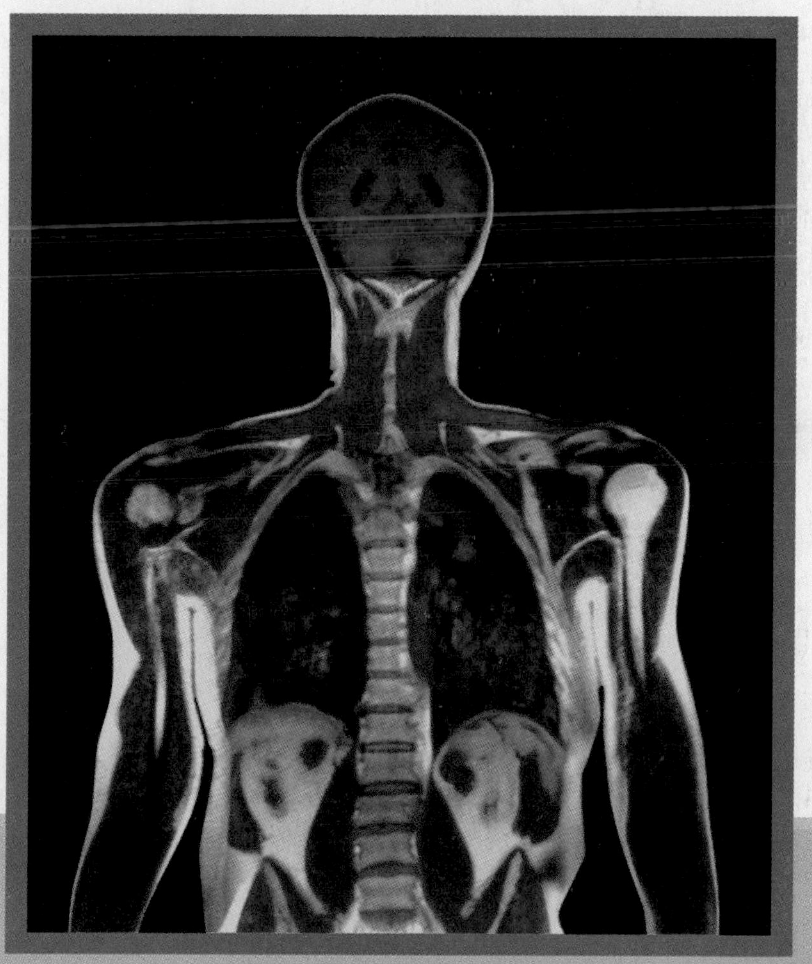

PRENTICE HALL
Needham, Massachusetts
Upper Saddle River, New Jersey

Human Biology and Health

Program Resources
Student Edition
Annotated Teacher's Edition
Teaching Resources Book with Color Transparencies
Human Biology and Health Materials Kits

Program Components
Integrated Science Laboratory Manual
Integrated Science Laboratory Manual, Teacher's Edition
Inquiry Skills Activity Book
Student-Centered Science Activity Books
Program Planning Guide
Guided Reading English Audiotapes
Guided Reading Spanish Audiotapes and Summaries
Product Testing Activities by Consumer Reports™
Event-Based Science Series (NSF funded)
Prentice Hall Interdisciplinary Explorations
Cobblestone, Odyssey, Calliope, and *Faces* Magazines

Media/Technology
Science Explorer Interactive Student Tutorial CD-ROMs
Odyssey of Discovery CD-ROMs
Resource Pro® (Teaching Resources on CD-ROM)
Assessment Resources CD-ROM with Dial-A-Test®
Internet site at www.science-explorer.phschool.com
Life, Earth, and Physical Science Videodiscs
Life, Earth, and Physical Science Videotapes

Science Explorer Student Editions

From Bacteria to Plants
Animals
Cells and Heredity
Human Biology and Health
Environmental Science
Inside Earth
Earth's Changing Surface
Earth's Waters
Weather and Climate
Astronomy
Chemical Building Blocks
Chemical Interactions
Motion, Forces, and Energy
Electricity and Magnetism
Sound and Light

Staff Credits

The people who made up the *Science Explorer* team—representing editorial, editorial services, design services, field marketing, market research, marketing services, on-line services/multimedia development, product marketing, production services, and publishing processes—are listed below. Bold type denotes core team members.

Kristen E. Ball, **Barbara A. Bertell,** Peter W. Brooks, **Christopher R. Brown, Greg Cantone,** Jonathan Cheney, **Patrick Finbarr Connolly,** Loree Franz, Donald P. Gagnon, Jr., **Paul J. Gagnon, Joel Gendler,** Elizabeth Good, Kerri Hoar, **Linda D. Johnson,** Katherine M. Kotik, Russ Lappa, Marilyn Leitao, David Lippman, **Eve Melnechuk, Natania Mlawer,** Paul W. Murphy, **Cindy A. Noftle,** Julia F. Osborne, Caroline M. Power, Suzanne J. Schineller, **Susan W. Tafler,** Kira Thaler-Marbit, Robin L. Santel, Ronald Schachter, **Mark Tricca,** Diane Walsh, Pearl B. Weinstein, Beth Norman Winickoff

Acknowledgment for page 256: Excerpts from *A Kind of Grace* by Jackie Joyner-Kersee. Copyright ©1997 by Jackie Joyner-Kersee. Reprinted by permission of Warner Books, Inc.

ISBN 0-13-434487-1
10 03 02 01

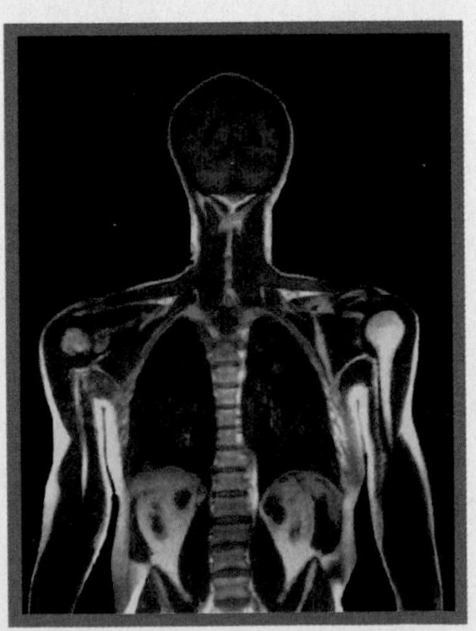

Cover: A magnetic resonance image (MRI) reveals structures within the human body.

Program Authors

Michael J. Padilla, Ph.D.
Professor
Department of Science Education
University of Georgia
Athens, Georgia

Michael Padilla is a leader in middle school science education. He has served as an editor and elected officer for the National Science Teachers Association. He has been principal investigator of several National Science Foundation and Eisenhower grants and served as a writer of the National Science Education Standards.

As lead author of *Science Explorer,* Mike has inspired the team in developing a program that meets the needs of middle grades students, promotes science inquiry, and is aligned with the National Science Education Standards.

Ioannis Miaoulis, Ph.D.
Dean of Engineering
College of Engineering
Tufts University
Medford, Massachusetts

Martha Cyr, Ph.D.
Director, Engineering Educational Outreach
College of Engineering
Tufts University
Medford, Massachusetts

Science Explorer was created in collaboration with the College of Engineering at Tufts University. Tufts has an extensive engineering outreach program that uses engineering design and construction to excite and motivate students and teachers in science and technology education.

Faculty from Tufts University participated in the development of *Science Explorer* chapter projects, reviewed the student books for content accuracy, and helped coordinate field testing.

Book Authors

Elizabeth Coolidge-Stolz, M.D.
Medical Writer
North Reading, Massachusetts

Dawn Graff-Haight, Ph.D., CHES
Associate Professor, Health Education
Linfield College
McMinnville, Oregon

Contributing Writers

Douglas E. Bowman
Health/Physical Education Teacher
Welches Middle School
Welches, Oregon

Patricia M. Doran
Science Teacher
Rondout Valley Junior High School
Stone Ridge, New York

Jorie Hunken
Science Consultant
Woodstock, Connecticut

Reading Consultant

Bonnie B. Armbruster, Ph.D.
Department of Curriculum and Instruction
University of Illinois
Champaign, Illinois

Interdisciplinary Consultant

Heidi Hayes Jacobs, Ed.D.
Teacher's College
Columbia University
New York, New York

Safety Consultants

W. H. Breazeale, Ph.D.
Department of Chemistry
College of Charleston
Charleston, South Carolina

Ruth Hathaway, Ph.D.
Hathaway Consulting
Cape Girardeau, Missouri

Tufts University Program Reviewers

Behrouz Abedian, Ph.D.
Department of Mechanical Engineering

Wayne Chudyk, Ph.D.
Department of Civil and Environmental Engineering

Eliana De Bernardez-Clark, Ph.D.
Department of Chemical Engineering

Anne Marie Desmarais, Ph.D.
Department of Civil and Environmental Engineering

David L. Kaplan, Ph.D.
Department of Chemical Engineering

Paul Kelley, Ph.D.
Department of Electro-Optics

George S. Mumford, Ph.D.
Professor of Astronomy, Emeritus

Jan A. Pechenik, Ph.D.
Department of Biology

Livia Racz, Ph.D.
Department of Mechanical Engineering

Robert Rifkin, M.D.
School of Medicine

Jack Ridge, Ph.D.
Department of Geology

Chris Swan, Ph.D.
Department of Civil and Environmental Engineering

Peter Y. Wong, Ph.D.
Department of Mechanical Engineering

Content Reviewers

Jack W. Beal, Ph.D.
Department of Physics
Fairfield University
Fairfield, Connecticut

W. Russell Blake, Ph.D.
Planetarium Director
Plymouth Community Intermediate School
Plymouth, Massachusetts

Howard E. Buhse, Jr., Ph.D.
Department of Biological Sciences
University of Illinois
Chicago, Illinois

Dawn Smith Burgess, Ph.D.
Department of Geophysics
Stanford University
Stanford, California

A. Malcolm Campbell, Ph.D.
Assistant Professor
Davidson College
Davidson, North Carolina

Elizabeth A. De Stasio, Ph.D.
Associate Professor of Biology
Lawrence University
Appleton, Wisconsin

John M. Fowler, Ph.D.
Former Director of Special Projects
National Science Teacher's Association
Arlington, Virginia

Jonathan Gitlin, M.D.
School of Medicine
Washington University
St. Louis, Missouri

Dawn Graff-Haight, Ph.D., CHES
Department of Health, Human Performance, and Athletics
Linfield College
McMinnville, Oregon

Deborah L. Gumucio, Ph.D.
Associate Professor
Department of Anatomy and Cell Biology
University of Michigan
Ann Arbor, Michigan

William S. Harwood, Ph.D.
Dean of University Division and Associate Professor of Education
Indiana University
Bloomington, Indiana

Cyndy Henzel, Ph.D.
Department of Geography and Regional Development
University of Arizona
Tucson, Arizona

Greg Hutton
Science and Health Curriculum Coordinator
School Board of Sarasota County
Sarasota, Florida

Susan K. Jacobson, Ph.D.
Department of Wildlife Ecology and Conservation
University of Florida
Gainesville, Florida

Judy Jernstedt, Ph.D.
Department of Agronomy and Range Science
University of California, Davis
Davis, California

John L. Kermond, Ph.D.
Office of Global Programs
National Oceanographic and Atmospheric Administration
Silver Spring, Maryland

David E. LaHart, Ph.D.
Institute of Science and Public Affairs
Florida State University
Tallahassee, Florida

Joe Leverich, Ph.D.
Department of Biology
St. Louis University
St. Louis, Missouri

Dennis K. Lieu, Ph.D.
Department of Mechanical Engineering
University of California
Berkeley, California

Cynthia J. Moore, Ph.D.
Science Outreach Coordinator
Washington University
St. Louis, Missouri

Joseph M. Moran, Ph.D.
Department of Earth Science
University of Wisconsin–Green Bay
Green Bay, Wisconsin

Joseph Stukey, Ph.D.
Department of Biology
Hope College
Holland, Michigan

Seetha Subramanian
Lexington Community College
University of Kentucky
Lexington, Kentucky

Carl L. Thurman, Ph.D.
Department of Biology
University of Northern Iowa
Cedar Falls, Iowa

Edward D. Walton, Ph.D.
Department of Chemistry
California State Polytechnic University
Pomona, California

Robert S. Young, Ph.D.
Department of Geosciences and Natural Resource Management
Western Carolina University
Cullowhee, North Carolina

Edward J. Zalisko, Ph.D.
Department of Biology
Blackburn College
Carlinville, Illinois

Teacher Reviewers

Stephanie Anderson
Sierra Vista Junior High School
Canyon Country, California

John W. Anson
Mesa Intermediate School
Palmdale, California

Pamela Arline
Lake Taylor Middle School
Norfolk, Virginia

Lynn Beason
College Station Jr. High School
College Station, Texas

Richard Bothmer
Hollis School District
Hollis, New Hampshire

Jeffrey C. Callister
Newburgh Free Academy
Newburgh, New York

Judy D'Albert
Harvard Day School
Corona Del Mar, California

Betty Scott Dean
Guilford County Schools
McLeansville, North Carolina

Sarah C. Duff
Baltimore City Public Schools
Baltimore, Maryland

Melody Law Ewey
Holmes Junior High School
Davis, California

Sherry L. Fisher
Lake Zurich Middle School North
Lake Zurich, Illinois

Melissa Gibbons
Fort Worth ISD
Fort Worth, Texas

Debra J. Goodding
Kraemer Middle School
Placentia, California

Jack Grande
Weber Middle School
Port Washington, New York

Steve Hills
Riverside Middle School
Grand Rapids, Michigan

Carol Ann Lionello
Kraemer Middle School
Placentia, California

Jaime A. Morales
Henry T. Gage Middle School
Huntington Park, California

Patsy Partin
Cameron Middle School
Nashville, Tennessee

Deedra H. Robinson
Newport News Public Schools
Newport News, Virginia

Bonnie Scott
Clack Middle School
Abilene, Texas

Charles M. Sears
Belzer Middle School
Indianapolis, Indiana

Barbara M. Strange
Ferndale Middle School
High Point, North Carolina

Jackie Louise Ulfig
Ford Middle School
Allen, Texas

Kathy Usina
Belzer Middle School
Indianapolis, Indiana

Heidi M. von Oetinger
L'Anse Creuse Public School
Harrison Township, Michigan

Pam Watson
Hill Country Middle School
Austin, Texas

Activity Field Testers

Nicki Bibbo
Russell Street School
Littleton, Massachusetts

Connie Boone
Fletcher Middle School
Jacksonville Beach, Florida

Rose-Marie Botting
Broward County School District
Fort Lauderdale, Florida

Colleen Campos
Laredo Middle School
Aurora, Colorado

Elizabeth Chait
W. L. Chenery Middle School
Belmont, Massachusetts

Holly Estes
Hale Middle School
Stow, Massachusetts

Laura Hapgood
Plymouth Community Intermediate School
Plymouth, Massachusetts

Sandra M. Harris
Winman Junior High School
Warwick, Rhode Island

Jason Ho
Walter Reed Middle School
Los Angeles, California

Joanne Jackson
Winman Junior High School
Warwick, Rhode Island

Mary F. Lavin
Plymouth Community Intermediate School
Plymouth, Massachusetts

James MacNeil, Ph.D.
Concord Public Schools
Concord, Massachusetts

Lauren Magruder
St. Michael's Country Day School
Newport, Rhode Island

Jeanne Maurand
Glen Urquhart School
Beverly Farms, Massachusetts

Warren Phillips
Plymouth Community Intermediate School
Plymouth, Massachusetts

Carol Pirtle
Hale Middle School
Stow, Massachusetts

Kathleen M. Poe
Kirby-Smith Middle School
Jacksonville, Florida

Cynthia B. Pope
Ruffner Middle School
Norfolk, Virginia

Anne Scammell
Geneva Middle School
Geneva, New York

Karen Riley Sievers
Callanan Middle School
Des Moines, Iowa

David M. Smith
Howard A. Eyer Middle School
Macungie, Pennsylvania

Derek Strohschneider
Plymouth Community Intermediate School
Plymouth, Massachusetts

Sallie Teames
Rosemont Middle School
Fort Worth, Texas

Gene Vitale
Parkland Middle School
McHenry, Illinois

Zenovia Young
Meyer Levin Junior High School (IS 285)
Brooklyn, New York

Contents

Human Biology and Health

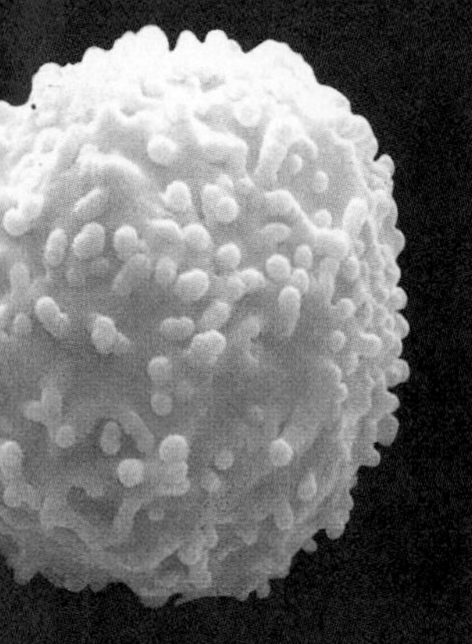

Activities

Inquiry Activities

CHAPTER PROJECT

Opportunities for long-term inquiry

Sharpen your Skills

Practice of specific science inquiry skills

DISCOVER

Exploration and inquiry before reading

TRY THIS

Reinforcement of key concepts

Skills Lab

In-depth practice of inquiry skills

Real-World Lab

Everyday application of science concepts

Interdisciplinary Activities

Math Toolbox

Science and History

Science and Society

Connection

Finding a Balance in NUTRITION

Nutritionist Alex Martinez's first experiment in science was on himself. Alex says that when he was growing up, he was quite chubby. Then as a high school freshman he began to play football and run track.

"My weight really hindered my athletic performance," he says. "It was very hard to turn down good cooking. But I knew if I wanted to get in shape, my eating habits would have to change." So Alex decided to change his diet by cutting back on fried foods and eating more fruits and vegetables. He also tried eating rice and chicken instead of beef, and he exercised.

"I became the subject of my own lab test, experimenting with different foods," Alex says. "And I could see the results. I lost weight and had more energy and endurance. I could run longer distances, and sometimes even passed my friends down the home stretch in the 100-yard dash. I felt a lot better about myself."

Alex Martinez, a Mexican American, grew up in New Mexico. He has a degree in nutrition and food science from New Mexico State University. He works as a roving health instructor, traveling to different cities in New Mexico to teach people about nutrition. An outdoor enthusiast, Alex spends his free time in the mountains—hiking, bicycling, and rock climbing.

That experience inspired Alex to pursue a career in nutrition, studying how the body uses food to grow and produce energy. Today, Alex is a nutritionist and health educator in New Mexico.

"For me, food is a science," Alex says. "Most people don't think of it that way. But food causes chemical reactions in the body. And those reactions all have specific effects."

Alex plans nutritious diets for people. At a camp for diabetic children, he helped young people plan diets to keep their blood sugar levels balanced. Currently he speaks to parent and student groups about healthy eating habits. He believes that eating right is not hard.

"There's no such thing as good food and bad food," Alex says. "All foods are good. We just have to balance them in our lives."

Talking With **Alex Martinez**

Q *How did you become interested in nutrition?*

A When I was training for track and football as a teen, I did a lot of reading about the right things to eat. My coaches were always talking about proper nutrition for athletes. When I found out there were college programs in nutrition, I knew that's what I wanted to study.

Q *How much science is involved in nutrition?*

A Quite a lot. I studied chemistry, biology, and human physiology. I learned how the body works—what allows me to run down the street, and how my body converts food into energy. Good nutrition is the starting point for this energy.

Q *Why should young people be concerned about nutrition?*

A Two reasons: Around the age of 11 or 12, teens start to go through growth spurts. A good, balanced diet is critically important to meet the demands of a changing body. Also, the habits young people develop at an early age stay with them for the rest of their life. If they want to be healthy when they grow up, they should be developing healthy eating habits right now.

Exercising (top) and eating a variety of nutritious foods (left) are keys to good health.

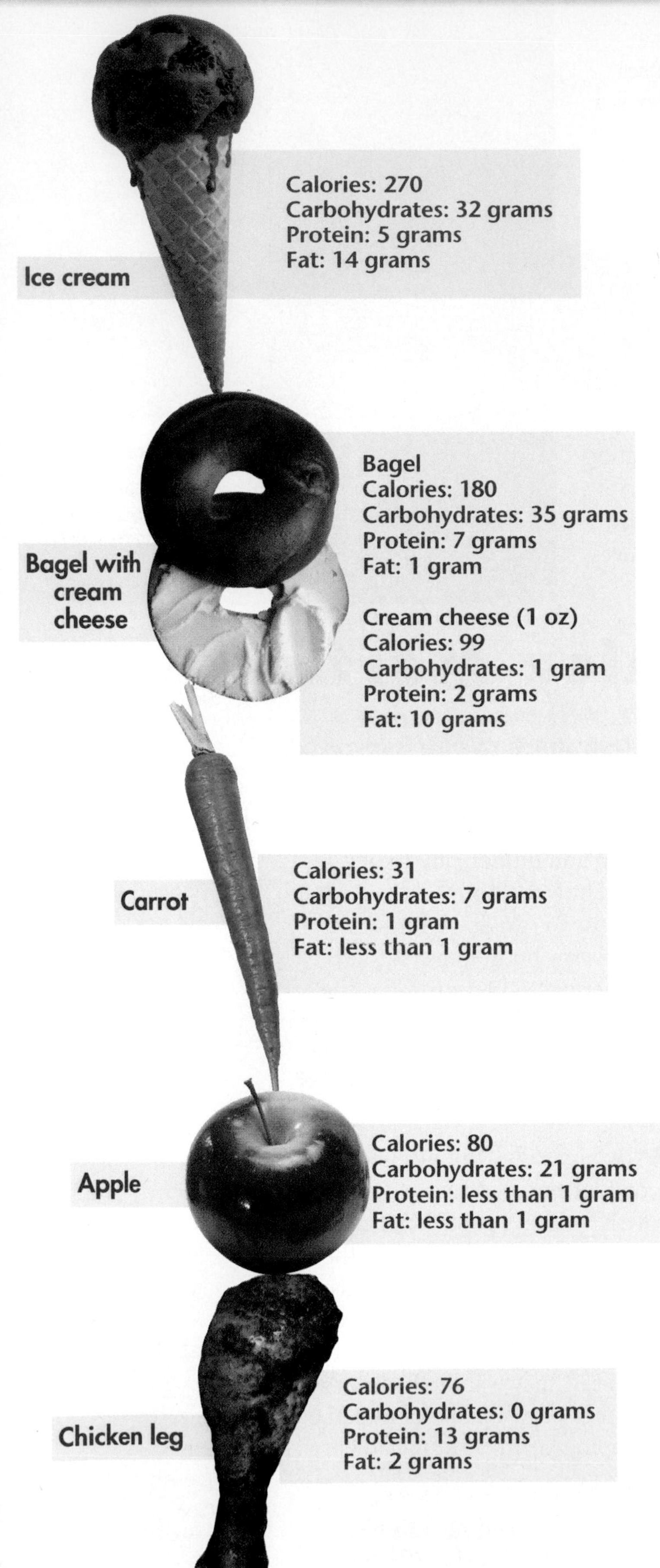

Q ***What ingredients in foods are important to teens?***

A Iron is very important for developing muscles and for helping to carry oxygen through the bloodstream. Without enough iron, people may feel overly tired. Calcium is also important. It plays a critical role in strong bone development. It's especially important for teenage girls to build strong bones. Later in life, women's bones tend to break more easily.

Q ***What about fat?***

A Fat is very important. It helps regulate hormones and vitamin absorption. But there are good fats and bad fats. Too many saturated fats, like those found in steak or hamburger, aren't good for people. Monounsaturated fats, found in foods such as nuts, are much healthier.

Q ***Is sugar important?***

A Yes, although like fat, people tend to eat too much of it. Sugar is a kind of carbohydrate. It's a person's primary energy source. But people shouldn't get sugar from candy bars and soda. Those are simple carbohydrates, low in nutrition. It's better to get sugar from foods such as fruits. They contain vitamins and minerals in addition to sugars.

Q ***Are there specific foods that young people should avoid?***

A My philosophy is that people can eat almost anything they want, as long as they balance it out. If they're dying for a hamburger and french fries one day, there's nothing wrong with that. They just have to balance it the next day by eating fruits and vegetables, and by getting more exercise.

Fresh fruits are good sources of carbohydrates, vitamins, and minerals.

Q ***What kinds of problems can an unbalanced diet create?***

A I'll give you an example. A patient of mine loves ice cream—she eats it all the time. Her diet was really high in fat and lacking in a lot of vitamins and minerals. She wasn't overweight. But she was always feeling tired.

Q ***What did you recommend?***

A I suggested that she eat less ice cream and instead add more natural sources of carbohydrates, such as grains, cereal, and fruit. She could still eat the same number of Calories, but from different, healthier sources.

Q ***How do you determine the proper diet for a person?***

A I use a formula based on age, weight, and a person's activity level to calculate the caloric intake—how much the person should eat every day. Then I try to get an idea about what he or she is already eating. Gradually I help the person convert to a healthy balance of about 60 percent carbohydrates and 30 percent fat.

Q ***Why is exercise important?***

A Every Calorie we take in, we have to burn off—otherwise, it stays around our hips and waist, especially when we get older. Also, exercising releases endorphins, a substance in our body that makes us feel good. Exercise keeps us healthy and feeling good about ourselves.

Q ***What goal should people set?***

A The goal is to be healthy. We can't all be professional athletes. But we can try to eat right and stay fit. And as long as we're trying, that makes a world of difference.

In Your Journal

Alex describes how his personal experiences influenced his career choice. Think about how experiences growing up can help a person choose a career many years later. Describe an experience in your life that might influence your career choice in the future.

CHAPTER 1

Healthy Body Systems

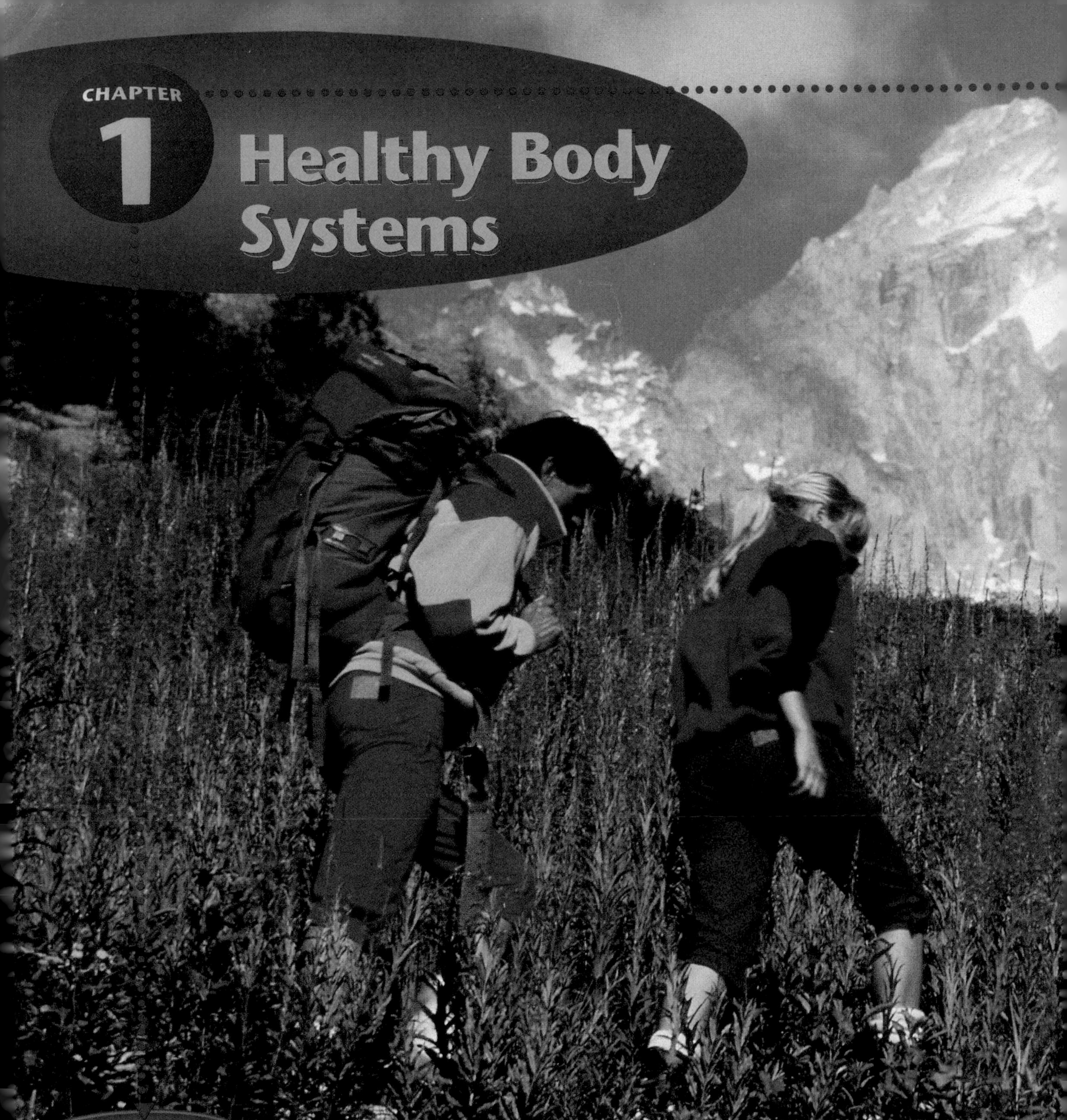

WHAT'S AHEAD

SECTION 1 How the Body Is Organized

Discover How Do You Lift Books?
Try This How Is a Book Organized?
Real-World Lab A Body of Knowledge

SECTION 2 Keeping the Body in Balance

Discover What Happens When You Are Startled?
Sharpen Your Skills Interpreting Data

SECTION 3 Wellness

Discover How Well Do You Take Care of Your Health?
Try This Wellness in the Balance

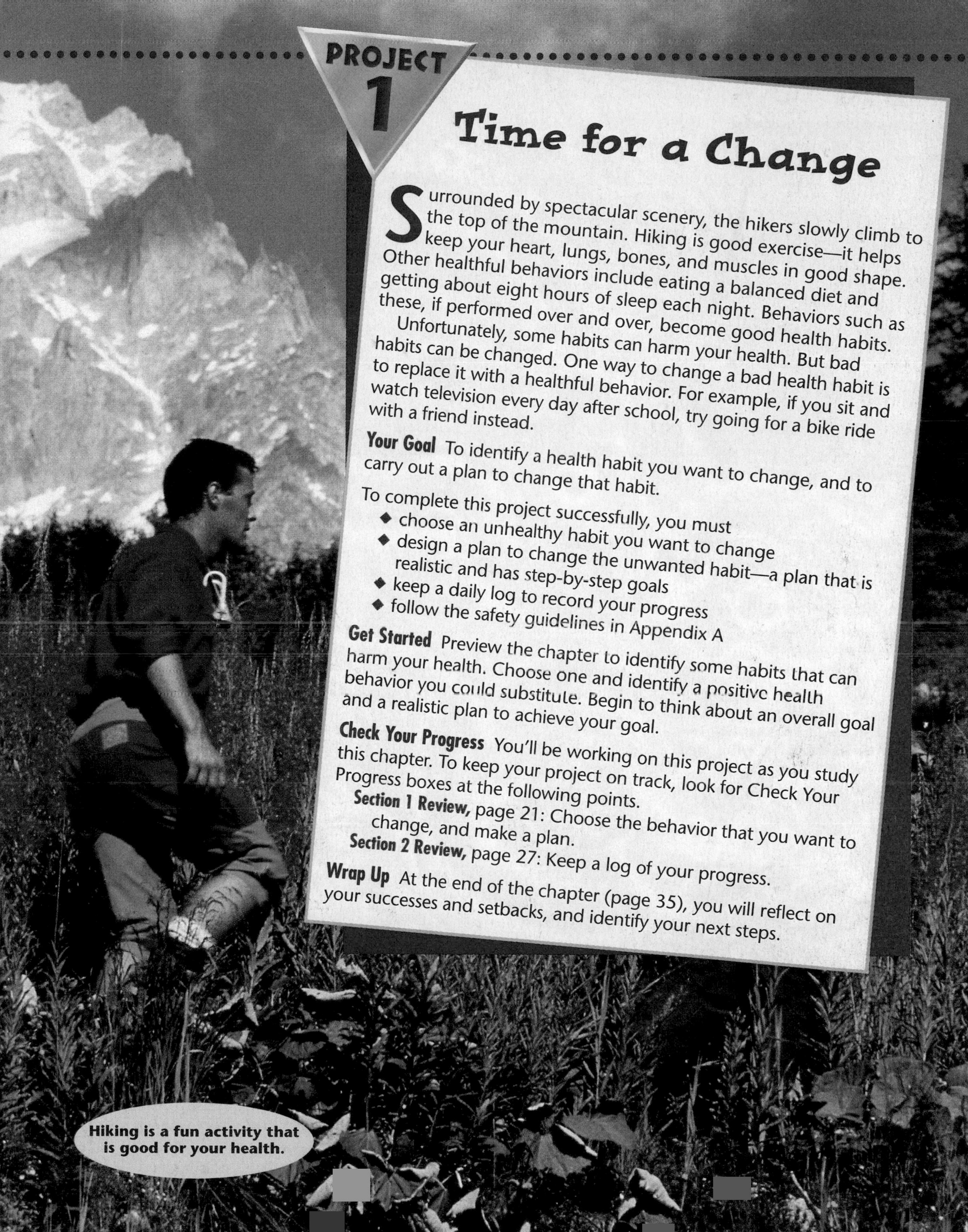

PROJECT 1

Time for a Change

Surrounded by spectacular scenery, the hikers slowly climb to the top of the mountain. Hiking is good exercise—it helps keep your heart, lungs, bones, and muscles in good shape. Other healthful behaviors include eating a balanced diet and getting about eight hours of sleep each night. Behaviors such as these, if performed over and over, become good health habits.

Unfortunately, some habits can harm your health. But bad habits can be changed. One way to change a bad health habit is to replace it with a healthful behavior. For example, if you sit and watch television every day after school, try going for a bike ride with a friend instead.

Your Goal To identify a health habit you want to change, and to carry out a plan to change that habit.

To complete this project successfully, you must

- choose an unhealthy habit you want to change
- design a plan to change the unwanted habit—a plan that is realistic and has step-by-step goals
- keep a daily log to record your progress
- follow the safety guidelines in Appendix A

Get Started Preview the chapter to identify some habits that can harm your health. Choose one and identify a positive health behavior you could substitute. Begin to think about an overall goal and a realistic plan to achieve your goal.

Check Your Progress You'll be working on this project as you study this chapter. To keep your project on track, look for Check Your Progress boxes at the following points.

Section 1 Review, page 21: Choose the behavior that you want to change, and make a plan.

Section 2 Review, page 27: Keep a log of your progress.

Wrap Up At the end of the chapter (page 35), you will reflect on your successes and setbacks, and identify your next steps.

Hiking is a fun activity that is good for your health.

How the Body Is Organized

DISCOVER ACTIVITY

How Do You Lift Books?

1. Stack one book on top of another one.
2. Lift the two stacked books in front of you so the lowest book is about level with your shoulders. Hold the books in this position for 30 seconds. While you are performing this activity, note how your body responds. For example, how do your arms feel at the beginning and toward the end of the 30 seconds?
3. Balance one book on the top of your head. Walk a few steps with the book on your head.

Think It Over

Inferring List all the parts of your body that worked together as you performed the activities in Steps 1 through 3.

GUIDE FOR READING

- What are the levels of organization in the body?
- What are the four basic types of tissue in the human body?

Reading Tip Before you read, preview *Exploring Levels of Organization in the Body.* Write down any unfamiliar words. Then, as you read, write their definitions.

The bell rings—lunchtime at last! You hurry down the noisy halls toward the cafeteria. The unmistakable aroma of hot pizza makes your mouth water. At last, after waiting in line, you pick up a plate with a slice of pizza and some salad. When you get to the cashier, you dig in your pocket for lunch money. Then, carefully balancing your tray, you scan the crowded cafeteria for your friends. You spot them, walk to their table, sit down, and begin to eat.

Think for a minute about how many parts of your body were involved in the simple act of getting and eating your lunch. You heard the bell with your ears and smelled the pizza with your nose. Bones and muscles worked together as you walked to the cafeteria, picked up your food, and sat down at the table. Without your brain, you couldn't have remembered where you put your lunch money. Once you began to eat, your teeth chewed the food and your throat muscles swallowed it. Then other parts of your digestive system, such as your stomach, began to process the food for your body to use.

Levels of Organization

Every minute of the day, whether you are eating, studying, playing basketball, or even sleeping, your body is busily at work. Each part of the body has a specific job to do, and all the different parts work together. This smooth functioning is due partly to the way in which the human body is organized. **The levels of organization in the human body consist of cells, tissues, organs, and organ systems.** The smallest unit is the cell, and the largest is the organ system. As you read about each level of organization, refer to *Exploring Levels of Organization in the Body,* which shows how your skeletal system is organized.

☑ ***Checkpoint*** *What is the largest level of organization in the human body?*

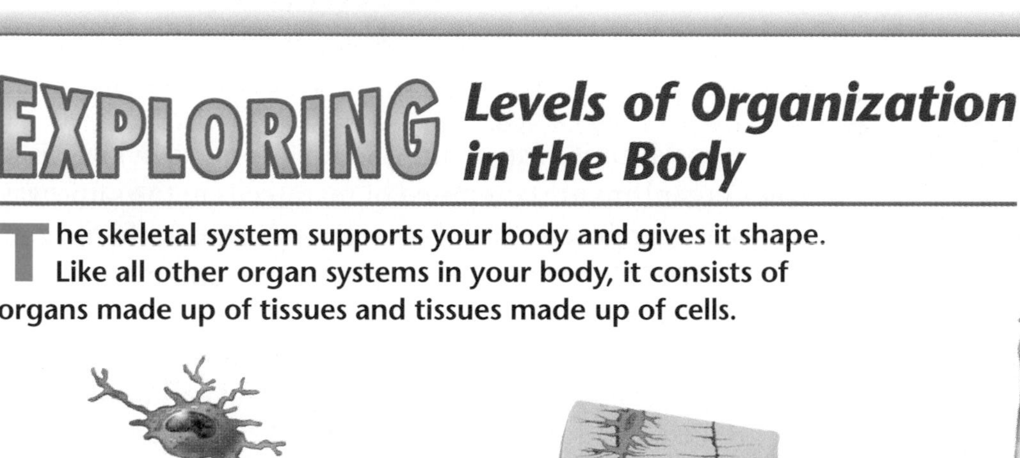

EXPLORING Levels of Organization in the Body

The skeletal system supports your body and gives it shape. Like all other organ systems in your body, it consists of organs made up of tissues and tissues made up of cells.

1 **Cell** Bone cells are responsible for bone growth and repair. Each bone cell has thin extensions that project into the nonliving material around it, which the cells produce.

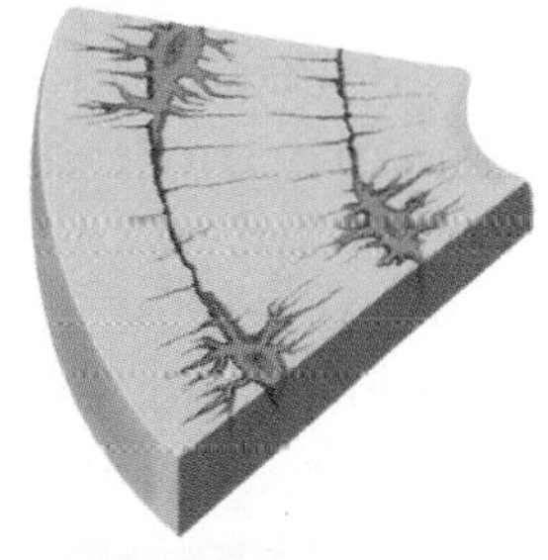

2 **Tissue** Bone tissue consists of living cells that are widely separated from one another by hard, nonliving material. This hard material gives bones their strength.

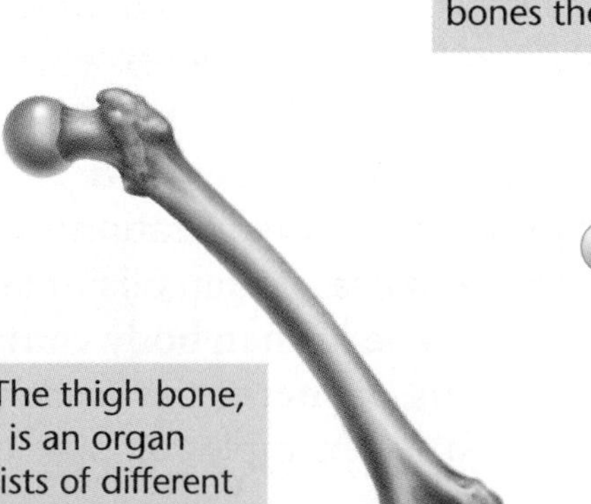

3 **Organ** The thigh bone, or femur, is an organ that consists of different kinds of tissues. Besides tissue made of bone cells, a bone contains blood and nerve tissue.

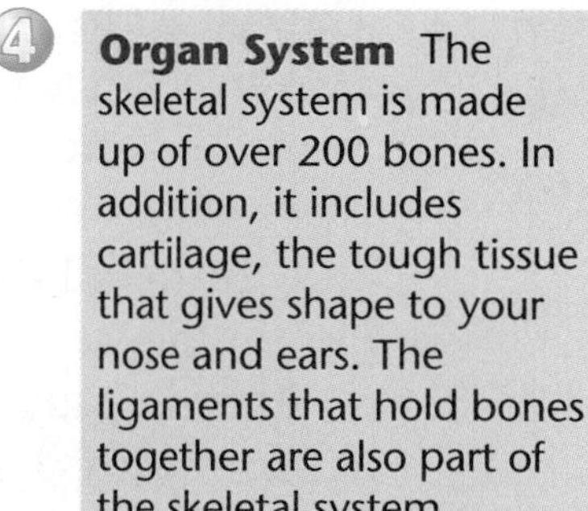

4 **Organ System** The skeletal system is made up of over 200 bones. In addition, it includes cartilage, the tough tissue that gives shape to your nose and ears. The ligaments that hold bones together are also part of the skeletal system.

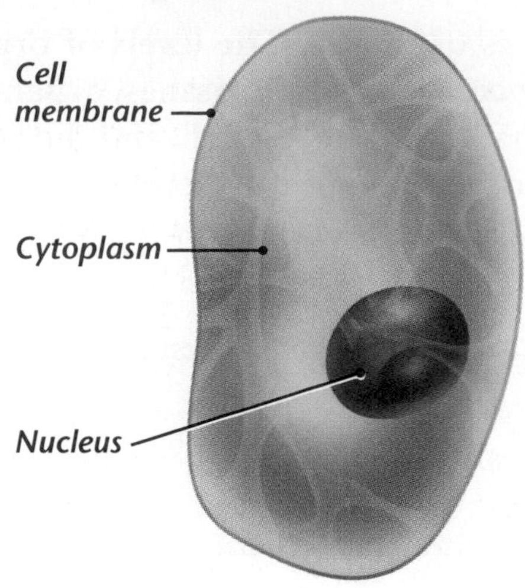

Figure 1 The cells in your body are surrounded by a cell membrane, and most have a nucleus. The cytoplasm is the area between the cell membrane and the nucleus.

How Is a Book Organized? ACTIVITY

In this activity, you will analyze the levels of organization in a book.

1. Examine this textbook to see how it is subdivided—into chapters, sections, and so on.
2. Make a concept map that shows this pattern of organization. Place the largest subdivision at the top of the map and the smallest at the bottom.
3. Compare the levels of organization in this book to those in the human body.

Making Models Which level of organization in the book represents cells? Which represent tissues, organs, and organ systems?

Cells

A **cell** is the basic unit of structure and function in a living thing. Complex organisms are composed of many cells in the same way a building is composed of many bricks. The human body contains about 100 trillion cells. Cells are quite tiny, and most cannot be seen without a microscope.

Most animal cells, including those in the human body, have a structure similar to the cell in Figure 1. The **cell membrane** forms the outside boundary of the cell. Inside the cell membrane is a large structure called the **nucleus.** The nucleus is the control center that directs the cell's activities and contains information that determines the cell's characteristics. When the cell divides, or reproduces, this information is passed onto the newly formed cells. The area between the cell membrane and the nucleus is called the **cytoplasm.** The cytoplasm contains a clear, jellylike substance in which many important cell structures are found.

Cells carry on the processes that keep organisms alive. Inside cells, for example, molecules from digested food undergo chemical reactions that provide energy for the body's activities.

☑ ***Checkpoint*** *What is the function of the nucleus?*

Tissues

The cell is the smallest unit of organization in your body; the next level is a tissue. A **tissue** is a group of similar cells that perform the same function. **The human body contains four basic types of tissue: muscle tissue, nerve tissue, connective tissue, and epithelial tissue.** To see examples of each of these tissues, look at Figure 2.

Like the muscle cells that form it, **muscle tissue** can contract, or shorten. By doing this, muscle tissue makes parts of your body move. When you turn the pages of this book or focus your eyes on this page, you are using muscle tissue.

While muscle tissue carries out movement, nerve tissue directs and controls it. **Nerve tissue** carries messages back and forth between the brain and every other part of the body. Your brain is made up mostly of nerve tissue.

Connective tissue provides support for your body and connects all its parts. Bone is one kind of connective tissue; its strength and hardness support your body and protect its delicate structures. Fat, which pads parts of your body, provides insulation from cold, and stores energy, is also a connective tissue. So is blood, which travels to all parts of your body.

Epithelial tissue (ep uh THEE lee ul) covers the surfaces of your body, inside and out. Some epithelial tissue, such as the outermost layer of your skin, protects the delicate structures that lie

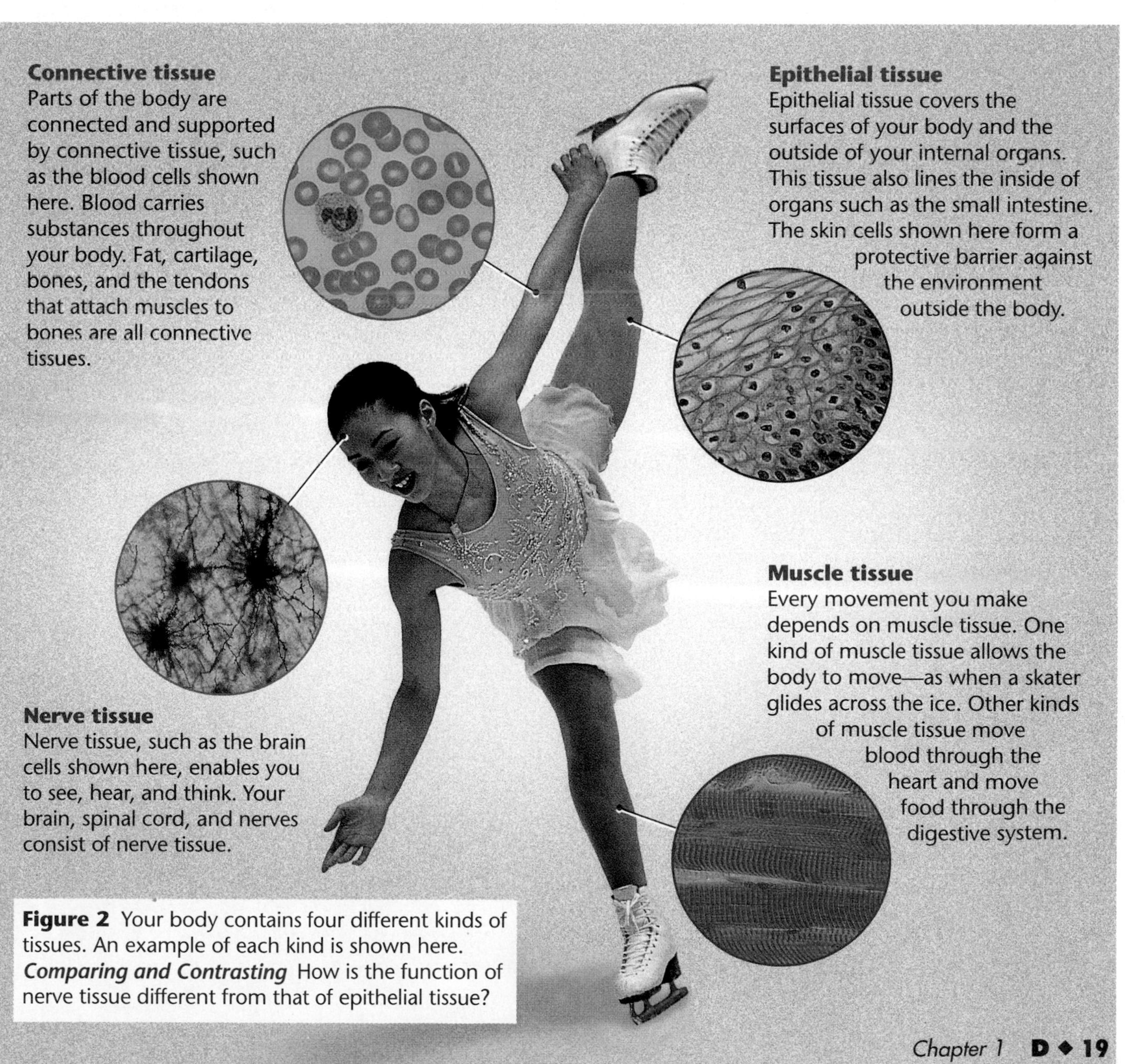

Figure 2 Your body contains four different kinds of tissues. An example of each kind is shown here. ***Comparing and Contrasting*** How is the function of nerve tissue different from that of epithelial tissue?

beneath it. Other kinds of epithelial tissue absorb or release substances. The lining of your digestive system consists of epithelial tissue. Some of the cells in this tissue release chemicals used in digestion, while others absorb digested food.

Organs and Organ Systems

Your stomach, heart, brain, and lungs are all organs. An **organ** is a structure that is composed of different kinds of tissue. Like a tissue, an organ performs a specific job. The job of an organ, however, is generally more complex than that of a tissue. The heart, for example, pumps blood throughout your body, over and over again. The heart contains all four kinds of tissue—muscle, nerve, connective, and epithelial. Each tissue type contributes to the overall job of pumping blood.

Each organ in your body is part of an **organ system,** a group of organs that work together to perform a major function. Your heart is part of your circulatory system, which carries oxygen and other materials throughout the body. Besides the heart, blood vessels are organs in the circulatory system. Figure 4 describes the major organ systems in the human body.

The different organ systems work together and depend on one another. You can compare the functioning of the human body to the work it takes to put on a school play. A play needs actors, of course, but it also needs a director, someone to make the costumes, and people to sell tickets. Similarly, when you ride a bike, you use your muscular and skeletal systems to steer and push the pedals. But you also need your nervous system to direct your arms and legs to move. Your respiratory, digestive, and circulatory systems work together to fuel your muscles with the energy they need. And your excretory system removes the wastes produced while your muscles are hard at work.

Figure 3 Each musician in the band contributes to the overall sound of the music. In the same way, each organ system in your body works with the other organ systems to keep you alive and healthy.

Organ Systems in the Human Body

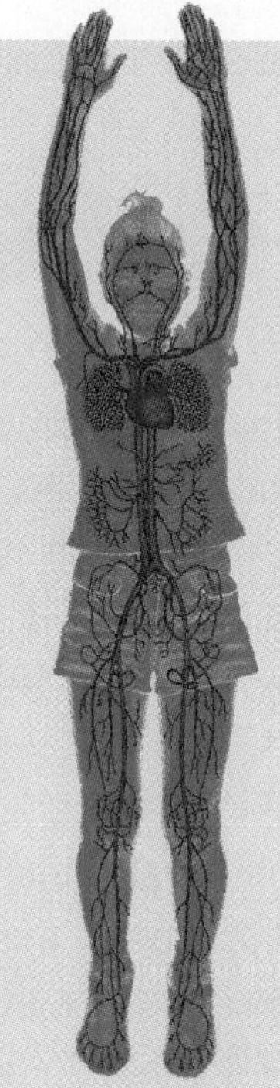

Endocrine Controls many body processes—such as intake of sugar by cells—by means of chemicals.

Excretory Removes wastes.

Immune Fights disease.

Muscular Enables the body to move; moves food through the digestive system; keeps the heart beating.

Nervous Detects and interprets information from the environment outside the body and from within the body; controls most body functions.

Reproductive Produces sex cells that can unite with other sex cells to create offspring; controls male and female characteristics.

Respiratory Takes oxygen into ▶ the body and eliminates carbon dioxide.

Skeletal Supports the body, protects it, and works with muscles to allow movement; makes blood cells and stores some materials.

Skin Protects the body, keeps water inside the body, and helps regulate body temperature.

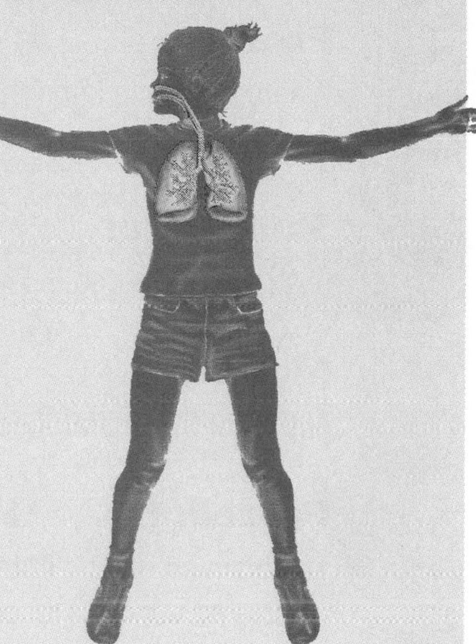

▲ **Circulatory** Carries needed materials to the body cells; carries wastes away from body cells; helps fight disease.

Digestive Takes food into the body, breaks food down, and absorbs the digested materials.

Figure 4 The human body is made up of eleven organ systems. ***Interpreting Charts*** Which two systems work together to get oxygen to your cells?

Section 1 Review

1. List the four levels of organization in the human body. Give an example of each level.
2. What are the four types of tissue found in the human body? What is the general function of each type?
3. Describe the structure of an animal cell.
4. **Thinking Critically Applying Concepts** What systems of the body are involved when you prepare a sandwich and then eat it?

Check Your Progress

CHAPTER PROJECT 1

Once you have chosen a behavior that you want to change, make a day-by-day plan. Get your teacher's approval for the plan. Then set up a log in which you will record your progress. Start now to work toward your first goal. (*Hint:* Your plan will be more successful if you set realistic intermediate goals along the way. For example, if you want to get more exercise, begin by exercising three times a week for a short period. Over time, you can gradually increase your exercise time and frequency.)

Real-World Lab

How It Works

A Body of Knowledge

In this lab, you will discover how much you already know about the human body.

Problem

Where are some important organs in the human body located?

Skills Focus

observing, inferring, posing questions

Materials

outline of the human body colored pencils

Procedure

1. Obtain an outline of the human body and five colored pencils. Notice that the outline shows a front view of the body, and that the right and left sides of the body are labeled.
2. Use one color to draw in the heart at the size and shape that you think it is. Draw the heart in the approximate place in the body where you think it is located. Label the heart on your drawing.
3. Select three different colors to represent the brain, lungs, and stomach. Draw each of these organs, showing its general size and shape and where you think it is located. Label each organ.
4. Choose one of the organs you just drew, and think of other organs that may be part of the same organ system. Draw those organs and label them. If the organs are part of a pathway, draw arrows to show the path.

Analyze and Conclude

1. Create a chart that lists the brain, heart, lungs, and stomach in the first column. In the second column, describe your understanding of the function of each of those organs.
2. Describe the role of the organ system you drew. How does it function in the body?
3. **Apply** For each organ in your chart, write one question you would like to have answered. Then write one question about the organ system you drew.

More to Explore

Find illustrations in this book that show the correct location of the organs you drew. Use a new body outline to make more accurate drawings of the organs and organ system.

Keeping the Body in Balance

DISCOVER — ACTIVITY

What Happens When You Are Startled?

1. Read this activity, and then close your eyes.
2. Your teacher is behind you and will pop a balloon at any moment.
3. Pay attention to how your body reacts when you hear the balloon pop. Observe whether you jump and whether your heartbeat rate and breathing rate change.
4. Observe how your body returns to normal after it responds to the sound.

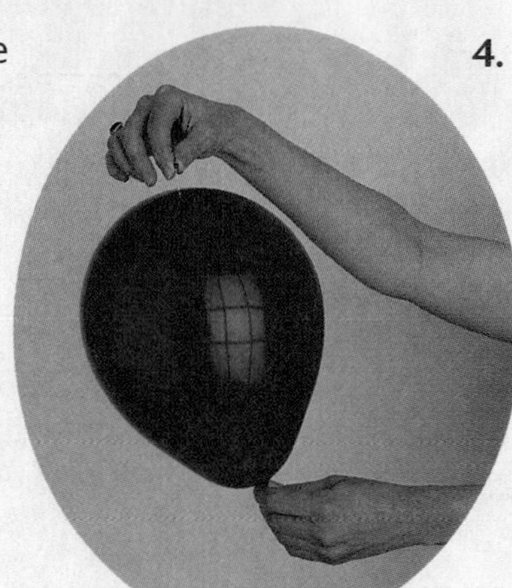

Think It Over

Predicting How might your body respond if you suddenly saw a huge, threatening animal rushing toward you? How might your response be an advantage to you?

GUIDE FOR READING

- What is homeostasis?
- What happens during the alarm stage of stress?

Reading Tip Before you read, write the headings in this section on a piece of paper, leaving a space after each. As you read, write a summary of the information under each heading.

Imagine that you are trapped in a damp, dark dungeon. Somewhere near you is a deep, water-filled pit into which you could fall. Overhead swings a pendulum with a razor-sharp edge. With each swing, the pendulum lowers closer and closer to your body.

The main character in Edgar Allan Poe's story "The Pit and the Pendulum" finds himself in that very situation. Here's his reaction: "A fearful idea now suddenly drove the blood in torrents upon my heart. . . . I at once started to my feet, trembling convulsively in every fibre. . . . Perspiration burst from every pore, and stood in cold, big beads upon my forehead."

Interpreting Data

ACTIVITY

A scientist fed a strong sugar solution to an animal. The scientist then checked the concentration of sugar in the animal's blood during the next three hours. The table below shows the results of the experiment.

Time After Eating Sugar (minutes)	Sugar Concentration (milligrams/ 100 milliliters)
0	75
30	125
60	110
90	90
120	75
150	75
180	75

Explain how the data show homeostasis at work. *(Hint:* Think about what happened to the blood-sugar level during the first hour and then during the next two hours.)

Homeostasis

Poe's character is reacting to danger. Your body, too, responds to threatening or startling events in specific ways. For example, your heart and breathing rates increase. Once you are no longer in danger or startled, your heart slows down. As the saying goes, you "breathe more easily."

The body's return to normal after a scare is one example of **homeostasis** (hoh mee oh STAY sis), the body's tendency to maintain an internal balance. **Homeostasis is the process by which an organism's internal environment is kept stable in spite of changes in the external environment.**

To see homeostasis in action, all you have to do is take your temperature when the air is chilly. Then take it again in an overheated room. No matter what the temperature of the air around you, your internal body temperature will be close to 37 degrees Celsius, as long as you are healthy. If you get sick, your body temperature may rise. But when you get well again, it returns to 37 degrees.

Your body has various ways of maintaining homeostasis. For example, you need food and water to stay alive. When your body is low on either of these substances, your brain sends signals that result in your feeling hungry or thirsty. When you eat or drink, you maintain homeostasis by providing your body with substances that it needs.

Figure 5 The wind is icy and the ground is covered with snow. In spite of the chill, the body temperatures of these sledders remain fairly constant at about 37° Celsius. ***Applying Concepts*** *What is the term for the body's tendency to maintain a stable internal environment?*

INTEGRATING CHEMISTRY When you perspire on a hot day, your body is maintaining its internal balance. When perspiration evaporates, the liquid water becomes water vapor, which is a gas. In order for a liquid to become a gas, heat must be added to it. As the water in perspiration evaporates, it absorbs heat from your body and carries it away. This removal of heat helps cool you down and enables your body to maintain a constant temperature on a hot day.

☑ ***Checkpoint*** *How do feelings of thirst help your body maintain homeostasis?*

Stress and Homeostasis

The rapid heartbeat and trembling of the character in "The Pit and the Pendulum" are both signs of stress. **Stress** is the reaction of your body and mind to threatening, challenging, or disturbing events. Many things can act as stressors, or events that cause stress. A snarling dog, an argument with a friend, or an upcoming oral report can all be stressors. Stress upsets homeostasis, and your body reacts in specific ways.

Physical Responses to Stress Figure 6 shows what happens in your body within seconds after you experience stress. During this stage, which is called the alarm stage, your body releases a

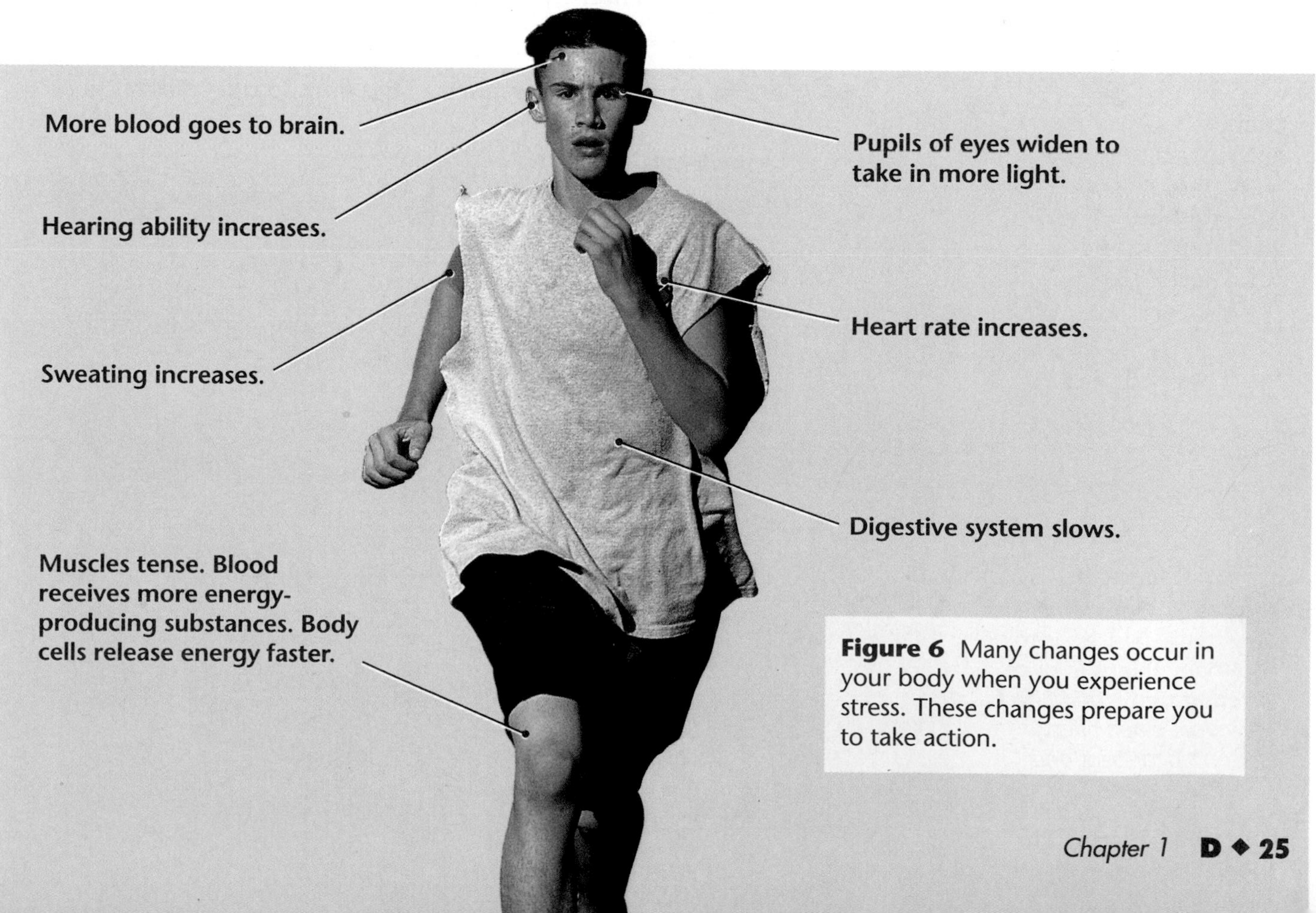

Figure 6 Many changes occur in your body when you experience stress. These changes prepare you to take action.

Language Arts CONNECTION

The quotation from "The Pit and the Pendulum" that you read at the beginning of this section (page 23) describes a character's reaction to extreme stress. Notice how the author, Edgar Allan Poe, uses detailed descriptions of the character's physical reactions, such as his rapid heartbeat and sweating, to convey the character's fear.

In Your Journal

Create a situation in which a character faces an extremely stressful situation. Describe the character's physical reactions and feelings. Make sure to use vivid and precise descriptive words that clearly convey the character's reactions.

chemical called **adrenaline** into your bloodstream. **Adrenaline gives you a burst of energy and causes many other changes in your body. These changes prepare you to take quick action.**

The effects of adrenaline, which take only a few seconds, are dramatic. Your breathing quickens, sending more oxygen to your body cells to provide energy for your muscles. That extra oxygen gets to your cells rapidly because your heart begins to beat faster. The faster heartbeat increases the flow of blood to your muscles and some other organs. In contrast, less blood flows to your skin and digestive system, so that more is available for your arms and legs. The pupils of your eyes become wider, allowing you to see better.

Fight or Flight The reactions caused by adrenaline are sometimes called the "fight-or-flight" response, because they prepare you either to fight the stressor or to take flight and escape. Scientists think that the fight-or-flight response was important for primitive people who faced wild-animal attacks and similar dangers. Today, the same reactions still occur with any stressor, whether it is a snarling dog or a social studies test.

During the fight-or-flight response, your body systems work together to respond to the stressor. For example, your respiratory system provides you with extra oxygen, which your circulatory system delivers to the parts of your body that need it. Your muscular system, in turn, works with your skeletal system to help you move—fast.

☑ *Checkpoint* *During the alarm stage, how do your eyes respond?*

Figure 7 Oops! One sure way to cause stress is to do too many things at once. ***Relating Cause and Effect*** *How does stress affect a person's heartbeat and breathing rates?*

Long-Term Stress

The alarm stage of stress only lasts for a short time. If the stress is over quickly, your body soon returns to its normal state. Some kinds of stressors, however, continue for a long time. Suppose, for example, you are stressed because you are moving to a new community. You cannot fight the stressor, and you cannot run away from it either. When a stressful situation does not go away quickly, your body cannot restore homeostasis. If you do not deal with the stress, you may become tired, irritable, and have trouble getting along with others. In addition, you may be more likely to become ill.

Figure 8 When you are under stress, it is important to find ways to relax.

Dealing With Stress

Stress is a normal part of life. No one can avoid stress entirely. When you are in a stressful situation, it is important that you recognize it and take action to deal with it, rather than pretending that the stressor doesn't exist. For example, suppose you aren't doing well in math class. If you accept the problem and deal with it—perhaps by asking your teacher for help—your stress will probably decrease.

In addition, when you are experiencing long-term stress, physical activity can help you feel better. Riding a bike, skating, or even raking leaves can take your mind off the stress. It is also important to talk about the situation and your feelings with friends and family members.

Section 2 Review

1. What is homeostasis?
2. Describe what happens during the alarm stage of stress.
3. Explain how your body temperature is an example of homeostasis.
4. What problems may result if a stressful situation does not go away quickly?
5. **Thinking Critically Making Judgments** What are three helpful ways of dealing with stress?

Check Your Progress

CHAPTER PROJECT 1

By now you should be carrying out your behavior-change plan. Keep a daily log to monitor your successes and setbacks. Don't be discouraged if things do not go exactly as you planned—just make adjustments to get yourself back on track. (*Hint:* Enlist your family and friends to support your effort. In addition, give yourself rewards, such as a trip to the movies, for reaching each intermediate goal you set.)

SECTION 3 Wellness

DISCOVER

How Well Do You Take Care of Your Health?

Answer *yes* or *no* to each question.

1. Do you engage in vigorous exercise, such as sports or brisk walking, several times a week?
2. Do you eat at least three servings of vegetables, two servings of fruit, and six servings of grain foods, such as bread, rice, and pasta, every day?
3. Do you get about eight hours of sleep each night?
4. Do you face and deal with stressful situations rather than ignore them?
5. Are you happy with yourself most of the time?
6. Do you have friends and family members you can turn to for help with a problem?

Think It Over

Making Judgments Add up the number of *yes* answers you gave. The more *yes* answers, the healthier the lifestyle you lead.

GUIDE FOR READING

- What are the three components of wellness?
- How can you think through a decision to make sure it is good for your health?

Reading Tip As you read, write a definition, in your own words, of each boldfaced term.

Tension is high as the soccer ball whizzes toward you. You aim your kick, and the ball soars into the net. You have scored the winning goal!

Playing soccer can be a great experience. The exercise is good for your body. But soccer does more than just keep your body healthy. It's fun to be part of a team and to share the thrill of competition. When your team plays well, you feel good about yourself and gain confidence in your abilities.

Components of Wellness

Everything you do, from playing soccer to going to the movies with friends, affects your overall level of health. **Wellness** is being at your best possible level of health—in your body, in your mind, and in your relationships with others. **Wellness has three components—physical health, mental health, and social health.**

Physical Health Your **physical health** consists of how well your body functions. When you are physically healthy, you have energy to carry out your daily tasks. To ensure your physical health, you need to eat healthy foods, exercise regularly, get enough sleep, and wear protective gear when you play sports. You also need to avoid harmful activities, such as smoking.

Mental Health Your **mental health** involves your feelings, or emotions—how you feel about yourself and how you handle the day-to-day demands of your life. When you are mentally healthy, you recognize your achievements and learn from your mistakes. Mentally healthy people handle stress well—by changing the stressful situation when they can, and by engaging in stress-relieving activities. In addition, people who are mentally healthy generally feel good about themselves.

Social Health **Social health** refers to how well you get along with others. When you are socially healthy, you have loving relationships, respect the rights of others, and give and accept help. Building healthy relationships with family members, making and keeping friends, and communicating your needs to others are all important for social health.

For teenagers especially, peer pressure can have an impact on social health. **Peer pressure** consists of pressure from your friends and classmates to behave in certain ways. Peer pressure can be good, if your friends encourage you to work hard in school and participate in sports and other healthy activities. Sometimes, however, you may experience peer pressure to do harmful things, such as drinking alcohol. Socially healthy people understand that it is okay to say no when they are asked to do things that can harm themselves or others.

Figure 9 Wellness means being at your best possible level of health. Having fun with friends (top) is part of social health. Physical health (middle) is important for demanding sports such as soccer. The feeling of accomplishment that comes from playing an instrument (bottom) helps develop mental health.

Wellness in the Balance

In this activity, you will make a mobile showing the three aspects of wellness.

1. Cut out a cardboard triangle about 20 cm on each side. Label the sides of the triangle "Physical Health," "Mental Health," and "Social Health." Tape a string to the center of the triangle.
2. Cut pictures from magazines showing activities that contribute to each of the three components of wellness.
3. Glue each picture onto a separate piece of cardboard. Tape one end of a string to each picture. Tape the other end to the appropriate side of the triangle. Hang the mobile from the center string.

Making Models How does your mobile show that all three components of wellness are important?

Overall Wellness Like three pieces in a jigsaw puzzle, your physical health, mental health, and social health are linked together. You can understand this if you think about what happens when a soccer team wins a game. To make the kick to score a goal, your body needs to be in good physical health. If you play well, you feel good about yourself—excited, happy, and proud. When you celebrate with your teammates, you enjoy good social relationships.

☑ ***Checkpoint*** *How is social health different from mental health? How are they related?*

Evaluating Your Wellness

Think for a minute about your overall level of health—physical, mental, and social. How healthy are you? You could think of your overall level of health as a point on a **continuum,** which is a gradual progression through many stages between one extreme and another. The illness-wellness continuum is shown in Figure 10. The far right end of the continuum represents perfect wellness, and the far left end represents very poor health, or even early death. The point in the middle is neutral—neither ill nor well. Your level of wellness is represented by a point somewhere between the two ends. For the most part, it is the behaviors that you choose that determine where on the continuum your level of health falls.

Figure 10 A person's level of health can be represented by a point on the illness-wellness continuum.
Making Judgments How can you improve your health and move closer to the wellness end of the continuum?

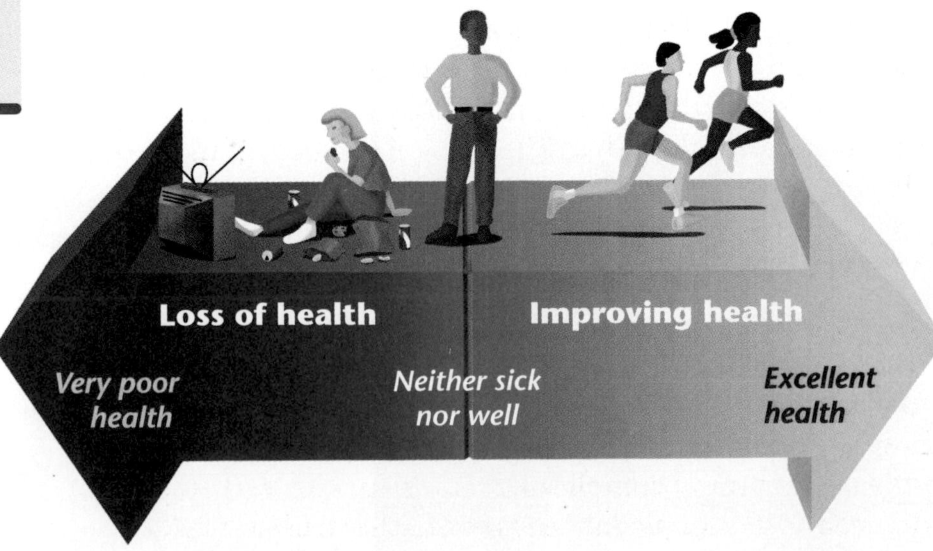

Figure 11 Snowboarding can affect your health in positive or negative ways. By taking proper precautions and being careful, snowboarding can be a positive experience.

Improving Your Health

Your health doesn't have to stay in the same place on the illness-wellness continuum. Working on wellness is a lot like keeping your room clean. You can't clean your room just once. After a few days, dirty clothes pile up, your trash basket overflows, and dust settles on everything. Like keeping your room tidy, you must work to improve your wellness every day.

Factors You Cannot Change Before you plan how to improve your wellness, you need to recognize that there are some health-related factors that you cannot change. Some of these may be traits that you inherited from your parents, such as skin that sunburns easily. However, you can still work toward wellness. You can use a sunscreen and limit your exposure to sunlight.

You probably cannot change the environment in which you live, even though it affects your health. Polluted air can damage the lungs and make the circulatory system struggle to get oxygen to the cells. Polluted water can carry chemicals and microorganisms that harm the body. Although you by yourself may not be able to change your environment, you can avoid some environmental risks. You can, for example, refuse to swim or fish in polluted water.

Making Wise Decisions Every day you make many decisions that affect your health. Some of these decisions, such as whether to wear a jacket on a cold day, are fairly simple. Others, such as how to deal with a friend who is pressuring you to use tobacco, may be a lot more complicated. For help with very important decisions, talk to a parent, teacher, or other trusted adult.

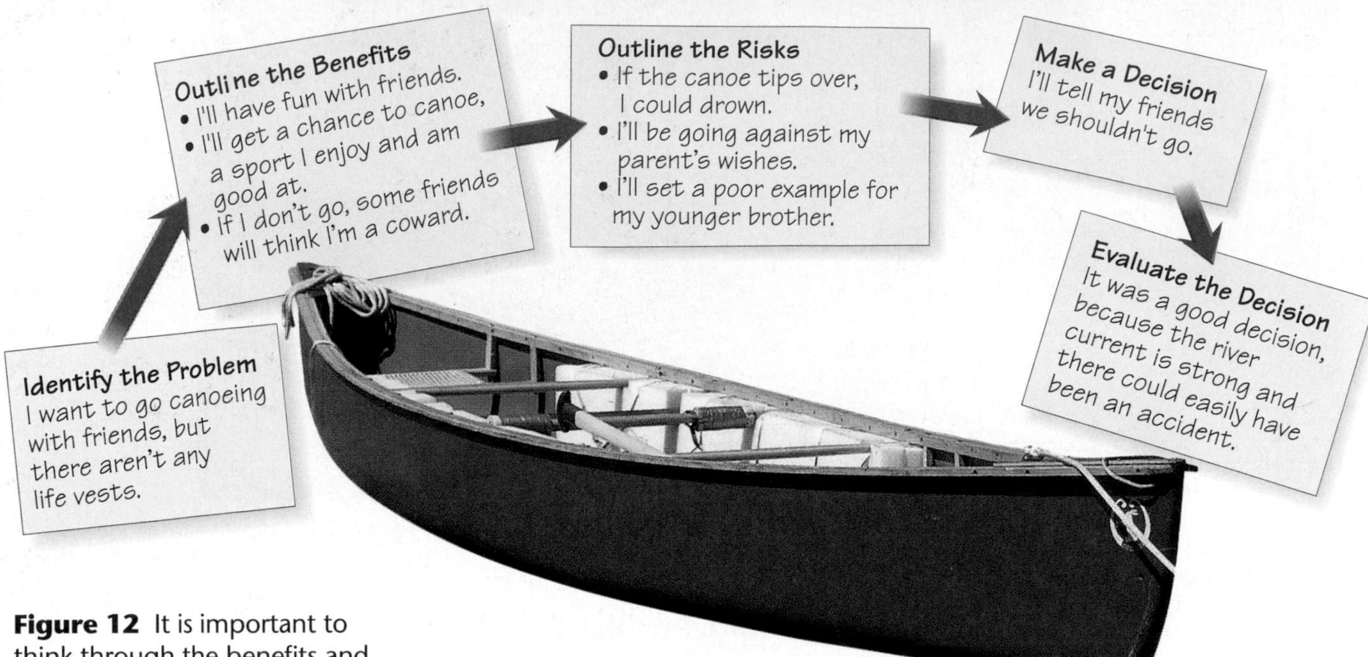

Figure 12 It is important to think through the benefits and risks of any decision you face. ***Problem Solving*** *What decision would you reach if you were faced with this problem?*

To make a healthy decision, it is important to think through the benefits and risks of an action you might take. You increase the likelihood of making a healthy decision if you think about it carefully beforehand. Evaluate the advantages and disadvantages of each choice you might make. Figure 12 shows how decision making can work in a real situation.

In this textbook, you will learn many ways to improve your health. You will discover that this textbook is something like an owner's manual. It will explain how your body works, and give you some suggestions for keeping your body healthy. The decision to do that is up to you.

Section 3 Review

1. Identify the three components of wellness. Briefly explain each one.
2. Explain the process involved in making a healthy decision.
3. Give an example of something that might change a person's position on the illness-wellness continuum. In which direction would the person move?
4. **Thinking Critically Inferring** How might having a friend who is very wellness-conscious affect your own level of wellness? Explain.

Science at Home

Explain to your family what the concept of wellness means. Then work with family members to identify four or five changes that you, as a family, could make to improve family wellness. Make sure to include changes that would improve mental and social health as well as physical health.

How the Body Is Organized

Key Ideas

- The levels of organization in the human body consist of cells, tissues, organs, and organ systems.
- The cell is the basic unit of structure and function in living things. The human body contains about 100 trillion cells.
- A tissue is a group of cells that perform the same function. The human body contains four basic types of tissue—muscle, nerve, connective, and epithelial.
- Organs, which are composed of different kinds of tissue, perform complex functions. An organ system is a group of organs that work together to perform a major function.

Key Terms

cell	nerve tissue
cell membrane	connective tissue
nucleus	epithelial tissue
cytoplasm	organ
tissue	organ system
muscle tissue	

Keeping the Body in Balance

Key Ideas

- Homeostasis is the process by which an organism's internal environment is kept stable in spite of changes in the external environment.
- Stress disturbs homeostasis. When under stress, the body releases adrenaline, which causes many changes in the body. The changes prepare the body to take quick action.
- Exercise and relaxing activities can help relieve stress.

Key Terms

homeostasis stress adrenaline

Wellness

INTEGRATING HEALTH

Key Ideas

- Wellness is being at the best possible level of health. The three components of wellness are physical health, mental health, and social health.
- Physical health consists of how well the body functions. Mental health consists of how you feel about yourself and how well you handle the demands of your life. Social health is how well you get along with other people.
- A person's overall level of wellness can range from very poor health to excellent health. Most people fall somewhere between those two points. Behavior can affect wellness, either by harming it or improving it.
- To make a health-related decision, you should consider both the benefits and the risks of any action.

Key Terms

wellness	social health
physical health	peer pressure
mental health	continuum

Reviewing Content

For more review of key concepts, see the Interactive Student Tutorial CD-ROM.

Multiple Choice

Choose the letter of the best answer.

1. A group of similar cells that perform a similar function is called a(n)
   a. cell.
   b. organ.
   c. tissue.
   d. organ system.
2. The control center of the cell is the
   a. cell membrane.
   b. cell fluid.
   c. cytoplasm.
   d. nucleus.
3. Which type of tissue is blood?
   a. muscle tissue
   b. epithelial tissue
   c. connective tissue
   d. nerve tissue
4. The term most closely associated with homeostasis is
   a. growth.
   b. stability.
   c. temperature.
   d. energy.
5. Which of the following is *not* a way to protect your social health?
   a. getting enough sleep
   b. making friends
   c. respecting the rights of others
   d. accepting help

True or False

If the statement is true, write true. If it is false, change the underlined word or words to make the statement true.

6. Epithelial tissue makes parts of your body move.
7. The circulatory system carries needed materials to the body cells.
8. The brain is an example of an organ.
9. The fight-or-flight response is part of the body's reaction to peer pressure.
10. Feeling good about yourself is one aspect of social health.

Checking Concepts

11. Explain the relationship between cells, tissues, organs, and organ systems.
12. What is the function of the respiratory system?
13. How does hunger help your body maintain homeostasis?
14. Think of a situation that might cause long-term stress. Identify some ways in which a person might deal with that stress.
15. List two possible health hazards in the environment, and explain how you might protect yourself from them.
16. **Writing to Learn** Imagine that you write a newspaper advice column called Ask Dr. Wellness. You receive the following letter:
    Dear Dr. Wellness: I am under a great deal of stress because I will soon be trying out for a major part in the school play. I want the part badly. How can I deal with this stress?
    Aspiring Actor
    Write an answer to this letter that gives Aspiring Actor some specific suggestions.

Thinking Visually

17. **Concept Map** The concept map below diagrams the three components of wellness. Copy the map and complete it. (For more on concept maps, see the Skills Handbook.)

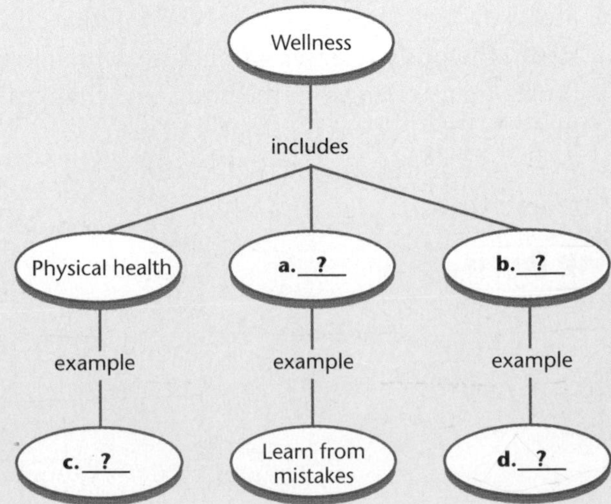

Applying Skills

The graph below shows the effects of the temperature of the environment on a girl's skin temperature and on the temperature inside her body. Use the graph to answer Questions 18–21.

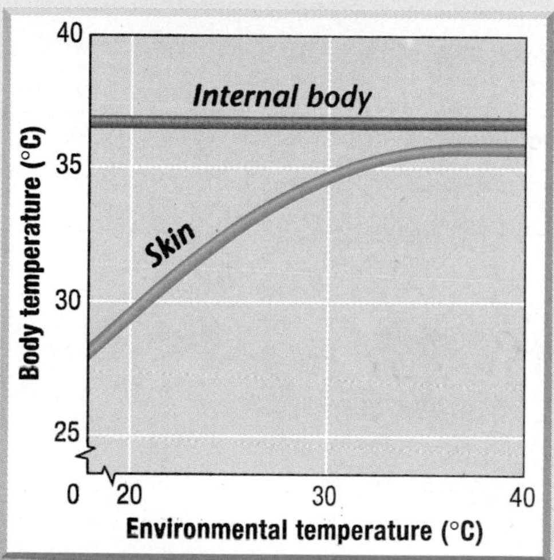

18. Interpreting Data As the temperature of the environment rises, what happens to the girl's internal temperature? How does this demonstrate homeostasis?

19. Inferring What happens to the temperature of the girl's skin? Why is this pattern different from the pattern shown by the girl's internal temperature?

20. Developing Hypotheses Suppose the girl went outdoors on a chilly fall morning. Write a hypothesis that predicts what would happen to her internal body temperature and skin temperature.

21. Designing Experiments Design an experiment to test your hypothesis from Question 20.

Thinking Critically

22. Making Judgments Suppose some friends were pressuring you to go skateboarding on a road with heavy traffic. Identify the benefits and risks of the choices you have. Then make a decision and explain your reasons.

23. Inferring Why do you think scientists classify blood as a connective tissue?

24. Making Generalizations How is homeostasis important to the survival of living things?

CHAPTER 1 REVIEW

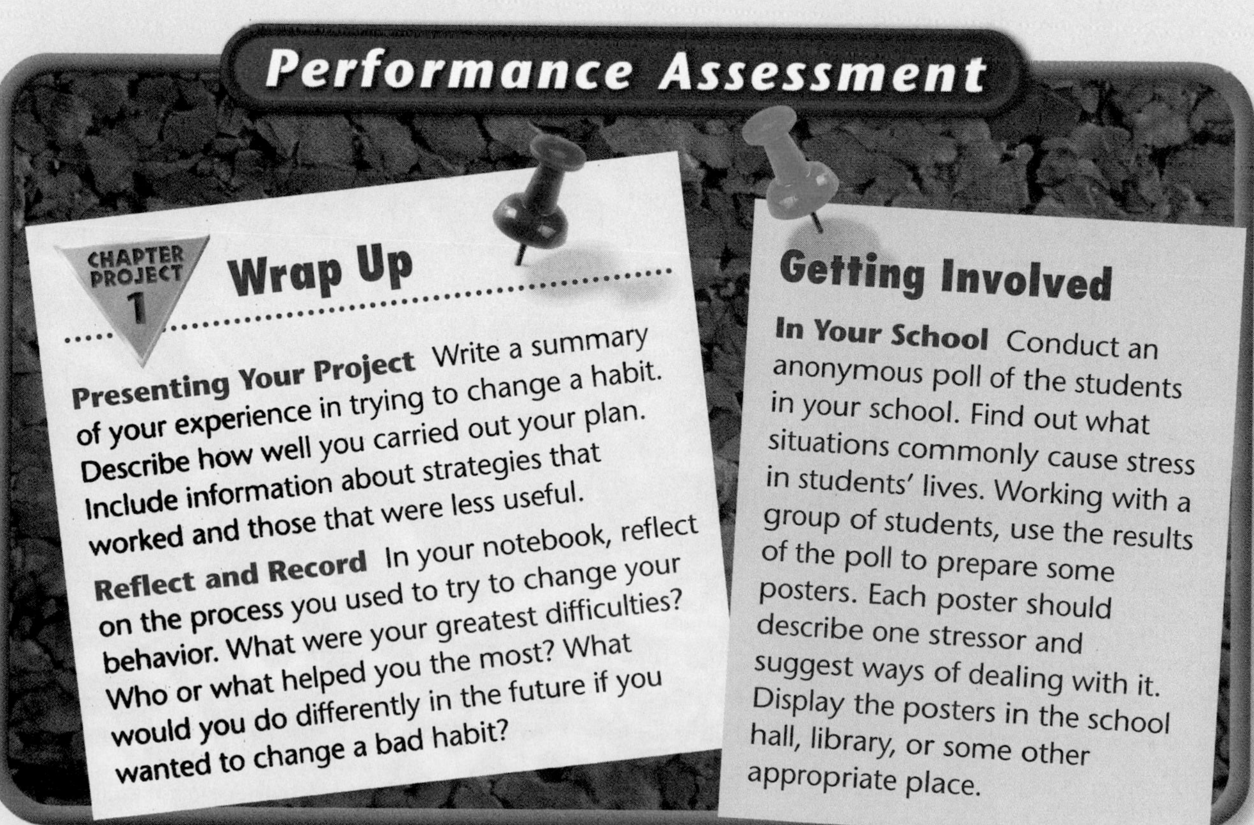

Performance Assessment

CHAPTER PROJECT 1

Wrap Up

Presenting Your Project Write a summary of your experience in trying to change a habit. Describe how well you carried out your plan. Include information about strategies that worked and those that were less useful.

Reflect and Record In your notebook, reflect on the process you used to try to change your behavior. What were your greatest difficulties? Who or what helped you the most? What would you do differently in the future if you wanted to change a bad habit?

Getting Involved

In Your School Conduct an anonymous poll of the students in your school. Find out what situations commonly cause stress in students' lives. Working with a group of students, use the results of the poll to prepare some posters. Each poster should describe one stressor and suggest ways of dealing with it. Display the posters in the school hall, library, or some other appropriate place.

CHAPTER 2

Bones, Muscles, and Skin

WHAT'S AHEAD

SECTION 1 The Skeletal System

Discover Hard as a Rock?
Try This Soft Bones?
Sharpen Your Skills Classifying

Integrating Technology

SECTION 2 Diagnosing Bone and Joint Injuries

Discover What Do X-Ray Images Show?

SECTION 3 The Muscular System

Discover How Do Muscles Work?
Try This Get a Grip
Skills Lab A Look Beneath the Skin

PROJECT 2

On the Move

People are able to perform an amazing variety of movements. For example, a baseball player can swing a bat, a chef can twirl pizza dough, and an artist can mold clay into a sculpture. Behind every human movement, there's a complex interaction of bones, muscles, and other parts of the body.

In this chapter, you'll find out how bones and muscles work. And in this project, you'll take a close look at a simple movement, such as stretching a leg, bending an arm at the elbow, or another movement you choose.

Your Goal To make a working model that shows how bones and muscles interact to move the body in a specific way.

To complete this project you will

- select a specific movement, and identify all of the major bones, joints, and muscles that are involved
- design an accurate physical model of the movement
- explain how the bones and muscles make the movement possible
- follow the safety guidelines in Appendix A

Get Started Let all group members name a motion from a sport or other familiar activity that they'd like to investigate. If the motion is long or complicated, discuss how to simplify it for the project. Also consider what kind of model you'll make, such as a wood or cardboard cutout, clay structure, or computer animation. Then write up a plan for your teacher's approval.

Check Your Progress You'll be working on this project as you study this chapter. To keep your project on track, look for Check Your Progress boxes at the following points.

Section 1 Review, page 45: Choose a simple motion to analyze and sketch.

Section 3 Review, page 54: Create your working model.

Wrap Up At the end of the chapter (page 65), you'll demonstrate your working model.

For this baseball player to hit the ball, his bones and muscles must work together in a coordinated manner.

SECTION 1 The Skeletal System

DISCOVER ACTIVITY

Hard as a Rock?

1. Your teacher will give you a leg bone from a cooked turkey or chicken and a rock.
2. Use a hand lens to examine both the rock and the bone.
3. Gently tap both the rock and the bone on a hard surface.
4. Pick up each object to feel how heavy it is.
5. Wash your hands. Then make notes of your observations.

Think It Over

Observing Based on your observations, why do you think bones are sometimes compared to rocks? List some ways in which bones and rocks are similar and different.

GUIDE FOR READING

- What are the functions of the skeleton?
- What role do movable joints play in the body?
- How can you keep your bones strong and healthy?

Reading Tip Before you read, rewrite the headings in the section as *how, why,* or *what* questions. As you read, write answers to the questions.

A construction site is a busy place. After workers have prepared the building's foundation, they begin to assemble thousands of steel pieces into a frame for the building. People watch as the steel pieces are joined to create a rigid frame that climbs toward the sky. By the time the building is finished, however, the building's framework will no longer be visible.

Like a building, you too have an inner framework, but it is made up of bones instead of steel. Your framework, or skeleton, is shown in Figure 2. The number of bones in your skeleton depends on your age. A newborn baby has about 275 bones. An adult, however, has about 206 bones. As a baby grows, some of the bones fuse together. For example, as a baby, you had many more individual bones in your skull than you do now. As you grew, some of your bones grew together to form the larger bones of your skull.

What the Skeletal System Does

Just as a building could not stand without its frame, you too would collapse without your skeleton. **Your skeleton has five major functions. It provides shape and support, enables you to move, protects your internal organs, produces blood cells, and stores certain materials until your body needs them.**

Figure 1 Like the steel beams that support a building, your skeleton supports your body.

Your skeleton determines the shape of your body, much as a steel frame determines the shape of a building. The backbone, or vertebral column, is the center of the skeleton. Locate the backbone in Figure 2. Notice that all the bones of the body are in some way connected to this column. If you move your fingers down the center of your back, you can feel the 26 small bones, or **vertebrae** (VUR tuh bray)(singular **vertebra**), that make up your backbone. Bend forward at the waist and feel the bones adjust as you move. You can think of each individual vertebra as a bead on a string. Just as a beaded necklace is flexible and able to bend, so too is your vertebral column. If your backbone were just one bone, you would not be able to bend or twist.

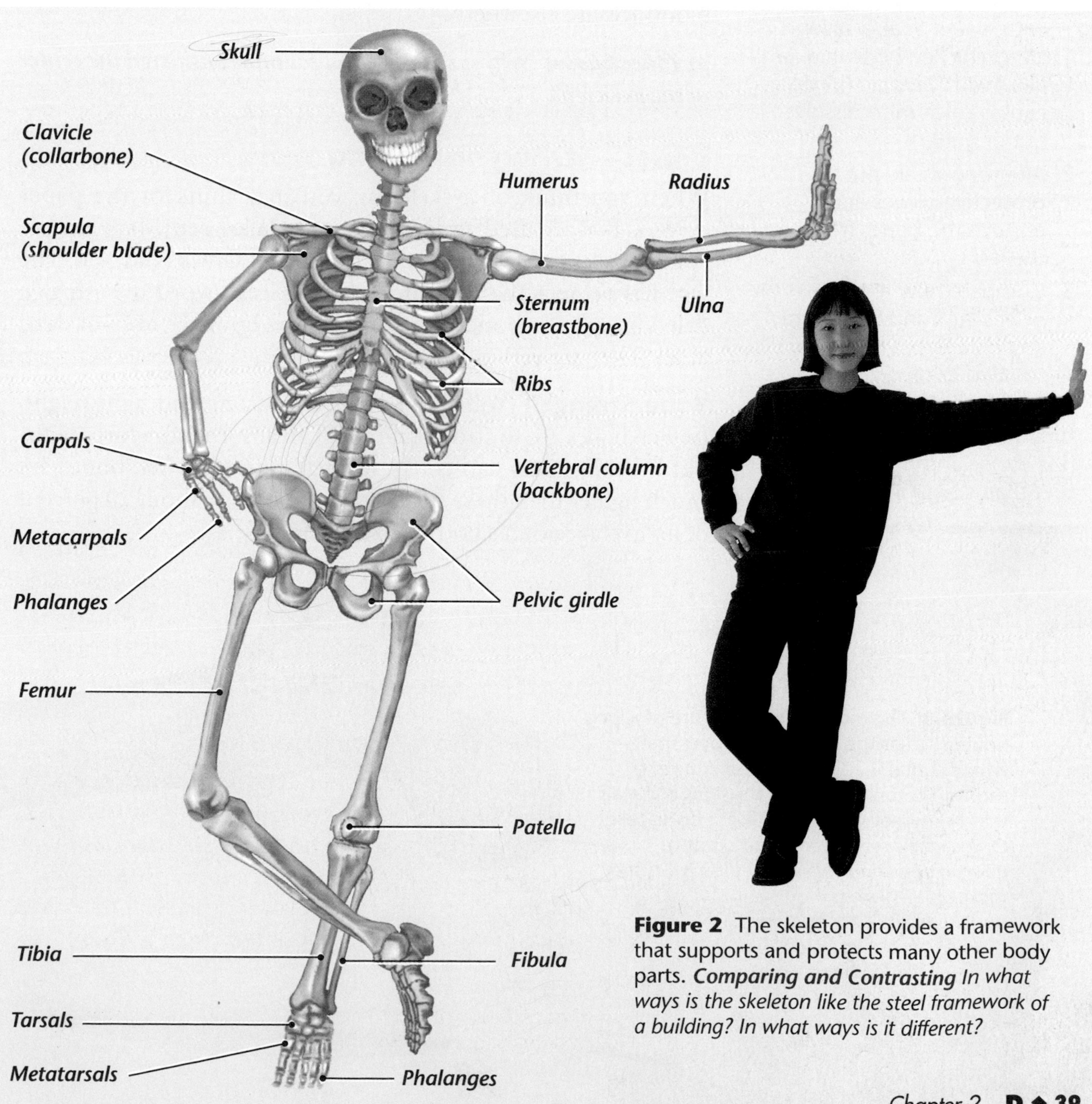

Figure 2 The skeleton provides a framework that supports and protects many other body parts. ***Comparing and Contrasting*** *In what ways is the skeleton like the steel framework of a building? In what ways is it different?*

Soft Bones?

ACTIVITY

In this activity, you will explore the role that calcium plays in bones.

1. Put on protective gloves. Soak one clean chicken bone in a jar filled with water. Soak a second clean chicken bone in a jar filled with vinegar. (Vinegar causes calcium to dissolve out of bone.)
2. After one week, put on protective gloves and remove the bones from the jars.
3. Compare how the two bones look and feel. Note any differences between the two bones.

Drawing Conclusions Based on your results, explain why it is important to consume a diet that is high in calcium.

Your skeleton also allows you to move. Most of the body's bones are associated with muscles. The muscles pull on the bones to make the body move. Bones also protect many of the organs in your body. For example, your skull protects your brain, and your breastbone and ribs form a protective cage around your heart and lungs.

Some of the bones in your body produce substances that your body needs. You can think of the long bones of your arms and legs as factories that make blood cells. Bones also store minerals such as calcium and phosphorus. Calcium and phosphorus make bones strong and hard. When the body needs these minerals, the bones release small amounts of them into the blood for use elsewhere.

☑ ***Checkpoint*** *Why is the vertebral column considered the center of the skeleton?*

Bones—Strong and Living

When you think of a skeleton, you may think of the paper cutouts that are used as decorations at Halloween. Many people connect skeletons with death. The ancient Greeks did, too. The word *skeleton* actually comes from a Greek word meaning "a dried body." The bones of your skeleton, however, are not dead at all. They are very much alive.

Bone Strength Your bones are both strong and lightweight. In fact, bones are so strong that they can absorb more force without breaking than can concrete or granite rock. Yet, bones are much lighter than these materials. In fact, only about 20 percent of an average adult's body weight is bone.

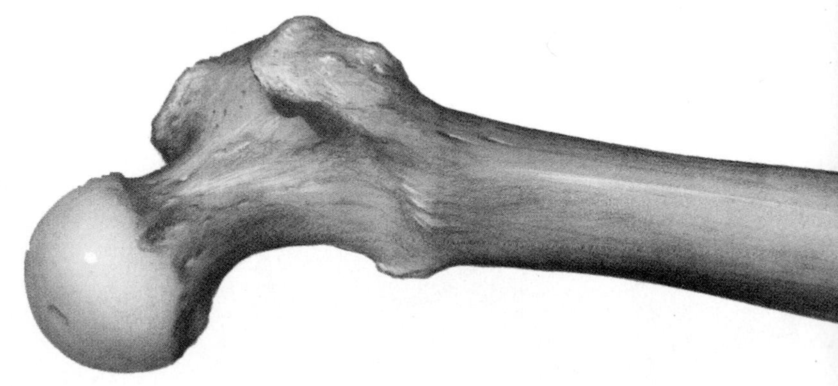

Figure 3 The most obvious feature of a long bone, such as the femur, is its long shaft, which contains compact bone. Running through compact bone is a system of canals that bring materials to the living bone cells. One canal is seen in the photograph. ***Interpreting Diagrams*** *What different tissues make up the femur?*

Have you ever heard the phrase "as hard as a rock"? Most rock is hard because it is made up of minerals that are packed tightly together. In a similar way, bones are hard because they are made up of two minerals—phosphorus and calcium.

Bone Growth Bones also contain cells and tissues, such as blood and nerves. And, because your bone cells are alive, they form new bone tissue as you grow. But even after you are grown, bone tissue continues to form within your bones. For example, every time you play soccer or basketball, your bones absorb the force of your weight. They respond by making new bone tissue.

Sometimes, new bone tissue forms after an accident. If you break a bone, for example, new bone tissue forms to fill the gap between the broken ends of the bone. The healed region of new bone may be stronger than the original bone.

The Structure of Bones

Figure 3 shows the structure of the femur, or thighbone. The femur, which is the body's longest bone, connects the pelvic bones to the lower leg bones. Notice that a thin, tough membrane covers all of the bone except the ends. Blood vessels and nerves enter and leave the bone through the membrane. Beneath the membrane is a layer of compact bone, which is hard and dense, but not solid. As you can see in Figure 3, small canals run through the compact bone. These canals carry blood vessels and nerves from the bone's surface to the living cells within the bone.

Just inside the compact bone is a layer of spongy bone. Spongy bone is also found at the ends of the bone. Like a sponge, spongy bone has many small spaces within it. This structure makes spongy bone lightweight but strong.

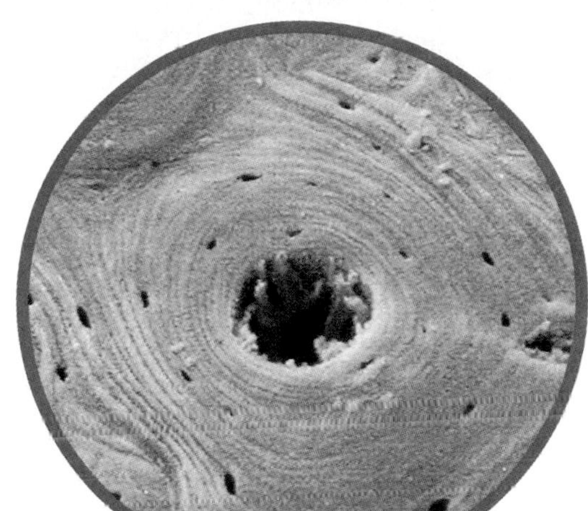

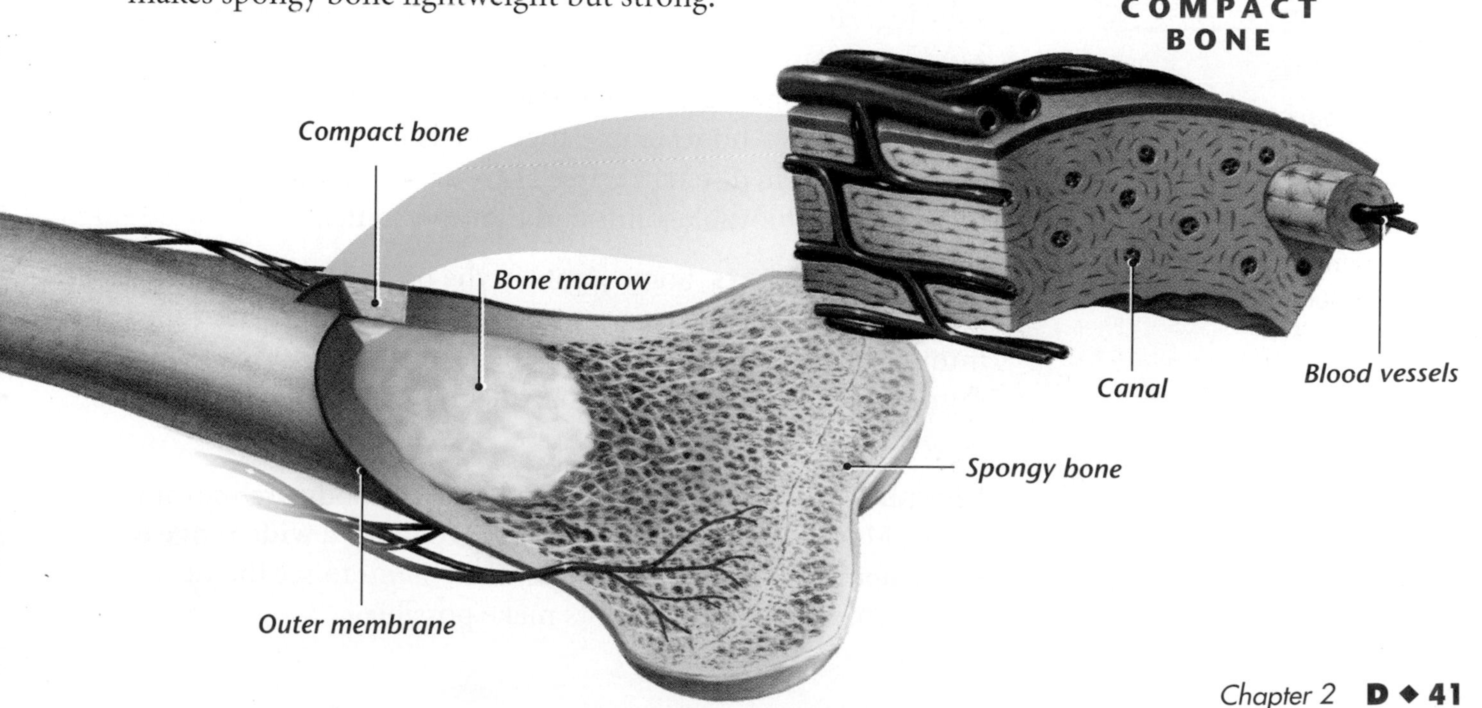

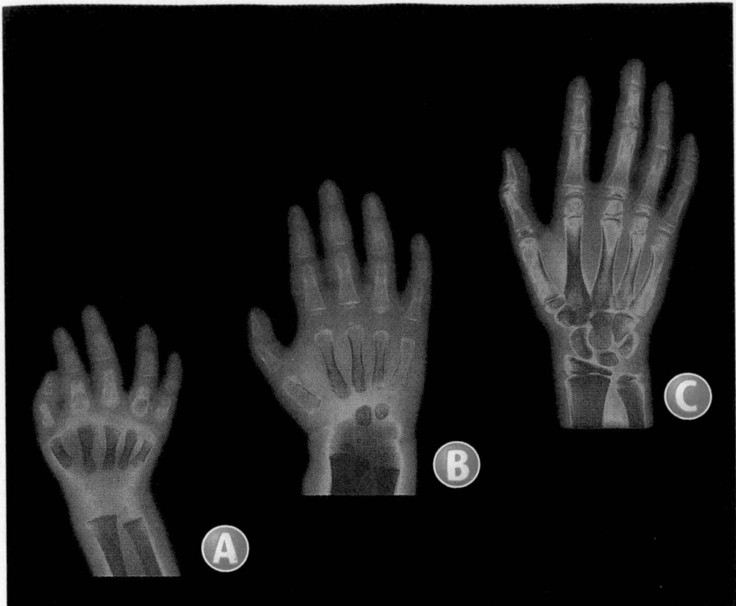

Figure 4 X-rays of the hands of a 1-year-old **(A)** and a 3-year-old **(B)** show that the cartilage in the wrist has not yet been replaced by bone. In the X-ray of the 13-year-old's hand **(C)**, the replacement of cartilage by bone is almost complete.

The spaces in bone contain a soft connective tissue called **marrow.** There are two types of marrow—red and yellow. Red bone marrow produces the body's blood cells. As a child, most of your bones contained red bone marrow. As a teenager, only the ends of your femur, your hip bones, and your sternum (breastbone) contain red marrow. Your other bones contain yellow marrow. This marrow stores fat that serves as an energy reserve.

How Bones Form

Try this activity: Move the tip of your nose from side to side between your fingers. Notice that the tip of your nose is not stiff. That is because it contains cartilage. **Cartilage** (KAHR tuh lij) is a connective tissue that is more flexible than bone. As an infant, much of your skeleton was cartilage. Over time, most of the cartilage has been replaced with hard bone tissue.

The replacement of cartilage by bone tissue usually is complete by the time you stop growing. But not all of your body's cartilage is replaced by bone. Even in adulthood, cartilage covers the ends of many bones. For example, in the knee, cartilage acts like a cushion that keeps your femur from rubbing against the bones of your lower leg.

☑ ***Checkpoint*** *What happens to cartilage as you grow?*

Joints of the Skeleton

Imagine what life would be like if your femur ran the length of your leg. How would you get out of bed in the morning? How would you run for the school bus? Luckily, your body contains many small bones rather than fewer large ones. A place in the body where two bones come together is a **joint.** Joints allow bones to move in different ways. There are two kinds of joints in the body—immovable joints and movable joints.

Immovable Joints Some joints in the body connect bones in a way that allows little or no movement. These joints are called immovable joints. The bones of the skull are held together by immovable joints. The joints that attach the ribs to the sternum are also immovable.

Movable Joints Most of the joints in the body are movable joints. **Movable joints allow the body to make a wide range of movements.** Look at *Exploring Movable Joints* to see the variety of movements that these joints make possible.

Classifying

Perform each of the activities listed below:

- move your arm in a circle
- push open a door
- lift a book from a desk
- kneel down
- wave your hand
- twist your head from side to side.

Determine which type of joint or joints is involved in performing each activity. Give a reason to support your classifications.

EXPLORING *Movable Joints*

Without movable joints, your body would be as stiff as a board. The four types of movable joints shown here allow your body to move in a variety of ways.

Ball-and-socket joint Ball-and-socket joints allow the greatest range of motion. In your shoulder, the top of the arm bone fits into the deep, bowl-like socket of the scapula (shoulder blade). The joint allows you to swing your arm freely in a circle. Your hips also have ball-and-socket joints.

Pivot joint A pivot joint allows one bone to rotate around another. The pivot joint in the top of your neck gives you limited ability to turn your head from side to side.

Gliding joint A gliding joint allows one bone to slide over another. The gliding joint in your wrist enables you to bend and flex your wrist, as well as make limited side-to-side motions. Your ankles also have gliding joints.

Hinge joint Like the hinge of a door, a hinge joint allows extensive forward or backward motion. Your knee is a hinge joint that allows you to bend and straighten your leg. Your elbow is also a hinge joint.

The bones in movable joints are held together by a strong connective tissue called a **ligament**. Cartilage that covers the ends of the bones keeps them from rubbing against each other. In addition, a fluid lubricates the ends of the bones, allowing them to move smoothly over each other.

Taking Care of Your Bones

INTEGRATING HEALTH Because your skeleton performs so many necessary functions, it is important to keep it healthy. This is especially true while you are still growing. **A combination of a balanced diet and regular exercise can start you on the way to a lifetime of healthy bones.**

One way to ensure healthy bones is to eat a well-balanced diet. A well-balanced diet includes enough calcium and phosphorus to keep your bones strong while they are growing. Meats, whole grains, and leafy green vegetables are all excellent sources of both calcium and phosphorus. Dairy products, including milk, are excellent sources of calcium.

Visual Arts CONNECTION

Leonardo da Vinci (1452–1519), was an Italian artist, inventor, and scientist. Although he is well known for his paintings, including the Mona Lisa, Leonardo also made accurate sketches of the human body. As a scientist, Leonardo used dissections and took precise measurements to create accurate drawings of bones, ligaments, tendons, and other body parts. His sketches are considered to be the first accurate drawings of the human body.

In Your Journal

Leonardo da Vinci relied on measurements and visual observations to make his drawings. Use a metric ruler to measure the lengths of the bones in your arm or leg. Then try to make an accurate drawing of your arm or leg.

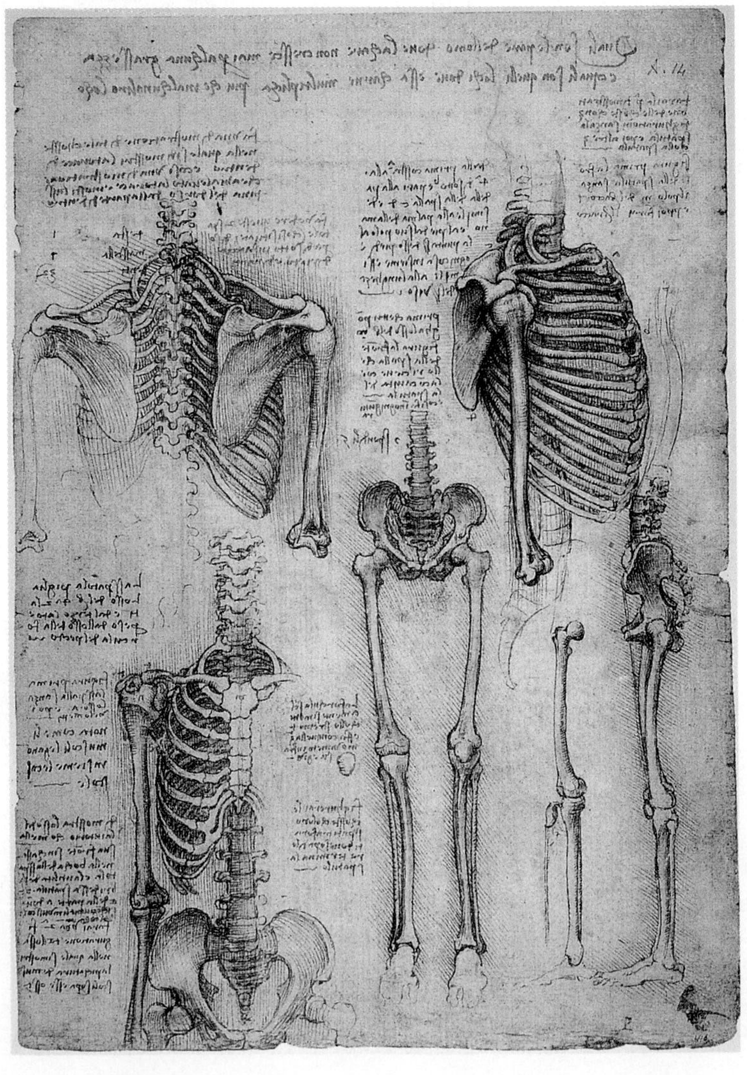

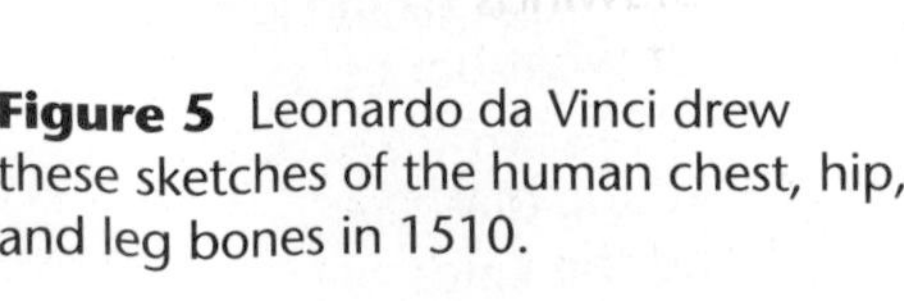

Figure 5 Leonardo da Vinci drew these sketches of the human chest, hip, and leg bones in 1510.

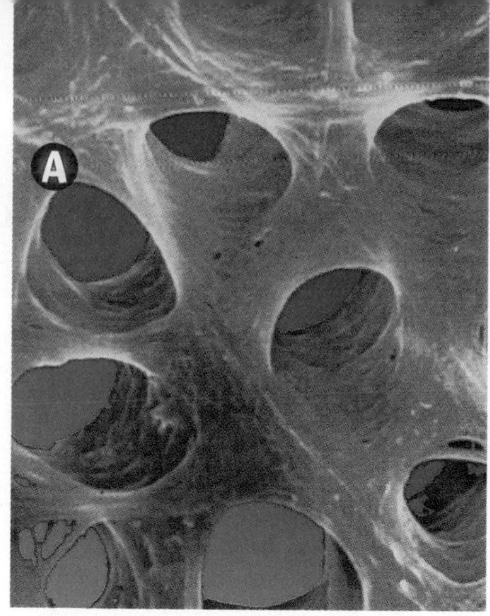

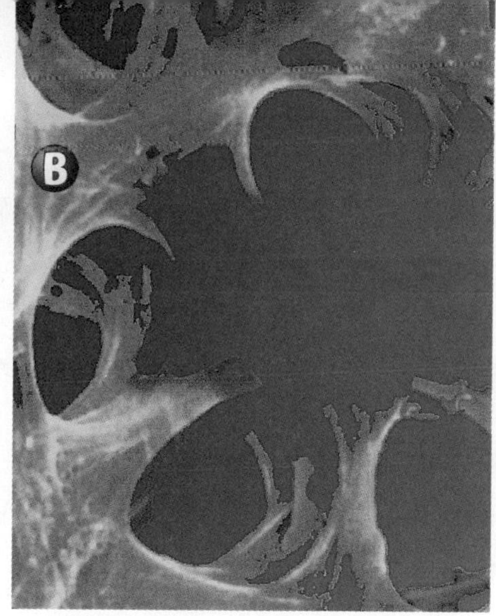

Figure 6 Without enough calcium in the diet, a person's bones weaken. **A.** This magnified view of healthy bone shows a continuous framework. **B.** Notice the large empty space in this bone from a person with osteoporosis. ***Relating Cause and Effect*** *What can you do to prevent osteoporosis?*

Another way to build and maintain strong bones is to get plenty of exercise. During activities such as walking, soccer, or basketball, your bones support the weight of your entire body. This helps your bones grow stronger and denser. Running, skating, and aerobics are other activities that help keep your bones healthy and strong.

As people become older, their bones begin to lose some of the minerals they contain. Mineral loss can lead to **osteoporosis** (ahs tee oh puh ROH sis), a condition in which the body's bones become weak and break easily. You can see the effect of osteoporosis in Figure 6B. Osteoporosis is more common in women than in men. Evidence indicates that regular exercise throughout life can help prevent osteoporosis. A diet with enough calcium can also help prevent osteoporosis. If you eat enough calcium-rich foods now, during your teenage years, you may help prevent osteoporosis later in life.

Section 1 Review

1. List five important functions that the skeleton performs in the body.
2. What is the role of movable joints in the body?
3. What behaviors are important for keeping your bones healthy?
4. Compare the motion of a hinge joint to that of a pivot joint.
5. **Thinking Critically Predicting** How would your life be different if your backbone consisted of just one bone?

Check Your Progress

CHAPTER PROJECT 2

By now, you should have your teacher's approval for modeling the movement you chose. Ask a classmate or friend to perform the movement. Make drawings to study the motion. Find out what bones are involved, and determine their sizes and shapes. (*Hint:* Notice the direction of bone movement and the kinds of joints that are involved.)

SECTION 2 Diagnosing Bone and Joint Injuries

DISCOVER ACTIVITY

What Do X-Ray Images Show?

1. Examine the photo below of an X-ray image.
2. Try to identify what part of the human body the X-ray shows.
3. Look at the X-ray to find the break in a bone.

Think It Over

Observing What types of structures are seen clearly in the X-ray? What types of structures cannot be seen?

GUIDE FOR READING

- How do X-rays help identify injuries of the skeletal system?
- How can bone and joint injuries be prevented?

Reading Tip As you read, create a table comparing X-rays and MRI. Include columns for the procedure involved, effect on body cells, cost, and types of injuries shown.

You call out, "Wait for me," as you run across an icy sidewalk to catch up to a friend. Suddenly, you slip. As you lose your balance, you put out your arms to break your fall. The next thing you know, you're on the ground. Your hands sting, and you notice they are scraped. One wrist is starting to swell, and it hurts! If you try to move your wrist, it hurts even more. You need to get to a doctor—and fast.

Common Skeletal System Injuries

On the way to the doctor, you 'd probably be wondering, "Is my wrist broken, or is it just bruised?" Your swollen wrist could be injured in one of three common ways: it could be fractured, sprained, or dislocated.

A **fracture,** or a break in a bone, can occur when you fall so that all of your weight is placed on only a few bones. A **sprain** occurs when ligaments are stretched too far and tear in places. If you have ever stumbled and turned an ankle, you may have felt a sharp pain. The pain probably occurred because the ligaments on the outside of your ankle stretched too far and tore. Sprains, especially of the ankle, are the most common joint injuries. Both sprains and fractures can cause swelling around the injured area.

A third injury of the skeletal system is a dislocation. A **dislocation** occurs when a bone comes out of its joint. For example, have you ever caught a ball with the tips of your fingers? You may have knocked a finger bone out of its joint. Sometimes a doctor can put back a dislocated bone without surgery. Other times surgery is needed.

▼ An X-ray image of a broken bone

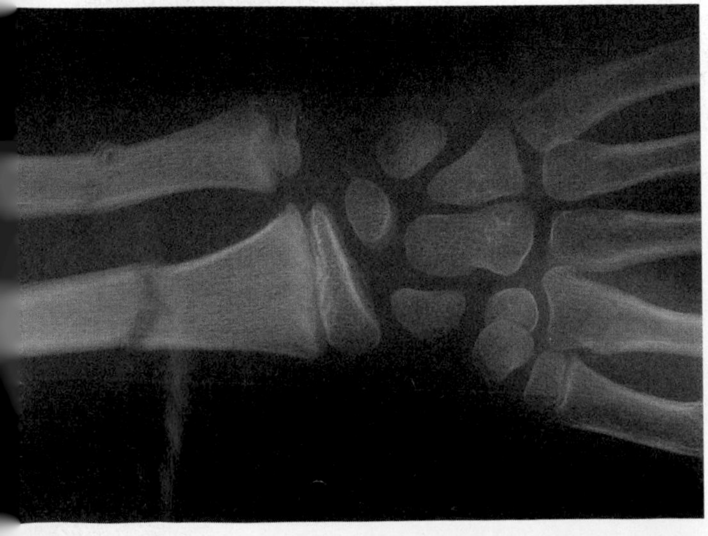

X-Rays—A Look Inside the Body

Integrating Physics X-ray images can determine whether bones have been broken. **X-rays,** like the light that your eyes can see, are a form of energy that travels in waves. Although the energy in the waves passes through some living tissue, it does not pass through bone.

Before an X-ray image is taken, a lead apron is placed on your body to protect you from unnecessary exposure to X-rays. Lead is a dense metal that absorbs X-rays. Photographic film is placed under the area to be viewed. Then a machine that emits a beam of X-rays is aimed at the area.

Because most X-rays pass through the skin and other body tissues, the X-rays strike the photographic film beneath the area. Unlike other body tissues, bone absorbs X-rays. Absorbed X-rays do not reach the film. After the film is developed, it shows bones as clearly defined white areas.

X-ray imaging has drawbacks. One limitation is that X-rays cannot be used to view injuries to soft tissues, such as the skin, muscle, connective tissue, and internal organs. In addition, the energy in X-rays can damage your body cells. This is why you should not have unnecessary X-ray images taken.

Magnetic Resonance Imaging

In 1970, a new method for taking clear images of both the bones and soft tissues of the body was developed. This method is called **magnetic resonance imaging,** or MRI. An MRI scanner is a large

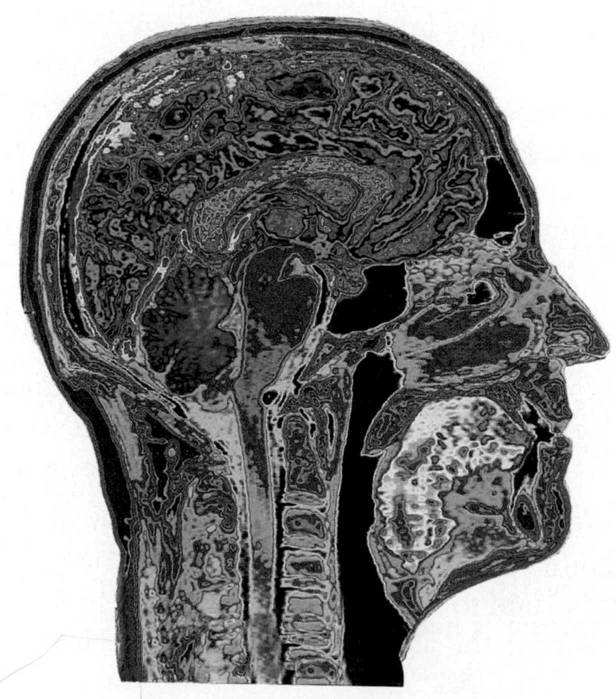

Figure 7 Magnetic resonance imaging can produce images of muscles and other soft tissues in the body.

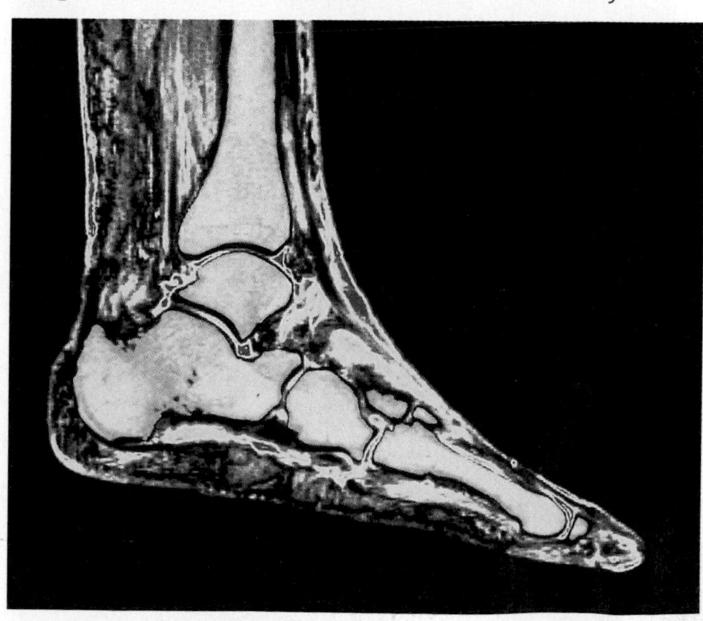

cylinder that contains electromagnets. The person is placed on a platform that slides into the center of the cylinder. The person is then exposed to short bursts of magnetic energy. This magnetic energy causes atoms within the body to vibrate, or resonate. A computer then analyzes the vibration patterns and produces an image of the area.

MRI images are amazingly sharp and clear. MRI can produce images of body tissues at any angle. In addition, it can show a clear image of muscles and other soft tissues that an X-ray image cannot show. Another advantage of MRI is that it does not damage cells. Because MRI machines are very expensive to buy and use, this technique is not used to examine broken bones.

☑ *Checkpoint* *What is one advantage that X-rays have over MRI?*

Arthroscopy

Before 1970, if you had a pain in a movable joint, a surgeon had to make a large incision into the joint to see what was causing the pain. Today, doctors make a small incision and insert a slim, tubelike instrument called an arthroscope (AHR thruh skohp) into the joint. The arthroscope allows doctors to look inside the joint to see what is wrong. After the problem is diagnosed, tiny instruments are inserted through a second small incision to make the necessary repairs. The arthroscope has helped to diagnose and repair many joint problems. Sometimes, however, a joint may be too damaged to repair. The damaged joint may then be replaced with an artificial joint.

Figure 8 To diagnose and treat a knee injury, this surgeon has inserted an arthroscope into the patient's knee.

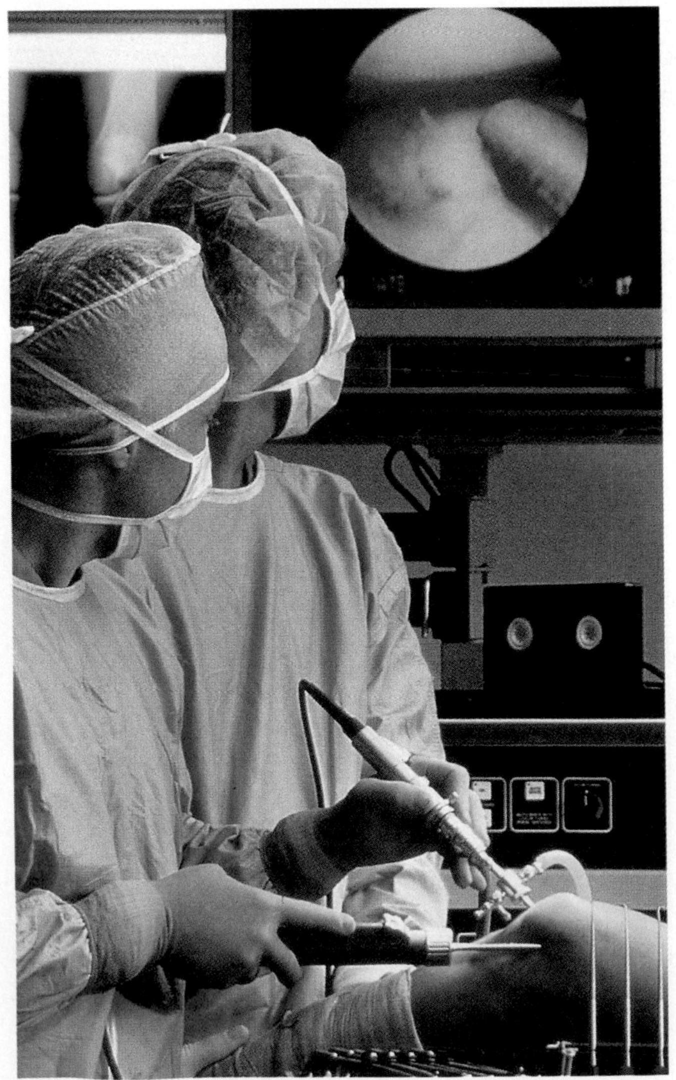

Preventing Skeletal System Injuries

INTEGRATING HEALTH Although injuries such as fractures, sprains, and dislocations are fairly common, they can be prevented. **Simple preventive measures include warming up before exercising, wearing appropriate protective equipment, and exercising in safe places.**

When you warm up before exercising, your joints become more flexible. This may help prevent a sprain or dislocation. In addition, it is important to wear the appropriate safety equipment for the activity you are doing. Helmets,

Figure 9 By wearing safety equipment, these hockey players can avoid bone and joint injuries. ***Observing*** *List all the safety equipment that these athletes are wearing.*

knee pads, shoulder pads, and padded gloves can help prevent injuries. You should also always wear shoes that are appropriate for your activity. Lastly, be aware of your surroundings. If you skate, run, or bike on a path or track, you are much less likely to be involved in an accident with a car or with another person.

If you do get injured, be sure to apply proper first aid. Placing ice on an injured area and elevating it can minimize pain and swelling. Make sure you tell a parent, coach, or other adult if you get hurt. If a trainer, doctor, or nurse gives you medical instructions, be sure you understand them, and then follow them exactly. Finally, don't return to regular activity until your injury has healed. By giving your bones or joints time to heal, you can help prevent further injury to the area.

Section 2 Review

1. What property of X-rays makes them useful for identifying injuries to the skeletal system?
2. What can you do to decrease the chances of injuring your skeletal system?
3. Describe three common bone and joint injuries.
4. List the advantages of MRI over X-rays.
5. **Thinking Critically Applying Concepts** Suppose that an X-ray image of your injured wrist did not show a fracture. But, after a month, your wrist is still painful and stiff. Why might your doctor order an MRI?

Science at Home

List the types of exercise you and your family members do. With your family, brainstorm a list of safety gear and precautions to use for each activity. (For example, for bicycling, you might list wearing a helmet, stretching before riding, and avoiding busy streets and nighttime riding.) How can you put these safety measures into practice?

SECTION 3 The Muscular System

DISCOVER ACTIVITY

How Do Muscles Work?

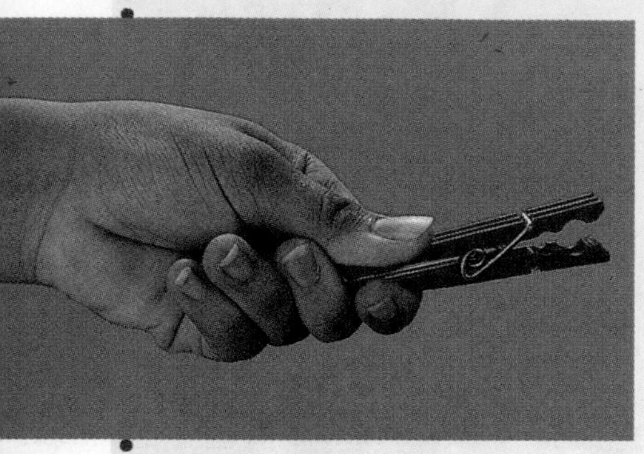

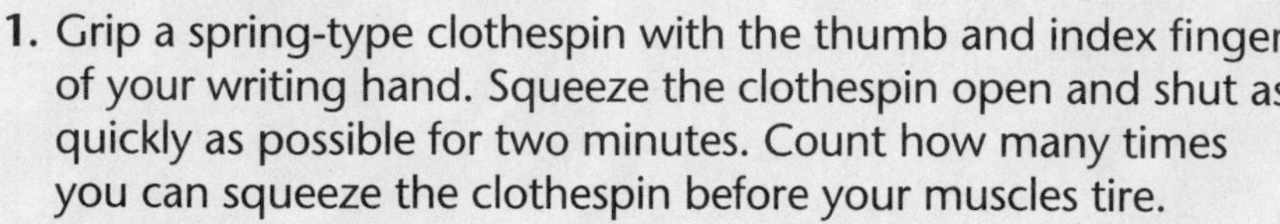

1. Grip a spring-type clothespin with the thumb and index finger of your writing hand. Squeeze the clothespin open and shut as quickly as possible for two minutes. Count how many times you can squeeze the clothespin before your muscles tire.
2. Rest for one minute. Then repeat Step 1.

Think It Over

Predicting What do you think would happen if you repeated Steps 1 and 2 with your other hand? Give a reason for your prediction. Then test your prediction.

GUIDE FOR READING

- **What three types of muscles are found in the body?**
- **Why do muscles work in pairs?**

Reading Tip **Before you read, preview Figure 10. Predict how skeletal, smooth, and cardiac muscles function.**

A rabbit becomes still when it senses danger. The rabbit sits so still that it doesn't seem to move a muscle. Could you sit without moving any muscles? If you tried to, you'd find that it is impossible to sit still for very long. Saliva builds up in your mouth. You swallow. You need to breathe. Your chest expands to let air in. All of these actions involve muscles.

There are about 600 muscles in your body. Muscles have many functions. For example, they keep your heart beating, pull your mouth into a smile, and move the bones of your skeleton.

Muscle Action

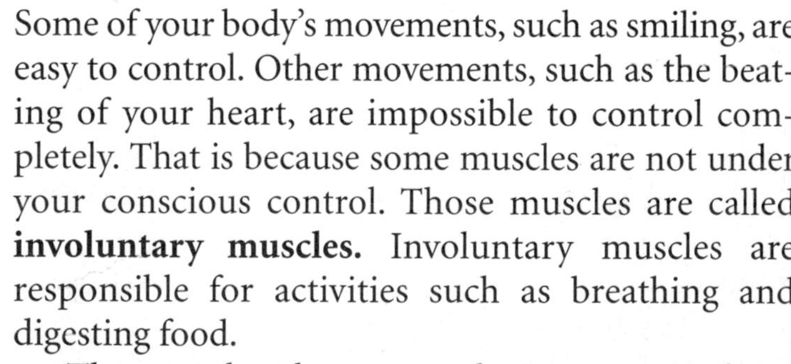

Some of your body's movements, such as smiling, are easy to control. Other movements, such as the beating of your heart, are impossible to control completely. That is because some muscles are not under your conscious control. Those muscles are called **involuntary muscles.** Involuntary muscles are responsible for activities such as breathing and digesting food.

The muscles that are under your control are called **voluntary muscles.** Smiling, turning a page in a book, and getting out of your chair when the bell rings are all actions controlled by voluntary muscles.

◄ **A rabbit "frozen" in place**

Types of Muscles

Your body has three types of muscle tissue—skeletal muscle, smooth muscle, and cardiac muscle. In Figure 10, you see a magnified view of each type of muscle in the body. Both skeletal and smooth muscles are found in many places in the body. Cardiac muscle is found only in the heart. Each muscle type performs specific functions in the body.

Skeletal Muscle Every time you type on a computer keyboard, shoot a basketball, or walk across a room, you are using skeletal muscles. As their name suggests, **skeletal muscles** are attached

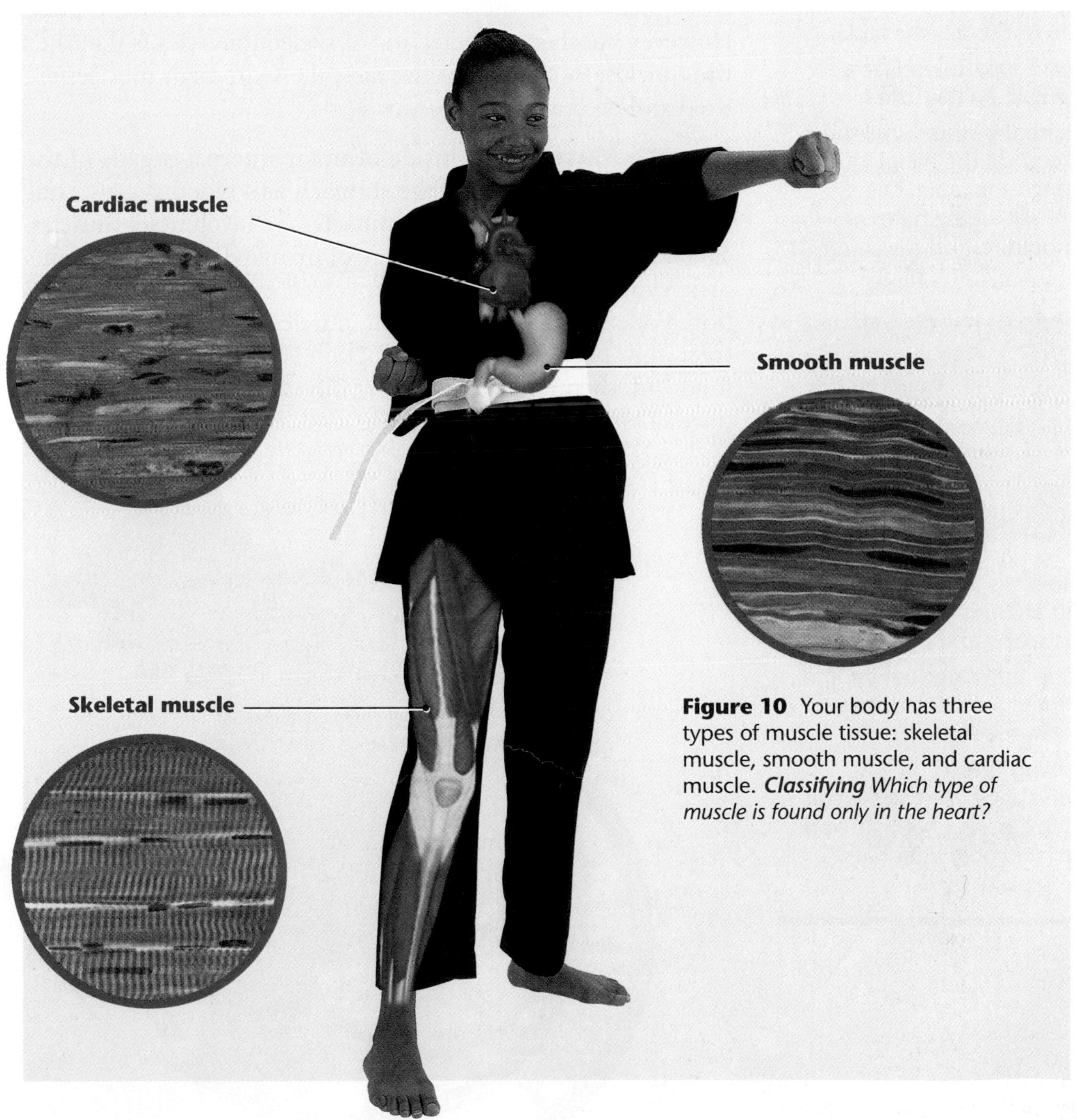

Figure 10 Your body has three types of muscle tissue: skeletal muscle, smooth muscle, and cardiac muscle. ***Classifying*** *Which type of muscle is found only in the heart?*

Get a Grip

ACTIVITY

Are skeletal muscles at work when you're not moving? Try this activity and see.

1. Hold a stirrer in front of you, parallel to a table top. Do not touch the table.
2. Have a partner place a hairpin on the stirrer.
3. Raise the stirrer until the "legs" of the hairpin just touch the table. The "head" of the hairpin should rest on the stirrer, as you see in the photo.

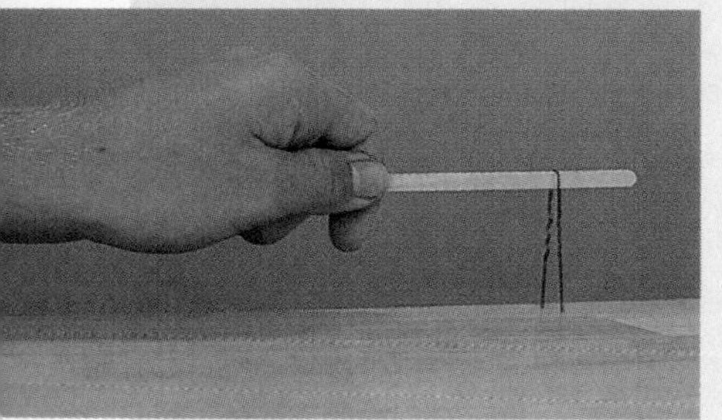

4. Hold the stirrer steady for 20 seconds. Observe what happens to the hairpin.
5. Grip the stirrer tighter and repeat Step 4. Observe what happens.

Inferring Based on your observations, are the skeletal muscles in your hand at work when you hold your hand still? Explain.

to the bones of your skeleton. These muscles provide the force that moves your bones. At each end of a skeletal muscle is a tendon. A **tendon** is a strong connective tissue that attaches muscle to bone. As you can see in Figure 10, skeletal muscle cells appear banded, or striated (STRY ay tid). For this reason, skeletal muscle is sometimes called striated muscle.

Because you have conscious control of skeletal muscles, they are classified as voluntary muscles. One characteristic of skeletal muscles is that they react very quickly. You can see an example of just how quickly skeletal muscle reacts by watching a swim meet. Immediately after the starting gun sounds, a swimmer's leg muscles quickly push the swimmer off the block into the pool. However, another characteristic of skeletal muscles is that they tire quickly. By the end of the race, the swimmer's muscles are tired and need a rest.

Smooth Muscle The inside of many internal organs of the body, such as the walls of the stomach and blood vessels, contain smooth muscles. **Smooth muscles** are involuntary muscles. They work automatically to control many types of movements inside your body, such as those involved in the process of digestion. For example, as the smooth muscles of your stomach contract, they produce a churning action. The churning mixes the food with chemicals produced by your stomach. This action and these chemicals help to digest the food.

Unlike skeletal muscles, smooth muscle cells are not striated. Smooth muscles behave differently than skeletal muscles, too. Smooth muscles react more slowly and tire more slowly.

Cardiac Muscle The tissue called **cardiac muscle** has characteristics in common with both smooth and skeletal muscles. Like smooth muscle, cardiac muscle is involuntary. Like skeletal muscle, cardiac muscle cells are striated. However, unlike skeletal muscle, cardiac muscle does not get tired. It can contract repeatedly. You call those repeated contractions heartbeats.

☑ *Checkpoint* *Which type of muscle reacts and tires quickly?*

Muscles at Work

Has anyone ever asked you to "make a muscle"? If so, you probably tightened your fist, bent your arm at the elbow, and made the muscles in your upper arm bulge. Like other skeletal muscles, the muscles in your arm do their work by contracting, or becoming shorter and thicker. Muscle cells contract when they receive messages from the nervous system. **Because muscle cells can only contract, not extend, skeletal muscles must work in pairs. While one muscle contracts, the other muscle in the pair returns to its original length.**

Figure 11 shows the muscle action involved in moving the lower arm. First, the biceps muscle on the front of the upper arm contracts to bend the elbow, lifting the forearm and hand. As the biceps contracts, the triceps on the back of the upper arm returns to its original length. Then to straighten the elbow, the triceps muscle contracts. As the triceps contracts to extend the arm, the biceps returns to its original length. Another example of muscles that work in pairs are those in your thigh that bend and straighten the knee joint.

Figure 11 Because muscles can only contract, or shorten, they must work in pairs. To bend the arm at the elbow, the biceps contracts while the triceps returns to its original length. ***Interpreting Diagrams*** *What happens to each muscle to straighten the arm?*

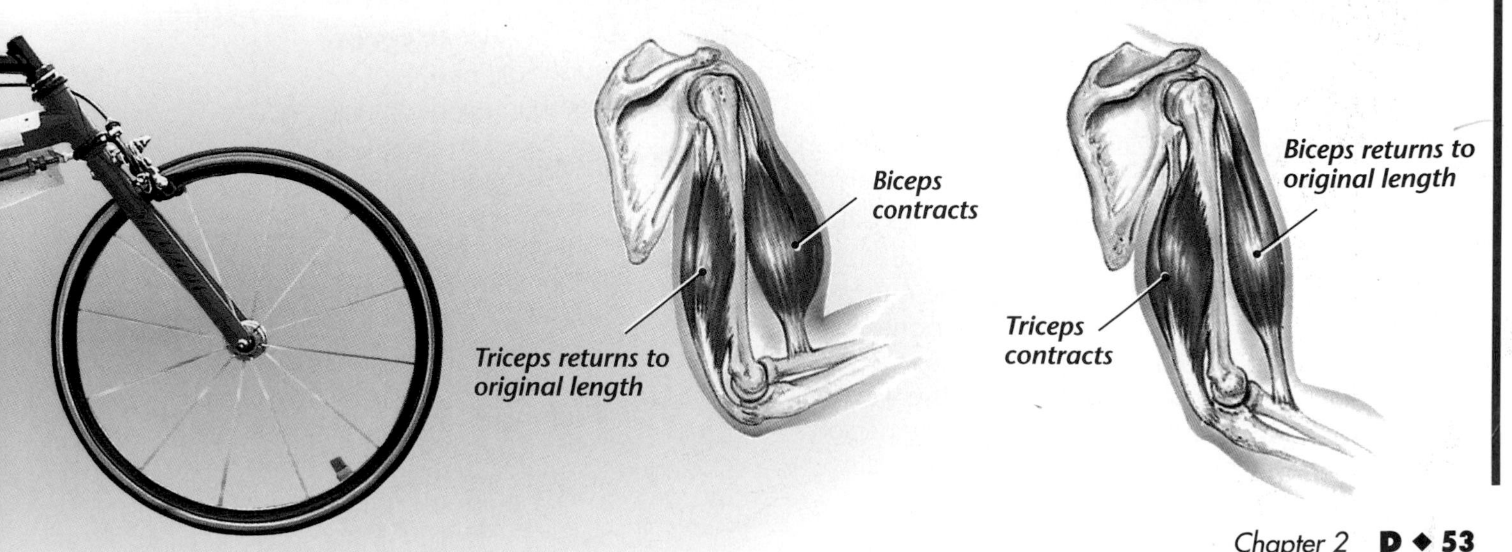

Figure 12 When you warm up before exercising, you increase the flexibility of your muscles.

Taking Care of Your Skeletal Muscles

INTEGRATING HEALTH Exercise is important for maintaining both muscular strength and flexibility. Exercise makes individual muscle cells grow wider. This, in turn, causes the whole muscle to become thicker. The thicker a muscle is, the stronger the muscle is. When you stretch and warm up thoroughly, your muscles become more flexible. This helps prepare your muscles for the work involved in exercising or playing.

Like your bones and joints, your skeletal muscles are subject to injuries. Some of the same precautions that help prevent bone and joint injuries can also help prevent muscle injuries. For example, warming up increases the flexibility of joints as well as muscles. In addition, using proper safety equipment can protect all of your tissues, including muscles and tendons.

Sometimes, despite taking proper precautions, muscles can become injured. A muscle strain, or a pulled muscle, can occur when muscles are overworked or overstretched. Tendons can also be overstretched or partially torn. After a long period of exercise, a skeletal muscle can cramp. When a muscle cramps, the entire muscle contracts strongly and stays contracted. If you injure a muscle or tendon, it is important to follow medical instructions and to rest the injured area until it heals.

Section 3 Review

1. Name the three types of muscle tissue. Where is each type found?
2. Describe how the muscles in your upper arm work together to bend and straighten your lower arm.
3. How do voluntary and involuntary muscles differ? Give an example of each type of muscle.
4. **Thinking Critically Predicting** The muscles that move your fingers are attached to the bones in your fingers by long tendons. Suppose one of the tendons in a person's index finger were cut all the way through. How would this injury affect the person's ability to move his or her index finger? Explain.

CHAPTER PROJECT 2

Check Your Progress

You should now be assembling your working model. Be sure that you include the muscles involved in the movement you are modeling. Also, remember that your model must show how muscle contractions produce the chosen movement. (*Hint:* After you have assembled your model, do a final check to be sure it functions the way it should.)

Observing

Skills Lab

A Look Beneath the Skin

In this lab, you will learn about your own skeletal muscles by observing the "arm" muscles of a chicken.

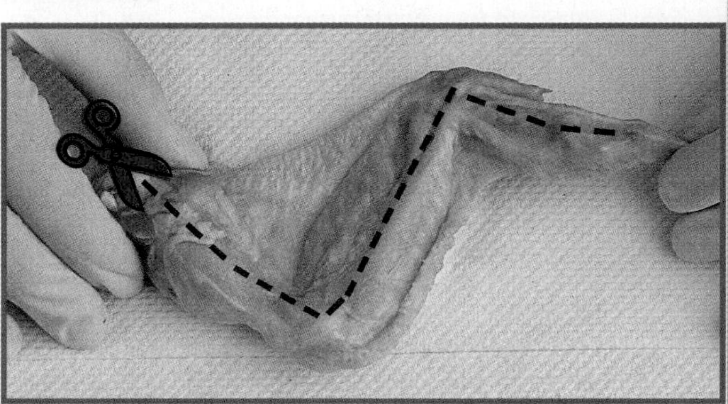

Problem

What are some characteristics of skeletal muscles? How do skeletal muscles work?

Materials

protective gloves
paper towels
scissors
water
dissection tray
uncooked chicken wing, treated with bleach

Procedure

1. Put on protective gloves. **CAUTION:** *Wear gloves whenever you handle the chicken.*
2. Your teacher will give you a chicken wing. Rinse it well with water, dry it with paper towels, and place it in a dissecting tray.
3. Carefully extend the wing to find out how many major parts it has. Draw a diagram of the external structure. Label the upper arm, elbow, lower arm, and hand (wing tip).
4. Use scissors to remove the skin. Cut along the cut line as shown in the photo. Only cut through the skin. **CAUTION:** *Cut away from your body and your classmates.*
5. Examine the muscles, the bundles of pink tissue around the bones. Find the two groups of muscles in the upper arm. Hold the arm down at the shoulder, and alternately pull on each muscle group. Observe what happens.
6. Find the two groups of muscles in the lower arm. Hold down the arm at the elbow, and alternately pull on each muscle group. Then make a diagram of the wing's muscles.
7. Find the tendons—shiny white tissue at the ends of the muscles. Notice what parts the tendons connect. Add the tendons to your diagram.
8. Remove the muscles and tendons. Find the ligaments, the whitish ribbonlike structures between bones. Add them to your diagram.
9. Dispose of the chicken parts according to your teacher's instructions. Wash your hands.

Analyze and Conclude

1. How does a chicken wing move at the elbow? How does the motion compare to how your elbow moves? What type of joint is involved?
2. What happened when you pulled on one of the arm muscles? What muscle action does the pulling represent?
3. Classify the muscles you observed as smooth, cardiac, or skeletal.
4. **Think About It** Why is it valuable to record your observations with accurate diagrams?

More to Explore

Use the procedures from this lab to examine an uncooked chicken thigh and leg. Compare how the chicken leg and a human leg move.

Section 4 The Skin

Discover Activity

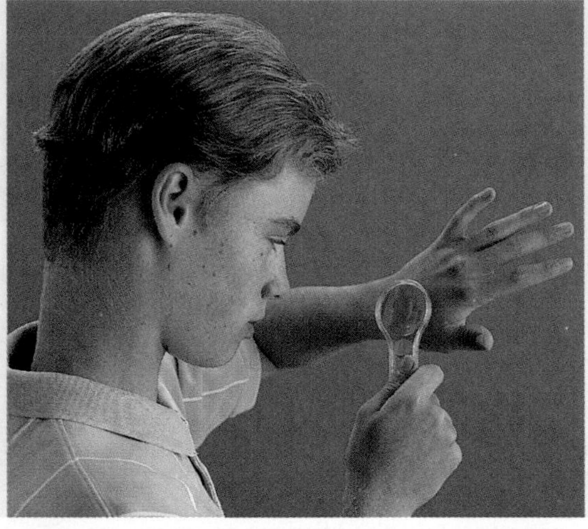

What Can You Observe About Skin?

1. Using a hand lens, examine the skin on your hand. Look for pores and hairs on both the palm and back of your hand.
2. Place a plastic glove on your hand. After five minutes, remove the glove. Then examine the skin on your hand with the hand lens.

Think It Over

Inferring Compare your hand before and after wearing the glove. What happened to the skin when you wore the glove? Why did this happen?

Guide for Reading

- **What are the functions of skin?**
- **What habits can help keep your skin healthy?**

Reading Tip **As you read, create a table that shows the two major layers of skin. Include columns to record the location, structures, and functions of each layer.**

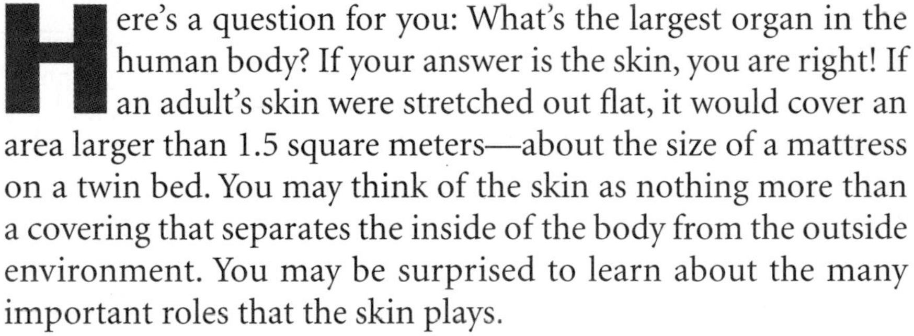

Here's a question for you: What's the largest organ in the human body? If your answer is the skin, you are right! If an adult's skin were stretched out flat, it would cover an area larger than 1.5 square meters—about the size of a mattress on a twin bed. You may think of the skin as nothing more than a covering that separates the inside of the body from the outside environment. You may be surprised to learn about the many important roles that the skin plays.

The Body's Tough Covering

The skin performs several major functions in the body. **The skin covers the body and prevents the loss of water. It protects the body from injury and infection. The skin also helps to regulate body temperature, eliminate wastes, gather information about the environment, and produce vitamin D.**

The skin protects the body by forming a barrier that keeps disease-causing microorganisms and harmful substances outside the body. In addition, the skin helps keep important substances inside the body. Like plastic wrap that keeps food from drying out, the skin prevents the loss of important fluids such as water.

Figure 13 The skin forms a barrier that protects the inside of the body from substances such as the chlorine in pool water.

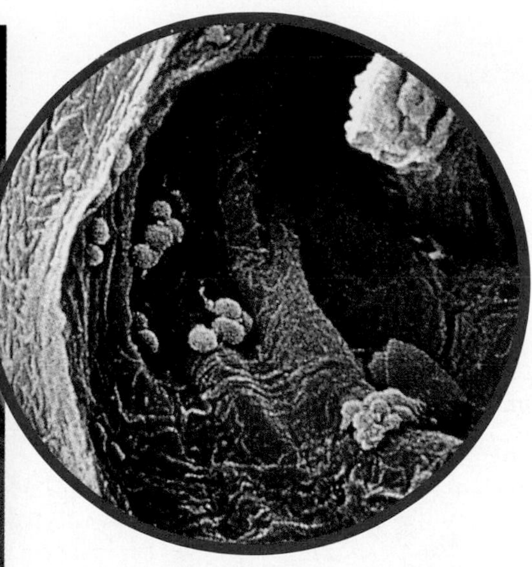

Figure 14 When you exercise, your body becomes warmer. Sweat glands in the skin produce perspiration, which leaves the body through pores like the one you see here. ***Relating Cause and Effect*** *How does perspiration help cool your body?*

Another function of the skin is to help the body maintain a steady temperature. Many blood vessels run through skin. When you become too warm, these blood vessels enlarge to increase the amount of blood that flows through them. This allows heat to move from your body into the outside environment. In addition, sweat glands in the skin respond to excess heat by producing perspiration. As perspiration evaporates from your skin, heat moves into the air. Because perspiration contains some dissolved waste materials, your skin also helps to eliminate wastes.

The skin also gathers information about the environment. To understand how the skin does this, place your fingertips on the skin of your arm and press down firmly. Then lightly pinch yourself. You have just tested some of the nerves in your skin. The nerves in skin provide information about such things as pressure, pain, and temperature. Pain messages are important because they warn you that something in your surroundings may have injured you.

Lastly, some skin cells produce vitamin D in the presence of sunlight. Vitamin D is important for healthy bones. This is because Vitamin D helps the cells in your digestive system to absorb the calcium in your food. Your skin cells need only a few minutes of sunlight to produce all the vitamin D you need in a day.

☑ ***Checkpoint*** *How does your skin help eliminate waste materials from your body?*

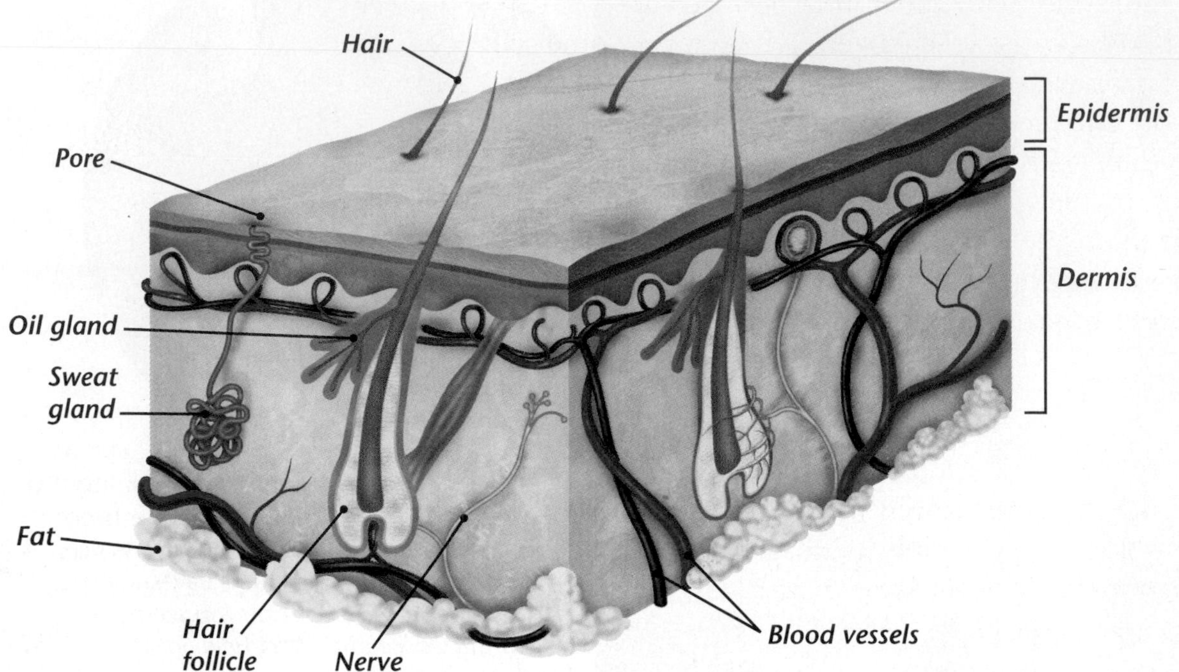

Figure 15 The skin is made of two main layers. The top layer is called the epidermis. The bottom layer is called the dermis. ***Interpreting Diagrams*** *In which layer of the skin do you find blood vessels?*

The Epidermis

The skin is organized into two main layers, the epidermis and the dermis. You can see these layers in Figure 15. The **epidermis** is the outermost layer of the skin. In most places, the epidermis is thinner than the dermis. The epidermis does not have nerves or blood vessels. This is why you usually don't feel pain from very shallow scratches and why shallow scratches do not bleed.

Dead or Alive? The cells in the epidermis have a definite life cycle. Each epidermal cell begins life deep in the epidermis, where cells divide to form new cells. The new cells gradually mature and move upward in the epidermis as new cells form beneath them. After about two weeks, the cells die and become part of the surface layer of the epidermis. Under a microscope, this surface layer of dead cells resembles flat bags laid on top of each other. Cells remain in this layer for about two weeks. Then they are shed and replaced by the dead cells below.

Protecting the Body In some ways, the cells of the epidermis are more valuable to the body dead than alive. Most of the protection provided by the skin is due to the layer of dead cells on the surface. The thick layer of dead cells on your fingertips, for example, protects and cushions your fingertips. The shedding of dead cells also helps to protect the body. As the cells fall away, they carry with them bacteria and other substances that settle on the skin. Every time you rub your hands together, you lose hundreds, even thousands, of dead skin cells.

Some cells in the inner layer of the epidermis help to protect the body, too. On your fingers, for example, some cells produce hard nails, which protect the fingertips from injury and help you scratch and pick up objects.

Other cells deep in the epidermis produce **melanin,** a pigment, or colored substance, that gives skin its color. The more melanin in your skin, the darker it is. Exposure to sunlight stimulates the skin to make more melanin. Melanin production helps to protect the skin from burning.

☑ *Checkpoint How do dead skin cells help to protect the body?*

The Dermis

The **dermis** is the lower layer of the skin. Find the dermis in Figure 15. Notice that it is located below the epidermis and above a layer of fat. This fat layer pads the internal organs and helps keep heat in the body.

The dermis contains nerves and blood vessels. The dermis also contains other structures as well—sweat glands, hairs, and oil glands. Sweat glands produce perspiration, which reaches the surface through openings called **pores.** Strands of hair grow within the dermis in structures called **follicles** (FAHL ih kulz). The hair that you see above the skin's surface is made up of dead cells. Oil produced in glands around the hair follicles waterproofs the hair. In addition, oil that reaches the surface helps to keep the skin moist.

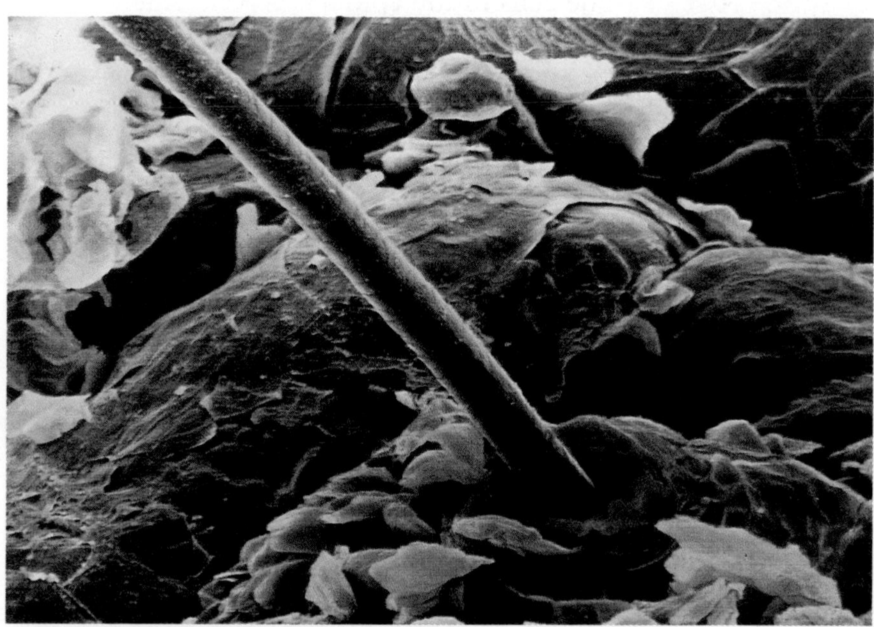

Figure 16 Hairs grow from follicles in the dermis of the skin. Hair is made of dead cells.

Sweaty Skin

ACTIVITY

This activity illustrates one of the skin's important functions.

1. Put on your safety goggles. Wrap a wet cotton ball around the bulb of one thermometer. Place a second thermometer next to the first one.

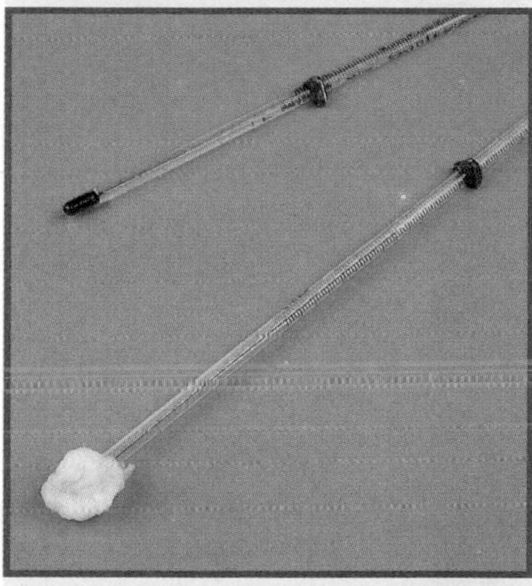

2. After two minutes, record the temperature reading on each thermometer.
3. Using a piece of cardboard, fan both thermometers for several minutes. The cardboard should be at least 10 cm from the thermometers. Then record the temperatures.

Measuring Which of the two thermometers had a lower temperature after Step 3? How does this activity relate to the role of skin in regulating body temperature?

Caring for Your Skin

Because your skin has so many important functions, it is important to take care of it. **Four simple habits can help you keep your skin healthy. Eat properly. Drink enough water. Limit your exposure to the sun. Keep your skin clean and dry.**

Eating Properly Your skin is always active. The cells in the epidermis are replaced, hair strands and nails grow, and oil is produced. These activities require energy—and a well-balanced diet provides the energy needed for these processes. You will learn more about healthy diets in Chapter 3.

Real-World Lab

You and Your Environment

Sun Safety

In this lab, you'll investigate how sunscreen products and various fabrics protect your skin from the sun.

Problem

How well do different materials protect the skin from the sun?

Skills Focus

predicting, observing, drawing conclusions

Materials

scissors
3 different fabrics
photosensitive paper
white construction paper
resealable plastic bag
2 sunscreens with SPF ratings of 4 and 30
pencil
plastic knife
metric ruler
stapler
staple remover

Procedure 

1. Read over the procedure. Then write a prediction about how well each of the sunscreens and fabrics will protect against the sun.
2. Use scissors to cut five strips of photosensitive paper that measure 5 cm by 15 cm.
3. Divide each strip into thirds by drawing lines across the strips as shown in the photo.
4. Cover one third of each strip with a square of white construction paper. Staple each square down.

Part 1 Investigating Sunscreens

5. Use a pencil to write the lower SPF (sun protection factor) rating on the back of the first strip. Write the other SPF rating on the back of a second strip.
6. Place the two strips side by side in a plastic bag. Seal the bag, then staple through the white squares to hold the strips in place.

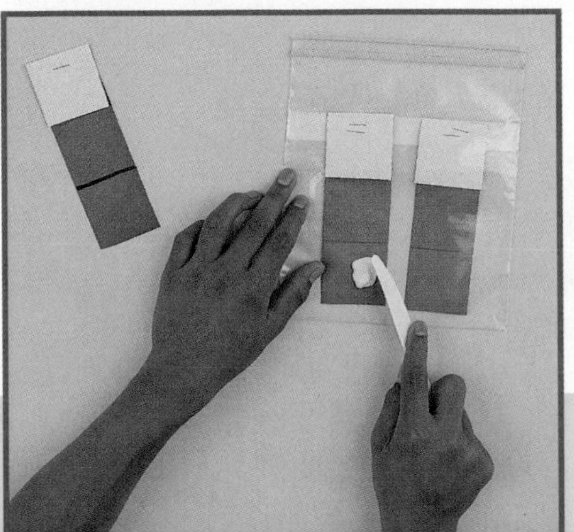

Drinking Water To keep your skin healthy, it is also important to drink plenty of water. When you participate in strenuous activities, such as playing soccer, you can perspire up to 10 liters of liquid a day. You need to replace the water lost in perspiration by drinking water or other beverages and by eating foods, such as fruits, that contain water.

Limiting Sun Exposure You can also take actions to protect your skin from cancer and early aging. **Cancer** is a disease in which some body cells divide uncontrollably. Repeated exposure to sunlight can damage skin cells and cause them to become

7. With a plastic knife, spread a thin layer of each sunscreen on the bag over the last square of each strip. Make certain each layer has the same depth. Be sure not to spread sunscreen over the middle squares.
8. Place the bag in direct sunlight with the sunscreen side up. Leave it there until the middle squares turn white.
9. Remove the strips from the bag, and take off the construction paper. Rinse the strips for one minute in cold water. Then dry them flat.
10. Observe all the squares. Record your observations.

Part 2 Investigating Fabrics

11. Obtain three fabrics of different thicknesses. Staple a square of each fabric over the last square of a photosensitive strip. Write a description of the fabric on the back of the strip.
12. Expose the strips to the sun, fabric-side up, until the middle square turns white. Then follow Steps 9 and 10.

Analyze and Conclude

1. Did the sunscreens protect against sun exposure? How do you know?
2. Which sunscreen provided more protection? Was your prediction correct?
3. Did the fabrics protect against sun exposure? How do you know?
4. Which fabric provided the most protection? The least protection? How did your results compare with your predictions?
5. **Apply** What advice would you give people about protecting their skin from the sun?

Design an Experiment

Design an experiment to find out whether ordinary window glass protects skin against sun exposure. Obtain your teacher's approval before carrying out this experiment.

Figure 17 This person is taking precautions to protect her skin from the sun. ***Applying Concepts*** *What other behaviors can provide protection from the sun?*

cancerous. In addition, exposure to the sun can cause the skin to become leathery and wrinkled.

There are many things you can do to protect your skin from damage by the sun. When you are outdoors, wear a hat and sunglasses and use a sunscreen on exposed skin. The clothing you wear can also protect you. Choose clothing made of tightly woven fabrics for the greatest protection. In addition, avoid exposure to the sun between the hours of 10 A.M. and 2 P.M. That is the time when sunlight is the strongest.

Keeping Skin Clean When you wash your skin with mild soap, you get rid of dirt and harmful bacteria. Good washing habits are particularly important during the teenage years when oil glands are more active. When oil glands become clogged with oil, bacterial infections can occur.

One bacterial infection of the skin that can be difficult to control is known as **acne.** If you develop acne, your doctor may prescribe an antibiotic to help control the infection. When you wash, you help to control oiliness and keep your skin from becoming infected with more bacteria.

Other organisms, called fungi, can also live on and infect the skin. Fungi grow best in warm, moist surroundings. Athlete's foot is a very common fungal infection that occurs on the feet, especially between the toes. You can prevent athlete's foot by keeping your feet, especially the spaces between your toes, clean and dry.

Section 4 Review

1. Describe the functions of the skin.
2. List three things you can do to keep your skin healthy.
3. Describe the structure of the two layers of skin.
4. **Thinking Critically Making Judgments** Do you think it is possible to wash your skin too much and damage it as a result? Why or why not?

Science at Home

With a family member, look for products in your home that provide protection from the sun. You may also want to visit a store that sells these products. Make a list of the products and place them in categories such as sunblocks, clothing, eye protectors, and other products. Explain to your family member why it is important to use such products.

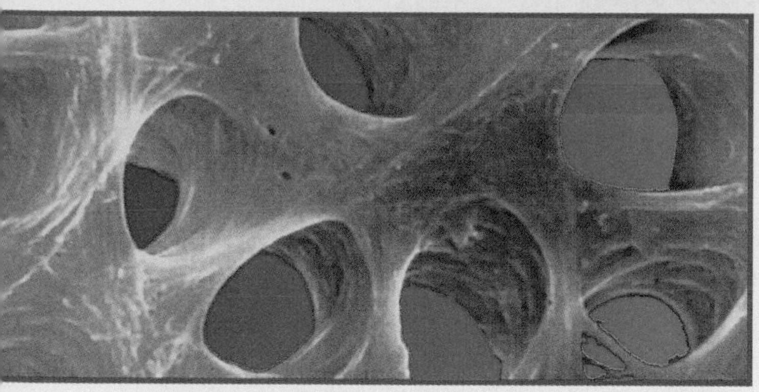

Section 1 The Skeletal System

Key Ideas

- The skeleton provides shape and support, enables movement, protects internal organs, produces blood cells, and stores materials.
- Movable joints allow the body to make a wide range of motions. Movable joints include gliding joints, hinge joints, pivot joints, and ball-and-socket joints.
- A combination of a balanced diet and regular exercise helps keep bones healthy.

Key Terms

vertebra
marrow
cartilage
joint
ligament
osteoporosis

Section 2 Diagnosing Bone and Joint Injuries

INTEGRATING TECHNOLOGY

Key Ideas

- X-rays are used to take images of bones. The waves of energy pass through the skin and other tissues and strike the photographic film underneath the area being observed.
- In magnetic resonance imaging (MRI), magnetic energy is used to produce an image of soft tissues.
- Skeletal injuries can be prevented by warming up, wearing protective equipment, and exercising in safe places.

Key Terms

fracture
sprain
dislocation
X-ray
magnetic resonance imaging

Section 3 The Muscular System

Key Ideas

- Skeletal muscles are voluntary muscles that are attached to the bones of the skeleton. Smooth muscles, which are involuntary muscles, line the walls of many internal organs and blood vessels. Cardiac muscles are involuntary muscles found only in the heart.
- Because muscles can only contract and not expand, skeletal muscles work in pairs. When one muscle contracts, the other muscle in the pair returns to its original length.

Key Terms

involuntary muscle
tendon
voluntary muscle
smooth muscle
skeletal muscle
cardiac muscle

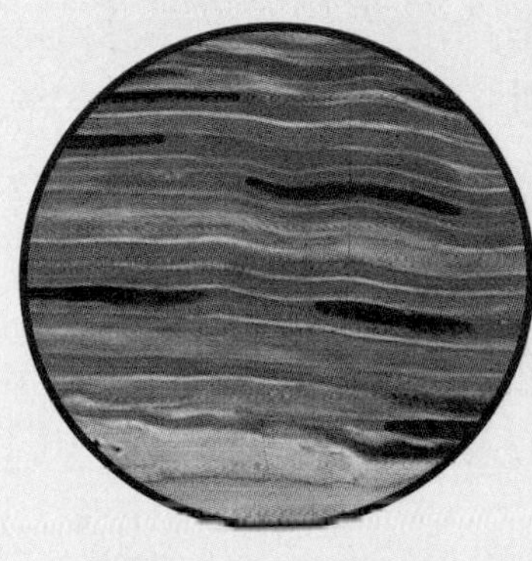

Section 4 The Skin

Key Ideas

- Skin covers and protects the body from injury and infection. It also helps to regulate body temperature, get rid of wastes, gather information about the environment, and produce vitamin D.
- The epidermis is the top layer of the skin. The dermis is the lower layer of the skin.
- For healthy skin, eat a well-balanced diet and drink enough water. Also limit your exposure to the sun and keep your skin clean.

Key Terms

epidermis
melanin
dermis
pore
follicle
cancer
acne

ACTIVITY

USING THE INTERNET

www.science-explorer.phschool.com

Reviewing Content

For more review of key concepts, see the Interactive Student Tutorial CD-ROM.

Multiple Choice

Choose the letter of the best answer.

1. Blood cells are produced in
  a. compact bone.
  b. marrow.
  c. cartilage.
  d. ligaments.

2. Joints that allow only forward or backward movement are
  a. pivot joints.
  b. ball and socket joints.
  c. hinge joints.
  d. gliding joints.

3. An injury in which the ligaments are overstretched and tear is called
  a. a fracture.
  b. a sprain.
  c. a dislocation.
  d. tendinitis.

4. Muscles that help the skeleton move are
  a. cardiac muscles.
  b. smooth muscles.
  c. skeletal muscles.
  d. involuntary muscles.

5. Which structures help to maintain body temperature?
  a. oil glands
  b. follicles
  c. sweat glands
  d. ligaments

True or False

If the statement is true, write true. If it is false, change the underlined word or words to make the statement true.

6. Spongy bone is filled with cartilage.

7. The connective tissue that connects the bones in a movable joint is called a tendon.

8. An X-ray is commonly used to diagnose soft tissue injuries.

9. Skeletal muscle is sometimes called striated muscle.

10. The epidermis contains nerve endings and blood vessels.

Checking Concepts

11. Describe the structure of a bone.

12. List the four kinds of movable joints. Describe how each kind of joint functions.

13. Why do X-ray images show bones but not muscles or other soft tissues?

14. How does the appearance of smooth muscle differ from that of skeletal muscle when viewed with a microscope?

15. Explain how skeletal muscles work in pairs to move a body part.

16. Why are smooth muscles called involuntary muscles?

17. Describe the life cycle of an epidermal cell.

18. Why is it important to limit your exposure to the sun?

19. Writing to Learn Write an article for your school newspaper about preventing skeletal and muscular injuries. The article should focus on ways in which athletes can decrease the risk of injuries during sports.

Thinking Visually

20. Concept Map Copy the concept map about muscles onto a separate sheet of paper. Then complete it and add a title. (For more information on concept maps, see the Skills Handbook.)

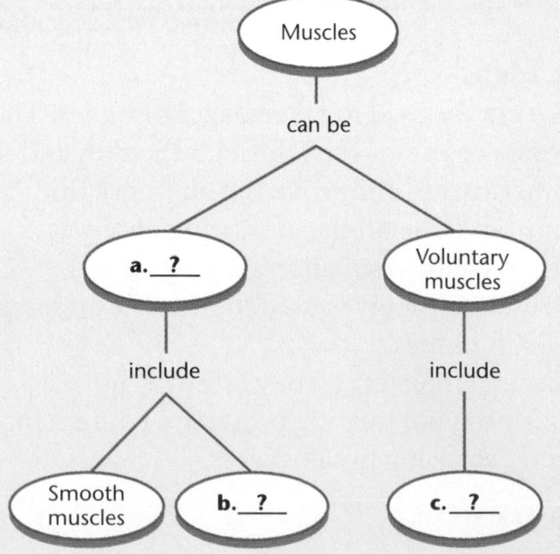

Applying Skills

The table below rates different activities as to how well they improve muscular strength and flexibility. Use the table to answer Questions 21–23.

Fitness Ratings of Physical Activities

Activity	Builds Muscular Strength	Improves Flexibility
Baseball/Softball	Low	Moderate
Gymnastics	Very High	Very High
Karate	Moderate	High
Soccer	Moderate	Moderate
Weight Training	Very High	Moderate

21. **Interpreting Data** Which activities rate highest for strength? For flexibility?
22. **Inferring** Would ballet improve muscular strength or flexibility? Why?
23. **Designing Experiments** Design an experiment to determine if an activity that you do increases muscular strength. How would you measure improvements in your strength?

Thinking Critically

24. **Inferring** Disks of rubbery cartilage are found between the vertebrae. What function do you think these disks serve?
25. **Applying Concepts** At birth, the joints in an infant's skull are flexible and not yet fixed. As the child develops, the bones become more rigid and grow together. Why is it important that the bones of an infant's skull not grow together too rapidly?
26. **Comparing and Contrasting** How are ligaments and tendons similar? How are they different?
27. **Predicting** If smooth muscle had to be consciously controlled, what problems could you foresee in day-to-day living?
28. **Relating Cause and Effect** A person who is exposed to excessive heat may suffer from a condition known as heat stroke. The first sign of heat stroke is that the person stops sweating. Why is this condition a life-threatening emergency?

Performance Assessment

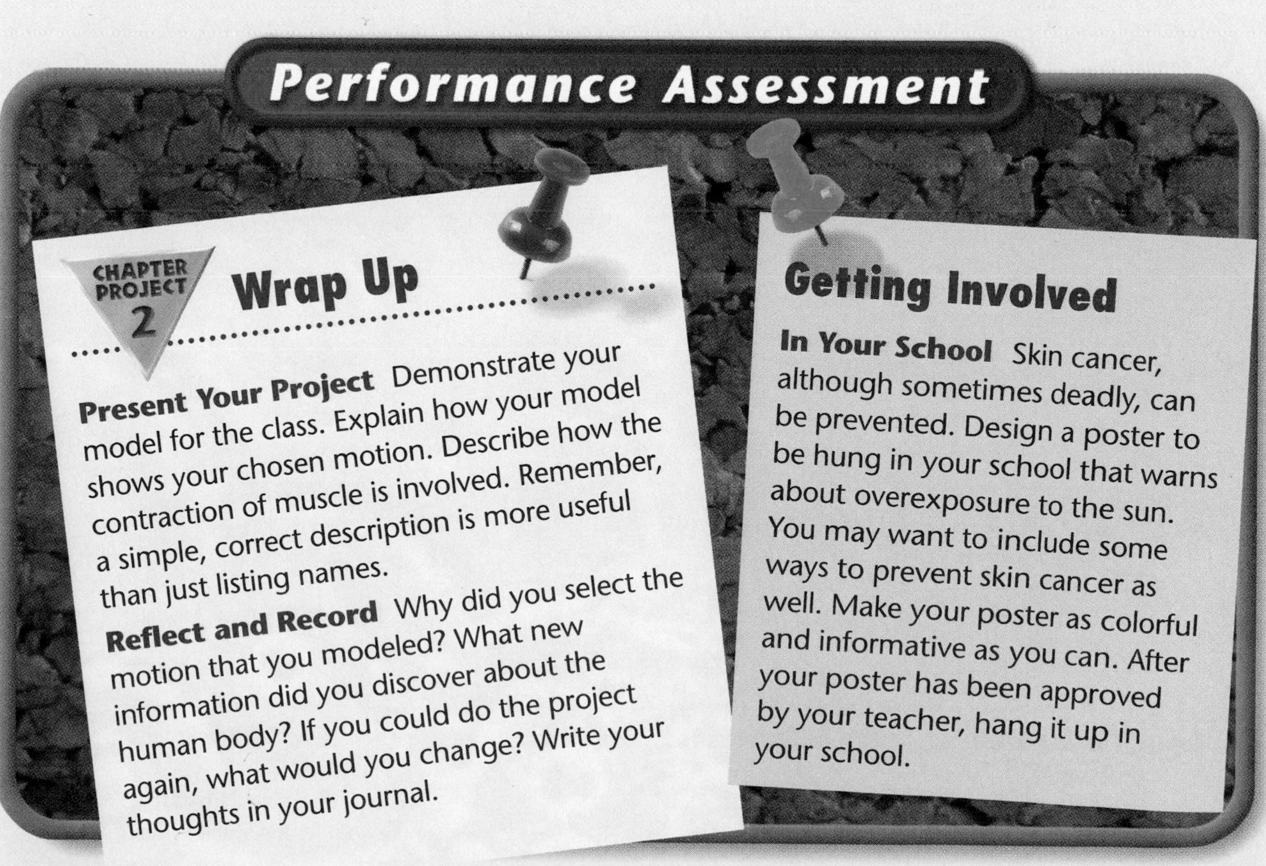

Chapter Project 2 Wrap Up

Present Your Project Demonstrate your model for the class. Explain how your model shows your chosen motion. Describe how the contraction of muscle is involved. Remember, a simple, correct description is more useful than just listing names.

Reflect and Record Why did you select the motion that you modeled? What new information did you discover about the human body? If you could do the project again, what would you change? Write your thoughts in your journal.

Getting Involved

In Your School Skin cancer, although sometimes deadly, can be prevented. Design a poster to be hung in your school that warns about overexposure to the sun. You may want to include some ways to prevent skin cancer as well. Make your poster as colorful and informative as you can. After your poster has been approved by your teacher, hang it up in your school.

CHAPTER 3

Food and Digestion

WHAT'S AHEAD

Section 1 Food and Energy

Discover Food Claims—Fact or Fiction?
Sharpen Your Skills Predicting
Real-World Lab Iron for Breakfast

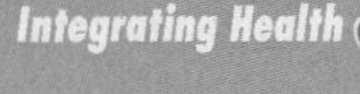

Integrating Health

Section 2 Healthy Eating

Discover Do Snack Foods Contain Fat?

Section 3 The Digestive Process Begins

Discover How Can You Speed up Digestion?
Try This Modeling Peristalsis
Skills Lab As the Stomach Churns

PROJECT 3

What's for Lunch?

When you see fresh vegetables in a market, which kinds appeal to you? In the school cafeteria at lunch time, which foods do you select? When you're hungry and grab a snack, what do you choose? This chapter looks at foods and the process of digestion that goes on in your body. It also explains how your food choices affect your health. In this project, you'll take a close look at the foods you select each day.

Your Goal To compare your eating pattern to the recommendations in the Food Guide Pyramid.

To complete this project successfully, you must

- keep an accurate record of everything you eat and drink for three days
- create graphs to compare your eating pattern with the recommendations in the Food Guide Pyramid
- make changes, if needed, during another three-day period to bring your diet closer to the recommendations in the Food Guide Pyramid

Get Started Begin by deciding how to best keep an accurate, complete food log. How will you make sure you record everything you eat, including snacks and drinks? How will you decide which category each food falls into? How will you determine serving sizes? Prepare a plan for keeping a food log, and give it to your teacher for approval.

Check Your Progress You'll be working on this project as you study this chapter. To keep your project on track, look for Check Your Progress boxes at the following points.

Section 1 Review, page 75: Keep a food log for three days.

Section 2 Review, page 81: Create graphs to compare your food choices to the recommended number of servings.

Section 4 Review, page 93: Make changes to improve your diet.

Wrap Up At the end of the chapter (page 97), you'll prepare a written summary of what you've learned.

Take your pick! Local markets offer a wide choice of tasty fruits and vegetables.

Final Digestion and Absorption

Discover **Which Surface Is Larger?**
Try This **Break Up!**

SECTION 1 Food and Energy

DISCOVER — ACTIVITY

Food Claims—Fact or Fiction?

1. Examine the list of statements at the right. Copy the list onto a separate sheet of paper.
2. Next to each statement, write *agree* or *disagree.* Give a reason for your response.
3. Discuss your responses with a small group of classmates. Compare the reasons you gave for agreeing or disagreeing with each statement.

Fact or Fiction?

a. Athletes need more protein in their diets than other people do.

b. The only salt that a food contains is the salt that you have added to it.

c. As part of a healthy diet, everyone should take vitamin supplements.

d. You can go without water for longer than you can go without food.

Think It Over

Posing Questions List some other statements about nutrition that you have heard. How could you find out whether the statements are true?

GUIDE FOR READING

- **What are the six nutrients needed by the body?**
- **What is the function of water in the body?**

Reading Tip **As you read, create a table that includes the function and sources of each nutrient group.**

Imagine a Thanksgiving dinner—roast turkey on a platter, delicious stuffing, and lots of vegetables—an abundance of colors and aromas. Food is an important part of many happy occasions, of times shared with friends and family. Food is also essential. Every living thing needs food to stay alive.

Why You Need Food

Foods provide your body with materials for growing and for repairing tissues. Food also provides energy for everything you do—running, playing a musical instrument, reading, and even sleeping. By filling those needs, food enables your body to maintain homeostasis. Recall that homeostasis is the body's ability to keep a steady internal state in spite of changing external conditions. Suppose, for example, that you cut your finger. Food provides both the raw materials necessary to grow new skin and the energy that powers this growth.

Your body converts the foods you eat into nutrients. **Nutrients** (NOO tre unts) are the substances in food that provide the raw materials and energy the body needs to carry out all the essential processes. **There are six kinds of nutrients necessary for human health—carbohydrates, fats, proteins, vitamins, minerals, and water.**

INTEGRATING PHYSICS Carbohydrates, fats, and proteins all provide the body with energy. When nutrients are used by the body for energy, the amount of energy they release can be measured in units called calories. One **calorie** is the amount of energy needed to raise the temperature of one gram of water by one Celsius degree. Most foods contain many thousands of calories of energy. Scientists usually use the term *Calorie,* with a capital *C,* to measure the energy in foods. One Calorie is the same as 1,000 calories. For example, one serving of popcorn may contain 60 Calories, or 60,000 calories, of energy. The more Calories a food has, the more energy it contains.

You need to eat a certain number of Calories each day to meet your body's energy needs. This daily energy requirement depends on a person's level of physical activity. It also changes as a person grows and ages. Infants and small children grow very rapidly, so they generally have the highest energy needs. Your current growth and level of physical activity affect the number of Calories you need. The more active you are, the higher your energy needs are.

Carbohydrates

The nutrients called **carbohydrates** (kar boh HY drayts), which are composed of carbon, oxygen, and hydrogen, are a major source of energy. One gram of carbohydrate provides your body with four Calories of energy. Carbohydrates also provide the raw materials to make parts of cells. Based on their chemical structure, carbohydrates are divided into two groups, simple carbohydrates and complex carbohydrates.

Figure 1 Your body obtains energy from carbohydrates. The sugars in fruits are simple carbohydrates. Starch is a complex carbohydrate found in grains and other plant products.

Sharpen your Skills

Predicting

ACTIVITY

Obtain food samples from your teacher. Write a prediction stating whether each food contains starch. Then test your predictions. First, put on your apron. Then use a plastic dropper to add three drops of iodine to each food sample. **CAUTION:** *Iodine can stain skin and clothing. Handle it carefully.* If the iodine turns blue-black, starch is present. Which foods contain starch?

Simple Carbohydrates Simple carbohydrates are also known as sugars. There are many types of sugars. They are found naturally in fruits, milk, and some vegetables. Sugars are also added to foods such as cookies, candies, and soft drinks. One sugar, **glucose** (GLOO kohs), is the major source of energy for your body's cells. However, most foods do not contain large amounts of glucose. The body converts other types of sugars into glucose, the form of sugar the body can use.

Complex Carbohydrates Complex carbohydrates are made up of many sugar molecules linked together in a chain. Starch is a complex carbohydrate found in plant foods such as potatoes, rice, corn, and grain products, such as pasta, cereals, and bread. To use starch as an energy source, your body first breaks it down into smaller, individual sugar molecules. Only then can your body release the molecules' energy.

Like starch, **fiber** is a complex carbohydrate found in plant foods. However, unlike starch, fiber cannot be broken down into sugar molecules by your body. Instead, the fiber passes through the body and is eliminated. Because your body cannot digest it, fiber is not considered a nutrient. Fiber is an important part of the diet, however, because it helps keep the digestive system functioning properly. Fruits, vegetables, and nuts contain fiber. So do products made with whole grains, such as some breads and cereals.

Nutritionists recommend that 50 to 60 percent of the Calories in a diet come from carbohydrates. When choosing foods containing carbohydrates, it is better to eat more complex carbohydrates than simple carbohydrates. Sugars can give a quick burst of energy, but starches provide a more even, long-term energy source. In addition, foods that are high in starch usually contain a variety of other nutrients. Foods made with a lot of sugar, such as candy, cookies, and soft drinks, usually have few valuable nutrients.

☑ ***Checkpoint*** *What are the two types of carbohydrates? Give an example of each.*

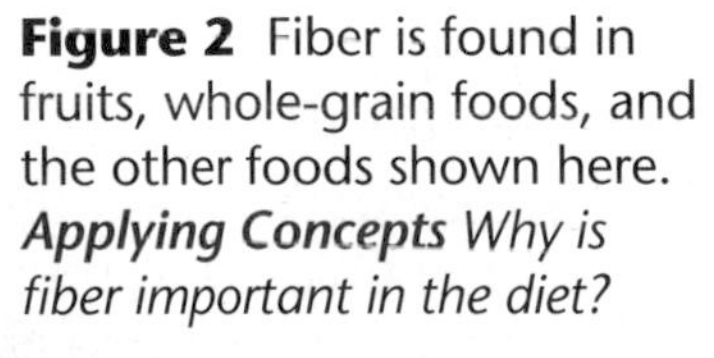

Figure 2 Fiber is found in fruits, whole-grain foods, and the other foods shown here. ***Applying Concepts*** *Why is fiber important in the diet?*

Figure 3 You obtain fats from foods such as steak, ice cream, and cooking oils.
Classifying *Which of these foods contain saturated fats?*

Fats

Like carbohydrates, **fats** are high-energy nutrients that are composed of carbon, oxygen, and hydrogen. However, fats contain more than twice as much energy as an equal amount of carbohydrates. In addition, fats perform other important functions. For example, they form part of the structure of cells. Fatty tissue also protects and supports your internal organs and acts as insulation to keep heat inside your body.

Fats are classified as either unsaturated fats or saturated fats, based on their chemical structure. **Unsaturated fats** are usually liquid at room temperature. Most oils, such as olive oil and canola oil, are unsaturated fats. Unsaturated fat is also found in some types of seafood, such as salmon. **Saturated fats** are usually solid at room temperature. Animal products, such as meat, dairy products, and egg yolks, contain relatively large amounts of saturated fat. Some oils, such as palm oil and coconut oil, are also high in saturated fat.

Foods that contain saturated fat often contain cholesterol as well. **Cholesterol** (kuh LES tur awl) is a waxy, fatlike substance found only in animal products. Like fats, cholesterol is an important part of your body's cells. But your liver makes all of the cholesterol your body needs. Therefore, cholesterol is not a necessary part of the diet.

Although people need some fats in their diet, they only need a small amount. Nutritionists recommend that no more than 30 percent of the Calories eaten each day come from fats. In particular, people should limit their intake of saturated fats and cholesterol. Extra fats and cholesterol in the diet can lead to a buildup of a fatty material in the blood vessels. This fatty buildup can cause heart disease. You will learn about the connections among fats, cholesterol, and heart disease in Chapter 4.

Math Toolbox

Calculating Percent

A percent (%) is a number compared to 100. For example, 30% means 30 out of 100.

Here is how to calculate the percent of Calories from fat in a person's diet. Suppose that a person eats a total of 2,000 Calories in one day. Of those Calories, 500 come from fats.

1. Write the comparison as a fraction:

$$\frac{500}{2,000}$$

2. Multiply the fraction by 100% to express it as a percent:

$$\frac{500}{2,000} \times \frac{100\%}{1} = 25\%$$

Calories from fat made up 25% of the person's diet that day.

Figure 4 Meats and these other foods are sources of protein.

Proteins

Proteins are nutrients that contain nitrogen as well as carbon, hydrogen, and oxygen. Proteins are needed for tissue growth and repair. They also play a part in chemical reactions within cells. Proteins can serve as a source of energy, but they are a less important source of energy than carbohydrates or fats. Foods that contain high amounts of protein include meat, poultry, fish, dairy products, nuts, beans, and lentils. About 12 percent of your daily Calorie intake should come from proteins.

Amino Acids Proteins are made up of small units called INTEGRATING CHEMISTRY **amino acids** (uh MEE noh), which are linked together chemically to form large protein molecules. Thousands of different proteins are built from only about 20 different amino acids. Your body can make about half of the amino acids it needs. The others, called essential amino acids, must come from the foods you eat.

Complete and Incomplete Proteins Proteins from animal sources, such as meat and eggs, are called complete proteins because they contain all the essential amino acids. Proteins from plant sources, such as beans, grains, and nuts, are called incomplete proteins because they are missing one or more essential amino acids. Different plant foods lack different amino acids. Therefore, to obtain all the essential amino acids from plant sources alone, people need to eat a variety of plant foods.

☑ ***Checkpoint*** *What is meant by the term* **incomplete protein?**

Vitamins

The life of a sailor in the 1700s could be difficult indeed. For one thing, sailors on long voyages ate hard, dry biscuits, salted meat, and not much else. In addition, many sailors developed a serious disease called scurvy. People with scurvy suffer from bleeding gums, stiff joints, and sores that do not heal.

Social Studies CONNECTION

Industry grew rapidly in the 1800s. During that time, many children of factory workers developed rickets, a condition in which the bones become soft. Rickets is caused by a lack of vitamin D. The main source of vitamin D is sunlight, which acts on skin cells to produce the vitamin.

Factory workers in the 1800s often lived in cities with dark, narrow streets. Air pollution from factories also blocked some sunlight. One researcher, Theobald A. Palm, wrote this statement in 1890: "It is in the narrow alleys, the haunts and playgrounds of the children of the poor, that this exclusion of sunlight is at its worst, and it is there that the victims of rickets are to be found in abundance."

In Your Journal

Write several questions that a newspaper reporter might have asked Dr. Palm about rickets among poor city residents. Then write the answers he might have given.

A Scottish doctor, James Lind, hypothesized that scurvy was the result of the sailors' poor diet. Lind divided sailors with scurvy into groups and fed different foods to each group. The sailors who were fed citrus fruits—oranges and lemons—quickly recovered from the disease. In 1754, Lind recommended that all sailors eat citrus fruits. When Lind's recommendations were finally carried out by the British Navy in 1795, scurvy disappeared from the navy.

Scurvy is caused by the lack of a nutrient called vitamin C. **Vitamins** act as helper molecules in a variety of chemical reactions within the body. The body needs only small amounts of vitamins. Figure 5 lists the vitamins necessary for health. The body can make a few of these vitamins. For example, bacteria that live in your intestines make small amounts of vitamin K.

Figure 5 Both fat-soluble vitamins and water-soluble vitamins are necessary to maintain health. ***Interpreting Charts*** *What foods provide a supply of both vitamins A and B_6?*

Essential Vitamins

Vitamin	Sources	Function
Fat-soluble		
A	Dairy products; eggs; liver; yellow, orange, and dark green vegetables; fruits	Maintains healthy skin, bones, teeth, and hair; aids vision in dim light
D	Fortified dairy products; fish; eggs; liver; made by skin cells in presence of sunlight	Maintains bones and teeth; helps in the use of calcium and phosphorus
E	Vegetable oils; margarine; green, leafy vegetables; whole-grain foods; seeds; nuts	Aids in maintenance of red blood cells
K	Green, leafy vegetables; milk; liver; made by bacteria in the intestines	Aids in blood clotting
Water-soluble		
B_1 (thiamin)	Pork; liver; whole-grain foods; legumes; nuts	Needed for breakdown of carbohydrates
B_2 (riboflavin)	Dairy products; eggs; leafy, green vegetables; whole-grain breads and cereals	Needed for normal growth
B_3 (niacin)	Many protein-rich foods; milk; eggs; meat; fish; whole-grain foods; nuts; peanut butter	Needed for release of energy
B_6 (pyridoxine)	Green and leafy vegetables; meats; fish; legumes; fruits; whole-grain foods	Helps in the breakdown of proteins, fats, and carbohydrates
B_{12}	Meats; fish; poultry; dairy products; eggs	Maintains healthy nervous system; needed for red blood cell formation
Biotin	Liver; meat; fish; eggs; legumes; bananas; melons	Aids in the release of energy
Folic acid	Leafy, green vegetables; legumes; seeds; liver	Needed for red blood cell formation
Pantothenic acid	Liver; meats; fish; eggs; whole-grain foods	Needed for the release of energy
C	Citrus fruits; tomatoes; potatoes; dark green vegetables; mangoes	Needed to form connective tissue and fight infection

However, people must obtain most vitamins from foods. If people eat a wide variety of foods, they will probably get enough of each vitamin. Most people do not need to take vitamin supplements.

Vitamins are classified as either fat-soluble or water-soluble. Fat-soluble vitamins dissolve in fat, and they are stored in fatty tissues in the body. Vitamins A, D, E, and K are all fat-soluble vitamins. Water-soluble vitamins dissolve in water and are not stored in the body. This fact makes it especially important to include sources of water-soluble vitamins—vitamin C and all the B vitamins—in your diet every day.

☑ ***Checkpoint*** *List the fat-soluble vitamins.*

Minerals

Like vitamins, minerals are needed by your body in small amounts. **Minerals** are nutrients that are not made by living things. They are present in soil and are absorbed by plants through their roots. You obtain minerals by eating plant foods or animals that have eaten plants. Figure 6 lists some minerals you

Figure 6 Eating a variety of foods each day provides your body with the minerals it needs. ***Interpreting Charts*** *Which minerals play a role in regulating water levels in the body?*

◀ Source of calcium

Essential Minerals		
Mineral	**Sources**	**Function**
Calcium	Milk; cheese; dark green, leafy vegetables; tofu; legumes	Helps build bones and teeth; important for blood-clotting, nerve and muscle function
Chlorine	Table salt; soy sauce; processed foods	Helps maintain water balance; aids in digestion
Fluorine	Fluoridated drinking water; fish	Helps form bones and teeth
Iodine	Seafood; iodized salt	Makes up part of hormones that regulate the release of energy
Iron	Red meats; seafood; green, leafy vegetables; legumes; dried fruits	Forms an important part of red blood cells
Magnesium	Green, leafy vegetables; legumes; nuts; whole-grain foods	Needed for normal muscle and nerve function; helps in the release of energy
Phosphorus	Meat; poultry; eggs; fish; dairy products	Needed for healthy bones and teeth; helps in the release of energy
Potassium	Grains; fruits; vegetables; meat; fish	Helps maintain water balance; needed for normal muscle and nerve function
Sodium	Table salt; soy sauce; processed foods	Helps maintain water balance; needed for normal nerve function

▼ Source of potassium

Source of sodium ▶

need. As you know from Chapter 2, calcium is needed for strong bones and teeth. Iron is needed for the proper function of red blood cells.

Water

Imagine that a boat is sinking. The people are getting into a lifeboat. They have room for one of the following: a bag of fruit, a can of meat, a loaf of bread, or a jug of water. Which item should they choose?

You might be surprised to learn that the lifeboat passengers should choose the water. Although people can probably survive for weeks without food, they will die within days without fresh water. Water is the most abundant substance in the body. It accounts for about 65 percent of the average person's body weight.

Figure 7 Like all living things, you need water. Without regular water intake, your body cannot carry out the processes that keep you alive.

Water is the most important nutrient because the body's vital processes—including chemical reactions such as the breakdown of nutrients—take place in water. Water makes up most of the body's fluids, including blood. Nutrients and other important substances are carried throughout the body dissolved in the watery part of the blood. Your body also needs water to produce perspiration.

Under normal conditions, you need to take in about 2 liters of water every day. You can do this by drinking water and other beverages, and by eating foods with lots of water, such as fruits and vegetables. If the weather is hot or you are exercising, you need to drink even more to replace the water that you lose in sweat.

Section 1 Review

1. List the six nutrients that are needed by the body.
2. Give three reasons why water is necessary for the body to function.
3. Why should you eat more complex carbohydrates than simple carbohydrates?
4. What is the difference between fat-soluble vitamins and water-soluble vitamins?
5. **Thinking Critically Applying Concepts** Why is it especially important that vegetarians eat a varied diet?

CHAPTER PROJECT 3

Check Your Progress

By now, you should have given your teacher your plan for keeping your food log. Adjust the plan as your teacher suggests. Then start your three days of record-keeping. If possible, your record-keeping should span two weekdays and one weekend day. Be sure to keep an accurate record of all the foods and beverages you consume. (*Hint:* Either make your log portable, or plan a method for recording your food intake when you're away from home.)

Real-World Lab

You, the Consumer

Iron for Breakfast

Have you ever looked at the nutrition facts on a cereal box? Some of the listed nutrients occur naturally in the cereal. Others are added as it is processed. In this lab, you will look for evidence that extra iron has been added to some cereals.

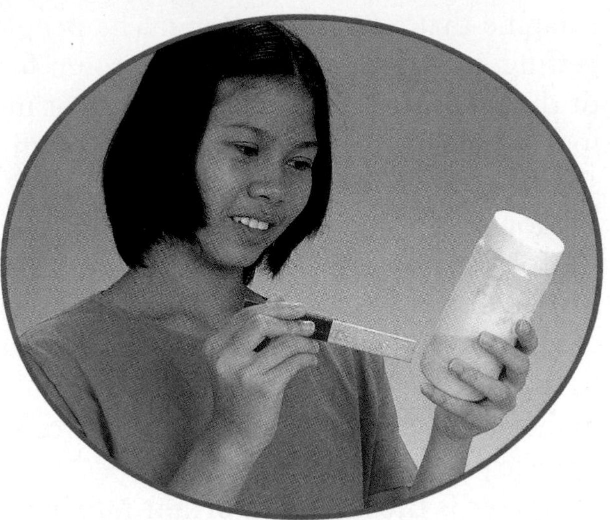

Problem

How can you test whether iron has been added to cereals?

Skills Focus

observing, predicting, interpreting data

Materials

long bar magnet
white paper towels
instant oatmeal
watch or clock
wooden dowel
2 dry breakfast cereals
3 sealable plastic freezer bags
plastic jar with sealable cover
balance
plastic spoon
warm water

Procedure

1. Read the nutrition facts listed on the packages of the cereals that you'll be testing. Record the percent of iron listed for each of the cereals.
2. Put a paper towel on the pan of a balance. Use a spoon to measure out 50 grams of instant oatmeal. **CAUTION:** *Do not eat any of the cereals in this lab.*
3. Place the oatmeal in a plastic bag. Push down gently on the bag to remove most of the air, then seal the bag. Roll a dowel over the cereal repeatedly to crush it into a fine powder.
4. Pour the powdered cereal into a plastic jar. Cover the cereal with warm water. Cover the jar tightly and shake it for about 15 minutes.
5. Move a bar magnet along the outside of the jar. Observe the results.
6. Repeat Steps 2 through 5 with your other cereal samples.

Analyze and Conclude

1. Describe the material you saw inside the jar near the magnet. What evidence do you have that this material is iron?
2. Which sample appeared to have the most added iron? The least? Were those results consistent with the listed amounts?
3. Why is it likely that any iron metal present in the cereal was added during the processing?
4. What roles does iron play in the body?
5. **Apply** Why might adding iron to breakfast cereal be a good way to ensure that children receive an adequate amount of that mineral?

More to Explore

Read the labels on five snack foods. Make a bar graph showing their iron content.

SECTION 2 Healthy Eating

DISCOVER ACTIVITY

Do Snack Foods Contain Fat?

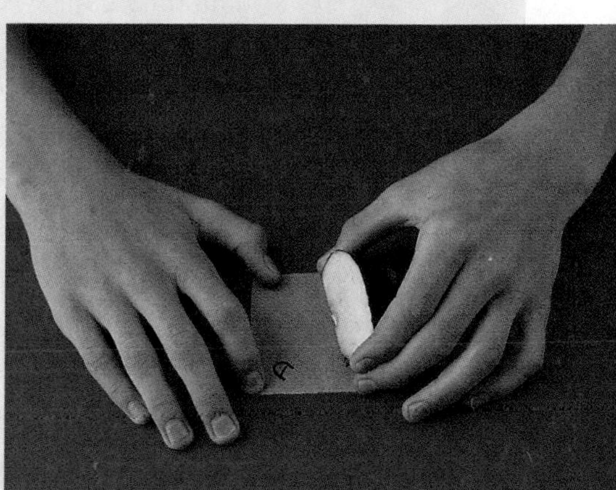

1. Cut four small squares from a brown paper bag. Label them *A, B, C,* and *D.*
2. Rub some crushed potato chips on square A. **CAUTION:** *Do not eat any of the foods in this activity.*
3. Repeat Step 2 using crushed pretzels (on square B), a piece of chocolate (on square C), and an apple slice (on square D).
4. Remove any food. Allow the paper squares to dry.
5. Note which squares have spots of oil on them.

Think It Over

Classifying If a food contains fat, it will leave oily spots on the brown paper. What does this tell you about the foods you tested?

GUIDE FOR READING

- **How can the Food Guide Pyramid help you plan a healthy diet?**
- **What kind of information is included on food labels?**

Reading Tip **Before you read, preview *Exploring the Food Guide Pyramid* on page 79. Write a list of questions about the pyramid. As you read, try to answer your questions.**

What does healthy eating mean to you? Eating more fresh fruits and vegetables? Not skipping breakfast? Cutting down on soft drinks and chips? You have just learned about the six types of nutrients—carbohydrates, fats, proteins, vitamins, minerals, and water—that are part of a healthy diet. You may now be wondering how you can use this information to make healthful changes in your diet.

With so many foods available, it may seem more difficult, not easier, to establish a healthful diet. Luckily, nutritionists have developed some aids—the Food Guide Pyramid and food labels.

Figure 8 Fruits and vegetables are essential parts of a healthy diet. Some people enjoy picking these foods right off the plant.

The Food Guide Pyramid

The **Food Guide Pyramid** was developed by nutritionists to help people plan a healthy diet. **The Food Guide Pyramid classifies foods into six groups. It also indicates how many servings from each group should be eaten every day to maintain a healthy diet.** You can combine the advice within the pyramid with knowledge of your own food preferences. By doing this, you can have a healthy diet containing foods you like.

You can see the six food groups in *Exploring the Food Guide Pyramid.* Notice that the food group at the base of the pyramid includes foods made from grains, such as bread, cereal, rice, and pasta. This bottom level is the widest part of the pyramid. The large size indicates that these foods should make up the largest part of the diet.

Figure 9 If you are very active, you need to eat more servings within the ranges specified for each food group in the Food Guide Pyramid.

The second level in the pyramid is made of two food groups, the Fruit group and the Vegetable group. Notice that this level is not as wide as the bottom level. This size difference indicates that people need fewer servings of these foods than of foods from the bottom level. The third level of the pyramid contains the Milk, Yogurt, and Cheese group, and the Meat, Poultry, Fish, Dry Beans, Eggs, and Nuts group. People need still smaller amounts of food from the third level.

At the top of the pyramid are foods containing large amounts of fat, sugar, or both. Notice that this is the smallest part of the pyramid. The small size indicates that intake of these foods should be limited. There is a good reason for this advice. Foods in the other groups already contain fats and sugars. Limiting intake of *additional* fats and sugars can help you prevent heart disease and other problems.

☑ ***Checkpoint*** *What types of foods should make up the largest portion of a person's diet?*

Food Labels

After a long day, you and your friends stop into a store on your way home from school. What snack should you buy? How can you make a wise choice? One thing you can do is to read the information provided on food labels. The United States Food and Drug Administration (FDA) requires that all food items except meat, poultry, fresh vegetables, and fresh fruit must be labeled with specific nutritional information.

EXPLORING the Food Guide Pyramid

The Food Guide Pyramid recommends the number of servings that a person should eat each day from six food groups. Note that each number of servings is listed as a range. Active, growing teenagers may need to eat the larger number of servings for each group.

Fats, Oils, and Sweets (Use sparingly.) Soft drinks, candy, ice cream, mayonnaise, and other foods in this group have few valuable nutrients. In addition, these foods are high in Calories. They should be eaten only in small quantities.

Milk, Yogurt, and Cheese Group (2–3 servings) Milk and other dairy products are rich in proteins, carbohydrates, vitamins, and minerals. Try to select low-fat dairy foods, such as low-fat milk.

Meat, Poultry, Fish, Dry Beans, Eggs, and Nuts Group (2–3 servings) These foods are high in protein. They also supply vitamins and minerals. Since eggs, nuts, and some meats are high in fat, they should be eaten sparingly.

Vegetable Group (3–5 servings) Vegetables are low-fat sources of carbohydrates, fiber, vitamins, and minerals.

Fruit Group (2–4 servings) Fruits are good sources of carbohydrates, fiber, vitamins, and water.

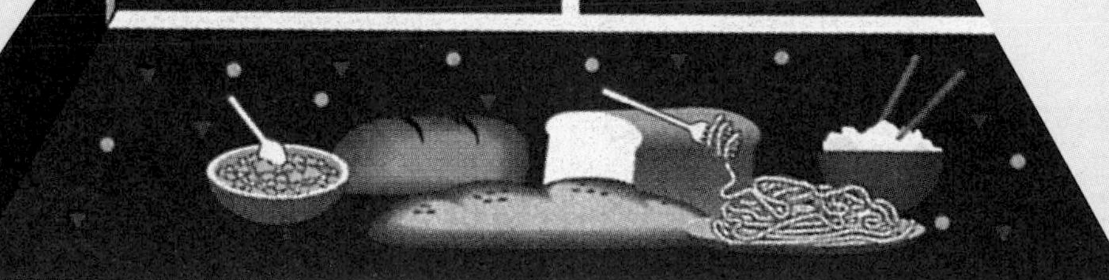

Bread, Cereal, Rice, and Pasta Group (6–11 servings) The foods at the base of the pyramid are rich in complex carbohydrates and also provide proteins, fiber, vitamins, and some minerals.

● *Fat (naturally occurring and added)*

▲ *Sugars (naturally occurring and added)*

Figure 10 shows a food label that might appear on a box of cereal. Refer to that label as you read about some of the important nutritional information it contains.

Serving Size Notice that the serving size and the number of servings in the container are listed at the top of the label. The FDA has established standard serving sizes for all types of foods. This means that all containers of ice cream, for example, use the same serving size on their labels. The information on the rest of the label, including Calorie counts and nutrient content, is based on the serving size. Therefore, if you eat a portion that's twice as large as the serving size, you'll consume twice the number of Calories and nutrients listed on the label.

Figure 10 By law, specific nutritional information must be listed on food labels. ***Calculating*** *How many servings of this product would you have to eat to get 90 percent of the Daily Value for iron?*

Nutrition Facts

Serving Size	1 cup (30g)
Servings Per Container	About 10

Amount Per Serving

Calories 110	Calories from Fat 15
	% Daily Value*
Total Fat 2g	**3%**
Saturated Fat 0g	**0%**
Cholesterol 0mg	**0%**
Sodium 280mg	**12%**
Total Carbohydrate 22g	**7%**
Dietary Fiber 3g	**12%**
Sugars 1g	
Protein 3g	

Vitamin A	10%	• Vitamin C	20%
Calcium	4%	• Iron	45%

* Percent Daily Values are based on a 2,000 Calorie diet. Your daily values may be higher or lower depending on your caloric needs:

	Calories	2,000	2,500
Total Fat	Less than	65g	80g
Sat. Fat	Less than	20g	25g
Cholesterol	Less than	300mg	300mg
Sodium	Less than	2,400mg	2,400mg
Total Carbohydrate		300g	375g
Fiber		25g	30g

Calories per gram:
Fat 9 • Carbohydrate 4 • Protein 4

Ingredients: Whole grain oats, sugar, salt, milled corn, oat fiber, dried whey, hon... almonds...

Calories from Fat The next item on the food label is the number of Calories in a serving and the number of Calories that come from fat. Notice that a single serving of this cereal supplies the body with 110 Calories of energy.

Recall that no more than 30 percent of the Calories you consume should come from fats. To calculate whether a specific food falls within this guideline, divide the number of Calories from fat by the total number of Calories, then multiply by 100%. For this cereal,

$$\frac{15}{110} \times \frac{100\%}{1} = 13.6\%.$$

That number shows you that a serving of this cereal is well within the recommended limits for fat intake.

Daily Values Locate the % Daily Value column on the label. The **Percent Daily Value** indicates how the nutritional content of one serving fits into the diet of a person who consumes a total of 2,000 Calories a day. One serving of this cereal contains 280 milligrams of sodium. That's 12 percent of the total amount of sodium a person should consume in one day.

As you have learned, the number of Calories you need daily depends on your age, size, and level of activity. An active teenager may require 2,500 Calories or more each day. If your needs exceed 2,000 Calories, you should take in more of each nutrient in your daily diet. Some food labels include a list of the nutrient needs for both a 2,000-Calorie and a 2,500-Calorie diet.

Ingredients Packaged foods, such as crackers and soup mixes, usually contain a mixture of ingredients. The food label lists those ingredients in order by weight, starting with the main ingredient. In a breakfast cereal, for example, that may be corn, oats, rice, or wheat. Often, sugar and salt are added for flavor. The list can alert you to substances that have been added to a food to improve its flavor or color, or to keep it from spoiling. In addition, some people can become sick or break out in a rash if they eat certain substances. By reading ingredients lists, people can avoid foods that contain those substances.

Using Food Labels You can use food labels to help you make healthful food choices. **Food labels allow you to evaluate a single food as well as to compare the nutritional value of two foods.** Suppose you are shopping for breakfast cereals. By reading the labels, you might find that one cereal contains little fat and a high percentage of the Daily Value for valuable nutrients such as complex carbohydrates and several vitamins. Another cereal might have fewer complex carbohydrates and vitamins and contain significant amounts of fat. You can see that the first cereal would be a better choice as a regular breakfast food. If you really enjoy the other cereal, however, you might make it an occasional treat rather than an everyday choice.

Figure 11 Food labels allow you to compare the nutritional content of similar kinds of foods.

Section 2 Review

1. What information does the Food Guide Pyramid provide? Into how many groups are foods classified?
2. Explain how food labels can help a person make healthy food choices.
3. Why are foods in the Bread, Cereal, Rice, and Pasta group placed at the bottom of the Food Guide Pyramid?
4. **Thinking Critically Applying Concepts** Why might a runner need more servings from the Bread, Cereal, Rice, and Pasta group than a less active person?

CHAPTER PROJECT 3

Check Your Progress

By this point, you should have completed three full days of record keeping. Now create bar graphs to compare your food intake to the recommended numbers of servings in the Food Guide Pyramid. Analyze your graphs to identify changes you could make in your diet.

The Digestive Process Begins

DISCOVER ACTIVITY

How Can You Speed up Digestion?

1. Obtain two plastic jars with lids. Fill the jars with equal amounts of water.
2. At the same time, place a whole sugar cube into one jar. Place a crushed sugar cube into the other jar.
3. Fasten the lids on the jars. Holding one jar in each hand, shake the two jars gently and equally.
4. Place the jars on a flat surface. Observe whether the whole cube or the crushed cube dissolves faster.

Think It Over

Predicting Use the results of this activity to predict which would take longer to digest: a large piece of food or one that has been cut up into many small pieces. Explain your answer.

GUIDE FOR READING

- **What general functions are carried out in the digestive system?**

Reading Tip **Before you read, preview the headings in this section. Predict the functions of the mouth, the esophagus, and the stomach.**

In June of 1822, nineteen-year-old Alexis St. Martin was wounded in the stomach while hunting. William Beaumont, a doctor with the United States Army, saved St. Martin's life. However, the wound left an opening in St. Martin's stomach that never closed completely. Beaumont realized that by looking through the opening, he could observe what was happening inside St. Martin's stomach.

Beaumont observed that milk changed chemically inside the stomach. He hypothesized that chemical reactions inside the stomach broke down foods into smaller particles. To test his hypothesis, Beaumont removed liquid from St. Martin's stomach. He had the liquid analyzed to determine what materials it contained. The stomach liquid contained an acid that could break down foods into simpler substances.

Dr. William Beaumont ▼

Functions of the Digestive System

Beaumont's observations helped scientists understand the role of the stomach in the digestive system. The digestive system has three main functions. **First, it breaks down food into molecules the body can use. Then, the molecules are absorbed into the blood and carried throughout the body. Finally, wastes are eliminated from the body.**

The process by which your body breaks down food into small nutrient molecules is called **digestion.** There are two kinds of digestion—mechanical and chemical. In mechanical digestion, foods are physically broken down into smaller pieces. Mechanical digestion occurs when you bite into a sandwich and chew it into small pieces. In chemical digestion, chemicals produced by the body break foods into their smaller chemical building blocks. For example, the starch in bread is broken down into individual sugar molecules.

After your food is digested, the molecules are ready to be transported throughout your body. **Absorption** (ab SAWRP shun) is the process by which nutrient molecules pass through the wall of your digestive system into your blood. Materials that are not absorbed, such as fiber, are eliminated from the body as wastes.

Figure 12 shows the organs of the digestive system, which is about nine meters long from beginning to end. As food moves through the digestive system, the processes of digestion, absorption, and elimination occur one after the other in an efficient, continuous process.

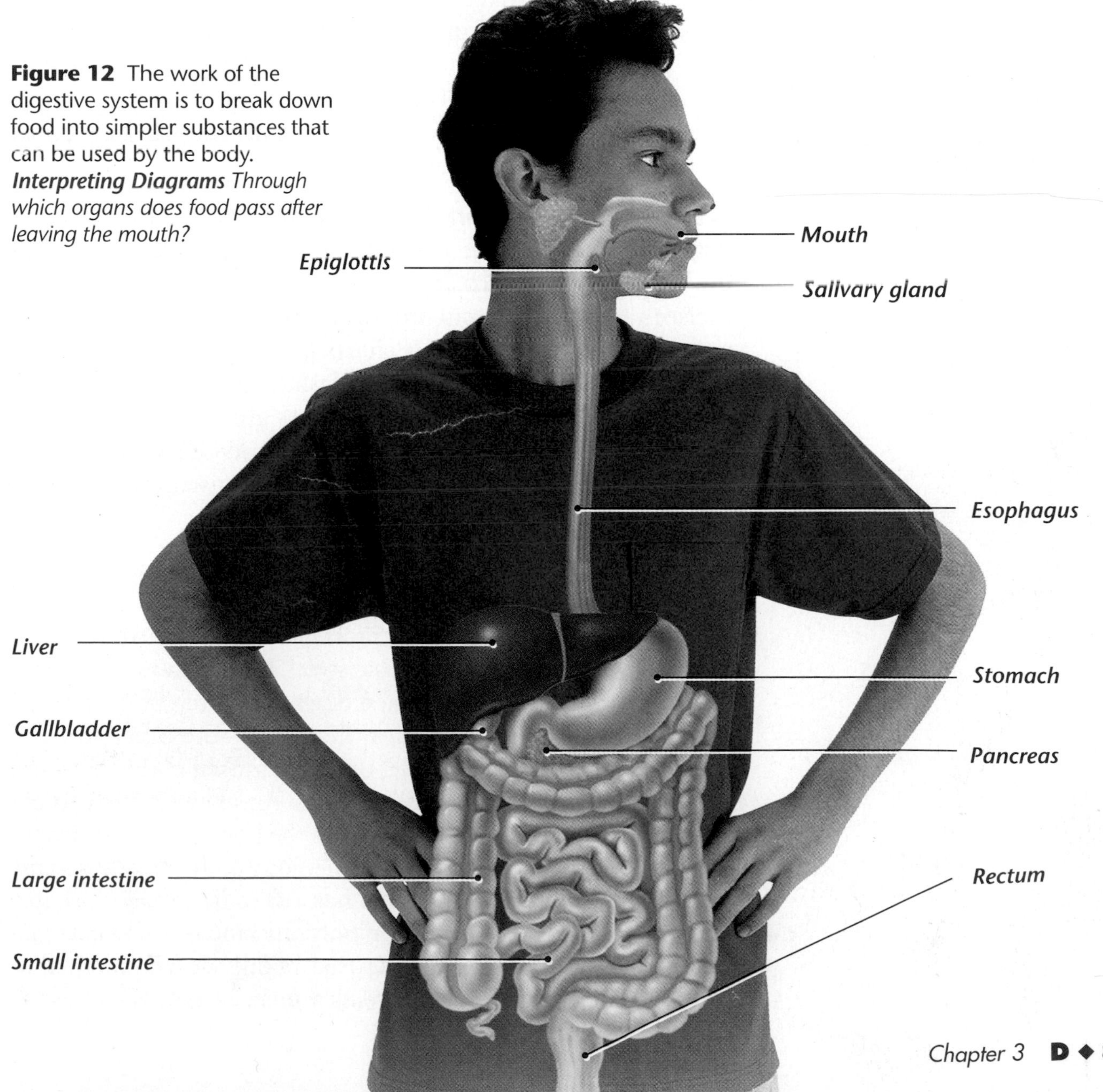

Figure 12 The work of the digestive system is to break down food into simpler substances that can be used by the body. ***Interpreting Diagrams*** *Through which organs does food pass after leaving the mouth?*

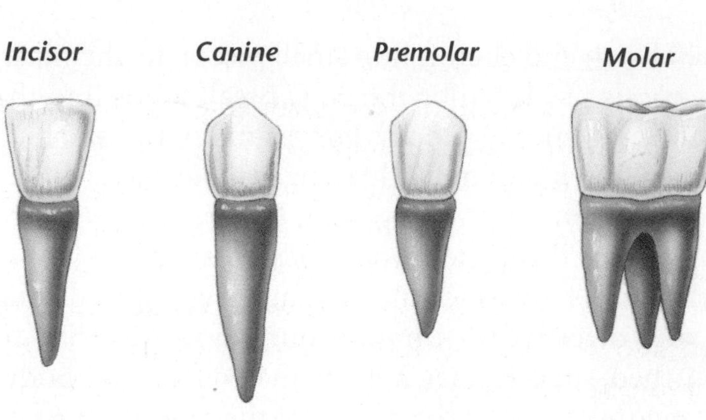

Figure 13 Mechanical digestion begins in the mouth, where the teeth cut and tear food into smaller pieces. ***Observing*** *Which teeth are specialized for biting into a juicy apple?*

The Mouth

Have you ever walked past a bakery or restaurant and noticed your mouth watering? Smelling or even just thinking about food when you're hungry is enough to start your mouth watering. This response isn't accidental. Your body is responding to hunger and thoughts of food by preparing for the delicious meal it expects. The fluid released when your mouth waters is called **saliva** (suh LY vuh). Saliva plays an important role in both the mechanical and chemical digestive processes that take place in the mouth.

Mechanical Digestion The process of mechanical digestion begins as you take your first bite of food. Your teeth carry out the first stage of mechanical digestion. Your center teeth, or incisors (in SY zurz), cut the food into bite-sized pieces. On either side of the incisors are sharp, pointy teeth called canines (KAY nynz). These teeth tear and slash the food in your mouth into smaller pieces. Behind the canines are the premolars and molars, which crush and grind the food. As the teeth do their work, saliva mixes with the pieces of food, moistening them into one slippery mass.

Chemical Digestion Like mechanical digestion, chemical

INTEGRATING CHEMISTRY

digestion begins in the mouth. If you take a bite of a cracker and roll it around your mouth, the cracker begins to taste sweet. It tastes sweet because a chemical in the saliva has broken down the starch in the cracker into sugar molecules. Chemical digestion—the breakdown of complex molecules into simpler ones—has taken place. Chemical digestion is accomplished by enzymes. An **enzyme** is a protein that speeds up chemical reactions in the body. The chemical in saliva that digests starch is an enzyme. Your body produces many different enzymes. Each enzyme has a specific chemical shape. Its shape enables it to take part in only one kind of chemical reaction. For example, the enzyme that breaks down starch into sugars cannot break down proteins into amino acids.

The Esophagus

If you've ever choked on food, someone may have said that your food "went down the wrong way." That's because there are two openings at the back of your mouth. One opening leads to your windpipe, which carries air into your lungs. Usually, your body keeps food out of your windpipe. As you swallow, muscles in your throat move the food downward. While this happens, a flap of tissue called the **epiglottis** (ep uh GLAHT is) seals off your windpipe, preventing the food from entering. As you swallow, food goes into the **esophagus** (ih SAHF uh gus), a muscular tube that connects the mouth to the stomach. The esophagus is lined with mucus. **Mucus** is a thick, slippery substance produced by the body. In the digestive system, mucus makes food easier to swallow and to be moved along.

Food remains in the esophagus for only about 10 seconds. After food enters the esophagus, contractions of smooth muscles push the food toward the stomach. These involuntary waves of muscle contraction are called **peristalsis** (pehr ih STAWL sis). The action of peristalsis is shown in Figure 14. Peristalsis also occurs in the stomach and farther down the digestive system. These muscular waves keep food moving in one direction.

Checkpoint *How is food prevented from entering the windpipe?*

Modeling Peristalsis

ACTIVITY

1. Obtain a clear, flexible plastic straw.
2. Put on your goggles. Hold the straw vertically and insert a small bead into the top of the straw. The bead should fit snugly into the straw. Do not blow into the straw.
3. Pinch the straw above the bead so that the bead begins to move down the length of the tubing.
4. Repeat Step 3 until the bead exits the straw.

Making Models How does this action compare with peristalsis? What do the bead and the straw represent in this model?

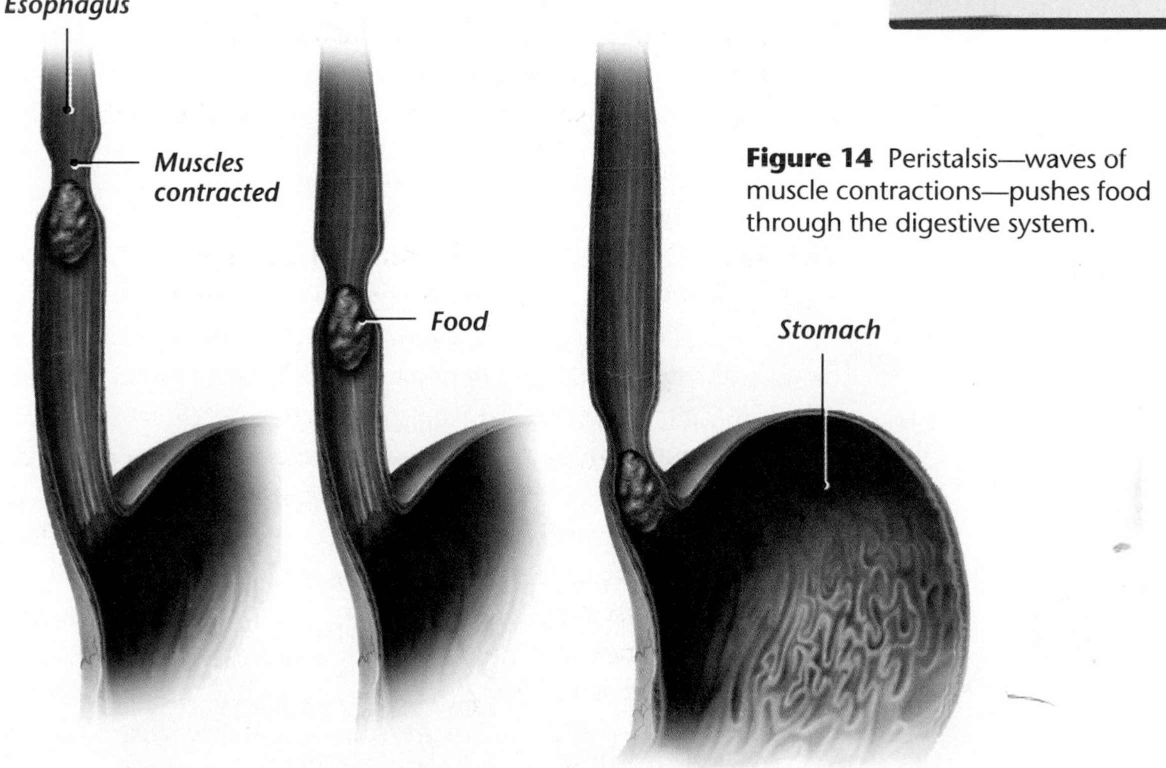

Figure 14 Peristalsis—waves of muscle contractions—pushes food through the digestive system.

The Stomach

When food leaves the esophagus, it enters the **stomach,** a J-shaped, muscular pouch located in the abdomen. As you eat, your stomach expands to hold all of the food that you swallow. An average adult's stomach holds about 2 liters of food.

Most mechanical digestion occurs in the stomach. Three strong layers of muscle contract to produce a churning motion. This action squeezes the food, mixing it with fluids in somewhat the same way that clothes and soapy water are mixed in a washing machine.

INTEGRATING CHEMISTRY While mechanical digestion is taking place, so too is chemical digestion. The churning of the stomach mixes food with digestive juice, a fluid produced by cells in the lining of the stomach.

Digestive juice contains the enzyme pepsin. Pepsin chemically digests the proteins in your food, breaking them down into amino acids. Digestive juice also contains hydrochloric acid, a very strong acid. This acid would burn a hole in clothes if it were spilled on them. Without this strong acid, however, your stomach could not function properly. First, pepsin works best in an acid environment. Second, the acid kills many bacteria that you swallow along with your food.

Since the acid is so strong, you may wonder why it doesn't burn a hole in your stomach. The reason is that digestive juice

Figure 15 As food passes through the digestive system, the digestive juices gradually break down large food molecules into smaller molecules. ***Interpreting Charts*** *Which enzymes aid in protein digestion?*

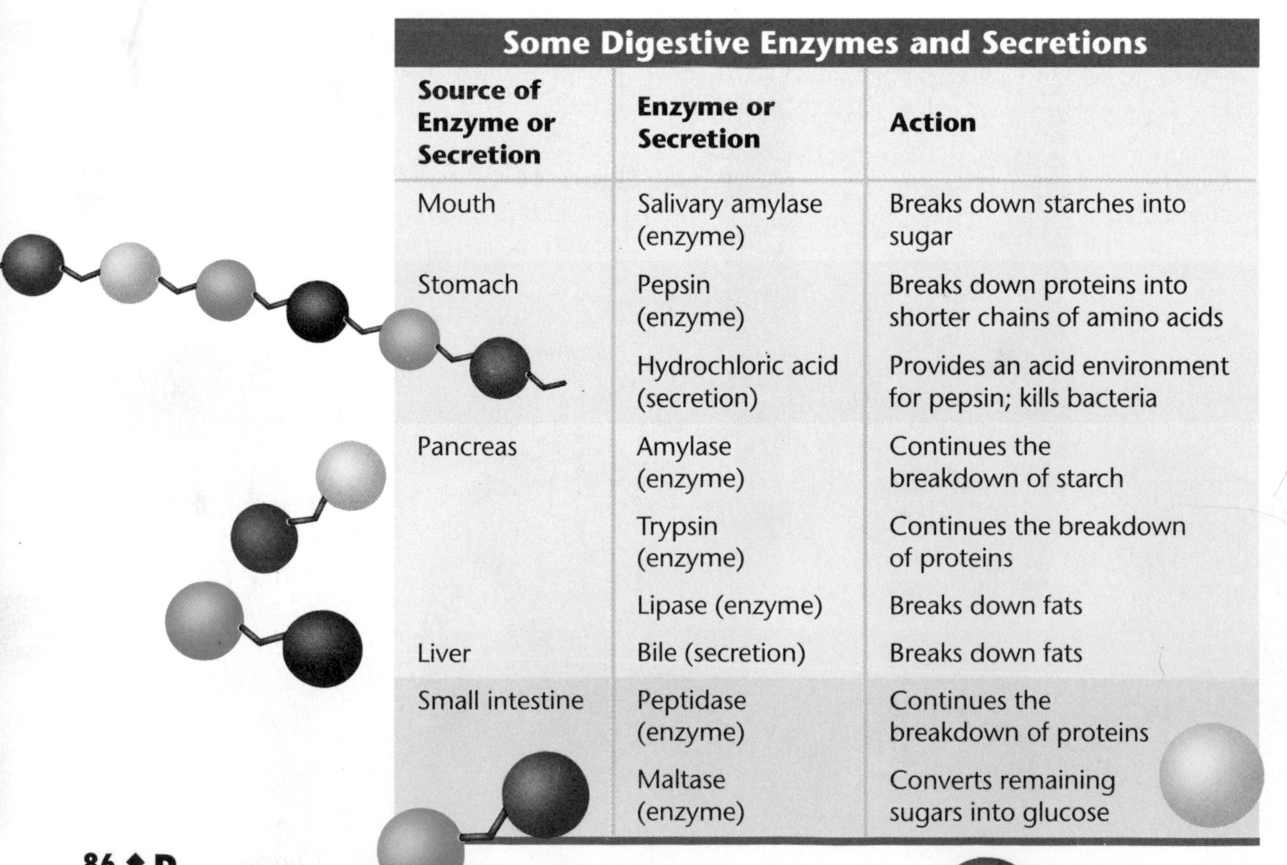

Some Digestive Enzymes and Secretions

Source of Enzyme or Secretion	Enzyme or Secretion	Action
Mouth	Salivary amylase (enzyme)	Breaks down starches into sugar
Stomach	Pepsin (enzyme)	Breaks down proteins into shorter chains of amino acids
	Hydrochloric acid (secretion)	Provides an acid environment for pepsin; kills bacteria
Pancreas	Amylase (enzyme)	Continues the breakdown of starch
	Trypsin (enzyme)	Continues the breakdown of proteins
	Lipase (enzyme)	Breaks down fats
Liver	Bile (secretion)	Breaks down fats
Small intestine	Peptidase (enzyme)	Continues the breakdown of proteins
	Maltase (enzyme)	Converts remaining sugars into glucose

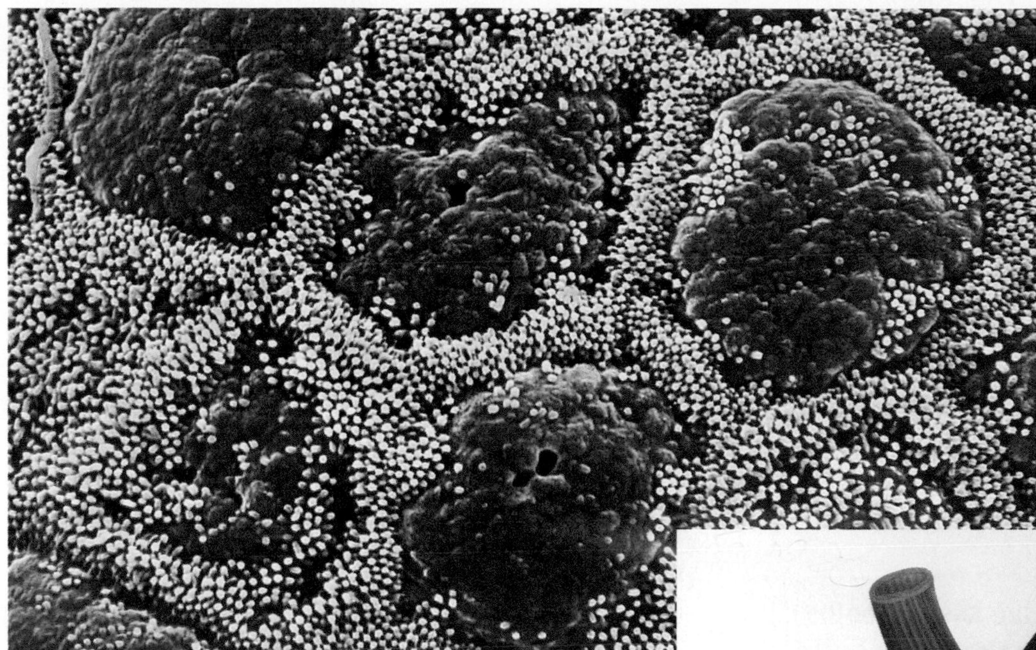

Figure 16 The stomach walls (left) produce mucus, shown here in yellow. Mucus protects the stomach from its own acid and enzymes. The stomach has powerful muscles (below) that help grind up food.

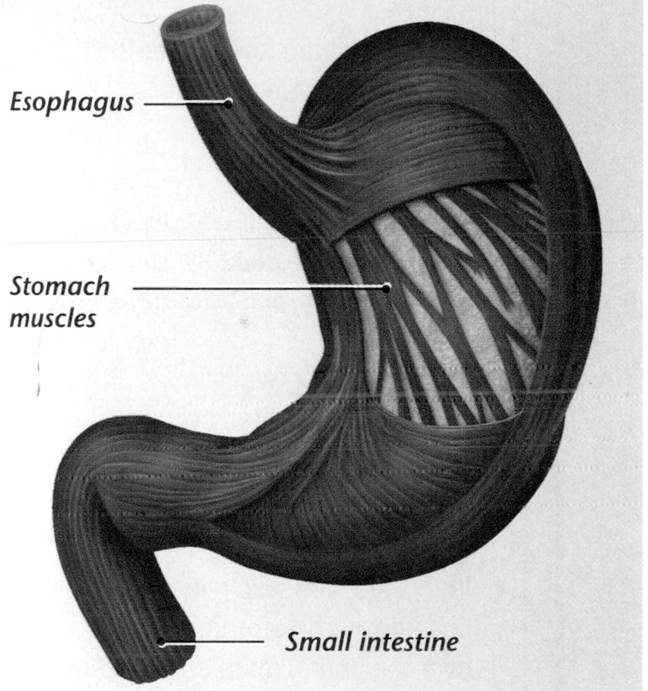

also contains mucus, which coats and protects the lining of your stomach. In addition, the cells that line the stomach are quickly replaced when they are damaged or worn out.

Food remains in the stomach until all of the solid material has been digested into liquid form. A few hours after you finish eating, the stomach completes mechanical digestion of the food. By that time, most of the proteins have been chemically digested into shorter chains of amino acids. The food, now a thick liquid, is released into the next part of the digestive system. That is where final chemical digestion and absorption will take place.

Section 3 Review

1. List the functions of the digestive system.
2. What role does saliva play in digestion?
3. Describe peristalsis and explain its function in the digestive system.
4. What is the function of pepsin?
5. **Thinking Critically Predicting** If your stomach could no longer produce acid, how do you think that would affect digestion?

Science at Home

Explain to your family what happens when people choke on food. With your family, find out how to recognize when a person is choking and what to do to help the person. Learn about the Heimlich maneuver and how it is used to help someone who is choking.

Skills Lab

Drawing Conclusions

AS THE STOMACH CHURNS

The proteins you eat are constructed of large, complex molecules. Your body begins to break down those complex molecules in the stomach. In this lab, you will draw conclusions about the process by which proteins are digested.

Problem

What conditions are needed for the digestion of proteins in the stomach?

Materials

test tube rack
marking pencil
pepsin
dilute hydrochloric acid
water
plastic stirrers
litmus paper
cubes of boiled egg white
10-mL plastic graduated cylinder
4 test tubes with stoppers

Procedure

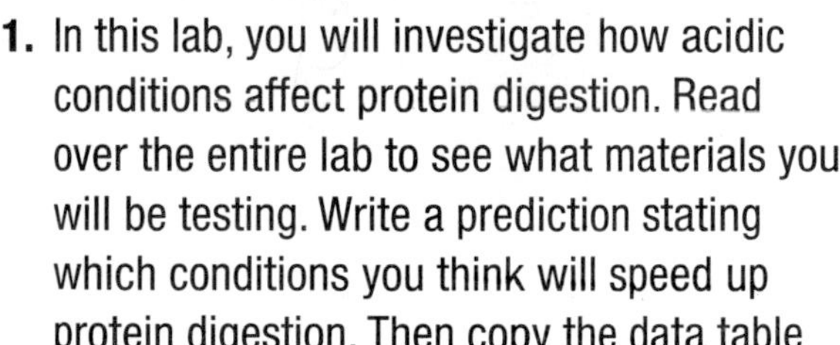

1. In this lab, you will investigate how acidic conditions affect protein digestion. Read over the entire lab to see what materials you will be testing. Write a prediction stating which conditions you think will speed up protein digestion. Then copy the data table into your notebook.
2. Label four test tubes *A, B, C,* and *D* and place them in a test tube rack.
3. In this lab, the protein you will test is boiled egg white, which has been cut into cubes about 1 cm on each side. Add 3 cubes to each test tube. Note and record the size and overall appearance of the cubes in each test tube. **CAUTION:** *Do not put any egg white into your mouth.*
4. Use a graduated cylinder to add 10 mL of the enzyme pepsin to test tube A. Observe the egg white cubes to determine whether an immediate reaction takes place. Record your observations under *Day 1* in your data table. If no changes occur, write "no immediate reaction."
5. Use a clean graduated cylinder to add 5 mL of pepsin to test tube B. Then rinse the graduated cylinder and add 5 mL of water to test tube B. Observe whether or not an immediate reaction takes place.
6. Use a clean graduated cylinder to add 10 mL of hydrochloric acid to test tube C. Observe whether or not an immediate reaction takes place. **CAUTION:** *Hydrochloric acid can burn skin and clothing. Avoid direct contact with it. Wash any splashes or spills with plenty of water, and notify your teacher.*

DATA TABLE

Test Tube	Egg White Appearance		Litmus Color	
	Day 1	Day 2	Day 1	Day 2
A				
B				
C				
D				

7. Use a clean graduated cylinder to add 5 mL of pepsin to test tube D. Then rinse the graduated cylinder and add 5 mL of hydrochloric acid to test tube D. Observe whether or not an immediate reaction takes place. Record your observations.
8. Obtain four strips of blue litmus paper. (Blue litmus paper turns pink in the presence of an acid.) Dip a clean plastic stirrer into the solution in each test tube, and then touch the stirrer to a piece of litmus paper. Observe what happens to the litmus paper. Record your observations.
9. Insert stoppers in the four test tubes and store the test tube rack as directed by your teacher.
10. The next day, examine the contents of each test tube. Note any changes in the size and overall appearance of the egg white cubes. Then test each solution with litmus paper. Record your observations in your data table.

Analyze and Conclude

1. Which material(s) were the best at digesting the egg white? What observations enabled you to determine this?
2. Do you think that the chemical digestion of protein in food is a fast reaction or a slow one? Explain.
3. What did this lab demonstrate about the ability of pepsin to digest protein?
4. Why was it important that the cubes of egg white all be about the same size?
5. **Think About It** How did test tubes A and C help you draw conclusions about protein digestion in this investigation?

Design an Experiment

Design a way to test whether protein digestion is affected by the size of the food pieces. Write down the hypothesis that you will test. Then create a data table for recording your observations. Obtain your teacher's permission before carrying out your plan.

Final Digestion and Absorption

DISCOVER

ACTIVITY

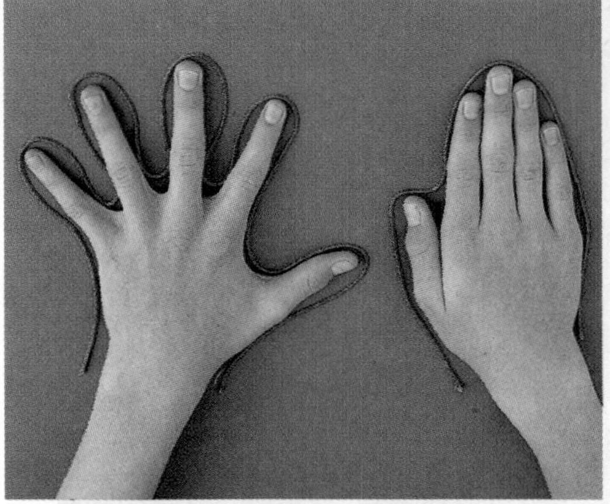

Which Surface Is Larger?

1. Work with a partner to carry out this investigation.
2. Begin by placing your hand palm-side down on a table. Keep your thumb and fingers tightly together. Lay string along the outline of your hand. Have your partner help you determine how long a string you need to outline your hand.
3. Use a metric ruler to measure the length of that string.

Think It Over

Predicting How long would you expect your hand outline to be if you spread out your thumb and fingers? Use string to test your prediction. Compare the two string lengths.

GUIDE FOR READING

- **What roles do the small intestine and large intestine play in digestion?**

Reading Tip **As you read, create a table with the headings *Small Intestine, Liver, Pancreas,* and *Large Intestine.* Under each heading, list that organ's digestive function.**

Have you ever been part of a huge crowd attending a concert or sports event? Barriers and passageways often guide people in the right direction. Ticket takers make sure that only those with tickets get in, and that they enter in an orderly fashion.

In some ways, the stomach can be thought of as the "ticket taker" of the digestive system. Once the food has been changed into a thick liquid, the stomach releases a little liquid at a time into the next part of the digestive system. This slow, smooth passage of food through the digestive system ensures that digestion and absorption take place smoothly.

The Small Intestine

After the thick liquid leaves the stomach, it enters the small intestine. The **small intestine** is the part of the digestive system where most of the chemical digestion takes place. If you look back at Figure 12, you may wonder how the small intestine got its name. After all, at about 6 meters—longer than some full-sized cars—it makes up two thirds of the digestive system. The small intestine was named for its small diameter. It is about two to three centimeters wide, about half the diameter of the large intestine.

When food reaches the small intestine, it has already been mechanically digested into a thick liquid. But chemical digestion has just begun. Although starches and proteins have been partially broken down, fats haven't been digested at all. **Almost all chemical digestion and absorption of nutrients takes place in the small intestine.**

The small intestine is bustling with chemical activity. As the liquid moves into the small intestine, it mixes with enzymes and secretions. The enzymes and secretions are produced in three different organs—the small intestine, the liver, and the pancreas. The liver and the pancreas deliver their substances to the small intestine through small tubes.

The Role of the Liver The **liver** is located in the upper portion of the abdomen. It is the largest and heaviest organ inside the body. You can think of the liver as an extremely busy chemical factory that plays a role in many body processes. For example, the liver breaks down medicines and other substances, and it helps eliminate nitrogen from the body. As part of the digestive system, the liver produces **bile,** a substance that breaks up fat particles. Bile flows from the liver into the **gallbladder,** the organ that stores bile. After you eat, bile passes through a tube from the gallbladder into the small intestine.

Bile is not an enzyme. It does not chemically digest foods. It does, however, break up large fat particles into smaller fat droplets. You can compare the action of bile on fats with the action of soap on oily skin. Soap physically breaks up the oil into small droplets that can mix with the soapy water and be washed away. Bile mixes with the fats in food to form small fat droplets. The droplets can then be chemically broken down by enzymes produced in the pancreas.

Break Up!

In this activity, you will model the breakup of fat particles in the small intestine. **ACTIVITY**

1. Fill two plastic jars half full of water. Add a few drops of oil to each jar.
2. Add $\frac{1}{4}$ teaspoon baking soda to one of the jars.
3. Stir the contents of both jars. Record your observations.

Observing In which jar did the oil begin to break up? What substance does the baking soda represent?

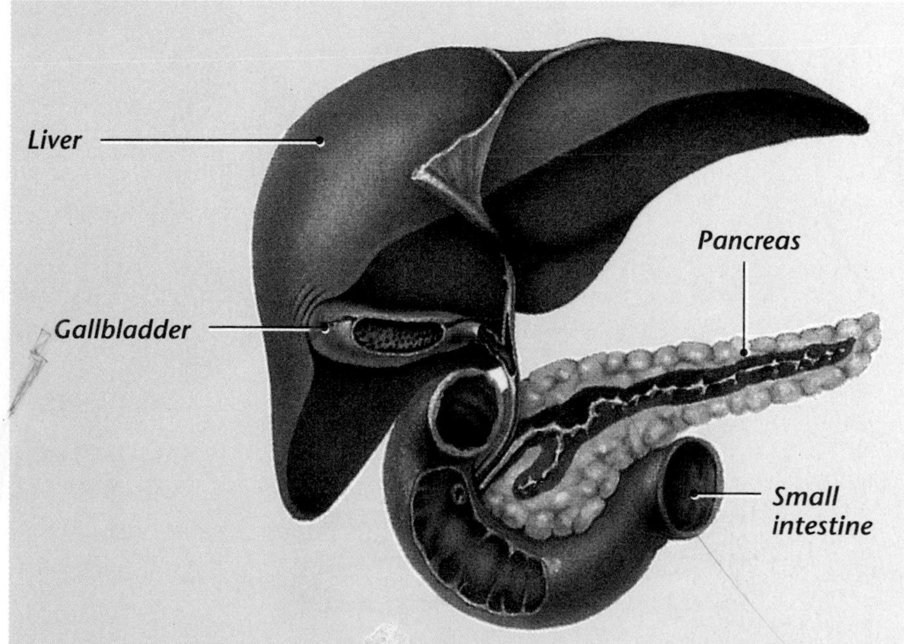

Figure 17 Substances produced by the liver and pancreas aid in the digestion of food.
Applying Concepts *Where is bile produced? Where is it stored before it is released into the small intestine?*

Help From the Pancreas The **pancreas** is a triangular organ that lies between the stomach and the first part of the small intestine. Like the liver, the pancreas plays a role in many body processes. As part of the digestive system, the pancreas produces enzymes that flow into the small intestine. These enzymes help break down starches, proteins, and fats.

The digestive enzymes produced by the pancreas and other organs do not break down all food substances, however. Recall that the fiber in food isn't broken down. Instead, fiber thickens the liquid material in the intestine. This makes it easier for peristalsis to push the material forward.

☑ *Checkpoint* *How does the pancreas aid in digestion?*

Absorption in the Small Intestine After chemical digestion takes place, the small nutrient molecules are ready to be absorbed by the body. The structure of the small intestine makes it well suited for absorption. The inner surface, or lining, of the small intestine looks bumpy. Millions of tiny finger-shaped structures called **villi** (VIL eye) (singular *villus*) cover the surface. The villi absorb nutrient molecules. Notice that tiny blood vessels run through the center of each villus. Nutrient molecules pass from cells on the surface of a villus into blood vessels. The blood carries the nutrients throughout the body for use by body cells.

The presence of villi increases the surface area of the small intestine. If all of the villi were laid out flat, the total surface area of the small intestine would be about as large as a tennis court.

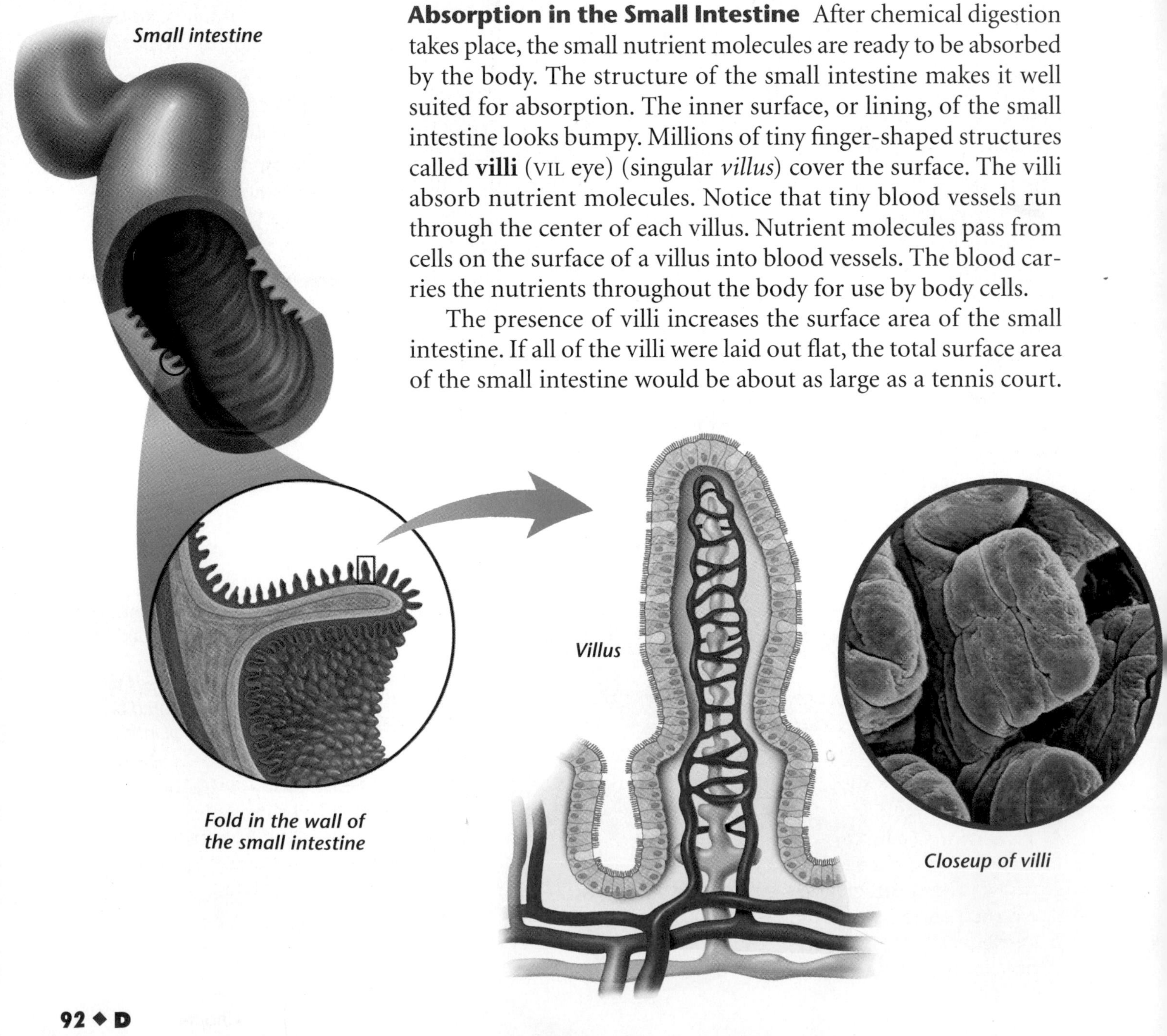

Figure 18 Tiny finger-shaped projections called villi line the inside of the small intestine. In the diagram, you can see that the blood vessels in the villi are covered by a single layer of cells. The photograph shows a closeup view of villi. ***Interpreting Diagrams*** *How does the structure of the villi help them carry out their function?*

Small intestine

Fold in the wall of the small intestine

Villus

Closeup of villi

This greatly increased surface enables digested food to be absorbed faster than if the walls of the small intestine were smooth.

The Large Intestine

By the time material reaches the end of the small intestine, most nutrients have been absorbed. The remaining material moves from the small intestine into the large intestine. The **large intestine** is the last section of the digestive system. It is about one and a half meters long—about as long as the average bathtub. As you can see in Figure 19, the large intestine is shaped somewhat like a horseshoe. It runs up the right-hand side of the abdomen, across the upper abdomen, and then down the left-hand side. The large intestine contains bacteria that feed on the material passing through. These bacteria normally do not cause disease. In fact, they are helpful because they make certain vitamins, including vitamin K.

The material entering the large intestine contains water and undigested food such as fiber. **As the material moves through the large intestine, water is absorbed into the bloodstream. The remaining material is readied for elimination from the body.**

The large intestine ends in a short tube called the **rectum.** Here waste material is compressed into a solid form. This waste material is eliminated from the body through the **anus,** a muscular opening at the end of the rectum.

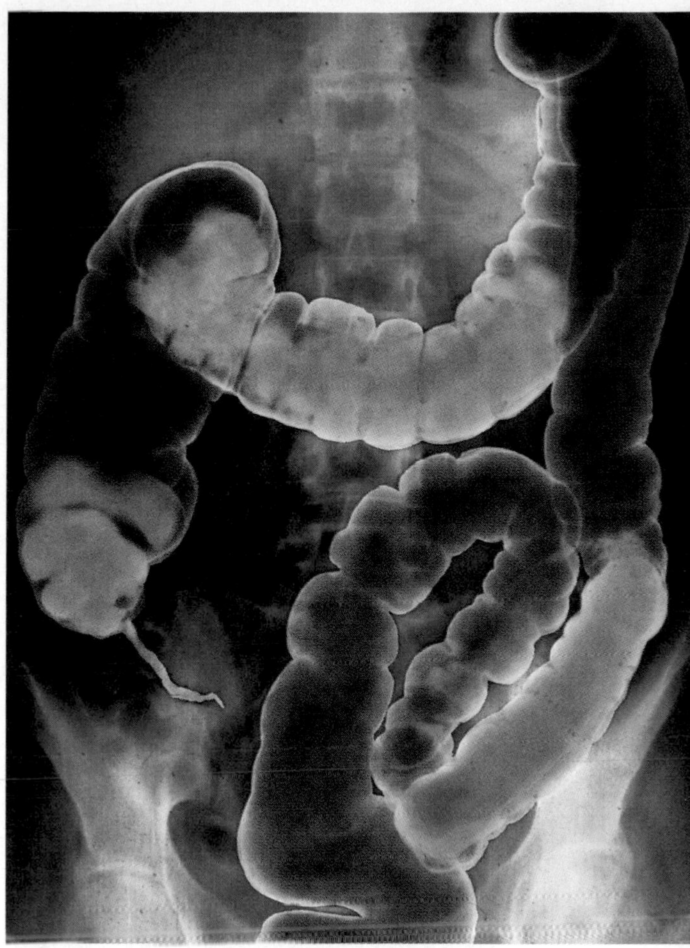

Figure 19 Notice the shape of the large intestine. As material passes through this structure, most of the water is absorbed by the body.

Section 4 Review

1. What two digestive processes occur in the small intestine? Briefly describe each process.
2. Which nutrient is absorbed in the large intestine?
3. How do the liver and pancreas function in the digestive process?
4. **Thinking Critically Relating Cause and Effect** Some people are allergic to a protein in wheat. When these people eat foods made with wheat, a reaction destroys the villi in the small intestine. What problems would you expect these people to experience?

CHAPTER PROJECT 3

Check Your Progress

You should now be trying to eat a more healthful diet. Be sure you keep an accurate log of your food intake during this three-day period. Then graph the results. (*Hint:* You might find it helpful to focus on one food category when trying to improve your eating habits.)

SCIENCE AND SOCIETY

Advertising and Nutrition

Millions of children enjoy Saturday morning television programs. As they watch, they see advertisements for high-sugar cereals, candy, soft drinks, and fat-filled foods. Such foods are not healthy choices. For example, in some cereals marketed to children, added sugar makes up almost half the cereal's weight. How greatly are children's eating habits influenced by food ads? Should these ads be allowed on children's television programs?

The Issues

Does Advertising Influence Children? Advertising products to children between the ages of four and twelve works. Overall, companies spend more than $300 million a year advertising to that age group. In turn, children influence adults to spend more than 500 times that amount—at least $165 billion a year.

Should Food Companies Advertise on Children's Television? Some people want to regulate food ads on children's shows. Evidence indicates that children choose particular foods based on ads. The foods children eat can affect their health not just during childhood but for the rest of their lives.

Other people point out that children don't try to buy every food they see advertised. It is usually parents, not children, who decide what foods to buy. In addition, companies pay for advertisements. Without this money, television producers might not be able to afford to make good programs.

What Responsibilities Do Families and Schools Have? Many people believe that parents and teachers should teach children about nutrition. These people argue that adults should teach children to read food labels and to recognize misleading advertisements. For the rest of children's lives, they will be surrounded by advertising. If they learn to analyze ads critically, children will become wise consumers as adults.

You Decide

1. Describe the Issue
Summarize the debate about food advertisements on children's television.

2. Analyze the Options
List some possible solutions to the problem of food advertisements on children's television. How would each solution affect children and advertisers?

3. Find a Solution
Prepare a leaflet proposing one solution to the problem. Use persuasive arguments to support your proposal.

Section 1 Food and Energy

Key Ideas

- Nutrients in food provide the body with energy and materials needed for growth, repair, and other life processes. The energy in foods is measured in Calories.
- The six nutrients necessary for human health are carbohydrates, fats, proteins, vitamins, minerals, and water.
- Water is the most important nutrient because it is necessary for all body processes.

Key Terms

nutrient
calorie
carbohydrate
glucose
fiber
fat
unsaturated fat
saturated fat
cholesterol
protein
amino acid
vitamin
mineral

Section 2 Healthy Eating

Integrating Health

Key Ideas

- The Food Guide Pyramid classifies foods into six major groups and tells how many servings from each group to eat.
- Food labels list the nutrients in foods and shows how the foods fit into your daily diet.

Key Terms

Food Guide Pyramid
Percent Daily Value

Section 3 The Digestive Process Begins

Key Ideas

- The functions of the digestive system are to break down food, absorb food molecules into the blood, and eliminate wastes.
- During mechanical digestion, food is ground into small pieces. During chemical digestion, large food molecules are broken into small molecules by enzymes.
- Food first passes from the mouth into the esophagus, and then into the stomach. Waves of muscle contractions, known as peristalsis, keep the food moving in one direction.

Key Terms

digestion
absorption
saliva
enzyme
epiglottis
esophagus
mucus
peristalsis
stomach

Section 4 Final Digestion and Absorption

Key Ideas

- Almost all chemical digestion and absorption of nutrients takes place in the small intestine.
- Nutrients are absorbed into the bloodstream through the villi of the small intestine.
- As material moves through the large intestine, water is absorbed. The remaining material is readied for elimination.

Key Terms

small intestine
liver
bile
gallbladder
pancreas
villus
large intestine
rectum
anus

www.science-explorer.phschool.com

CHAPTER 3 REVIEW

Reviewing Content

For more review of key concepts, see the Interactive Student Tutorial CD-ROM.

Multiple Choice

Choose the letter of the best answer.

1. Which nutrient makes up about 65 percent of the body's weight?
   a. carbohydrate
   b. protein
   c. water
   d. fat
2. According to the Food Guide Pyramid, from which group should you eat the most servings?
   a. Milk, Yogurt, and Cheese
   b. Meat, Poultry, Fish, Beans, Eggs, and Nuts
   c. Vegetables
   d. Bread, Cereal, Rice, and Pasta
3. Most mechanical digestion takes place in the
   a. mouth. b. esophagus.
   c. stomach. d. small intestine.
4. The enzyme in saliva chemically breaks down
   a. fats. b. proteins.
   c. sugars. d. starches.
5. Bile is produced by the
   a. liver. b. pancreas.
   c. small intestine. d. large intestine.

True or False

If the statement is true, write true. If it is false, change the underlined word or words to make the statement true.

6. Proteins that come from animal sources are incomplete proteins.
7. Vitamins that are stored in the fatty tissue of the body are water-soluble.
8. To determine which of two cereals supplies more iron, you can check the Percent Daily Value on the food label.
9. The physical breakdown of food is called mechanical digestion.
10. Most materials are absorbed into the bloodstream in the large intestine.

Checking Concepts

11. How does a person's level of physical activity affect his or her daily energy needs?
12. Why is fiber necessary in a diet even though it's not considered a nutrient?
13. Why does the Food Guide Pyramid give the recommended daily servings as a range instead of a single number?
14. Describe the function of the epiglottis.
15. Explain the role of peristalsis in the digestive system.
16. What is the function of villi? Where are villi located?
17. **Writing to Learn** Imagine that you are a bacon, lettuce, and tomato sandwich. Describe your journey through a person's digestive system, ending with absorption.

Thinking Visually

18. **Flowchart** Copy the incomplete flowchart onto a separate sheet of paper. Complete the flowchart with the names and functions of the missing organs. (For more on flowcharts, see the Skills Handbook.)

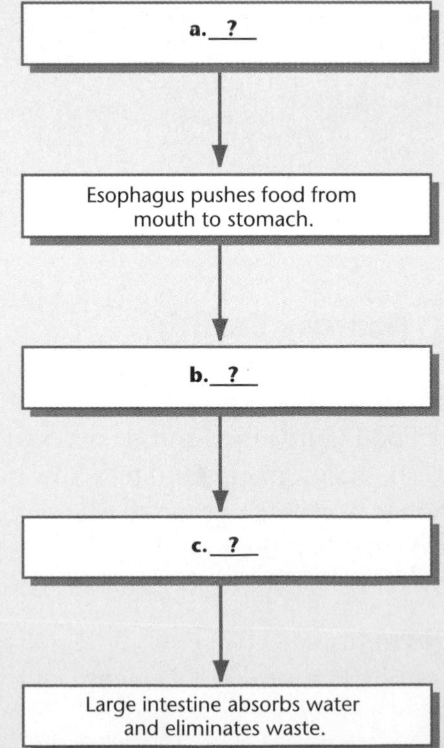

Applying Skills

Use the chart below to answer Questions 19–21.

Food (1 cup)	Calcium (% Daily Value)	Calories	Calories from Fat
Chocolate milk	30	230	80
Low-fat milk	35	110	20
Plain Yogurt	35	110	35

19. Classifying To which group in the Food Guide Pyramid do the foods in the chart belong? What is the recommended range of daily servings for that group?

20. Interpreting Data How many cups of low-fat milk provide the daily recommended amount of calcium?

21. Calculating Which of the foods meet the recommendation that no more than 30 percent of a food's Calories come from fat? Explain.

Thinking Critically

22. Applying Concepts Before winter arrives, animals that hibernate often prepare by eating foods that contain a lot of fat. How is this behavior helpful?

23. Comparing and Contrasting The digestive system is sometimes said to be "an assembly line in reverse." Identify some similarities and some differences between your digestive system and an assembly line.

24. Relating Cause and Effect "Heartburn" occurs when stomach acid enters the esophagus. Use your knowledge of the digestive system to explain how this condition affects the esophagus and how "heartburn" got its name.

25. Inferring Why is it important to chew your food thoroughly before swallowing?

26. Relating Cause and Effect Suppose a medicine killed all the bacteria in your body. How might this affect vitamin production in your body? Explain.

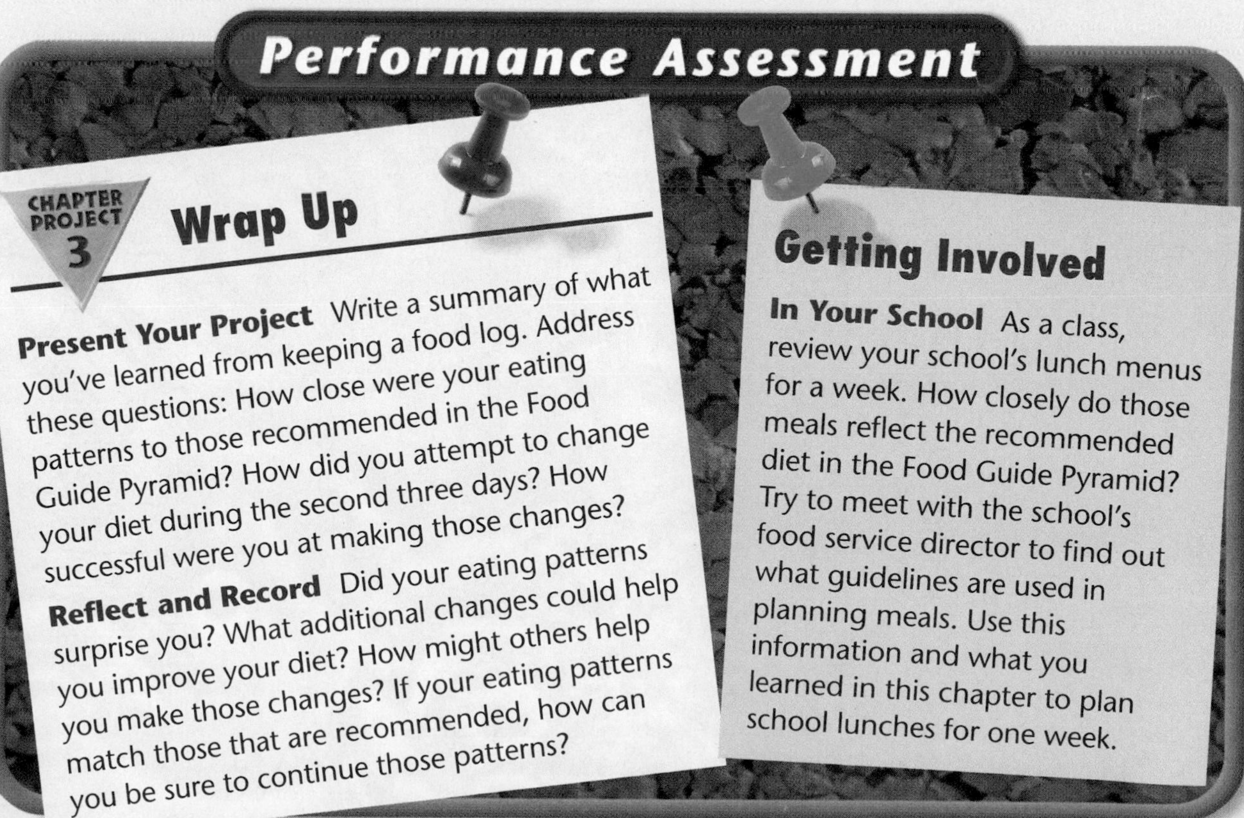

Performance Assessment

CHAPTER PROJECT 3

Wrap Up

Present Your Project Write a summary of what you've learned from keeping a food log. Address these questions: How close were your eating patterns to those recommended in the Food Guide Pyramid? How did you attempt to change your diet during the second three days? How successful were you at making those changes?

Reflect and Record Did your eating patterns surprise you? What additional changes could help you improve your diet? How might others help you make those changes? If your eating patterns match those that are recommended, how can you be sure to continue those patterns?

Getting Involved

In Your School As a class, review your school's lunch menus for a week. How closely do those meals reflect the recommended diet in the Food Guide Pyramid? Try to meet with the school's food service director to find out what guidelines are used in planning meals. Use this information and what you learned in this chapter to plan school lunches for one week.

4 Circulation

What's Ahead

The Body's Transportation System

Discover How Hard Does Your Heart Work?

A Closer Look at Blood Vessels

Discover How Does Pressure Affect the Flow of Blood?
Sharpen Your Skills Creating Data Tables
Skills Lab Heart Beat, Health Beat

Blood and Lymph

Discover What Kinds of Cells Are in Blood?
Try This Caught in the Web
Real-World Lab Do You Know Your A-B-O's?

PROJECT 4

Travels of a Red Blood Cell

Every day, you travel from home to school and then back home again. Your path makes a loop, or circuit, ending where it began. In this chapter, you'll learn how your blood also travels in circuits. You'll find out how your heart pumps your blood throughout your body, bringing that essential fluid to all your living cells. As you learn more about the heart and circulatory system, you'll create a display to show how blood circulates throughout the body.

Your Goal To design and construct a display showing a complete journey of a red blood cell through the human body.

To complete the project successfully, your display must

- show a red blood cell that leaves from the heart and returns to the same place
- show where the red blood cell picks up and delivers oxygen and carbon dioxide
- provide written descriptions of the circuits made by the red blood cell, either with captions or in a continuous story
- be designed following the safety guidelines in Appendix A

Get Started Look ahead at the diagrams in the chapter. Then discuss the kinds of displays you could use, including a three-dimensional model, posters, a series of drawings, a flip-book, or a video animation. Write down any content questions you'll need to answer.

Check Your Progress You'll be working on this project as you study this chapter. To keep your project on track, look for Check Your Progress boxes at the following points.

Section 1 Review, page 106: Make a sketch of your display.
Section 2 Review, page 111: Begin to construct your display.
Section 3 Review, page 118: Add a written description to your display.

Wrap Up At the end of the chapter (page 127), you will use your display to show how blood travels through the body.

Blood cells travel in blood vessels to all parts of the body.

Integrating Health

SECTION 4 **Cardiovascular Health**

Discover **Which Foods Are "Heart Healthy"?**
Try This **Blocking the Flow**

The Body's Transportation System

DISCOVER

How Hard Does Your Heart Work?

1. Every minute, your heart beats about 75 to 85 times. With each beat, it pumps about 60 milliliters of blood. Can you work as hard and fast as your heart does?
2. Cover a table or desk with newspapers. Place two large plastic containers side by side on the newspapers. Fill one with 2.5 liters of water, which is about the volume of blood that your heart pumps in 30 seconds. Leave the other container empty.
3. With a plastic cup that holds about 60 milliliters, transfer water as quickly as possible into the empty container without spilling any. Have a partner time you for 30 seconds. As you work, count how many transfers you make in 30 seconds.
4. Multiply your results by 2 to find the number of transfers for one minute.

Think It Over

Inferring Compare your performance with the number of times your heart beats every minute. What do your results tell you about the strength and speed of a heartbeat?

GUIDE FOR READING

- **What is the function of the cardiovascular system?**
- **What role does the heart play in the cardiovascular system?**
- **What path does blood take through the circulatory system?**

Reading Tip **As you read, create a flowchart that shows the path that blood follows as it circulates through the body.**

In the middle of the night, a truck rolls rapidly through the darkness. Loaded with fresh fruits and vegetables, the truck is headed for a city supermarket. The driver steers off the interstate and onto a smaller highway. Finally, after driving through narrow city streets, the truck reaches its destination. As dawn begins to break, store workers unload the cargo. They work quickly, because other trucks—carrying meats, canned goods, and freshly baked breads—are waiting to be unloaded. And while workers fill the store with products to be sold, a garbage truck removes yesterday's trash. All these trucks have traveled long distances over roads. Without a huge network of roads, big and small, the supermarket couldn't stay in business.

Movement of Materials

Like the roads that link all parts of the country, your body has a "highway" network, called the cardiovascular system, that links all parts of your body. The **cardiovascular system,** or circulatory system, consists of the heart, blood vessels, and blood. **The cardiovascular system carries needed substances to cells and carries waste products away from cells.** In addition, blood contains cells that fight disease.

Needed Materials Most substances that need to get from one part of the body to another are carried by blood. For example, blood carries oxygen from your lungs to your body cells. Blood also transports the glucose your cells use to produce energy.

Waste Products The cardiovascular system also picks up wastes from cells. For example, when cells use glucose, they produce carbon dioxide as a waste product. The carbon dioxide passes from the cells into the blood. The cardiovascular system then carries carbon dioxide to the lungs, where it is exhaled.

Disease Fighters The cardiovascular system also transports cells that attack disease-causing microorganisms. This process can keep you from becoming sick. If you do get sick, these disease-fighting blood cells will kill the microorganisms to help you get well.

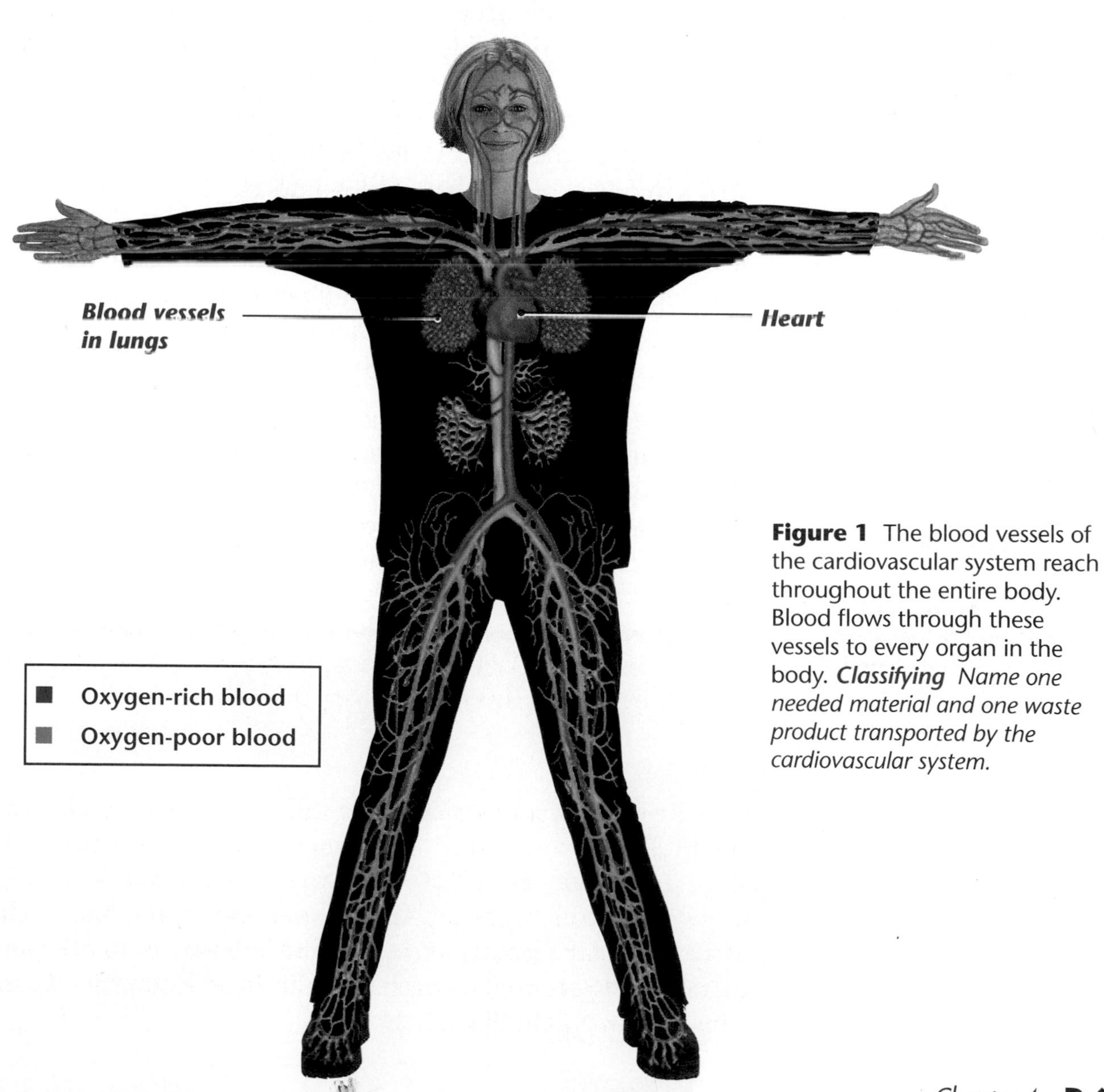

Figure 1 The blood vessels of the cardiovascular system reach throughout the entire body. Blood flows through these vessels to every organ in the body. ***Classifying*** *Name one needed material and one waste product transported by the cardiovascular system.*

Figure 2 This small stone sculpture, created by ancient Egyptians, represents the heart. Ancient Egyptians believed that feelings, thoughts, and memories were created by the heart.

The Heart

Without the heart, blood wouldn't go anywhere. The **heart** is a hollow, muscular organ that pumps blood throughout the body. Your heart, which is about the size of your fist, is located in the center of your chest. The heart lies beneath the breastbone and inside the ribs. These bones protect the heart from injury.

Each time the heart beats, it pushes blood through the blood vessels of the cardiovascular system. As you learned in Chapter 2, the heart is made of cardiac muscle, which can contract over and over without getting tired. The heart beats continually throughout a person's life, resting only between beats. During your lifetime, your heart may beat over 3 billion times. In a year, it pumps enough blood to fill over 30 competition-size swimming pools.

The Heart's Structure Look closely at *Exploring the Heart* as you read about the structure of the heart. Notice that the heart has two sides—a right side and a left side—completely separated from each other by a wall of tissue. Each side has two compartments, or chambers—an upper and a lower chamber. Each of the two upper chambers, called an **atrium** (AY tree um) (plural *atria*), receives blood that comes into the heart. Each lower chamber, called a **ventricle,** pumps blood out of the heart. The atria are separated from the ventricles by valves. A **valve** is a flap of tissue that prevents blood from flowing backward. Valves are also located between the ventricles and the large blood vessels that carry blood away from the heart.

How the Heart Works The action of the heart has two main phases. In one phase, the heart muscle relaxes and the heart fills with blood. In the other phase, the heart muscle contracts and pumps blood forward. A heartbeat, which sounds something like *lub-dup,* can be heard during the pumping phase.

Figure 3 As blood flows out of the heart and toward the lungs, it passes through the valve shown in the photograph. The illustration shows how blood flows through the open valve.
Applying Concepts *What is the function of the valves in the heart?*

When the heart muscle relaxes, blood flows into the chambers. Then the atria contract. This muscle contraction squeezes blood out of the atria, through the valves, and then into the ventricles. Next the ventricles contract. This contraction closes the valves between the atria and ventricles, making the *lub* sound and squeezing blood into large blood vessels. As the valves between the ventricles and the blood vessels snap shut, they make the *dup* sound. All of this happens in less than a second.

☑ ***Checkpoint*** *Contrast the functions of atria and ventricles.*

EXPLORING the Heart

Every second of your life, your heart pumps blood through your body. The right side of the heart pumps blood to the lungs, while the left side pumps blood to the rest of the body.

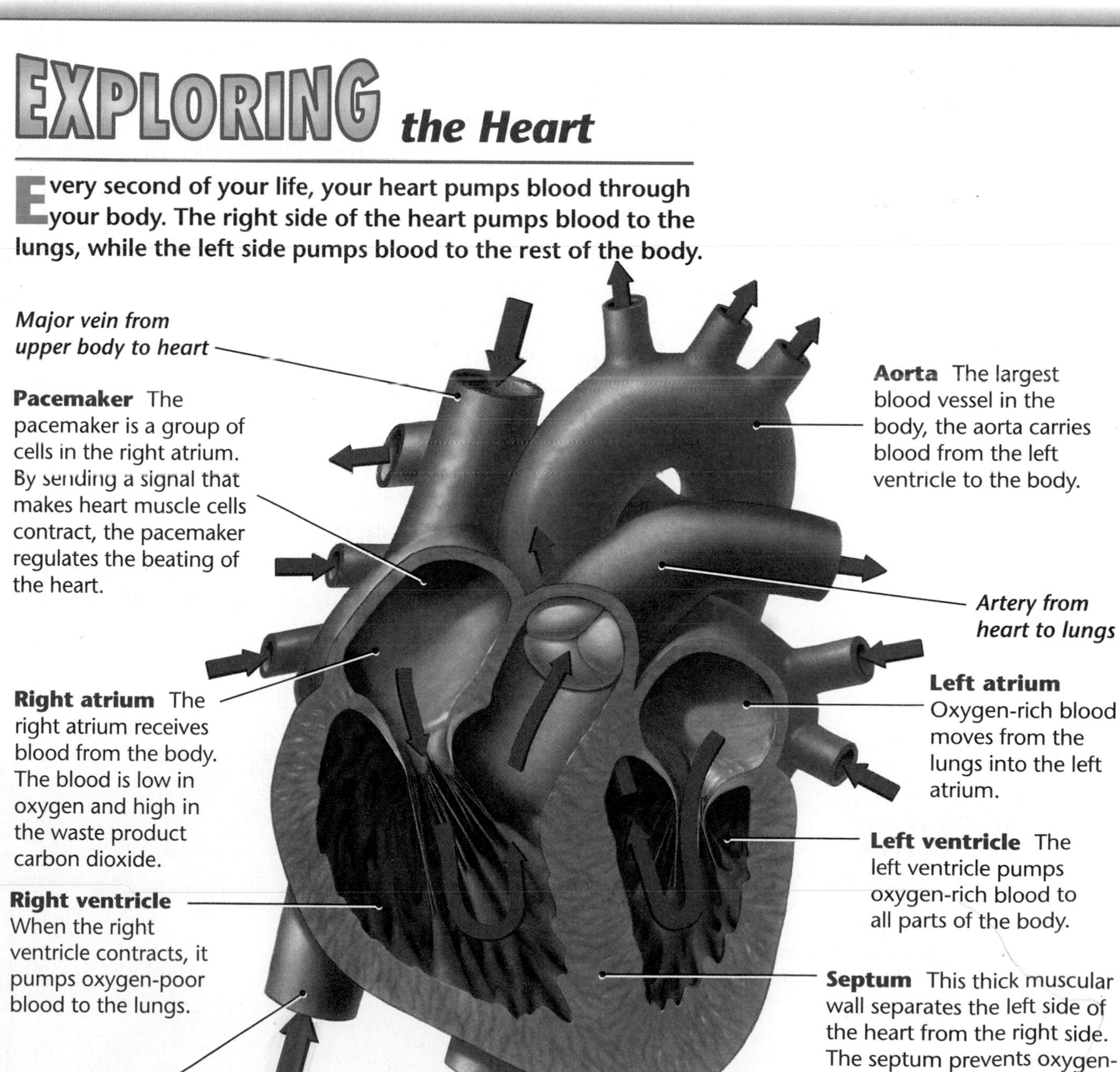

Language Arts CONNECTION

When you say that a person has a "heart of gold," you mean that the person is kind and generous—not that the person's heart is actually made of gold metal. "Heart of gold" is an idiom—an expression with a meaning that cannot be understood from the ordinary meanings of the words in it. The words *heart* and *blood* are found in many idioms. For example, a "blood-chilling scream" frightens you, but it doesn't lower the temperature of your blood.

In Your Journal

Learn what each of the following idioms means:
- a change of heart
- a heart-to-heart talk
- make the blood boil

Then write a sentence using each of these idioms.

Regulation of Heartbeat

A group of cells called the **pacemaker,** which is located in the right atrium, sends out signals that make the heart muscle contract. The pacemaker constantly receives messages about the body's oxygen needs. It then adjusts the heart rate to match. Your heart beats much faster when you are exercising than when you are sitting quietly. When you are exercising, the entire process from the beginning of one heartbeat to the beginning of the next can take less than half a second. Your muscles need more oxygen during exercise. Your rapid heartbeat supplies blood that carries the oxygen.

INTEGRATING TECHNOLOGY In some people, the pacemaker becomes damaged as a result of disease or an accident. This often results in an irregular or slow heartbeat. In the 1950s, doctors and engineers developed an artificial, battery-operated pacemaker. The artificial pacemaker is implanted beneath the skin and connected by wires to the heart. Tiny electric impulses travel from the battery through the wires. These impulses make the heart contract at a normal rate.

Checkpoint *What is the function of the pacemaker?*

Two Loops

After leaving the heart, blood travels in blood vessels through the body. Your body has three kinds of blood vessels—arteries, capillaries, and veins. **Arteries** are blood vessels that carry blood away from the heart. From the arteries, blood flows into tiny vessels called **capillaries.** In the capillaries, substances are exchanged between the blood and body cells. From capillaries, blood flows into **veins,** which are the vessels that carry blood back to the heart.

The overall pattern of blood flow through the body is something like a figure eight. The heart is at the center where the two

Figure 4 Activities such as swimming require a lot of energy. A person's heart beats fast in order to supply the muscles with the blood they need. The heart's pacemaker regulates the speed at which the heart beats.

loops cross. **In the first loop, blood travels from the heart to the lungs and then back to the heart. In the second loop, blood is pumped from the heart throughout the body and then returns again to the heart.** The heart is really two pumps, one on the right and one on the left. The right side pumps blood to the lungs, and the left side pumps blood to the rest of the body.

Blood travels in only one direction. If you were a drop of blood, you could start at any point in the figure eight and eventually return to the same point. The entire trip would take less than a minute. As you read about the path that blood takes through the cardiovascular system, trace the path in Figure 5.

Loop One: to the Lungs and Back When blood from the body flows into the right atrium, it contains little oxygen but a lot of carbon dioxide. This oxygen-poor blood is dark red. The blood then flows from the right atrium into the right ventricle. Then the ventricle pumps oxygen-poor blood into the arteries that lead to the lungs.

As blood flows through the lungs, large blood vessels branch into smaller ones. Eventually, blood flows through tiny capillaries that are in close contact with the air that comes into the lungs. The air in the lungs has more oxygen than the blood in the capillaries, so oxygen moves from the lung into the blood. In contrast, carbon dioxide moves in the opposite direction—from the blood into the lung. As the blood leaves the lungs, it is now rich in oxygen and poor in carbon dioxide. This blood, which is bright red, flows to the left side of the heart to be pumped through the second loop.

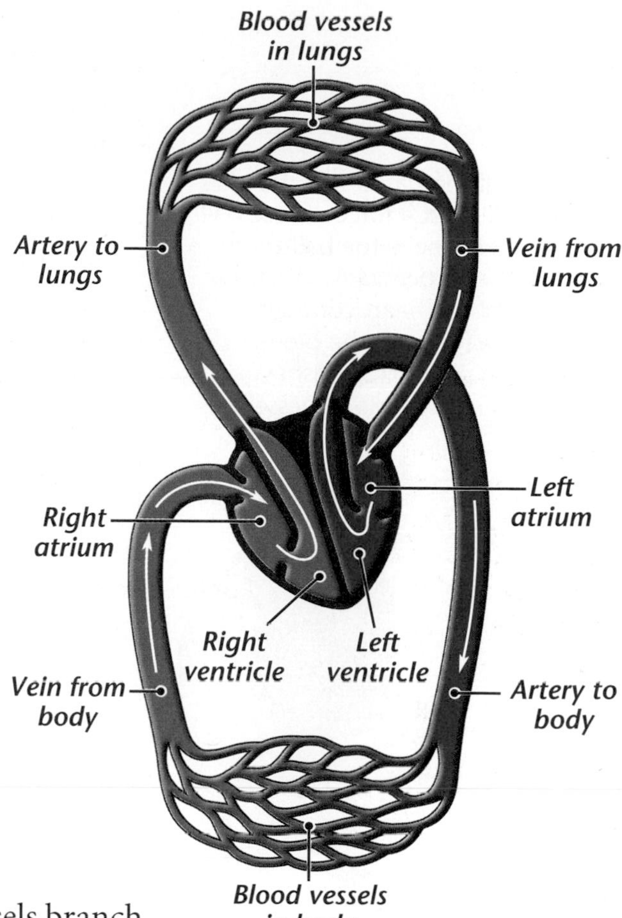

Figure 5 Blood circulates through the body in two loops with the heart at the center. Use the arrows to trace the path of blood, beginning at the right atrium. ***Interpreting Diagrams*** *Where does the blood that enters the left atrium come from?*

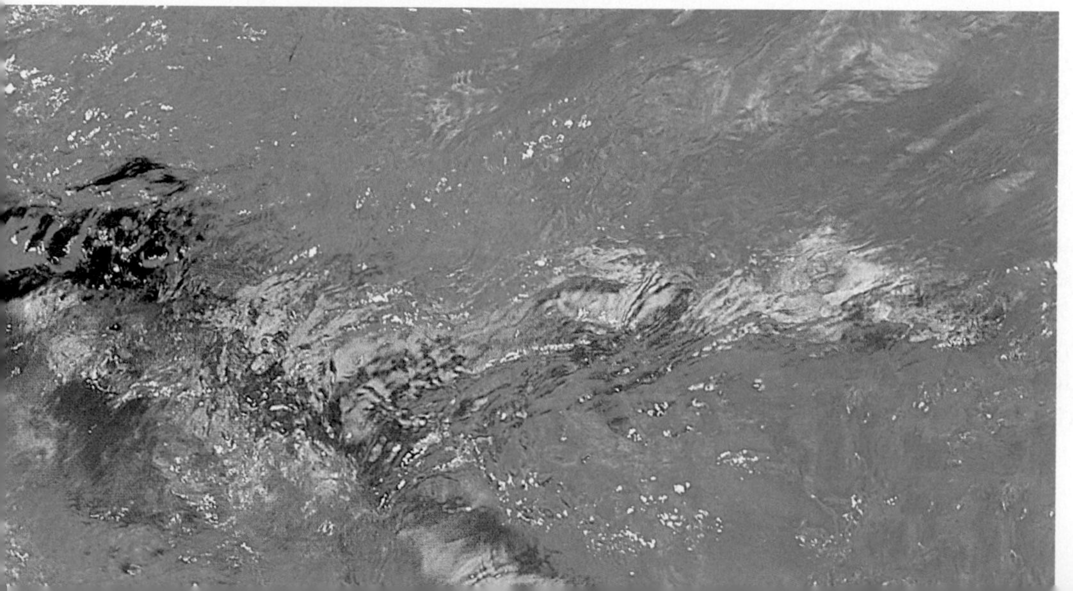

Loop Two: to the Body and Back The second loop begins as the left atrium fills with oxygen-rich blood coming from the lungs. The blood then moves into the left ventricle. From the left ventricle, the blood is pumped into the **aorta** (ay AWR tuh), the largest artery in the body.

Eventually, after passing through branching arteries, blood flows through tiny capillaries in different parts of your body, such as your brain, liver, and legs. These vessels are in close contact with body cells. Oxygen moves out of the blood and into the body cells. At the same time, carbon dioxide passes from the body cells and into the blood. The blood then flows back to the right atrium of the heart through veins, completing the second loop.

Figure 6 If the batter hits the ball, the bat will exert a force on the ball. This force will make the ball zoom through the air. Similarly, when the ventricles of the heart contract, they exert a force on the blood inside them. This force pushes blood through the blood vessels.

The Force of the Ventricles

INTEGRATING PHYSICS

When the ventricle muscles contract, they exert a force on the blood that is inside them. A **force** is a push or a pull. You see examples of forces all around you. When you lift a book off a table, for example, you exert a force on the book, making it move upward. The force exerted by the ventricles moves blood out of your heart and into arteries.

The contraction of the left ventricle exerts much more force than the contraction of the right ventricle. The right ventricle only pumps blood to the lungs. In contrast, the left ventricle pumps blood throughout the body. As a way of understanding this, think of the force it would take to bunt a baseball. Then think about how hard you would need to hit the ball if you wanted to hit a home run.

Section 1 Review

1. What is the function of the cardiovascular system?
2. What function does the heart perform?
3. Describe the route that blood takes through the cardiovascular system. Begin with blood leaving the left ventricle.
4. What is the heart's pacemaker? What causes the pacemaker to change the rate at which the heart beats?
5. **Thinking Critically Comparing and Contrasting** Most of the arteries in the body carry oxygen-rich blood away from the heart. One artery, however, carries blood that has little oxygen away from the heart. From which ventricle does that artery carry blood? To where does that artery carry blood?

Check Your Progress

CHAPTER PROJECT 4

At this point, you should have sketched out the two loops your red blood cell will travel. Make sure each pathway forms a complete circuit back to the heart. Begin to plan how you will construct your display. Keep a running list of the materials or equipment you'll need. (*Hint:* Think about how you will show the movement of the blood cell in your display.)

A Closer Look at Blood Vessels

DISCOVER ACTIVITY

How Does Pressure Affect the Flow of Blood?

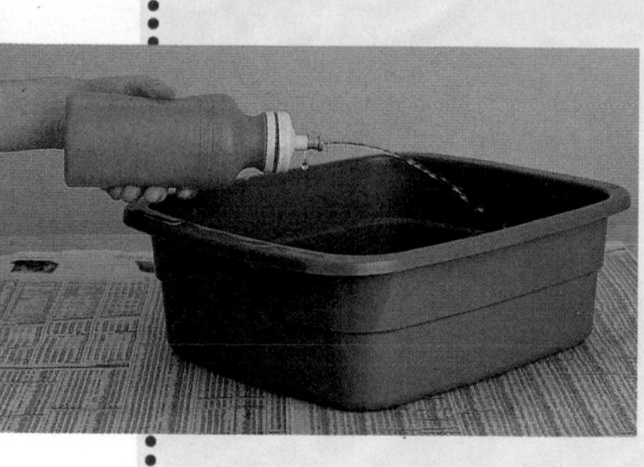

1. Spread newspapers over a table or desktop. Then fill a plastic squeeze bottle with water.
2. Hold the bottle over a dishpan. Squeeze the bottle with one hand. Observe how far the water travels.
3. Now grasp the bottle with both hands and squeeze again. Observe how far the water travels this time.

Think It Over

Inferring Blood is pushed through arteries with much more force than it is pushed through veins. Which part of the activity models an artery? Which part models a vein? Which organ in the body provides the pushing force?

GUIDE FOR READING

- **What are the functions of arteries, capillaries, and veins?**
- **What causes blood pressure?**

Reading Tip **As you read, use the text headings to make an outline of the information in this section.**

Like corridors in a large building, blood vessels run through all of the tissues of your body. While some blood vessels are as wide as your thumb, most of them are much finer than a human hair. If all the arteries, capillaries, and veins in your body were hooked together, end to end, they would stretch a distance of almost 100,000 kilometers. That's long enough to wrap around Earth twice—with a lot left over!

Arteries

When blood leaves the heart, it travels through arteries. The right ventricle pumps blood into the arteries that go to the lungs. The left ventricle pumps blood into the aorta, the largest artery in your body. Every organ receives blood from arteries that branch off the aorta. The first branches, called the **coronary arteries,** carry blood to the heart itself. Other branches carry blood to the brain, intestines, and other organs. Each artery branches into smaller and smaller arteries.

Artery Structure The walls of arteries are generally very thick. In fact, artery walls consist of three layers. The innermost layer, which is made up of epithelial

Figure 7 If all the blood vessels in your body were joined end to end, they would wrap around the world almost two and a half times.

Math TOOLBOX

Pulse Rate

A rate is the speed at which something happens. When you calculate a rate, you compare the number of events with the time period in which they occur. Here is how you can calculate the pulse rate of a person whose heart beats 142 times in 2 minutes.

1. Write the comparison as a fraction.

$$\frac{142 \text{ heartbeats}}{2 \text{ minutes}}$$

2. Divide the numerator and the denominator by the denominator.

$$\frac{142 \div 2}{2 \div 2} = \frac{71}{1}$$

The person's pulse rate is 71 heartbeats per minute.

tissue, is smooth. This smooth surface enables blood to flow freely. The middle layer consists mostly of muscle tissue. The outer wall is made up of flexible connective tissue. Because of this layered structure, arteries have both strength and flexibility. Arteries are able to withstand the enormous pressure of blood pumped by the heart, and to expand and relax in response to that pumping.

Pulse If you lightly touch the inside of your wrist, you can feel the artery in your wrist rise and fall repeatedly. The pulse that you feel is caused by the alternating expansion and relaxation of the artery wall. Every time the heart's ventricles contract, they send a spurt of blood out through all the arteries in your body. As this spurt travels through the arteries, it pushes the artery walls and makes them expand. After the spurt passes, the artery walls become narrower again. When you count the number of times an artery pulses beneath your fingers, you are counting heartbeats. By taking your pulse rate, you can determine how fast your heart is beating.

Regulating Blood Flow The muscles in the middle wall of an artery are involuntary muscles, which contract without your thinking about it. When they contract, the opening in the artery becomes smaller. When they relax, the opening becomes larger. These muscles act as control gates, adjusting the amount of blood sent to different organs. For example, after you eat, your stomach

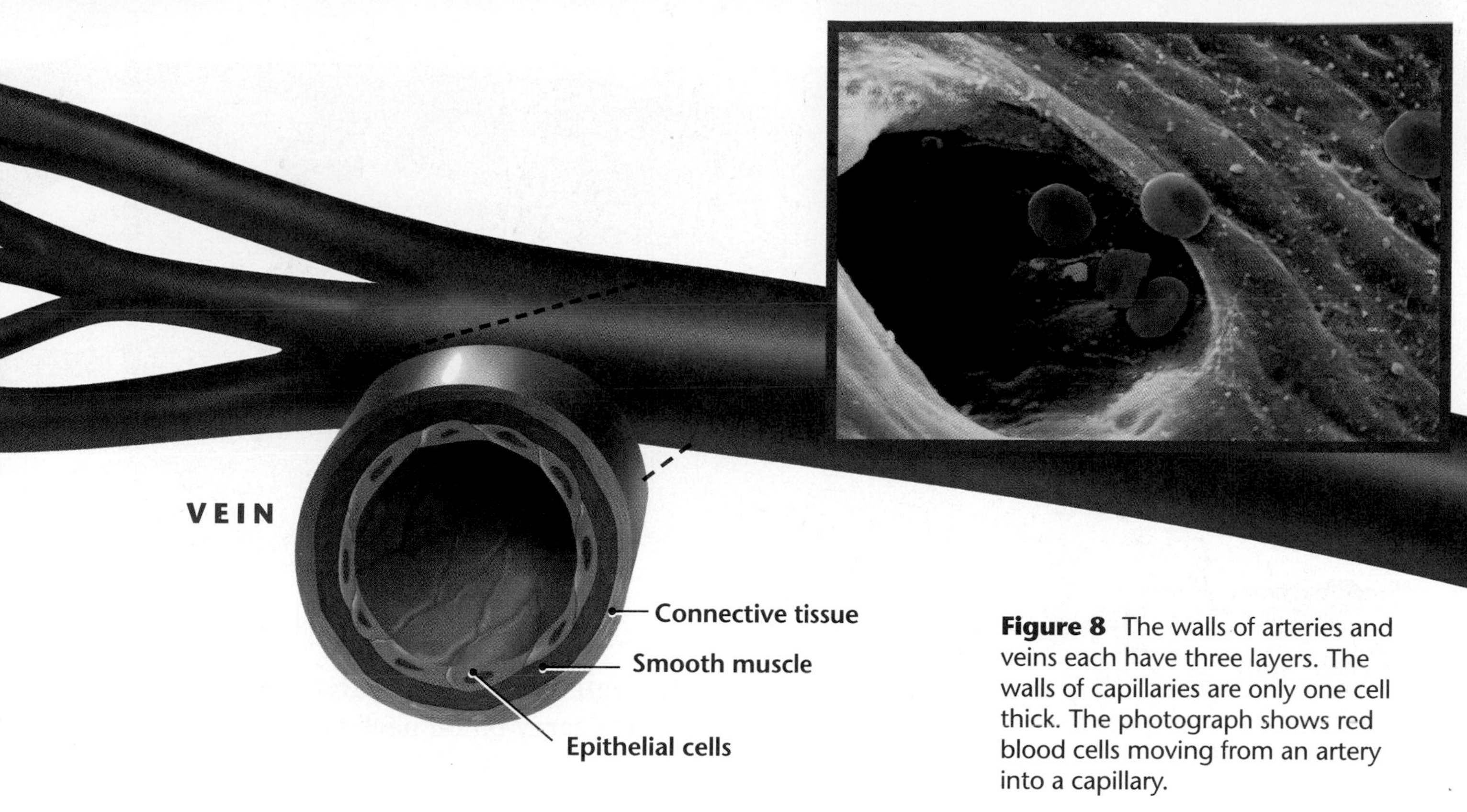

Figure 8 The walls of arteries and veins each have three layers. The walls of capillaries are only one cell thick. The photograph shows red blood cells moving from an artery into a capillary.

and intestines need a greater blood supply to help power digestion. The arteries leading to those organs become larger, so that more blood flows through them. In contrast, when you are running, your stomach and intestines need less blood than the muscles in your legs. The arteries leading to the stomach and intestines become narrower, decreasing the blood flow to those organs.

☑ *Checkpoint* *What causes the pulse that you feel in your wrist?*

Capillaries

Eventually, blood flows from small arteries into the tiny capillaries. **In the capillaries, materials are exchanged between the blood and the body's cells.** Capillary walls are only one cell thick. Because capillaries have thin walls, materials can pass easily through them. Materials such as oxygen and glucose pass from blood, through the thin capillary walls, to the cells. Cellular waste products travel in the opposite direction—from cells, through the capillary walls, and into blood.

INTEGRATING CHEMISTRY One way in which materials are exchanged between the blood and the body cells is by diffusion. **Diffusion** is the process by which molecules move from an area in which they are highly concentrated to an area in which they are less concentrated. For example, glucose is more highly concentrated in blood than it is in the body cells. Therefore, glucose diffuses from the blood, through the capillary wall, and into the body cells.

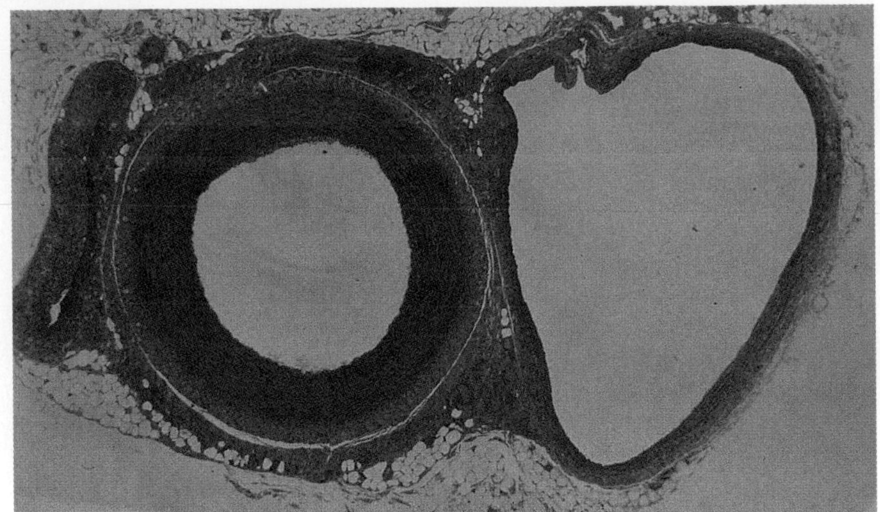

Figure 9 The wall of the artery (left) is much thicker than that of the vein (right).
Making Generalizations *Why is it important for artery walls to be both strong and flexible?*

Sharpen your Skills

Creating Data Tables

ACTIVITY

Scientists measured the volume of blood that different organs receive, first when a person was resting and then when the person was engaged in vigorous exercise.

- At rest, the organs of the abdomen received approximately 1,400 mL of blood per minute (mL/min). During vigorous exercise, they received 600 mL/min.
- At rest, skeletal muscles received about 1,200 mL/min. During vigorous exercise, the same muscles received about 12,500 mL/min.
- At rest, the kidneys received about 1,100 mL/min. During vigorous exercise, they received 600 mL/min.

Create a table to record these data. Then use the data to explain why some organs receive more blood during exercise, while some receive less.

Veins

After blood moves through capillaries, it enters larger blood vessels called veins, which carry blood back to the heart. The walls of veins, like those of arteries, have three layers, with muscle in the middle layer. However, the walls of veins are generally thinner than those of arteries.

By the time blood flows into veins, the pushing force of the heart has less effect than it did in the arteries. Several factors help move blood through veins. First, the muscles inside veins contract, narrowing the opening and pushing blood along, like toothpaste squeezed through a tube. Second, because many veins are located near skeletal muscles, the contraction of the muscles helps push the blood along. For example, as you run or walk, the skeletal muscles in your legs contract and squeeze the veins in your legs. Third, larger veins in your body have valves in them that prevent blood from flowing backward.

☑ ***Checkpoint*** *How do skeletal muscles help move blood in veins?*

Blood Pressure

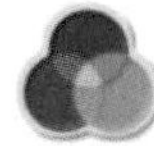

INTEGRATING PHYSICS

Suppose that you are washing a car. You attach the hose to the faucet and turn on the faucet. The water flows out in a slow, steady stream. Then, while your back is turned, your little brother turns the faucet on all the way. Suddenly, the water spurts out rapidly, and the hose almost jumps out of your hand.

As water flows through a hose, it pushes against the walls of the hose, creating pressure on the walls. **Pressure** is the force that something exerts over a given area. When your brother turned on the faucet all the way, the additional water flow increased the pressure exerted on the inside of the hose. The extra pressure made the water spurt out of the nozzle faster.

What Causes Blood Pressure? Blood traveling through blood vessels behaves in a manner similar to that of water moving through a hose. Blood exerts a pressure, called **blood pressure,** against the walls of blood vessels. **Blood pressure is caused by the force with which the ventricles contract.** In general, as blood moves away from the heart, its pressure decreases. This happens because the farther away from the heart the blood moves, the lower the force of the ventricles. Blood flowing through arteries exerts the highest pressure. Blood pressure in capillaries and veins is much lower than in the arteries.

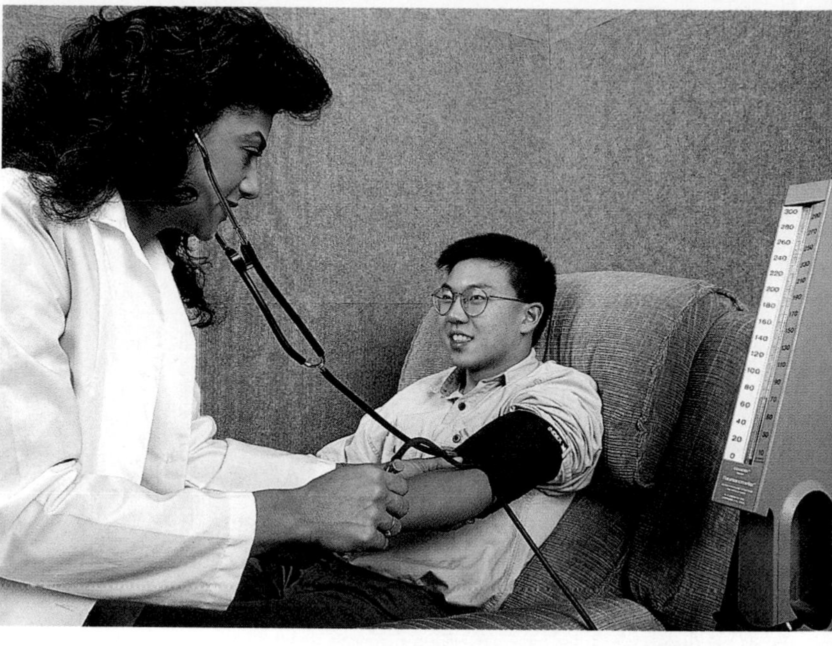

Figure 10 Blood pressure is measured with a sphygmomanometer. The cuff is wrapped around the patient's arm. His blood pressure is recorded by the height of the mercury column in the instrument on the right.

Measuring Blood Pressure Blood pressure can be measured with an instrument called a **sphygmomanometer** (sfig moh muh NAHM uh tur). Many sphygmomanometers contain a tube of mercury. Blood pressure is expressed in millimeters of mercury and is recorded as two numbers. The first number is a measure of the blood pressure while the ventricles contract and pump blood into the arteries. The second number, which is lower, measures the blood pressure while the ventricles relax between heartbeats. The two numbers are expressed as a fraction: the contraction pressure over the relaxation pressure. A typical blood pressure reading for a young adult is 120/80. You will learn about the effects of high blood pressure in Section 4.

Section 2 Review

1. Contrast the functions of arteries, capillaries, and veins.
2. What causes blood pressure?
3. Explain the factors that enable blood in your leg veins to return to the heart in spite of the downward pull of gravity.
4. **Thinking Critically Applying Concepts** Arteries adjust the amount of blood flowing to different parts of the body, depending on where blood is needed. Use this fact to explain why it may not be a good idea to exercise vigorously shortly after you eat.

Check Your Progress CHAPTER PROJECT 4

By now you should have begun constructing your display. Make sure that the blood vessels are depicted accurately. Also check that your display correctly shows the path of a red blood cell and the place where the red blood cell picks up oxygen. *(Hint: Start to prepare a rough draft of your written description.)*

Skills Lab

Measuring

Heart Beat, Health Beat

Problem

How does physical activity affect your pulse rate?

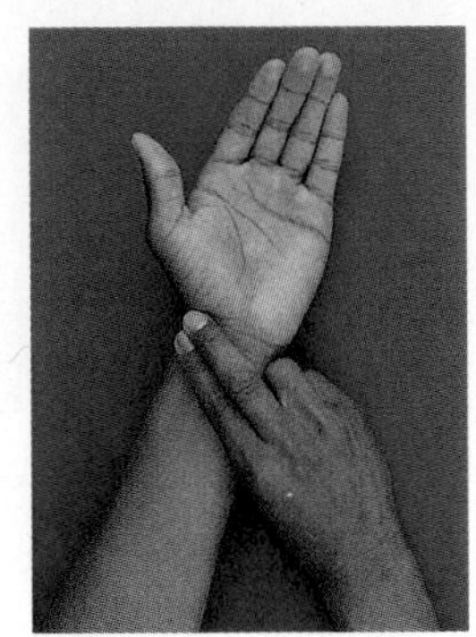

Materials

watch or clock with second hand
graph paper

Procedure

1. Predict how your pulse rate will change as you go from resting to being active, then back to resting again. Then copy the data table into your notebook.
2. Locate your pulse by placing the index and middle finger of one hand on your other wrist at the base of your thumb. Move the two fingers slightly until you feel your pulse.
3. Work with a partner for the rest of this lab. Begin by determining your resting pulse rate. Count the number of beats in your pulse for exactly one minute while your partner times you. Record the number in your data table. **CAUTION:** *Do not complete the rest of these procedures if there is any medical reason why you should avoid physical activities.*

DATA TABLE

Activity	Pulse Rate
Resting	
Walking	
Running	
Resting after Exercise	
(1 min) Resting after Exercise	
(3+ min) Resting after Exercise	

4. Walk in place for one minute while your partner times you. Stop and immediately take your pulse for one minute. Record the number in your data table.
5. Run in place for one minute. Take your pulse again, and record the result.
6. Sit down right away, and have your partner time you as you rest for one minute. Then take your pulse rate again.
7. Have your partner time you as you rest for 3 more minutes. Then take your pulse rate again and record it.

Analyze and Conclude

1. Use the data you obtained to create a bar graph of your pulse rate under the different conditions you tested.
2. What conclusion can you draw about the relationship between physical activity and a person's pulse rate?
3. What happens to the pulse rate when the physical activity has stopped?
4. What can you infer about the heartbeat when the pulse rate increases?
5. **Think About It** Do you think the pulse measurements you made are completely accurate? Why or why not? How could you improve the accuracy of your measurements?

Design an Experiment

Do the resting pulse rates of adults, teens, and young children differ? Write a plan to answer this question. Obtain your teacher's permission before carrying out your plan.

SECTION 3 Blood and Lymph

DISCOVER ACTIVITY

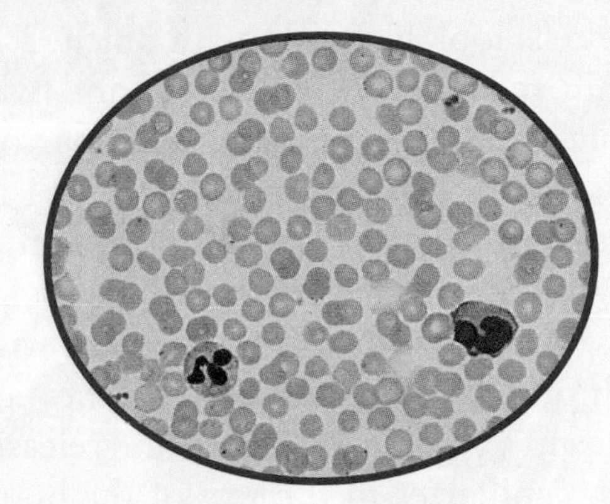

What Kinds of Cells Are in Blood?

1. Obtain a microscope slide of human blood. Look at the slide under the microscope, first under low power and then under high power.
2. Look carefully at the different kinds of cells that you see.
3. Make several drawings of each kind of cell. Use red pencil for the red blood cells.

Think It Over

Observing How many kinds of cells did you see? How do they differ from each other?

If someone fills a test tube with blood and lets it sit for a while, the blood separates into layers. The top layer is a clear, yellowish liquid. A dark red material rests on the bottom. The top layer is **plasma,** which is the liquid part of blood. The red material at the bottom is a mixture of blood cells. **Blood is made up of four components: plasma, red blood cells, white blood cells, and platelets.** About 45 percent of the volume of blood is made up of cells. The rest consists of plasma.

GUIDE FOR READING

- **What are the four components of blood?**
- **What determines the type of blood that a person can receive in transfusion?**

Reading Tip **As you read, write definitions for each boldfaced term in your own words.**

Plasma

Blood, as you have learned, transports materials from one part of the body to another. Most of those materials travel in plasma. In fact, 10 percent of plasma is made up of these dissolved materials. The other 90 percent of plasma is water.

Plasma carries molecules that come from the breakdown of digested food, such as glucose and fats. The vitamins and minerals your body needs also travel in plasma. Plasma also carries chemical messengers that direct body activities such as the uptake of glucose by your cells. In addition, many wastes produced by cell processes are carried away by plasma.

Protein molecules give plasma its yellow color. There are three groups of plasma proteins. One group helps to regulate the amount of water in blood. The second group, which is produced by white blood cells, helps fight disease. The third group of proteins interacts with platelets to form blood clots.

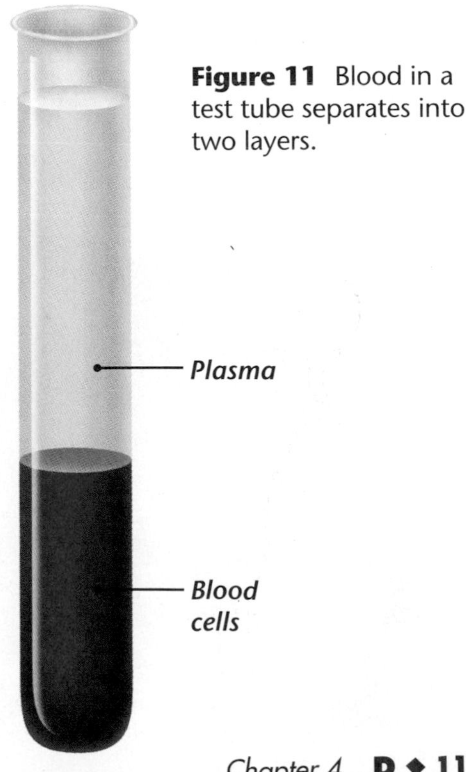

Figure 11 Blood in a test tube separates into two layers.

Red Blood Cells

Without red blood cells, your body could not use the oxygen that you breathe in. **Red blood cells** take up oxygen in the lungs and deliver it to cells elsewhere in the body. Red blood cells, like most blood cells, are produced in bone marrow.

Exploring Blood Cells shows what red blood cells look like. Under a microscope, these cells look like disks with pinched-in centers. Because they are thin, red blood cells can bend and twist easily. This flexibility enables them to squeeze through narrow capillaries.

A red blood cell is made mostly of **hemoglobin** (HEE muh gloh bin), which is an iron-containing protein that binds chemically to oxygen molecules. When hemoglobin combines with oxygen, the cells become bright red. Without oxygen, they are dark red. Hemoglobin picks up oxygen in the lungs and releases it as blood travels through capillaries in the rest of the body. Hemoglobin also picks up some of the carbon dioxide produced by cells. However, most of the carbon dioxide is carried by plasma. The blood carries the carbon dioxide to the lungs, where it is released from the body.

EXPLORING *Blood Cells*

Blood consists of liquid plasma and three kinds of cells—red blood cells, white blood cells, and platelets.

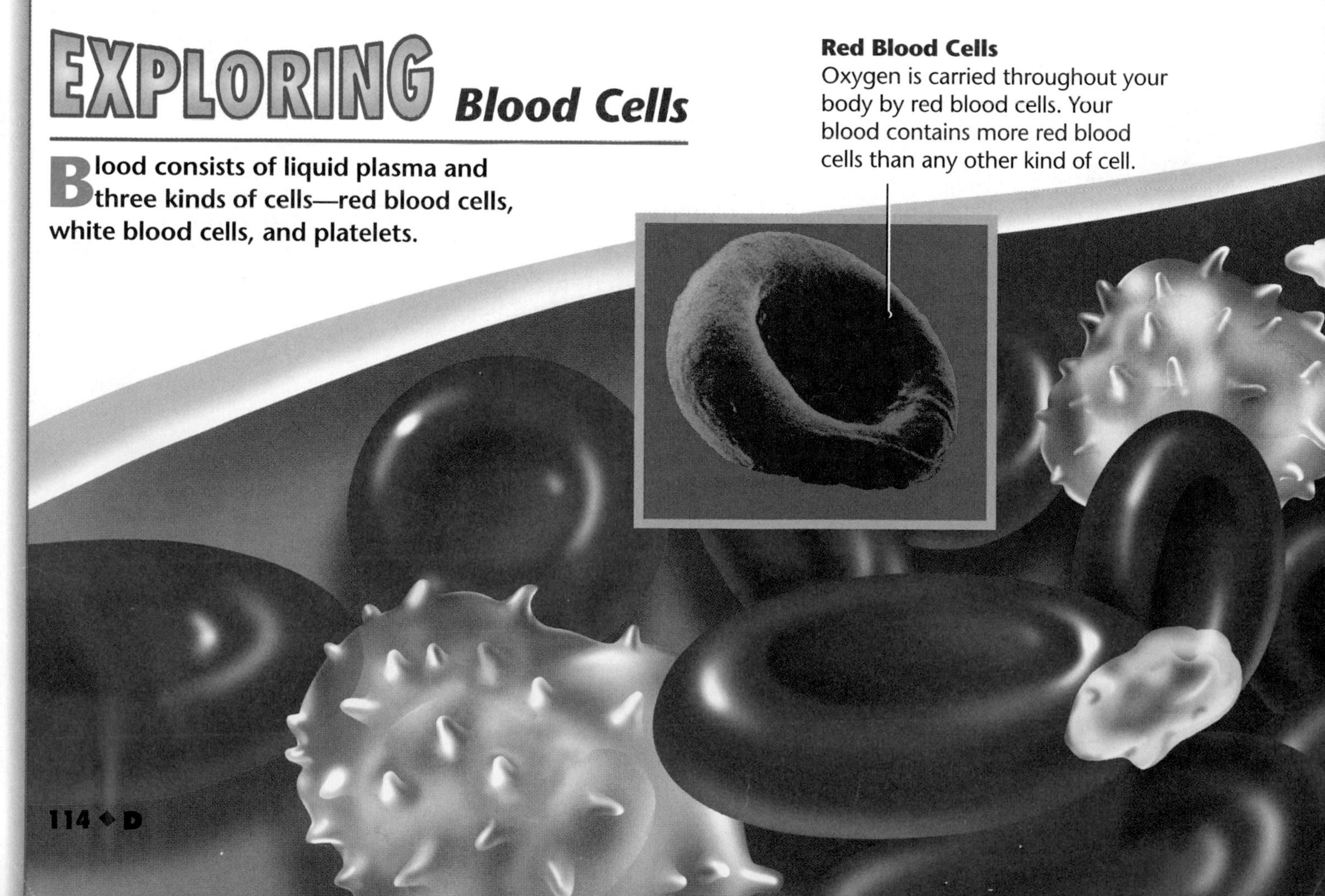

Red Blood Cells
Oxygen is carried throughout your body by red blood cells. Your blood contains more red blood cells than any other kind of cell.

Red blood cells have no nuclei. Without a nucleus, a red blood cell cannot live very long. In fact, red blood cells live only about 120 days. Every second, about 2 million red blood cells in your body die. Fortunately, your bone marrow produces new red blood cells at the same rate.

☑ *Checkpoint* *What is the shape of a red blood cell?*

White Blood Cells

Like red blood cells, white blood cells begin their existence in bone marrow. **White blood cells** are the body's disease fighters. Some white blood cells recognize disease-causing organisms such as bacteria, and alert the body that it has been invaded. Other white blood cells produce chemicals to fight the invaders. Still others surround and kill the organisms. You will learn more about the functions of white blood cells in Chapter 6.

White blood cells are different from red blood cells in several important ways. There are fewer of them—only about one white blood cell for every 500 to 1,000 red blood cells. White blood cells are also bigger than red blood cells, and they have nuclei. And most white blood cells live for months or even years.

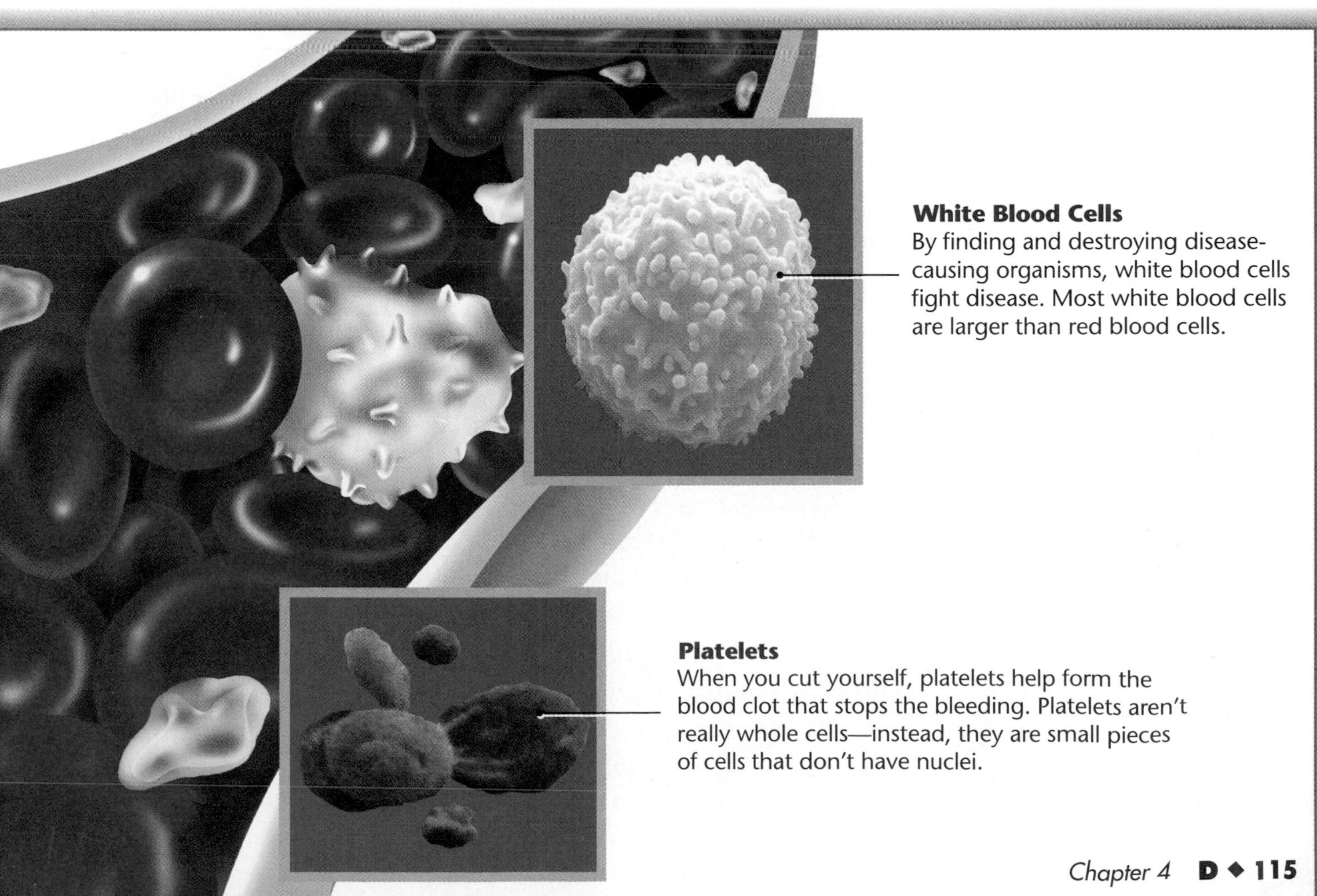

White Blood Cells
By finding and destroying disease-causing organisms, white blood cells fight disease. Most white blood cells are larger than red blood cells.

Platelets
When you cut yourself, platelets help form the blood clot that stops the bleeding. Platelets aren't really whole cells—instead, they are small pieces of cells that don't have nuclei.

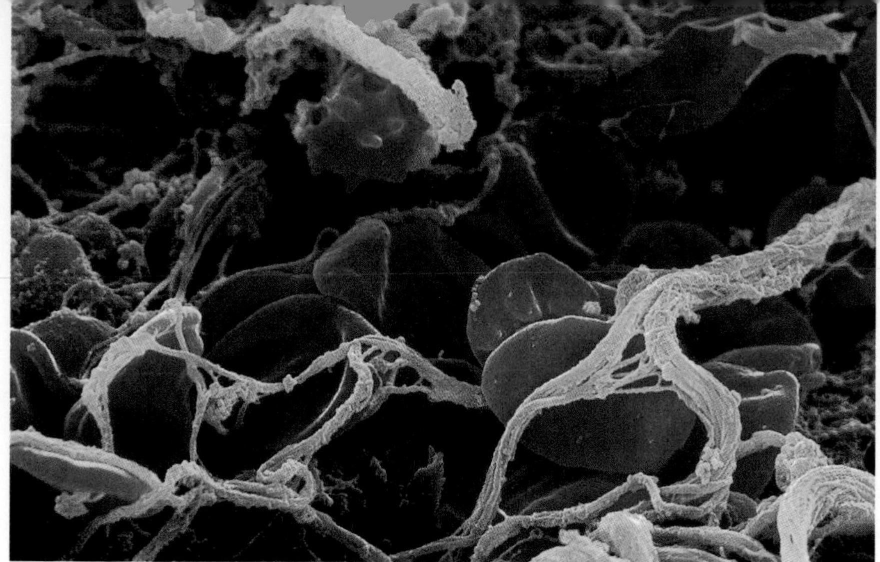

Figure 12 When you cut your skin, a blood clot forms. The blood clot consists of blood cells trapped in a fiber net. Platelets produce the material of which the fibers are made.

Platelets

When you cut your finger, blood flows out of the cut. After a short time, however, a blood clot forms, stopping the blood flow. **Platelets** (PLAYT lits) are cell fragments that play an important part in forming blood clots.

When a blood vessel is cut, platelets collect and stick to the vessel at the site of the wound. The platelets release chemicals that start a chain reaction. This series of reactions eventually produces a chemical called **fibrin** (FY brin). Fibrin gets its name from the fact that it weaves a net of tiny fibers across the cut in the blood vessel. The fiber net traps blood cells. As more and more platelets and blood cells become trapped in the net, a blood clot forms. A scab is a dried blood clot on the skin surface.

☑ *Checkpoint* *What role do platelets play in forming blood clots?*

Caught in the Web

ACTIVITY

In this activity, you will model part of the process by which a blood clot forms.

1. Cover the opening of a sturdy plastic cup with a piece of cheesecloth. Use a rubber band to hold the cheesecloth in place.
2. Put some water, paper clips, and coins in another cup.
3. Carefully pour the water, coins, and paper clips into the middle of the cheesecloth.

Making Models The paper clips and coins represent blood cells. What does the cheesecloth represent? What starts the production of the substance that the cheesecloth represents?

Blood Types

If a person loses a lot of blood—from a wound or during surgery—he or she may be given a **blood transfusion.** A blood transfusion is the transference of blood from one person to another. Most early attempts at blood transfusion failed, but no one knew why until the early 1900s. At that time Karl Landsteiner, an Austrian American physician, tried mixing blood samples from pairs of people. Sometimes the two blood samples blended smoothly. In other cases, however, the red blood cells clumped together. This clumping accounted for the failure of many blood transfusions. If clumping occurs within the body, it clogs the capillaries and may kill the person.

Marker Molecules Landsteiner went on to discover that there are four types of blood—A, B, AB, and O. Blood types are determined by marker molecules on red blood cells. If your blood type is A, you have the A marker. If your blood type is B, you have the B marker. People with type AB blood have both A and B markers. The red blood cells of people with type O blood contain neither A nor B markers.

Your plasma contains clumping proteins that recognize red blood cells with "foreign" markers and make those cells clump together. For example, if you have blood type A, your blood contains clumping proteins that act against cells with B markers. So if you receive a transfusion of type B blood, your clumping proteins will make the "foreign" type B cells clump together.

Safe Transfusions Landsteiner's work led to a better understanding of transfusions. **The marker molecules on your red blood cells determine your blood type and the type of blood that you can safely receive in transfusions.** A person with type A blood can receive transfusions of either type A or type O blood. Neither of these two blood types has B markers. Thus they would not be recognized as foreign by the clumping proteins in type A blood. A person with type AB blood can receive all blood types in transfusion, because type AB blood has no clumping proteins. Figure 13 shows which transfusions are safe for each blood type.

If you ever receive a transfusion, your blood type will be checked. Then donated blood that you can safely receive will be found. This process is called cross matching. You may have heard a doctor on a television show give the order to "type and cross." The doctor wants to find out what blood type the patient has and then cross match it against donated blood.

Blood Types

Blood Type	Marker Molecules on Red Blood Cells	Clumping Proteins	Blood Types That Can Be Safely Received in a Transfusion
A	A, A, A, A, A, A	anti-B	A and O
B	B, B, B, B, B, B	anti-A	B and O
AB	A, B, B, A, A, B	no clumping proteins	A, B, AB, and O
O		anti-A and anti-B	O

Figure 13 The chemical markers on a person's red blood cells determine the types of blood he or she can safely receive in a transfusion. ***Interpreting Charts*** *What types of blood can be given safely to a person with blood type AB? Who can safely receive blood type O?*

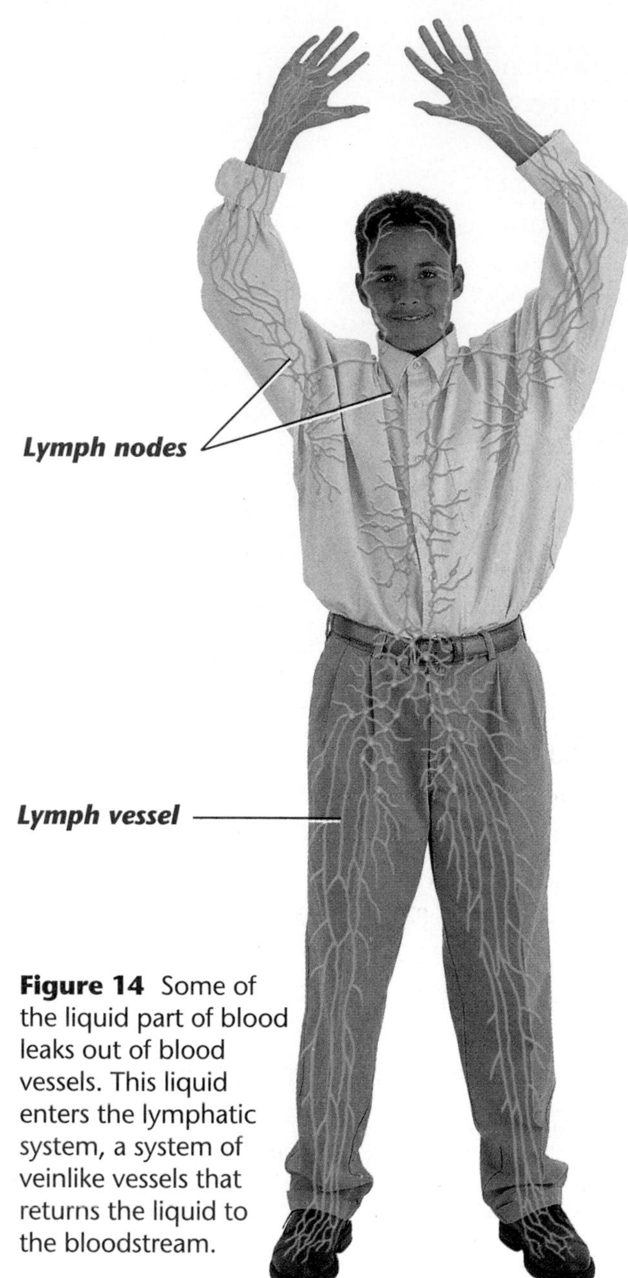

Figure 14 Some of the liquid part of blood leaks out of blood vessels. This liquid enters the lymphatic system, a system of veinlike vessels that returns the liquid to the bloodstream.

The Lymphatic System

As blood travels through the capillaries in the cardiovascular system, some of the fluid leaks out. It moves through the walls of capillaries and into surrounding tissues. This fluid carries materials that the cells in the tissues need.

After bathing the cells, this fluid moves into the lymphatic system. The **lymphatic system** (lim FAT ik) is a network of veinlike vessels that returns the fluid to the bloodstream. The lymphatic system acts something like rain gutters after a rainstorm, carrying the fluid away.

Lymph Once the fluid is inside the lymphatic system, it is called **lymph.** Lymph consists of water and dissolved materials such as glucose. It also contains some white blood cells that have left the capillaries.

The lymphatic system has no pump, so lymph moves slowly. Lymphatic vessels, which are part of the cardiovascular system, connect to large veins in the chest. Lymph empties into these veins and once again becomes part of blood plasma.

Lymph Nodes As lymph flows through the lymphatic system, it passes through small knobs of tissue called **lymph nodes.** Lymph nodes filter the lymph, trapping bacteria and other microorganisms that cause disease. When the body is fighting an infection, the lymph nodes enlarge. If you've ever had "swollen glands" when you've been sick, you've actually had swollen lymph nodes.

Section 3 Review

1. List the four components of blood. Identify whether each is a cell, a part of a cell, or a liquid.
2. Explain why a person with type O blood cannot receive a transfusion of type A blood.
3. Where does lymph come from? What happens to lymph after it travels through the lymphatic system?
4. **Thinking Critically Relating Cause and Effect** People with the disease hemophilia do not produce the chemical fibrin. Explain why hemophilia is a serious disease.

CHAPTER PROJECT 4

Check Your Progress

By now, you should be completing your display. Write out your description using the correct names of blood vessels and other terms that you've learned in this chapter. *(Hint:* If your display has moving parts, test it to make sure that it works the way you expect it to.)

You and Your Community

Real-World Lab

Do You Know Your A-B-O's?

Donated blood is used for blood transfusions. But not every type of blood can be safely donated to every individual. In this lab, you'll investigate why type O blood is especially useful in blood transfusions.

Problem

Which blood types can safely receive transfusions of type A blood? Which can receive type O blood?

Materials

4 paper cups
4 plastic droppers
white paper
four model "blood" types
marking pen
8 plastic petri dishes
toothpicks

Procedure

1. Write down your ideas about why type O blood might be in higher demand than other blood types. Then make two copies of the data table in your notebook.
2. Label 4 paper cups A, B, AB, and O. Fill each cup about one-third full with the model "blood" supplied by your teacher. Insert one clean plastic dropper into each cup. Use each dropper to transfer only that one type of blood.
3. Label the side of each of 4 petri dishes with a blood type: A, B, AB, or O. Place the petri dishes on a sheet of white paper.
4. Use the plastic droppers to place 10 drops of each type of blood in its labeled petri dish. Each sample represents the blood of a potential receiver of a blood transfusion. Record the original color of each sample in your data table as yellow, blue, green, or colorless.

DATA TABLE

Donor: Type ______

Potential Receiver	Original Color	Final Color of Mixture	Safe or Unsafe?
A			
B			
AB			
O			

5. Label your first data table Donor: Type A. To test whether each potential receiver can safely receive type A blood, add 10 drops of type A blood to each sample. Stir each mixture with a separate, clean toothpick.
6. Record the final color of each mixture in the data table. If the color stayed the same, write "safe" in the last column. If the color of the mixture changed, write "unsafe."
7. Label your second data table Donor: Type O. Obtain four clean petri dishes, and repeat Steps 3 through 6 to determine who could safely receive type O blood.

Analyze and Conclude

1. Which blood types can safely receive a transfusion of type A blood? Type O blood?
2. If some blood types are not available, how might type O blood be useful?
3. **Apply** Why should hospitals have an adequate supply of different types of blood?

More to Explore

Repeat this activity to find out which blood types can safely receive donations of type B and type AB blood.

Section 4 Cardiovascular Health

DISCOVER ACTIVITY

Which Foods Are "Heart Healthy"?

1. Your teacher will give you an assortment of foods. If they have nutrition labels, read the information.
2. Sort the foods into three groups. In one group, put those foods that you think are good for your cardiovascular system. In the second group, put foods that you think might damage your cardiovascular system if eaten often. Place foods you aren't sure about in the third group.

Think It Over

Forming Operational Definitions How did you define a "heart-healthy" food?

GUIDE FOR READING

- **What behaviors can help maintain cardiovascular health?**

Reading Tip **Before you read, rewrite the headings in the section as questions that begin with *how, why,* or *what.* Write short answers to these questions as you read.**

Shortly after sunrise, when most people are just waking up, the rowers are already out on the river. Rhythmically, with perfectly coordinated movement, the rowers pull on the oars, making the boat glide swiftly through the water. Despite the chilly morning air, sweat glistens on the rowers' faces and arms. And inside their chests, their hearts are pounding, delivering blood to the arm and chest muscles that power the oars.

Rowers cannot perform at their peaks unless their cardiovascular systems are in excellent condition. But cardiovascular health is important to all people, not just athletes. Cardiovascular

disease is the leading cause of death in the United States. However, people can practice behaviors that decrease their risks of developing cardiovascular problems.

Cardiovascular Disease

Compare the two arteries shown in Figure 15. The one on the left is a healthy artery. It has a large space in the center through which blood can flow easily. The artery on the right, in contrast, has a thick wall and only a small space in the middle. This artery exhibits **atherosclerosis** (ath uh roh skluh ROH sis), a condition in which an artery wall thickens as a result of the buildup of fatty materials. One of these fatty materials is cholesterol, a waxy, fat-like substance. Atherosclerosis restricts the flow of blood in the arteries.

Atherosclerosis can develop in the coronary arteries that supply the heart. When that happens, the heart muscle receives less blood and therefore less oxygen. This condition may lead to a heart attack. A **heart attack** occurs when blood flow to part of the heart muscle is blocked. Cells die in the part of the heart that does not receive blood. This permanently damages the heart.

Treatment for mild atherosclerosis usually includes a low-fat diet and a moderate exercise program. In addition, medications that lower the levels of cholesterol and fats in the blood may be prescribed. People with severe atherosclerosis may need to undergo surgery or other procedures to unclog blocked arteries.

☑ ***Checkpoint*** *Why is atherosclerosis especially serious when it affects the coronary arteries?*

Hypertension

High blood pressure, or **hypertension** (hy pur TEN shun), is a disorder in which a person's blood pressure is consistently higher than normal—greater than 140/90. Hypertension makes the heart work harder. It also may damage the walls of the blood

Blocking the Flow

ACTIVITY

Use this activity to find out how fatty deposits affect the flow of blood through an artery.

1. Put a funnel in the mouth of a plastic jar. The funnel will represent an artery.
2. To model blood flowing through the artery, slowly pour 100 mL of water into the funnel. Have your partner time how many seconds it takes for all the water to flow through the funnel. Then discard the water.
3. Use a plastic knife to spread a small amount of peanut butter along the bottom of the funnel's neck. Then, with a toothpick, carve out a hole in the peanut butter so that the funnel is partly, but not completely, clogged.
4. Repeat Steps 1 and 2.

Predicting If the funnels were arteries, which one—blocked or unblocked—would do a better job of supplying blood to tissues? Explain.

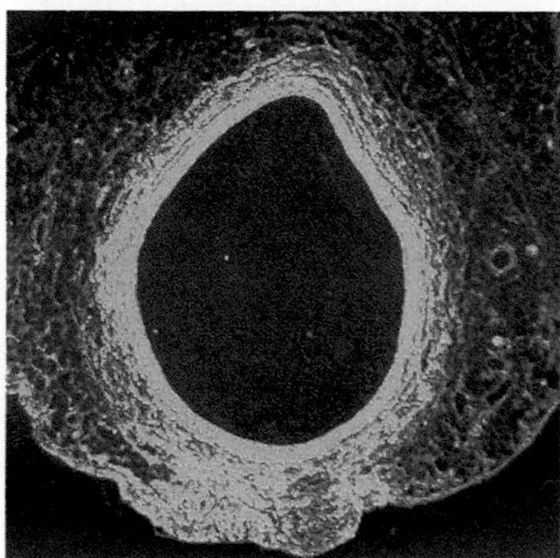

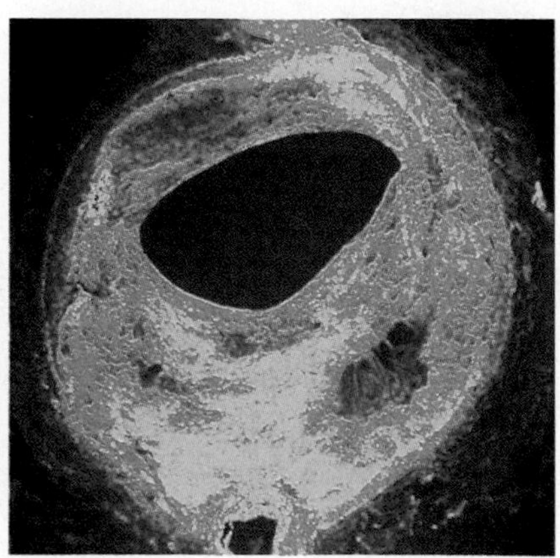

Figure 15 The healthy artery on the left is unblocked. In contrast, notice the narrow opening in the artery on the right. This person has atherosclerosis, which is caused by fatty deposits on the artery walls. ***Relating Cause and Effect*** *What kind of diet can lead to atherosclerosis?*

vessels. Over time, both the heart and arteries can be severely harmed by hypertension. Because people with hypertension often have no obvious symptoms to warn them, hypertension is sometimes called the "silent killer."

Hypertension and atherosclerosis are closely related. As the arteries narrow, blood pressure increases. Being overweight and failing to get enough exercise can also increase a person's risk of developing hypertension.

Cardiovascular Advances in the Twentieth Century

Scientists today have an in-depth understanding of how the cardiovascular system works and how to treat cardiovascular problems. This time line describes some advances of the twentieth century.

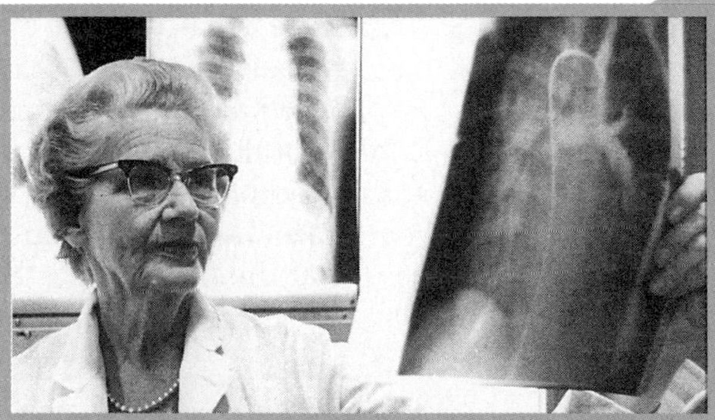

1944
Treatment for "Blue Babies"

Helen Taussig identified the heart defect that causes the skin of some newborn babies to be bluish in color. The blood of these "blue babies" does not receive an adequate amount of oxygen. Taussig and another surgeon, Alfred Blalock, developed an operation to correct the defect and save these babies' lives.

1900 **1920** **1940**

1901
Discovery of Blood Types

Karl Landsteiner demonstrated that people have different blood types, which are determined by marker molecules on their red blood cells. Landsteiner's discovery enabled blood transfusions to be done safely.

1930s–1940s
Blood Banks

Charles Drew demonstrated that emergency transfusions could successfully be done with plasma if whole blood was not available. During World War II, Drew established blood banks for storing donated blood. His work helped save millions of lives on and off the battlefield.

For mild hypertension, regular exercise and careful food choices may be enough to lower blood pressure. People with hypertension need to limit their intake of sodium, which can increase their blood pressure. Sodium is found in salt and in processed foods such as soups and packaged snack foods. For some people who have hypertension, however, medications are needed to reduce their blood pressure.

☑ ***Checkpoint*** *Why is hypertension called the "silent killer"?*

In Your Journal

Choose one of the scientists whose work is described here. Imagine that you are on a committee that has chosen him or her to receive an award. Write the speech you would give at the award ceremony. The speech should explain the importance of the scientist's contributions.

1967

First Heart Transplant

Christiaan Barnard, a South African surgeon, performed the first transplant of a human heart. Louis Washkansky, the man who received the heart, lived for only 18 days after the transplant. But Barnard's work paved the way for future successes in transplanting hearts and other organs.

1992

Laser Beam Unclogs Arteries

The United States government approved a device that uses a laser beam to burn away the material causing blockage in some arteries. This device can help some people with atherosclerosis.

1960 **1980** **2000**

1982

Artificial Heart

An artificial heart, developed by Robert Jarvik, was implanted into a patient by surgeon William DeVries at the University of Utah. Barney Clark, the man who received the artificial heart, lived for 112 days. Today artificial hearts are sometimes used temporarily in people waiting for heart transplants.

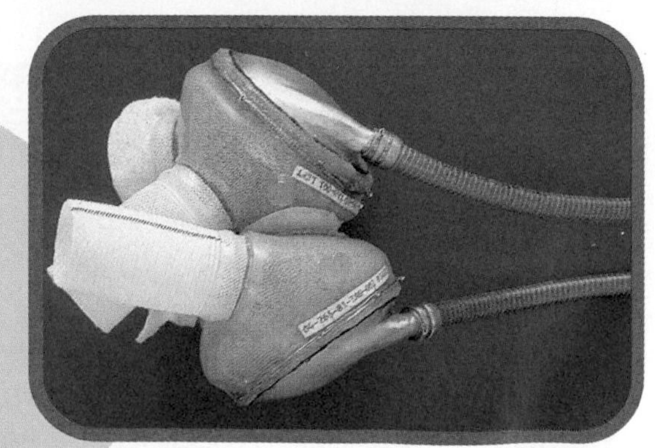

Keeping Your Cardiovascular System Healthy

Few young people have heart attacks, but atherosclerosis can begin to develop in people as young as 20 years old. You can establish habits now that will lessen your risk of developing atherosclerosis and hypertension. **To help maintain cardiovascular health, people should exercise regularly; eat a balanced diet that is low in fat, cholesterol, and sodium; and avoid smoking.**

Figure 16 Eating foods that are low in fat can help keep your cardiovascular system healthy.

Exercise Do you participate in sports, ride a bike, swim, dance, or climb stairs instead of taking the elevator? Every time you do one of those activities, you are helping to maintain your cardiovascular health. Exercise strengthens your heart muscle and also helps prevent atherosclerosis.

A Balanced Diet Foods that are high in cholesterol and fats can lead to a buildup of fatty deposits on artery walls. In addition, eating too many high-fat foods can lead to excessive weight gain. Foods such as red meats, eggs, and cheese are high in cholesterol. These foods also contain substances that your body needs. Therefore, a smart approach might be to eat them, but only in small quantities. Some foods that are especially high in fat include butter and margarine, potato chips, doughnuts, and fried foods such as French fries. Eat high-fat foods only occasionally, if at all.

Avoid Smoking Smokers are more than twice as likely to have a heart attack than are nonsmokers. Every year, almost 180,000 people in the United States die from cardiovascular disease caused by smoking. If smokers quit, however, their risk of death from cardiovascular disease decreases.

Section 4 Review

1. List three things you can do to help your cardiovascular system stay healthy.
2. What is atherosclerosis?
3. How does hypertension affect blood vessels?
4. **Thinking Critically Relating Cause and Effect** Coronary heart disease is much less common in some countries than it is in the United States. What factors might account for this difference?

Science at Home

With your family, discuss some things that you all can do to maintain healthy cardiovascular systems. Make a list of exercise activities, such as bicycling and swimming, that family members can enjoy together. You might also work with your family to cook and serve a "heart-healthy," low-fat meal.

Section 1 The Body's Transportation System

Key Ideas

- The cardiovascular system consists of the heart, blood vessels, and blood.
- The heart pumps blood through the blood vessels. The heart has four chambers. The two atria receive blood, and the two ventricles pump blood out of the heart.
- Blood travels from the heart to the lungs and back to the heart. It is then pumped to the body and returns again to the heart.
- A group of cells called the pacemaker regulates the rate at which the heart beats.

Key Terms

cardiovascular system
heart
atrium
ventricle
valve
pacemaker
artery
capillary
vein
aorta
force

Section 2 A Closer Look at Blood Vessels

Key Ideas

- Arteries carry blood from the heart to capillaries. In the capillaries, materials are exchanged between the blood and the body's cells. From the capillaries, blood flows into veins that carry it back to the heart.
- Blood pressure is caused by the force with which the ventricles contract. Blood pressure is highest in arteries and lowest in veins.

Key Terms

coronary artery
diffusion
pressure
blood pressure
sphygmomanometer

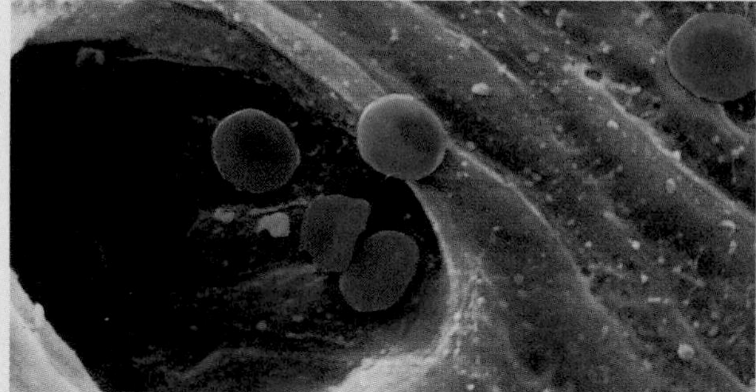

Section 3 Blood and Lymph

Key Ideas

- Plasma, the liquid part of blood, transports materials such as glucose, vitamins, and waste products.
- Red blood cells, which contain hemoglobin, carry oxygen and deliver it to body cells. White blood cells fight disease. Platelets are important in forming blood clots.
- There are four blood types—A, B, AB, and O. A person's blood type determines the types of blood he or she can receive in transfusions.
- Some fluid escapes from blood vessels. The lymphatic system transports this fluid, called lymph, and empties it back into the blood.

Key Terms

plasma
red blood cell
hemoglobin
white blood cell
platelet
fibrin
blood transfusion
lymphatic system
lymph
lymph node

Section 4 Cardiovascular Health

INTEGRATING HEALTH

Key Ideas

- Atherosclerosis is a condition in which an artery wall thickens due to the buildup of cholesterol and other fatty materials.
- Hypertension is a disorder in which the blood pressure is higher than normal.
- To help prevent atherosclerosis and hypertension, people need to exercise regularly; eat a diet low in fat, cholesterol, and salt; and avoid smoking.

Key Terms

atherosclerosis
cholesterol
heart attack
hypertension

www.science-explorer.phschool.com

CHAPTER 4 REVIEW

Reviewing Content

For more review of key concepts, see the Interactive Student Tutorial CD-ROM.

Multiple Choice

Choose the letter of the best answer.

1. The heart's upper chambers are called
   a. ventricles.
   b. atria.
   c. valves.
   d. hemoglobins.
2. Oxygen-rich blood enters the heart through the
   a. left atrium.
   b. right atrium.
   c. left ventricle.
   d. right ventricle.
3. Which of the following is *not* important in moving blood through veins?
   a. the force with which the atria contract
   b. valves
   c. muscles in the walls of veins
   d. the contraction of skeletal muscles
4. Platelets help the body to
   a. control bleeding.
   b. carry oxygen.
   c. fight infection.
   d. regulate the amount of water in plasma.
5. Cholesterol is a fatlike substance associated with
   a. lymph nodes.
   b. fibrin.
   c. atherosclerosis.
   d. salt.

True or False

If the statement is true, write true. If it is false, change the underlined word or words to make the statement true.

6. The two lower heart chambers are called ventricles.
7. White blood cells contain hemoglobin.
8. The capillaries are the narrowest blood vessels in the body.
9. A person with blood type B can receive a transfusion of blood types B and AB.
10. Elevated blood pressure is called hypertension.

Checking Concepts

11. A red blood cell is moving through an artery in your leg. Describe the path that blood cell will follow back to your heart. Identify the chamber of the heart to which it will return.
12. Contrast the forces with which the right and left ventricles contract. How does this relate to each ventricle's function?
13. How is a capillary's structure adapted to its function?
14. What is the function of hemoglobin?
15. Give two reasons why the food choices that people make are important to their cardiovascular health.
16. **Writing to Learn** Write an ad that encourages teenagers to exercise. Your ad will appear in a teen magazine. The ad should point out the health benefits of exercise and identify some ways that teenagers can exercise.

Thinking Visually

17. **Compare/Contrast Table** Compare the three types of blood vessels by copying and completing the table below. (For more on compare/contrast tables, see the Skills Handbook.)

Blood Vessel	Function	Structure of Wall
Artery	a. ?	3 layers: inner–epithelial tissue middle–muscle outer–connective tissue
b. ?	exchange of materials between cells and blood	c. ?
Vein	d. ?	e. ?

Applying Skills

The graph below shows how average blood pressure, measured when the ventricles contract, changes as men and women grow older. Use the graph to answer Questions 18–20.

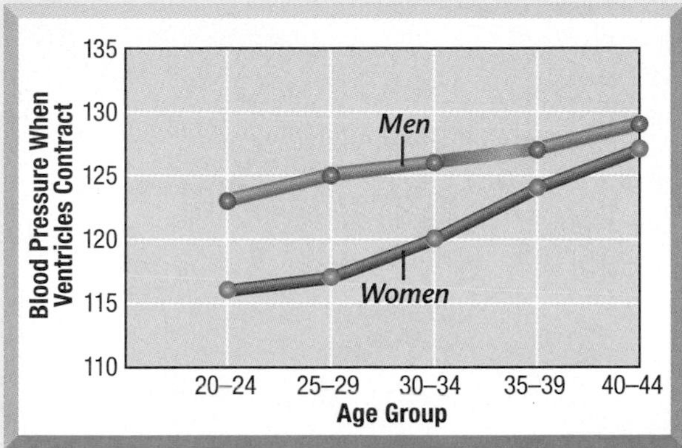

18. Interpreting Data At age 20, who is likely to have the higher blood pressure—a man or a woman?

19. Drawing Conclusions In general, what happens to people's blood pressure as they age?

20. Predicting Do you think that there is some age at which both men and women have about the same blood pressure? Use the graph lines to explain your prediction.

Thinking Critically

21. Predicting Some babies are born with an opening between the left and right ventricles. How would this heart defect affect the ability of the cardiovascular system to deliver oxygen to body cells?

22. Comparing and Contrasting Contrast the direction of movement of oxygen in lung capillaries and other capillaries in the body.

23. Relating Cause and Effect People who do not have enough iron in their diets sometimes develop a condition in which their blood cannot carry a normal amount of oxygen. Explain why this is so.

24. Making Generalizations Why are atherosclerosis and hypertension sometimes called "lifestyle diseases"?

CHAPTER 4 REVIEW

Performance Assessment

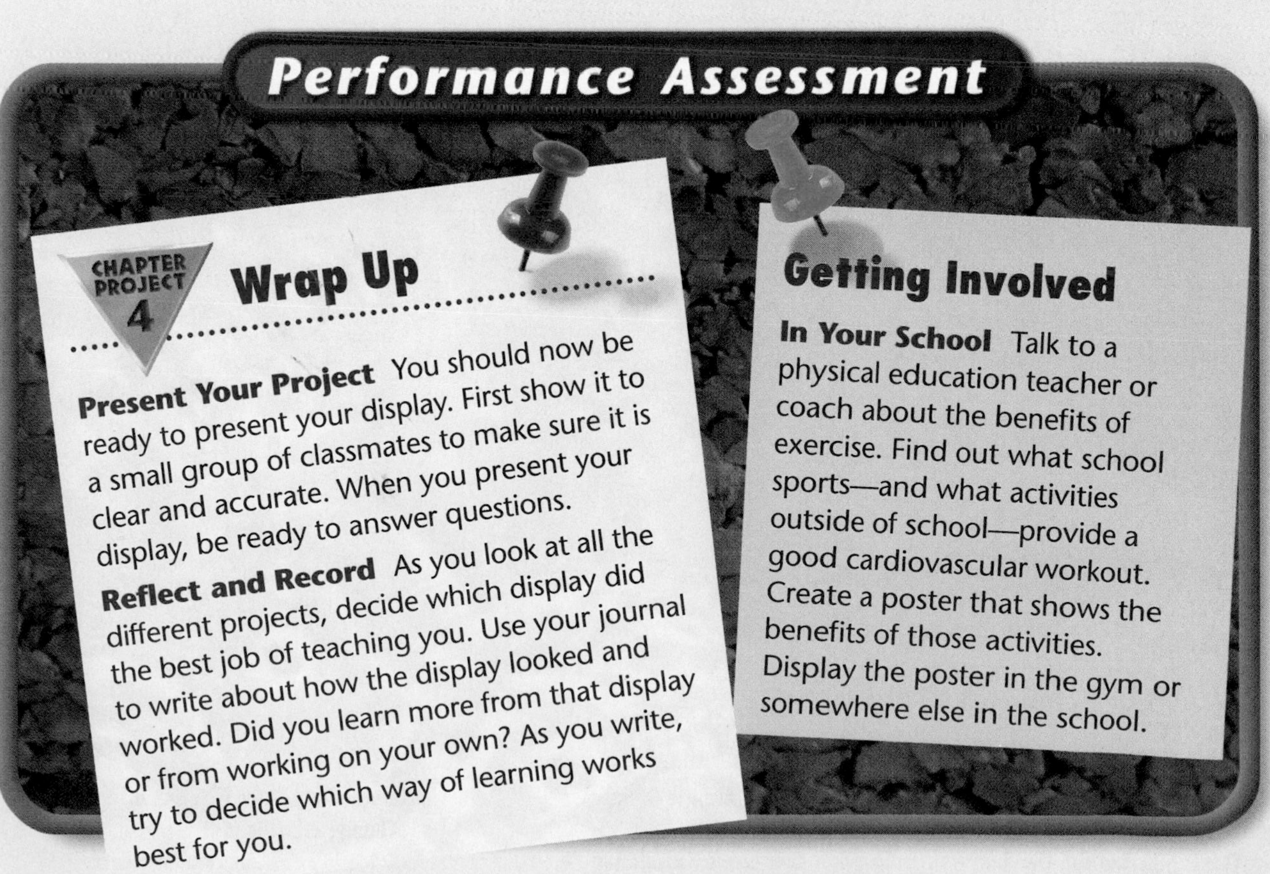

CHAPTER PROJECT 4

Wrap Up

Present Your Project You should now be ready to present your display. First show it to a small group of classmates to make sure it is clear and accurate. When you present your display, be ready to answer questions.

Reflect and Record As you look at all the different projects, decide which display did the best job of teaching you. Use your journal to write about how the display looked and worked. Did you learn more from that display or from working on your own? As you write, try to decide which way of learning works best for you.

Getting Involved

In Your School Talk to a physical education teacher or coach about the benefits of exercise. Find out what school sports—and what activities outside of school—provide a good cardiovascular workout. Create a poster that shows the benefits of those activities. Display the poster in the gym or somewhere else in the school.

CHAPTER 5 Respiration and Excretion

WHAT'S AHEAD

SECTION 1 The Respiratory System

Discover **How Big Can You Blow Up a Balloon?**
Try This **Do You Exhale Carbon Dioxide?**
Skills Lab **A Breath of Fresh Air**

Integrating Health

SECTION 2 Smoking and Your Health

Discover **What Are the Dangers of Smoking?**
Sharpen Your Skills **Calculating**

SECTION 3 The Excretory System

Discover **How Does Filtering a Liquid Change What Is in It?**
Real-World Lab **Clues About Health**

PROJECT 5

Get the Message Out

Lively music fills the air as the band marches along the parade route. To play many musical instruments, you need powerful, healthy lungs, which are part of the respiratory system. In this chapter, you will learn about the respiratory and excretory systems.

One way that people can keep their respiratory systems healthy is by choosing not to smoke. You've probably seen antismoking advertisements on television and in magazines. Imagine that you're part of a team of writers and designers who create advertisements. You've just been given the job of creating antismoking ads for different age groups. As you learn about the respiratory system, you can use your knowledge in your ad campaign.

Your Goal To create three different antismoking ads: one telling young children about the dangers of smoking; the second one discouraging teenagers from trying cigarettes; and the third encouraging adult smokers to quit.

To complete the project successfully, each ad must

- accurately communicate at least three health risks associated with smoking
- address at least two pressures that influence people to start or continue smoking
- use images and words in convincing, creative ways that gear your message to each audience

Get Started Brainstorm a list of reasons why people smoke. Consider the possible influence of family and friends as well as that of ads, movies, videos, and television. Also decide which types of ads you will produce, such as magazine ads or billboards. Begin to plan your ads.

Check Your Progress You'll be working on this project as you study this chapter. To keep your project on track, look for Check Your Progress boxes at the following points.

Section 2 Review, page 144: Plan your ads.
Section 3 Review, page 150: Design and produce your ads.

Wrap Up At the end of the chapter (page 153), you will display your completed ads. Be prepared to discuss your reasons for choosing the images and persuasive messages that you used.

Trombone players in a marching band need strong, healthy lungs.

Section 1 The Respiratory System

Discover ACTIVITY

How Big Can You Blow Up a Balloon?

1. Take a normal breath, then blow as much air as possible into a balloon. Twist the end and hold it closed. Have your partner measure around the balloon at its widest point.
2. Let the air out of the balloon. Repeat Step 1 and calculate the average of the two measurements.
3. Compare your results with those of your classmates. The bigger the circumference, the greater the volume of air exhaled.

Think It Over

Inferring What factors might affect the volume of air a person can exhale?

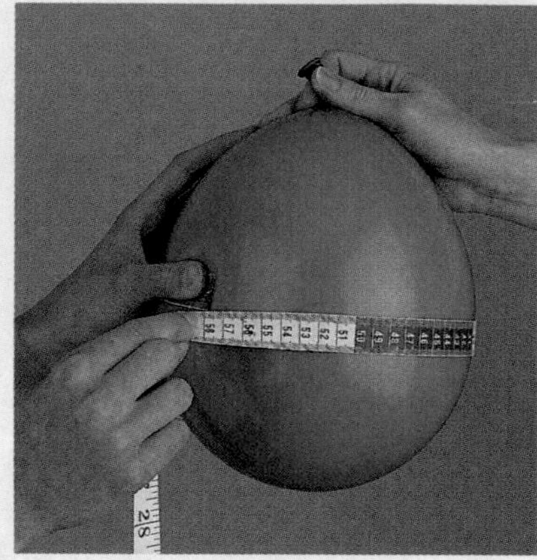

GUIDE FOR READING

- **What are the functions of the respiratory system?**
- **What structures does air pass through as it travels to the lungs?**
- **How do oxygen, carbon dioxide, and water move in the lungs?**

Reading Tip **Before you read, preview *Exploring the Respiratory System* on page 133. Write down any unfamiliar terms.**

Jerry, the main character in Doris Lessing's story "Through the Tunnel," is on vacation at the seaside. Day after day, he watches some older boys dive into deep water on one side of a huge rock. The boys mysteriously reappear on the other side. Jerry figures out that there must be an underwater tunnel in the rock. He finds the tunnel beneath the water and decides to swim through it. Once inside, though, he is terrified. The walls are slimy, and rocks scrape his body. He can barely see where he is going. But worst of all, Jerry has to hold his breath for far longer than ever before. The author describes Jerry this way: "His head was swelling, his lungs were cracking."

Jerry's behavior could have killed him. No one can go for very long without breathing. Your body cells need oxygen, and they get that oxygen from the air you breathe. **The respiratory system moves oxygen from the outside environment into the body. It also removes carbon dioxide and water from the body.**

Why the Body Needs Oxygen

The energy-releasing chemical reactions that take place inside your cells require oxygen. As a result of these reactions, your cells are able to perform all the tasks that keep you alive. Like a fire, which cannot burn without oxygen, your cells cannot "burn" enough substances to keep you alive without oxygen.

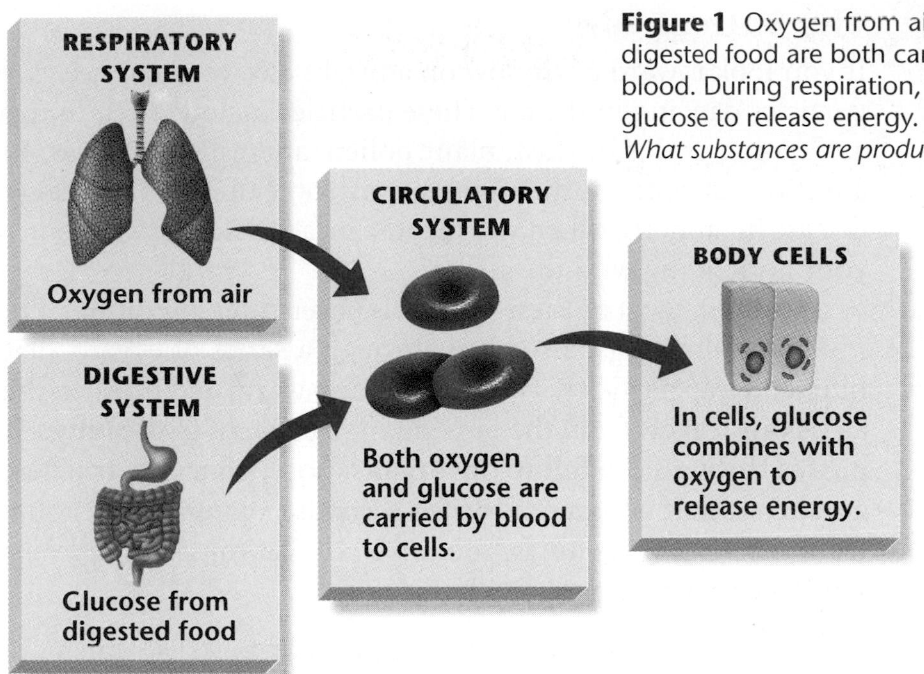

Figure 1 Oxygen from air and glucose from digested food are both carried to cells by the blood. During respiration, oxygen reacts with glucose to release energy. ***Applying Concepts*** *What substances are produced during respiration?*

Respiration is the process in which oxygen and glucose undergo a complex series of chemical reactions inside cells. These chemical reactions release the energy that fuels growth and other cell processes. Besides releasing energy, respiration produces carbon dioxide and water. Your body eliminates the carbon dioxide and some of the water through your lungs. To a scientist, *breathing* and *respiration* mean different things. Respiration, which is also called cellular respiration, refers to the chemical reactions inside cells. Breathing refers to the movement of air into and out of the lungs.

Your respiratory system gets oxygen into your lungs. However, respiration could not take place without your circulatory and digestive systems. The digestive system absorbs glucose from food. The circulatory system carries both oxygen from your lungs and glucose from food to your cells.

✓ *Checkpoint* *Why does your body need oxygen?*

The Air You Breathe

INTEGRATING EARTH SCIENCE The oxygen your body needs comes from the atmosphere, which is the blanket of gases that surrounds Earth. The atmosphere is made up of a mixture of gases. Only about 21 percent of air is oxygen. Nitrogen makes up about 78 percent, and the remaining 1 percent includes carbon dioxide, helium, and other gases. Your body doesn't use most of the air that you breathe into your lungs. When you exhale, most of the air goes back into the atmosphere.

The Path of Air

If you look toward a window on a bright day, you may see tiny particles dancing in the air. These particles include such things as floating grains of dust, plant pollen, and ash from fires. In addition, air contains microorganisms, some of which can cause disease in humans. When you breathe in, all these materials enter your body along with the air.

However, most of these materials never enter your lungs. On its way to the lungs, air passes through a series of organs that filter and trap particles. These organs also warm and moisten the air. **As air travels from the outside environment to the lungs, it passes through the following organs: nose, pharynx, trachea, and bronchi.** It takes air only a few seconds to complete the route from the nose to the lungs. You can trace that route in *Exploring the Respiratory System.*

The Nose Your nose has two openings, or nostrils, which are separated by a thin wall. Air enters the body through the nostrils and then moves into the nose cavities, or nasal cavities. The lining of the nasal cavities contains many blood vessels. Warm blood flowing through these vessels heats the air. Some of the cells lining the cavities produce mucus. This sticky material moistens the air and keeps the delicate tissue from drying out. Mucus also traps particles, such as dust and bacteria. The cells that line the nasal cavities have **cilia** (SIL ee uh), tiny hairlike extensions that can move together like whips. The whiplike motion of these cilia sweeps the mucus into the throat, where you swallow it. In the stomach, the mucus, along with the particles and bacteria trapped in it, is destroyed by stomach acid.

Some particles and bacteria never make it to your stomach. They irritate the lining of your nose or throat, and you sneeze. The powerful force of a sneeze shoots the particles and bacteria out of your nose and into the air.

Figure 2 The cilia that line the nasal passages help remove trapped particles. The brown particles in the photograph are dust; the orange particles are pollen grains. When a person sneezes, many of the trapped particles are shot out into the air.

The Pharynx After flowing through the nasal cavities, air enters the **pharynx** (FAR ingks), or throat. The pharynx is the only part of the respiratory system that is shared with another system—the digestive system. If you look at *Exploring the Respiratory System,* you can see that both the nose and the mouth connect to the pharynx.

☑ ***Checkpoint*** *To what two body systems does the pharynx belong?*

The Trachea From the pharynx, air moves into the **trachea** (TRAY kee uh), or windpipe. You can feel your trachea if you gently run your fingers down the center of your neck. The trachea feels like a tube with a series of ridges. The firm ridges are rings of cartilage that strengthen the trachea and keep it open.

The trachea, like the nose, is lined with cilia and mucus. The cilia in the trachea sweep upward, moving mucus toward the pharynx, where it is swallowed. The trachea's cilia and mucus

EXPLORING *the Respiratory System*

On its path from outside the body into the lungs, air passes through several structures that clean, warm, and moisten it. Once in the lungs, the oxygen in the air can enter your bloodstream.

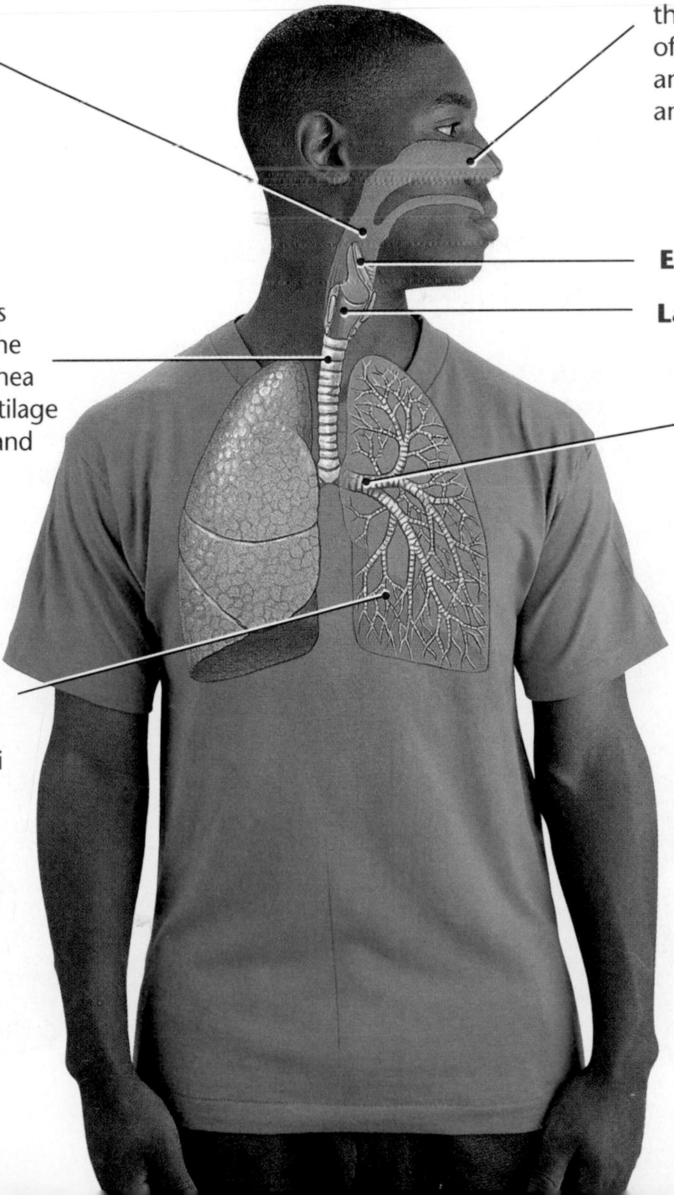

Pharynx Air moves from the nose downward into the throat, or pharynx. Part of the pharynx is also a passageway for food.

Nose Air enters the body through two nostrils. The lining of the nose is coated with cilia and mucus, which trap particles and warm and moisten the air.

Epiglottis

Larynx

Trachea The trachea leads from the pharynx toward the lungs. The walls of the trachea are made up of rings of cartilage which protect the trachea and keep it from collapsing.

Bronchi Air moves from the trachea into the right and left bronchi. One bronchus leads to each lung. Part of each bronchus is outside the lung and part is inside.

Lungs After it reaches the lungs, air moves through smaller and smaller bronchi until it reaches the alveoli. In the alveoli, oxygen passes into the blood and carbon dioxide passes out of the blood.

continue the cleaning and moistening of air that began in the nose. If particles irritate the lining of the trachea, you cough. A cough, like a sneeze, sends harmful materials flying out of your body and into the air.

Normally, only air—not food—enters the trachea. If food does enter the trachea, the food can block the opening and prevent air from getting to the lungs. When that happens, a person chokes. Fortunately, food rarely gets into the trachea. Remember from Chapter 3 that the epiglottis is a small flap of tissue that folds over the trachea. The epiglottis seals the trachea off while you swallow.

The Bronchi and Lungs Air moves from the trachea to the **bronchi** (BRAHNG ky)(singular *bronchus*), the passages that direct air into the lungs. The **lungs** are the main organs of the respiratory system. The left bronchus leads into the left lung, and the right bronchus leads into the right lung. Inside the lungs, each bronchus divides into smaller and smaller tubes in a pattern that resembles the branches of a tree.

At the end of the smallest tubes are small structures that look like bunches of grapes. The "grapes" are **alveoli** (al VEE uh ly) (singular *alveolus*), tiny sacs of lung tissue specialized for the movement of gases between air and blood. Notice in Figure 3 that each alveolus is surrounded by a network of capillaries. It is here that the blood picks up its cargo of oxygen from the air.

☑ ***Checkpoint*** *Describe the structure of the bronchi.*

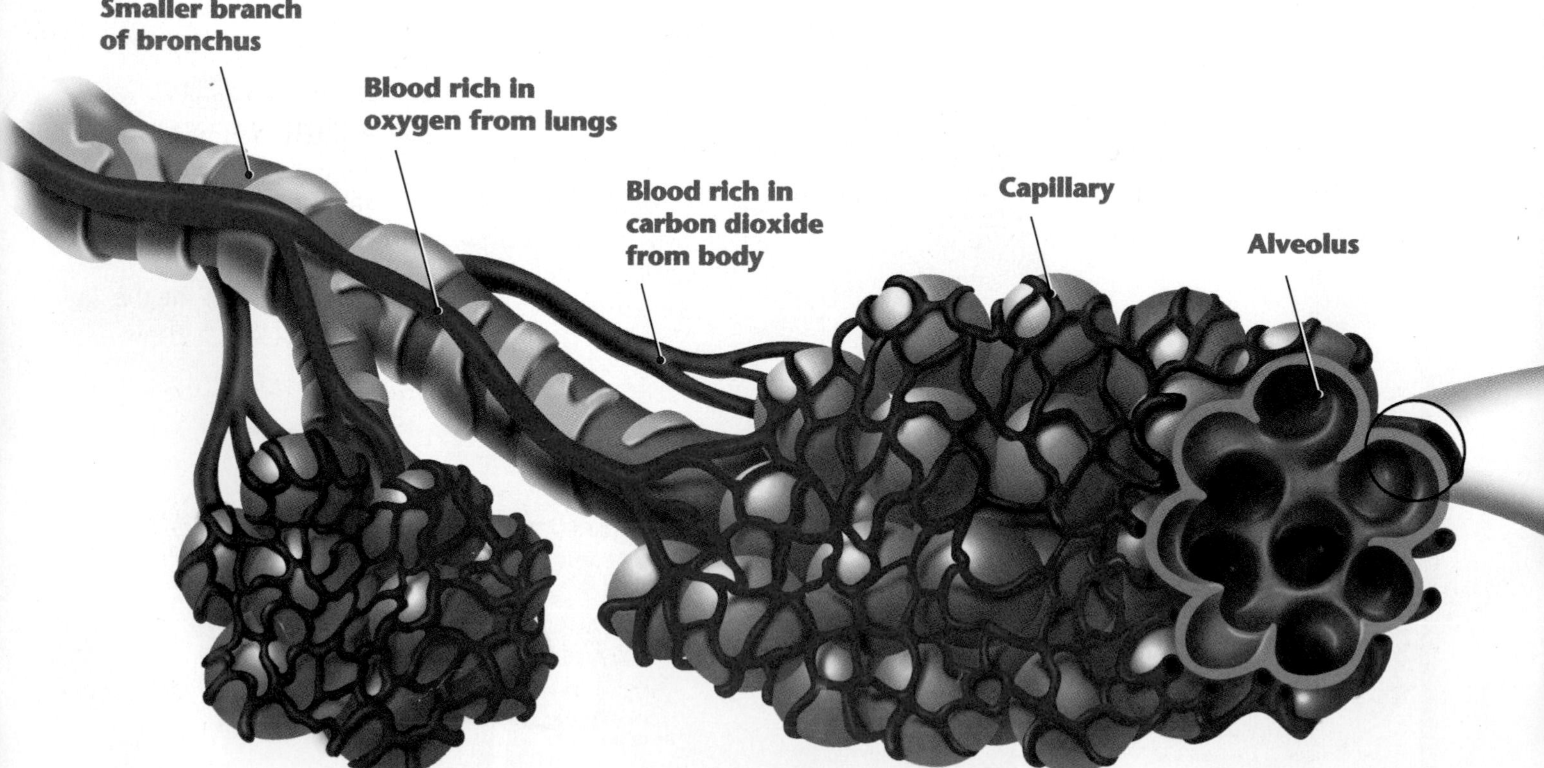

Gas Exchange

Because the walls of both the alveoli and the capillaries are very thin, materials can pass through them easily. **After air enters an alveolus, oxygen passes through the wall of the alveolus and then through the capillary wall into the blood. Carbon dioxide and water pass from the blood into the alveoli.** This whole process is known as gas exchange.

How Gas Exchange Occurs Imagine that you are a drop of blood beginning your journey through a capillary that wraps around an alveolus. When you begin that journey, you are carrying a lot of carbon dioxide and little oxygen. As you move through the capillary, oxygen gradually attaches to the hemoglobin in your red blood cells. At the same time, you are getting rid of carbon dioxide. At the end of your journey around the alveolus, you are rich in oxygen and poor in carbon dioxide.

A Large Surface Area Your lungs can absorb a large amount of oxygen because of the large surface area of the alveoli. An adult's lungs contain about 300 million alveoli. If you removed the alveoli, opened them, and spread them out on a flat surface, you would have a surface area of about 70 square meters. That's about the area of three lanes in a bowling alley!

INTEGRATING MATHEMATICS

The huge surface area of the alveoli enables the lungs to absorb a large amount of oxygen. The lungs can therefore supply the oxygen that people need—even when they are performing strenuous activities. When you play a musical instrument or a fast-paced game of basketball, you have your alveoli to thank.

Your lungs are not the only organs that provide a large surface area in a relatively small space. Remember that the small intestine contains numerous, tiny villi that increase the surface available to absorb food molecules.

Do You Exhale Carbon Dioxide?

ACTIVITY

Learn whether carbon dioxide is present in exhaled air.

1. Put on your goggles. Label two test tubes A and B.
2. Fill each test tube with 10 mL of water and a few drops of bromthymol blue solution. Bromthymol blue solution turns green or yellow in the presence of carbon dioxide.
3. Using a straw, blow air into the liquid in test tube A for a few seconds. Blow gently—if you blow hard, the liquid will bubble out of the test tube. **CAUTION:** *Use the straw to exhale only. Do not suck the solution back through the straw.*
4. Compare the solutions in the test tubes. Wash your hands when you have finished.

Predicting Suppose you had exercised immediately before you blew into the straw. Predict how this would have affected the results.

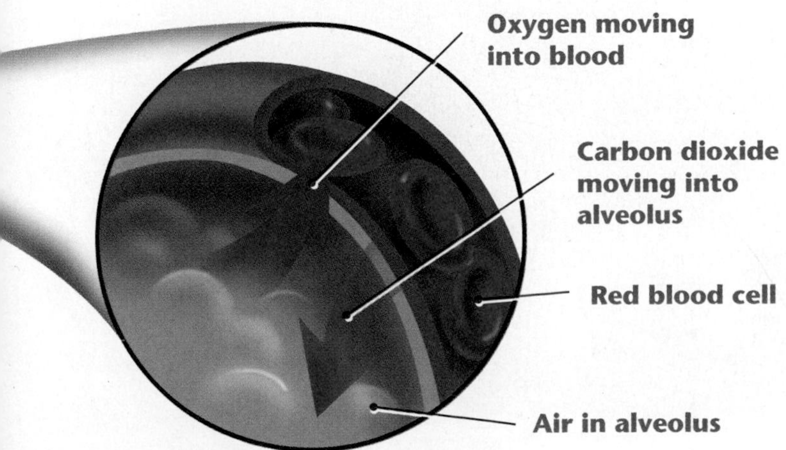

Figure 3 Alveoli are hollow air sacs surrounded by capillaries. As blood flows through the capillaries, oxygen moves from the alveoli into the blood. At the same time, carbon dioxide moves from the blood into the alveoli. ***Interpreting Diagrams*** *How is the structure of the alveoli important for gas exchange?*

Social Studies CONNECTION

Have you ever seen movies or read about climbers scaling mountains in the Andes or Himalayas? Some of the peaks in the Andes rise to almost 7,000 meters. Mount Everest in the Himalayas, which rises to 8,848 meters, is the world's tallest mountain. People who climb these mountains usually experience mountain sickness—dizziness, headaches, and shortness of breath. Their symptoms are due to a shortage of oxygen in their blood. The amount of oxygen in air decreases the farther one goes above sea level.

In contrast to visitors, people who live high in these mountain ranges do not experience these symptoms. Their respiratory and circulatory systems have adjusted to compensate for the low levels of oxygen. For example, they inhale a greater volume of air with each breath than do people at lower levels. In addition, their blood contains a greater number of red blood cells for transporting oxygen.

In Your Journal

Locate the Andes Mountains and Himalaya Mountains on a globe or map. Then imagine that you are climbing a mountain in one of these ranges. Write a diary entry describing your physical reactions and what you might see.

How You Breathe

In an average day, you may breathe more than 20,000 times. The rate at which you breathe depends on your body's need for oxygen. When you exercise, your body needs a lot of oxygen to supply energy. The more oxygen you need, the faster you breathe.

Muscles for Breathing Pay attention to your breathing as you read this paragraph. Can you feel the air flowing in and out through your nose? Do you notice the gentle lift and fall of your chest?

Breathing, like other body movements, is controlled by muscles. Figure 5 shows the structure of the chest, including the muscles that enable you to breathe. Notice that the lungs are surrounded by the ribs, which have muscles attached to them. At the base of the lungs is the **diaphragm** (DY uh fram), a large, dome-shaped muscle that plays an important role in breathing.

The Process of Breathing Here is what happens when you

INTEGRATING PHYSICS

inhale, or breathe in. The rib muscles contract, lifting the chest wall upward and outward. At the same time, the diaphragm contracts and moves downward. The combined action of these muscles makes the chest cavity larger, providing extra space for the lungs to expand.

When the chest cavity has expanded, there is more room for air. For a brief moment, however, there is no extra air to fill the space. Because the same amount of air now occupies a larger

Figure 4 These people live high in the Andes Mountains in Ecuador. Despite the low oxygen levels, these people experience no symptoms of mountain sickness. Their respiratory systems have adjusted in order to get enough oxygen into their bodies.

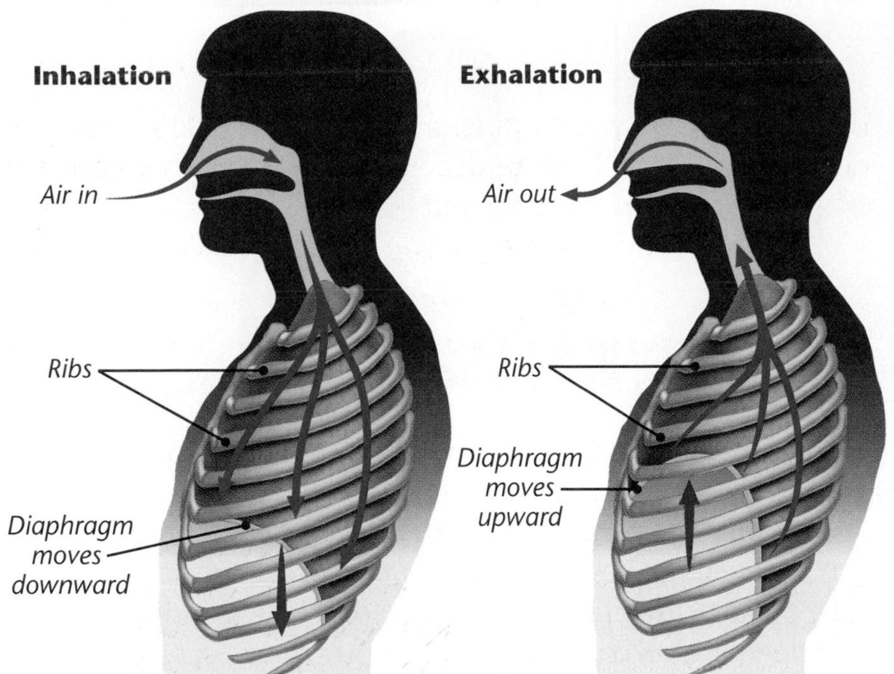

Figure 5 When you inhale, the diaphragm moves downward, allowing more room in the lungs for air. In contrast, when you exhale, the diaphragm moves upward. This upward movement increases the pressure in the lungs and pushes the air out. ***Interpreting Diagrams*** *How does the downward movement of the diaphragm affect the pressure of air inside the chest cavity?*

space, the pressure of the air inside your lungs decreases. This means that the pressure of air inside the chest cavity is lower than the pressure of the atmosphere pushing on the body. Because of this difference in air pressure, air rushes into your chest, in the same way that air is sucked into a vacuum cleaner. You have inhaled.

In contrast, when you exhale, or breathe out, the rib muscles and diaphragm relax, and the chest cavity becomes smaller. This decrease in size squeezes air out of the lungs, the way squeezing a container of ketchup pushes ketchup out of the opening.

☑ ***Checkpoint*** *What muscles cause the chest to expand during breathing?*

How You Speak

The **larynx** (LAR ingks), or voice box, is located in the top part of the trachea, underneath the epiglottis. You can see the larynx if you look back at *Exploring the Respiratory System* on page 133. Place your fingers on your Adam's apple, which sticks out from the front of your neck. You can feel some of the cartilage that makes up the larynx. Two **vocal cords,** which are folds of connective tissue that produce your voice, stretch across the opening of the larynx.

How the Vocal Cords Work If you've ever let air out of a balloon while stretching its neck, you've heard the squeaking sound that the air makes. The neck of the balloon is something like your vocal cords.The vocal

INTEGRATING PHYSICS

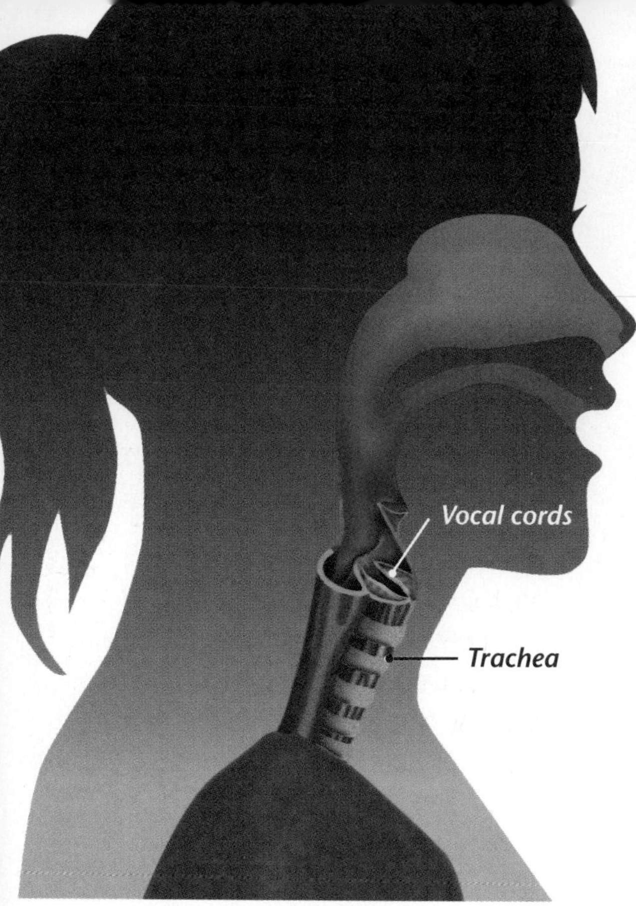

Figure 6 Air moving over this singer's vocal cords causes them to vibrate and produce sound. When her vocal cords contract, or shorten, she sings higher notes. When her vocal cords lengthen, she sings lower notes.

cords have a slitlike opening between them. When you speak, muscles make the vocal cords contract, narrowing the opening. Air from the lungs rushes through this opening. The movement of the vocal cords makes the air particles vibrate, or move rapidly back and forth. This vibration creates a sound—your voice.

High and Low Tones The length of the vocal cords affects whether you produce low or high tones. When the vocal cords contract and shorten, you speak in a higher voice. When they are longer and in a relaxed position, you speak in a lower voice.

The length of vocal cords changes during a person's lifetime. Small children have high-pitched voices because their larynxes are small and their vocal cords are short. The vocal cords of both boys and girls are about the same length. During the teenage years, however, the vocal cords of boys grow longer than those of girls. This is why men have deeper voices than women.

Section 1 Review

1. List the functions of the respiratory system.
2. Describe the path that a molecule of oxygen takes as it moves from the air into the alveoli.
3. Explain what happens to carbon dioxide in the blood that flows through capillaries in the alveoli.
4. Why does air rush into your body when you inhale?
5. **Thinking Critically Relating Cause and Effect** When there is a lot of dust in the air, people often cough and sneeze. Explain why this happens.

Science at Home

Use a shoe box and a set of blocks to show your family how the alveoli increase the surface area of the lungs. The shoe box represents a lung, and each block represents an alveolus. Fill the box with as many blocks as will fit inside. Then have your family imagine how much surface would be covered if all of the blocks were opened up and put together to form a large sheet. How would the surface area of the blocks compare with that of the shoe box?

Making Models

Skills Lab

A Breath of Fresh Air

How does air get into your lungs? In this lab, you will make a model of the lungs to demonstrate how breathing takes place.

Problem

What causes your body to inhale and exhale air?

Materials

small balloon   large balloon
scissors
transparent plastic bottle with narrow neck

Procedure 

1. In your notebook, explain how you think air gets into the lungs during the breathing process.
2. Cut off and discard the bottom of a small plastic bottle. Trim the cut edge so there are no rough spots.
3. Stretch a small balloon, then blow it up a few times to stretch it further. Insert the round end of the balloon through the mouth of the bottle. Then, with a partner holding the bottle, stretch the neck of the balloon and pull it over the mouth of the bottle.
4. Stretch a large balloon, then blow it up a few times to stretch it further. Cut off the balloon's neck, and discard it.
5. Have a partner hold the bottle while you stretch the remaining part of the balloon over the bottom opening of the bottle, as shown in the photo.
6. Use one hand to hold the bottle firmly. With the knuckles of your other hand, push upward on the large balloon, causing it to form a dome. Remove your knuckles from the balloon, letting the balloon flatten. Repeat this procedure a few times. Observe what happens to the small balloon. Record your observations in your notebook.

Analyze and Conclude

1. Make a diagram of the completed model in your notebook. Add labels to show which parts of your model represent the chest cavity, diaphragm, lungs, and trachea.
2. In this model, what is the position of the diaphragm just after you have exhaled? What do the lungs look like just after you have exhaled?
3. In this model, how does the diaphragm move? How do these movements of the diaphragm affect the lungs?
4. **Think About It** How does this model show that pressure changes are responsible for breathing?

More to Explore

How could you improve on this model to more closely show what happens in the chest cavity during the process of breathing? Obtain your teacher's permission before making a new model.

SECTION 2 Smoking and Your Health

DISCOVER

What Are the Dangers of Smoking?

Pair up with a partner. Read each question below and decide on a reasonable answer based on your current knowledge.

1. In the United States, about how many people die each year from smoking-related illnesses?
2. What percentage of lung cancer deaths are related to smoking?
3. On the average, how much longer do nonsmokers live than smokers?
4. What percentage of smokers say they want to quit smoking?
5. What percentage of smokers actually succeed in quitting?

Think It Over

Inferring Why do you think people start smoking when they know that smoking can cause serious health problems?

GUIDE FOR READING

- **What harmful chemicals are contained in tobacco smoke?**
- **How does tobacco smoke harm the respiratory and circulatory systems?**

Reading Tip **Before you read, make a list of smoking-related health problems that you already know about. Add to your list as you read.**

Whoosh! Millions of tiny but dangerous aliens are invading the respiratory system. The aliens are pulled into the nose with an inhaled breath. The cilia in the nasal cavities trap some aliens, and others get stuck in mucus. But many aliens get past these defenses. After tumbling in air currents, thousands of the invaders enter the lungs. The aliens implant themselves in the alveoli!

The "aliens" are not tiny creatures from space. They are the substances found in cigarette smoke. In this section you will learn how tobacco smoke damages the respiratory system.

Chemicals in Tobacco Smoke

With each puff, a smoker inhales over 4,000 different chemicals. **Some of the most deadly chemicals in tobacco smoke are tar, carbon monoxide, and nicotine.**

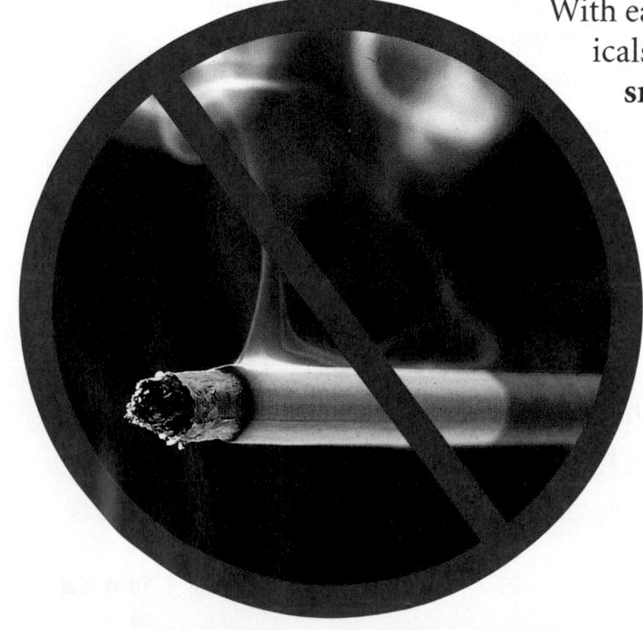

Tar The dark, sticky substance that forms when tobacco burns is called **tar.** When someone inhales tobacco smoke, some tar settles on cilia that line the trachea and other respiratory organs. Tar makes cilia clump together so they can't function to prevent harmful materials from getting into the lungs. Tar also contains chemicals that have been shown to cause cancer.

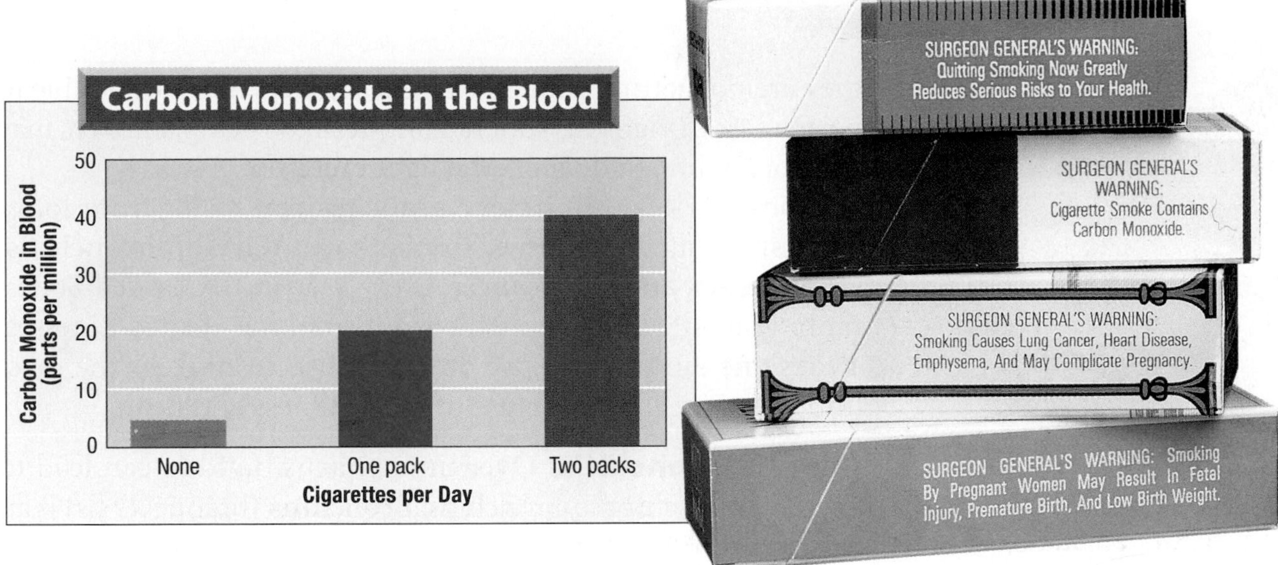

Figure 7 The more cigarettes a person smokes, the more carbon monoxide he or she inhales. ***Relating Cause and Effect*** *How does carbon monoxide deprive the body of oxygen?*

Carbon Monoxide When substances—including tobacco—are burned, a colorless, odorless gas called **carbon monoxide** is produced. Carbon monoxide is dangerous to inhale because its molecules bind to hemoglobin in red blood cells. When carbon monoxide binds to hemoglobin, it takes the place of some of the oxygen that the red blood cells normally carry. The carbon monoxide molecules are something like cars that have taken parking spaces reserved for other cars.

When carbon monoxide binds to hemoglobin, red blood cells carry less than their normal load of oxygen throughout the body. To make up for the decrease in oxygen, the breathing rate increases and the heart beats faster. Smokers' blood may contain too little oxygen to meet their bodies' needs.

Nicotine Another dangerous chemical found in tobacco smoke is **nicotine.** Nicotine is a drug that speeds up the activities of the nervous system, heart, and other organs. It makes the heart beat faster and blood pressure rise. Nicotine produces an **addiction,** or physical dependence. Smokers feel an intense need, or craving, for a cigarette if they go without one. Addiction to nicotine is one reason why smokers have difficulty quitting.

☑ ***Checkpoint*** *How does the tar in cigarette smoke affect the body?*

Respiratory System Problems

Tobacco smoke harms the respiratory system in several ways. For example, because their cilia can't sweep away mucus, many smokers have a frequent cough. The mucus buildup also limits the space for air flow, and this decreases oxygen intake. Because they are not getting enough oxygen, smokers may not be able to participate in vigorous sports. Long-term or heavy smokers may be short of breath during even light exercise.

Some serious respiratory problems can result from long-term smoking. **Over time, smokers can develop bronchitis, emphysema, and lung cancer.** Every year in the United States, more than 400,000 people die from smoking-related illnesses. That's one out of every five deaths. Tobacco smoke is the most important preventable cause of major illness and death.

Chronic Bronchitis Over time, mucus buildup can lead to long-term, or chronic, bronchitis. **Bronchitis** (brahng KY tis) is an irritation of the breathing passages in which the small passages become narrower than normal and may be clogged with mucus. These people have a hard time breathing. If bronchitis lasts a long time, it can cause permanent damage to the breathing passages. Chronic bronchitis is often accompanied by infection with disease-causing microorganisms. Chronic bronchitis is five to ten times more common in heavy smokers than in nonsmokers.

Figure 8 These people stay healthy by exercising and by choosing not to smoke.

Emphysema The chemicals in tobacco smoke damage lung tissue as well as breathing passages. **Emphysema** (em fuh SEE muh) is a serious disease that destroys lung tissue and causes difficulty in breathing. People with emphysema do not get enough oxygen and cannot adequately eliminate carbon dioxide. Therefore, they are always short of breath. Some people with emphysema even have trouble blowing out a match. Unfortunately, the damage caused by emphysema is permanent, even if a person stops smoking.

Lung Cancer About 140,000 Americans die each year from lung cancer caused by smoking. Cigarette smoke contains over 40 different chemicals that cause cancer, including chemicals in tar. Cancerous growths, or tumors, take away space in the lungs that should be used for gas exchange. Unfortunately, lung cancer is difficult to detect early, when treatment would be most effective.

☑ ***Checkpoint*** *How does emphysema affect a person's lungs?*

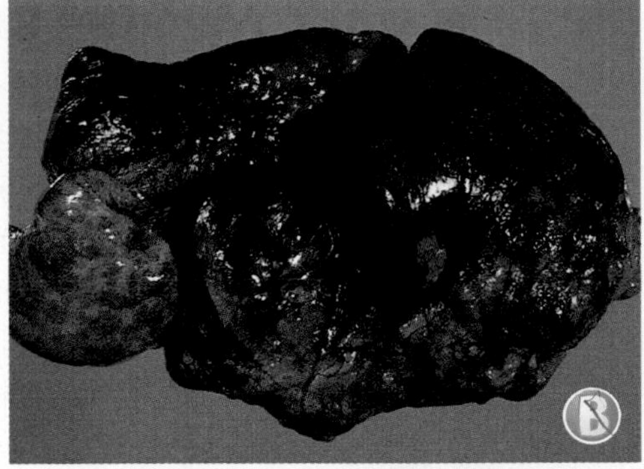

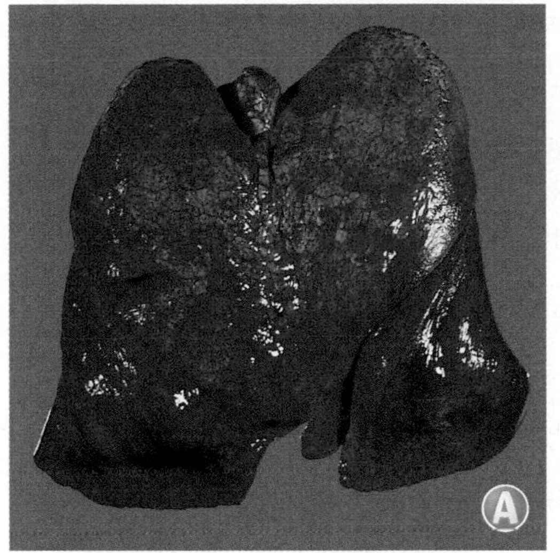

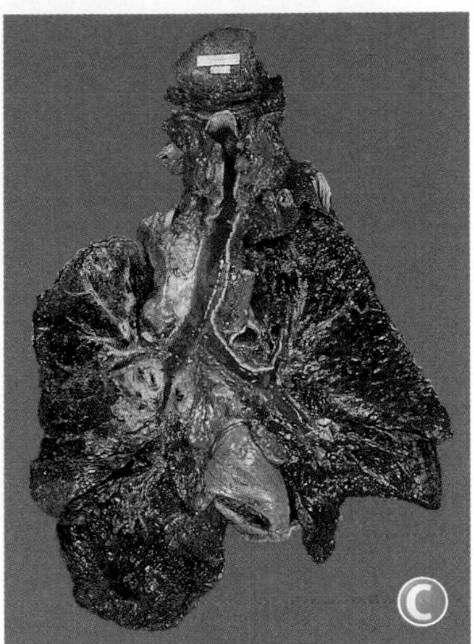

Figure 9 Over time, smoking damages the lungs and leads to serious health problems. Compare the lungs of a nonsmoker **(A)** to those of a person with emphysema **(B)** and a person with lung cancer **(C)**.

Circulatory System Problems

The chemicals in tobacco smoke that damage the lungs also harm the circulatory system. Some of the chemicals get into the blood and are absorbed by the blood vessels. The chemicals then irritate the walls of the blood vessels. This irritation contributes to the buildup of the fatty material that causes atherosclerosis. Atherosclerosis can lead to heart attacks. **Compared to nonsmokers, smokers are more than twice as likely to have heart attacks.**

Conditions that harm the lungs, such as bronchitis and emphysema, also strain the circulatory system. The respiratory and circulatory systems work together to get oxygen to the cells and to remove carbon dioxide from the body. If either system is damaged, the other one must work harder.

Passive Smoking

Smokers are not the only people to suffer from the effects of tobacco smoke. In **passive smoking,** people involuntarily inhale the smoke from other people's cigarettes, cigars, or pipes. Since this smoke contains the same harmful chemicals that smokers inhale, it can cause health problems. Each year, passive smoking causes about 300,000 young children in the United States to develop respiratory problems such as bronchitis. In addition, long-term exposure to cigarette smoke increases people's risks of heart disease and cancer.

Calculating

ACTIVITY

Heavy smokers may smoke two packs of cigarettes every day. Find out what one pack of cigarettes costs. Then use that price to calculate how much a person would spend on cigarettes if he or she smoked two packs a day for 30 years.

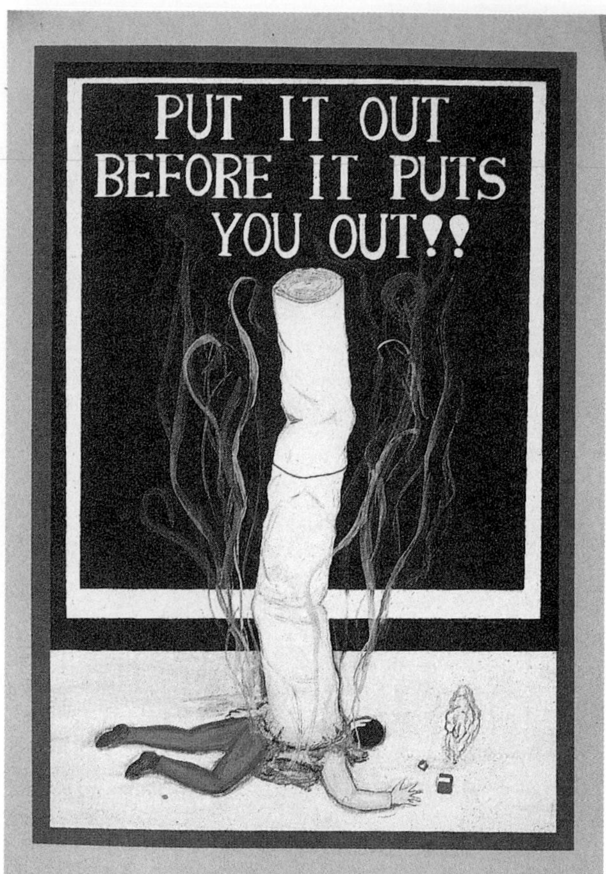

Figure 10 This antismoking advertisement was created by a teenager to encourage smokers to quit.

Choosing Not to Smoke

Today about 50 million Americans are smokers. Of those people, more than 90 percent began smoking when they were teenagers. Studies show that if people do not start smoking when they are teenagers, they probably will not start smoking later in life.

You may be tempted to try smoking. Friends may pressure you, or advertisements may appeal to you. Tobacco advertisements show smokers as young, attractive, popular people. The ads try to make you think that you will be like these people if you use tobacco products.

It is important to remember that it's very hard to quit smoking once you start. Many teenage smokers think that they will quit when they are older—but because nicotine is addictive, they have trouble doing so. And smoking hurts people right away, not just later in life. The lungs of teenagers who smoke develop more slowly than those of nonsmokers and may never reach the same peak level of functioning. In addition, teenage smokers may develop coughs and bronchitis. If someone asks you to try a cigarette, think of your health and politely refuse.

Section 2 Review

1. Name three harmful substances in tobacco smoke. Describe the effects of each substance.
2. Identify three respiratory problems caused by smoking.
3. Describe the effect of smoking on the circulatory system.
4. Identify two factors that may pressure teenagers to try smoking.
5. **Thinking Critically Relating Cause and Effect** Scientists estimate that about 3,000 nonsmoking Americans die every year from smoking-related lung cancer. Explain why.

Check Your Progress

CHAPTER PROJECT 5

By now you should have sketched what your ads might look like and written what they might say. In planning your ads, be sure to consider all the effects of smoking, not just those related to health—for example, the expense of smoking. Plan to use ideas and images that are appropriate for each age group. (*Hint:* Look through a variety of magazines to find ads aimed at different age groups. Which techniques seem to work best? How can you use those techniques in your ads?)

SECTION 3

The Excretory System

DISCOVER ACTIVITY

How Does Filtering a Liquid Change What Is in It?

1. Your teacher will give you 50 milliliters of a liquid in a small container. Pour a small amount of sand into the liquid.
2. Use a glucose-test strip to determine whether glucose is present in the liquid.
3. Put filter paper in a funnel. Then put the funnel into the mouth of a second container. Slowly pour the liquid through the funnel into the second container.

4. Look for any solid material on the filter paper. Remove the funnel and carefully examine the liquid that passed through the filter.
5. Test the liquid again to see whether it contains glucose.

Think It Over

Observing Which substances passed through the filter, and which did not? How might a filtering device be useful in the body?

GUIDE FOR READING

- What is the function of the excretory system?
- How is urine produced in the kidneys' nephrons?
- In addition to the kidneys, what other organs play a role in excretion?

Reading Tip As you read, write a brief summary of the information under each heading.

The human body faces a challenge that is a bit like trying to keep a home clean. You learned in Chapter 3 that the body takes in foods through the digestive system and breaks them down into nutrients. As cells use those nutrients in respiration and other processes, wastes are created. **The excretory system is the system in the body that collects wastes produced by cells and removes the wastes from the body.** The removal process is known as **excretion.**

If wastes were not taken away, they would pile up and make you sick. Excretion helps maintain homeostasis by keeping the body's internal environment stable and free of harmful materials.

The Kidneys

As you already know, some wastes that your body must eliminate are carbon dioxide and excess water. Another waste product is urea. **Urea** (yoo REE uh) is a chemical that comes from the breakdown of proteins. Your two **kidneys,** which are the major organs of the excretory system, eliminate urea, excess water, and some other waste materials. These wastes are eliminated in **urine,** a watery fluid produced by your kidneys.

The kidneys act something like filters. As blood flows through the kidneys, they remove wastes from the blood. After the process is complete, urine flows from the kidneys through two narrow tubes called **ureters** (yoo REE turz). The ureters carry the urine to the **urinary bladder,** a sacklike muscular organ that stores urine. When the bladder is full enough that its walls are stretched, you feel a need to urinate. Urine flows from the body through a small tube called the **urethra** (yoo REE thruh), which you can see in *Exploring a Kidney.*

☑ ***Checkpoint*** *What is the role of the ureters?*

The Filtering Process

The kidneys are champion filters. Every drop of blood in your body passes through your kidneys and is filtered more than 300 times a day. Contrast this to a typical swimming-pool filter, which only cleans the pool water about 5 times a day.

Each of your kidneys contains about a million tiny filtering factories called **nephrons.** The nephrons are the tiny structures that remove wastes from blood and produce urine. **Urine formation takes place in a number of stages. First, both wastes and needed materials, such as glucose, are removed from the blood. Then, much of the needed material is returned to the blood.**

Filtering Out Wastes After entering the kidneys, blood flows through smaller and smaller arteries. Eventually it reaches a cluster of capillaries in a nephron. These capillaries are surrounded

EXPLORING *a Kidney*

Each kidney contains about a million tiny filtering units called nephrons. Urine is produced in the nephrons.

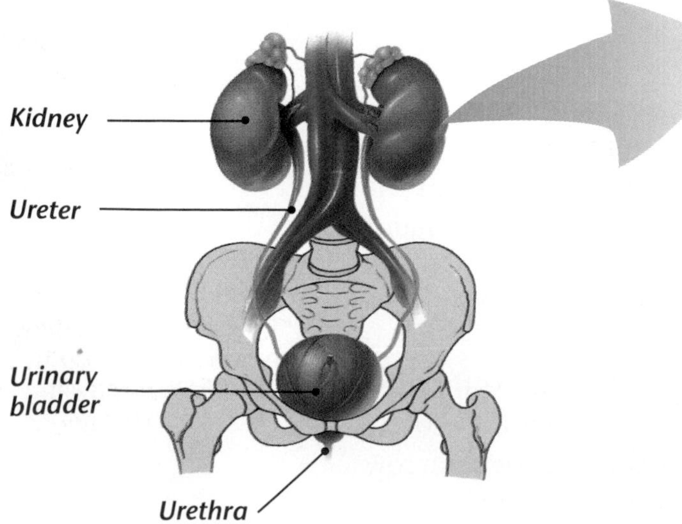

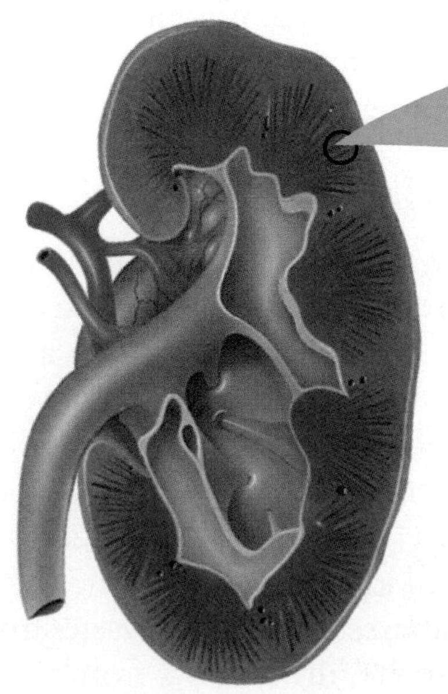

by a thin-walled, hollow capsule that is connected to a long tube. Find the capillary cluster, the capsule, and the tube in *Exploring a Kidney*. In the capillary cluster, urea, glucose, other chemicals, and some water move out of the blood and into the capsule. In contrast, blood cells and most protein molecules do not move into the capsule. Instead, they remain in the capillaries.

Formation of Urine Urine forms from the filtered material that passes into the capsule. This filtered material flows through the long, twisting tube. Some of the substances that collect in the capsule are needed by the body. As the liquid moves through the tube, many of these substances are reabsorbed, or returned to the blood. Normally all the glucose, most of the water, and small amounts of other materials pass back into the blood in the capillaries that surround the tube. In contrast, urea and other wastes remain in the tube.

The filtering process is something like cleaning your locker by throwing everything in your locker into a wastebasket, and then putting back the things that you want to keep. You can think of the locker as your blood and the wastebasket as the capsule. After the entire filtering and reabsorbing process is complete, the fluid that remains in the tube is urine.

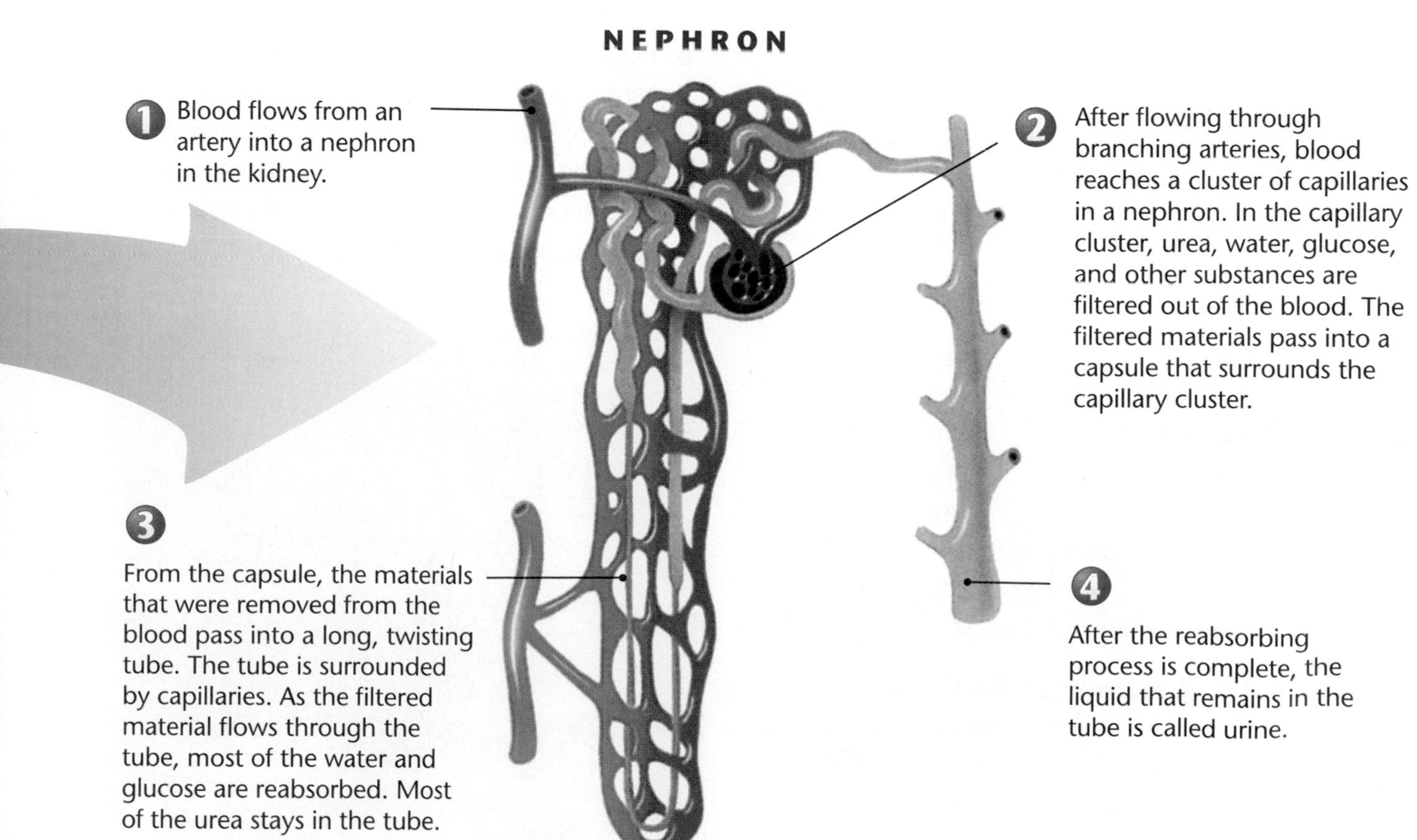

Analyzing Urine for Signs of Disease  *INTEGRATING HEALTH* When people go to a doctor for a medical checkup, they usually have their urine analyzed. A chemical analysis of urine can be useful in detecting some medical problems. Normally, urine contains almost no glucose or protein. If glucose is present in urine, it may indicate that a person has diabetes, a condition in which body cells cannot absorb enough glucose from the blood. Protein in urine can be a sign that the kidneys are not functioning properly.

Real-World Lab

You Solve the Mystery

CLUES ABOUT HEALTH

In this lab, you'll become a medical detective as you carry out urine tests to uncover evidence of disease.

Problem

How can you test urine for the presence of glucose and protein?

Skills Focus

observing, interpreting data, drawing conclusions

Materials

test tubes, 6
plastic droppers, 6
glucose solution
marking pencil
glucose test strips
simulated urine samples, 3
test tube rack
water
protein solution
white paper towels
Biuret solution

Procedure 

Part 1 Testing for Glucose

1. Label six test tubes as follows: "W" for water, "G" for glucose, "P" for protein, and "A," "B," and "C" for three patients' "urine samples."
2. Place the test tubes in a test tube rack. Label six glucose test strips with the same letters.
3. Copy the data table into your notebook.
4. Fill each test tube about 3/4 full with the solution that corresponds to its label.
5. Place the W glucose test strip on a clean, dry section of a paper towel. Then use a clean plastic dropper to place 2 drops of the water from test tube W on the test strip. Record the resulting color of the test strip in your data table. If no color change occurs, write "no reaction."

Water Balance in the Body

The kidneys also help maintain homeostasis by regulating the amount of water in your body. Remember that as urine is being formed, water passes from the tube back into the bloodstream. The exact amount of water that is reabsorbed depends on conditions both outside and within the body. Suppose that it's a hot day. You've been sweating a lot, and you haven't had much to drink. In that situation, almost all of the water in the tube will be reabsorbed, and you will excrete only a small amount of urine. If,

DATA TABLE

Test for	W (water)	G (glucose)	P (protein)	A (Patient A)	B (Patient B)	C (Patient C)
	Test Tube					
Glucose						
Protein						

6. Use the procedure in Step 5 to test each of the other five solutions with the correctly labeled glucose test strip. Record the color of each test strip in the data table.

Part 2 Testing for Protein

7. Obtain a dropper bottle containing Biuret solution. Record the original color of the solution in your notebook.
8. Carefully add 10 drops of Biuret solution to test tube W. **CAUTION:** *Biuret solution can harm skin and damage clothing. Handle it with care.* Gently swirl the test tube to mix the two solutions together. Hold the test tube against a white paper towel to help you detect any color change. Observe the color of the final mixture, and record that color in your data table.
9. Repeat Step 8 for each of the other test tubes.

Analyze and Conclude

1. Which of the three patients' urine samples tested normal? How do you know?
2. Which urine sample(s) indicated that diabetes might be present? How do you know?
3. Which urine sample(s) indicated that kidney disease might be present? How do you know?
4. When a person's health is normal, how are the kidneys involved in keeping glucose and protein out of urine?
5. **Apply** Do you think a doctor should draw conclusions about the presence of a disease based on a single urine sample? Explain.

More to Explore

Propose a way to determine whether a patient with glucose in the urine could reduce the level through changes in diet.

however, the day is cool and you've drunk a lot of water, less water will be reabsorbed. Your body will produce a larger volume of urine.

Every day, you need to take at least 2 liters of water into your body. You can do this either by drinking or by eating foods such as apples that contain a lot of water. This helps your kidneys maintain the proper water balance in your body.

Figure 11 Your skin and lungs also function as excretory organs. Water and some chemical wastes are excreted in perspiration. And when you exhale on a cold morning, you can see the water in your breath. ***Applying Concepts*** *What other waste product does your exhaled breath contain?*

Other Organs of Excretion

Most of the wastes produced by the body are removed through the kidneys, but not all. **The other organs of excretion are the lungs, skin, and liver.** You've already learned how the lungs and skin remove wastes. When you breathe out, carbon dioxide and some water are removed from the body. Sweat glands also function in excretion, because water and some chemical wastes are excreted in perspiration.

Have you ever torn apart a large pizza box so that it could fit in a wastebasket? If so, then you can understand that some wastes need to be broken down before they can be excreted. The liver performs this function. For example, urea, which comes from the breakdown of proteins, is produced by the liver. The liver also converts part of the hemoglobin molecule from old red blood cells into substances such as bile. Recall from Chapter 3 that bile helps break down fats during digestion. Because the liver produces a usable material from old red blood cells, you can think of the liver as a recycling factory.

Section 3 Review

1. What is the function of the excretory system?
2. Describe the two stages of urine formation.
3. What roles do the lungs, skin, and liver play in excretion?
4. How do the kidneys help regulate the amount of water in the body?
5. **Thinking Critically Predicting** On a long bus trip, Laura does not drink any water for several hours. How will the volume of urine she produces that day compare to the volume on a day when she drinks several glasses of water? Explain.

CHAPTER PROJECT 5

Check Your Progress

By now you should be creating your ads. If you are producing ads for a newspaper or magazine, you need to create original drawings or use images from other sources. If you are preparing television or radio ads, you need to arrange for actors and any necessary props. Write and edit the text or script of your ads. Arrange for a place to display your ads or for a time to present the ads.

STUDY GUIDE

CHAPTER 5 REVIEW

Section 1 The Respiratory System

Key Ideas

- The respiratory system moves oxygen into the body and removes carbon dioxide from the body.
- In the process of respiration in cells, glucose is broken down using oxygen to produce energy.
- As air travels from the outside environment to the lungs, it passes through the nose, pharynx, trachea, and bronchi. The air is warmed, moistened, and filtered.
- In the alveoli, oxygen moves from the air into the blood, while carbon dioxide and water pass from the blood into the air. This process is known as gas exchange.
- During inhalation, the diaphragm and rib muscles make the chest cavity expand. The air pressure inside the lungs decreases, and air rushes into the lungs. During exhalation, the chest cavity becomes smaller, pushing air out of the body.
- When air passes over the vocal cords, which are folds of tissue in the larynx, they vibrate to produce sound.

Key Terms

respiration
cilia
pharynx
trachea
bronchi
lungs
alveoli
diaphragm
larynx
vocal cords

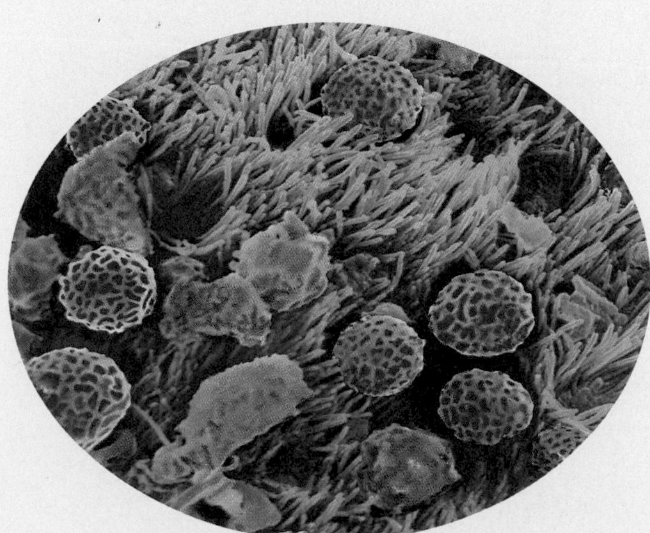

Section 2 Smoking and Your Health

INTEGRATING HEALTH

Key Ideas

- The most harmful substances in tobacco smoke are tar, carbon monoxide, and nicotine.
- When people inhale tobacco smoke, they increase their chances of developing respiratory diseases such as bronchitis, emphysema, and lung cancer.
- Smokers are more likely to have heart attacks than are nonsmokers.

Key Terms

tar
carbon monoxide
nicotine
addiction
bronchitis
emphysema
passive smoking

Section 3 The Excretory System

Key Ideas

- The excretory system removes carbon dioxide, urea, water, and other wastes from the body.
- The kidneys are the major organs of excretion. By filtering the blood, the kidneys produce urine.
- Urine travels from the kidneys through the ureters to the urinary bladder. Urine is eliminated through the urethra.
- In the kidney's nephrons, wastes and other materials are filtered from the blood. Some useful substances, such as glucose and water, are then reabsorbed into the blood.
- The lungs, skin, and liver are also organs of excretion.

Key Terms

excretion
urea
kidney
urine
ureters
urinary bladder
urethra
nephron

ACTIVITY

USING THE INTERNET

www.science-explorer.phschool.com

CHAPTER 5 REVIEW

Reviewing Content

For more review of key concepts, see the Interactive Student Tutorial CD-ROM.

Multiple Choice

1. The process in which glucose and oxygen react in cells to release energy is called
   a. digestion.
   b. respiration.
   c. breathing.
   d. gas exchange.
2. The trachea divides into two tubes called
   a. bronchi.
   b. alveoli.
   c. windpipes.
   d. diaphragms.
3. Your voice is produced by the
   a. pharynx.
   b. larynx.
   c. trachea.
   d. alveoli.
4. The disease in which the respiratory passages become narrower than normal is called
   a. bronchitis.
   b. lung cancer.
   c. diabetes.
   d. emphysema.
5. Normal urine contains both
   a. water and carbon monoxide.
   b. water and large amounts of glucose.
   c. urea and proteins.
   d. urea and water.

True or False

If the statement is true, write true. If it is false, change the underlined word or words to make the statement true.

6. Dust particles trapped in mucus are swept away by tiny, hairlike blood vessels.
7. The clusters of air sacs in the lungs are called alveoli.
8. Tar is a chemical in tobacco smoke that makes the heart beat faster.
9. The ureter is the tube through which urine leaves the body.
10. The lungs are excretory organs.

Checking Concepts

11. Explain the difference between breathing and respiration.
12. Explain how the alveoli provide a large surface area for gas exchange.
13. Describe how the diaphragm and rib muscles control inhaling and exhaling.
14. Why do men have deeper voices than women?
15. Describe what happens when carbon monoxide enters the body. How does this affect the body?
16. Explain two ways in which the kidneys maintain homeostasis.
17. **Writing to Learn** Imagine that you are a molecule of oxygen. Write an adventure story that describes what happens to you between the time you are inhaled through someone's nose and the time you are used in respiration in a body cell.

Thinking Visually

18. **Flowchart** The kidneys eliminate wastes from the body in a series of steps. Copy the flowchart below and complete it by filling in the missing steps. (For more on flowcharts, see the Skills Handbook.)

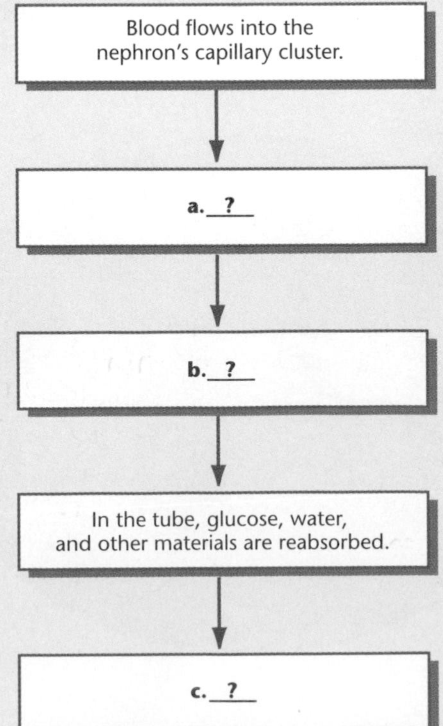

Applying Skills

Use your knowledge of the respiratory system and the information in the data table to answer Questions 19–21.

Gases in Inhaled and Exhaled Air		
Gas	**Inhaled Air**	**Exhaled Air**
Nitrogen	78%	78%
Oxygen	21%	16%
Carbon dioxide	0.03%	4%

19. **Interpreting Data** Which gas makes up a higher percentage of exhaled air than inhaled air? How can you account for this difference?
20. **Drawing Conclusions** Based on the data, which gas is used by the body? How is this gas used?
21. **Inferring** Explain why the percentage of nitrogen is the same in both inhaled air and exhaled air.

Thinking Critically

22. **Inferring** If you exhale onto a mirror, the mirror will become clouded with a thin film of moisture. Explain why this happens.
23. **Applying Concepts** Explain how babies can develop smoking-related respiratory problems.
24. **Predicting** If the walls of the capillary cluster in a nephron were damaged or broken, what substance might you expect to find in urine that is not normally present? Explain.
25. **Making Judgments** Do you think that drugstores, which sell medicines, should also sell cigarettes and other tobacco products? Why or why not?
26. **Comparing and Contrasting** How is respiration similar to the burning of fuel? How is it different?

Performance Assessment

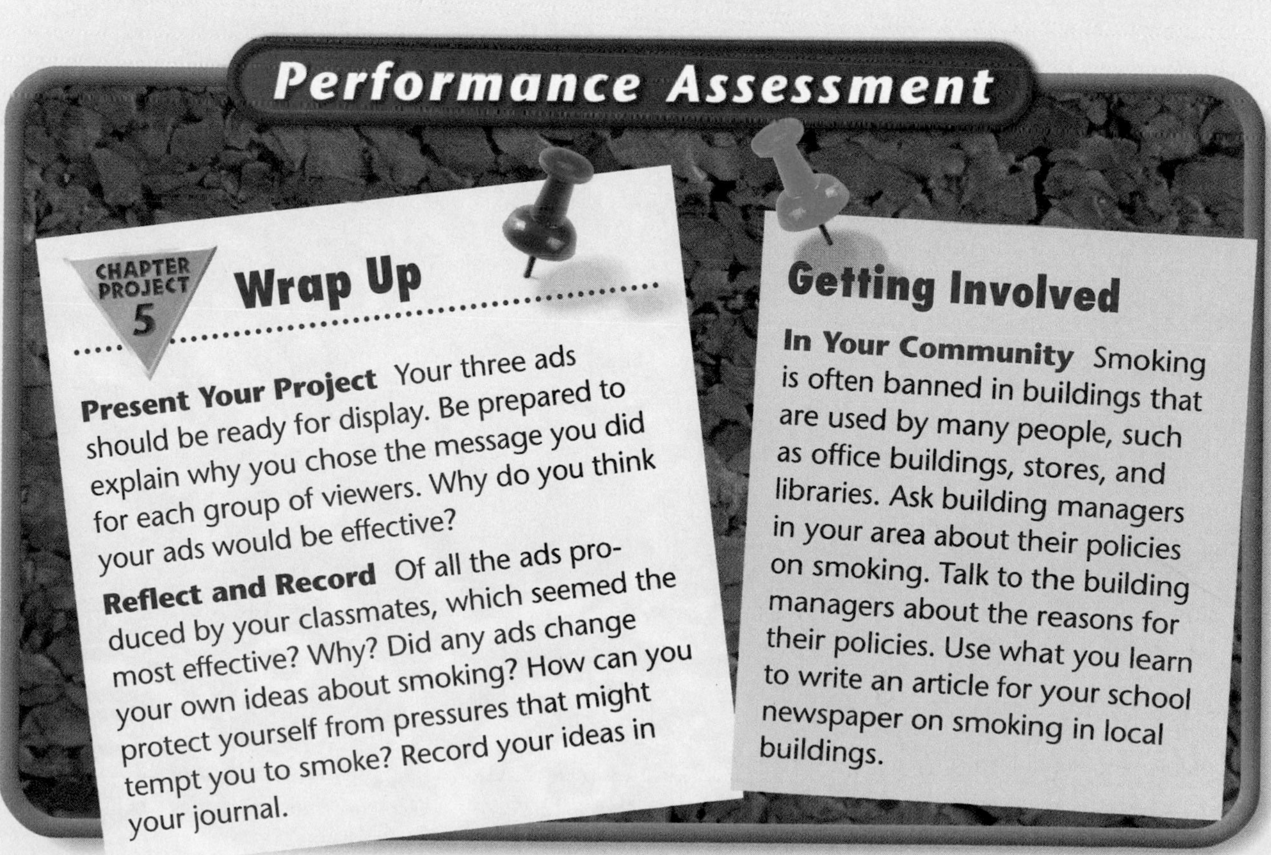

CHAPTER PROJECT 5

Wrap Up

Present Your Project Your three ads should be ready for display. Be prepared to explain why you chose the message you did for each group of viewers. Why do you think your ads would be effective?

Reflect and Record Of all the ads produced by your classmates, which seemed the most effective? Why? Did any ads change your own ideas about smoking? How can you protect yourself from pressures that might tempt you to smoke? Record your ideas in your journal.

Getting Involved

In Your Community Smoking is often banned in buildings that are used by many people, such as office buildings, stores, and libraries. Ask building managers in your area about their policies on smoking. Talk to the building managers about the reasons for their policies. Use what you learn to write an article for your school newspaper on smoking in local buildings.

6 Fighting Disease

A white blood cell (shown in purple) attacks a cancer cell (yellow).

WHAT'S AHEAD

Infectious Disease

Discover How Does a Disease Spread?
Sharpen Your Skills Posing Questions

The Body's Defenses

Discover Which Pieces Fit Together?
Try This Stuck Together
Real-World Lab The Skin as a Barrier

Preventing Infectious Disease

Discover What Substances Can Kill Pathogens?

PROJECT 6

Stop the Invasion!

When you catch a cold, your body is being attacked. The attackers are cold viruses. If they're not stopped, they'll multiply in great numbers and cause infection. Many other diseases are also caused in this way—by viruses or bacteria that invade your body. In this chapter, you'll learn how your body defends itself against such invasions. And you'll put that knowledge to use as you develop a series of informative news reports in this chapter project.

Your Goal To create a series of imaginary news broadcasts from "battlefield sites" where the body is fighting an infectious disease.

To complete the project successfully you must

- choose a specific disease and represent the sequence of events that occur when that disease strikes the body
- describe the stages of the disease as if they were battles between two armies
- present your story creatively in at least three reports using newspaper, radio, or television news-reporting techniques

Get Started With some classmates, list your ideas about delivering a good newspaper, radio, or television news report. Think about what techniques reporters use to make stories interesting or to explain complicated information. Also, recall the times you've had a cold, flu, or other infectious disease. Write down how your body responded, how long you were sick, and any other useful information you can remember.

Check Your Progress You'll be working on this project as you study this chapter. To keep your project on track, look for Check Your Progress boxes at the following points.

Section 1 Review, page 160: Select a specific disease to research. Learn how it affects the body and how the body responds.
Section 2 Review, page 167: Write scripts for your news reports.
Section 5 Review, page 184: Make any necessary revisions, and practice your presentation.

Wrap Up At the end of the chapter (page 187), you will "broadcast" your news reports for the rest of the class.

Infectious Disease

Discover Activity

How Does a Disease Spread?

1. On a sheet of paper, write three headings: *Round 1, Round 2,* and *Round 3.*
2. Everyone in the class should shake hands with two people. Under *Round 1,* record the names of the people whose hand you shook.
3. Now shake hands with two different people. Record the name of each person whose hand you shook under *Round 2.*
4. Once again, shake hands with two additional people. Under *Round 3,* record the names of the people whose hand you shook.

Think It Over

Calculating Suppose you had a disease that was spread by shaking hands. Everyone whose hand you shook has caught the disease. So has anyone who later shook those people's hands. Calculate how many people you "infected."

Guide for Reading

- **What kinds of organisms cause disease?**
- **Where do pathogens come from?**

Reading Tip **As you read, use the headings in the section to make an outline. Write the important concepts under each heading.**

Before the twentieth century, surgery was a very risky business. Even if people lived through an operation, they were not out of danger. After the operation, many patients' wounds became infected, and the patients often died. No one knew what caused these infections.

In the 1860s, a British surgeon named Joseph Lister hypothesized that microorganisms caused the infections. To protect his patients, Lister used carbolic acid, a chemical that kills microorganisms. Before performing an operation, Lister washed his hands and surgical instruments with carbolic acid. After the surgery, he covered the patient's wounds with bandages dipped in carbolic acid.

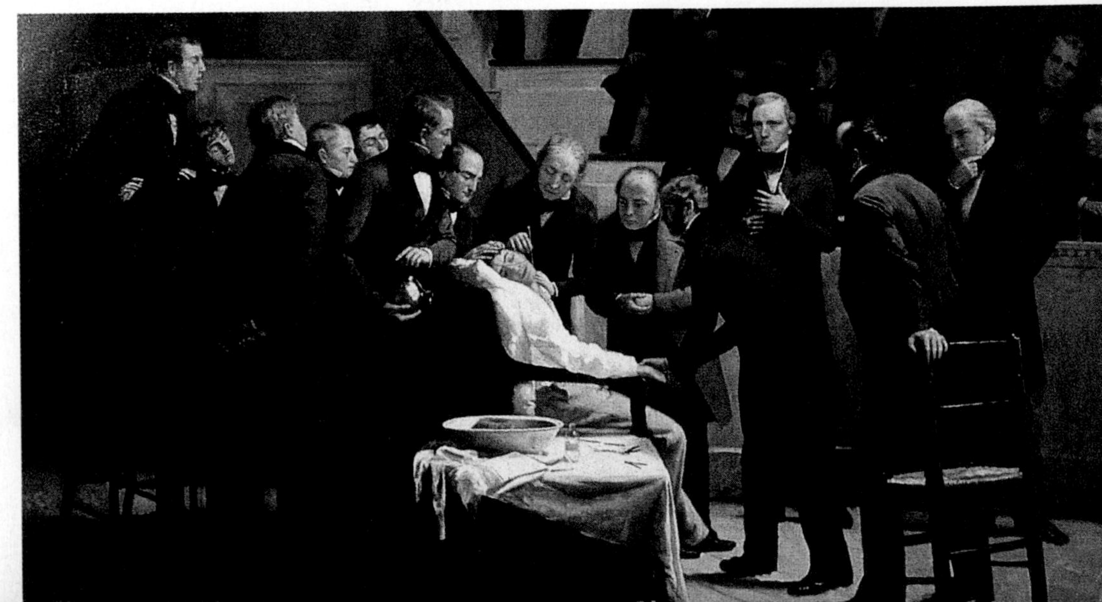

Figure 1 Doctors at Massachusetts General Hospital perform surgery on a patient in 1846. In the 1800s, surgery was performed under conditions that were very different from those used today.

Lister's results were dramatic. Before he used his new method, about 45 percent of his surgical patients died from infection. With Lister's new techniques, only 15 percent died.

Disease and Pathogens

Like the infections that Lister observed after surgery, many illnesses, such as ear infections and food poisoning, are caused by living things that are too small to see. Organisms that cause disease are called **pathogens.** Diseases caused by pathogens are infectious. An **infectious disease** is a disease that can pass from one organism to another.

When you have an infectious disease, pathogens have gotten inside your body and harmed it. Pathogens make you sick by damaging individual cells, even though you may feel pain in a whole organ or throughout your body. For example, when you have strep throat, pathogens have damaged cells in your throat.

☑ *Checkpoint What causes infectious disease?*

Understanding Infectious Disease

Until Lister's time, few people thought that living organisms could cause disease. Before that, people believed that things like evil spirits or swamp air made people sick.

Several scientists in the late 1800s contributed to the understanding of infectious diseases. Joseph Lister was influenced by the work of Louis Pasteur, a French scientist. In the 1860s, Pasteur showed that microorganisms cause certain kinds of diseases. In addition, Pasteur showed that killing the microorganisms could prevent the spread of those diseases. In the 1870s and 1880s, a German physician named Robert Koch demonstrated that each infectious disease is caused by a specific kind of pathogen. In other words, one kind of pathogen causes pneumonia, another kind causes chicken pox, and still another kind causes rabies.

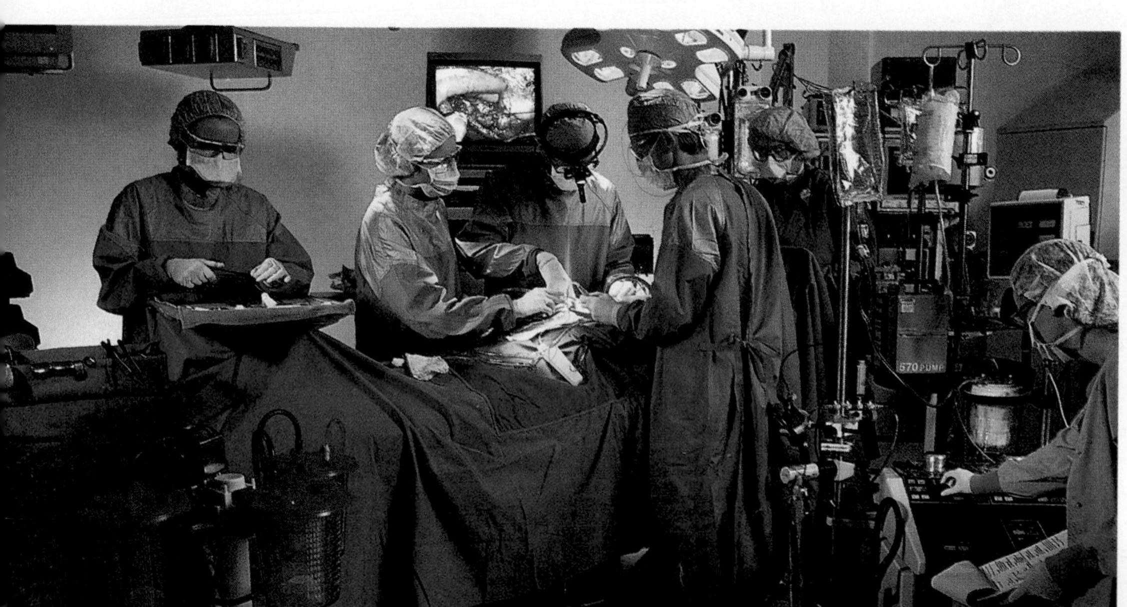

Figure 2 Surgery today is performed in operating rooms that have been cleaned thoroughly to eliminate disease-causing organisms. ***Comparing and Contrasting*** *Contrast Figures 1 and 2. How does surgery today differ from surgery in 1846?*

Kinds of Pathogens

You share Earth with many kinds of organisms. Most are harmless, but some can make you sick. Some diseases are caused by many-celled animals, such as worms. However, most pathogens are too small to be seen without a microscope. **The four major groups of human pathogens are bacteria, viruses, fungi, and protists.** Look at Figure 3 to see examples of pathogens.

Bacteria Bacteria are one-celled microorganisms. They cause a wide variety of diseases, including ear infections, food poisoning, and tuberculosis, which is a disease of the lungs. Some bacterial pathogens damage body cells directly. Strep throat, for example, is caused by streptococcus bacteria that invade cells in your throat. Other bacterial pathogens do not enter cells, but instead produce a poison, or **toxin,** that damages cells. For example, when the bacteria that cause tetanus get into a wound, they can produce a toxin that damages the nervous system. Tetanus is also called lockjaw because the nerve damage can lock the muscles that control the jaws.

Figure 3 Most infectious diseases are caused by microscopic organisms. **A.** Bacteria like this rod-shaped one cause tetanus, a disease that harms the nervous system. **B.** When you have a cough and a sore throat, this round virus, called an adenovirus may be to blame. **C.** This fungus causes ringworm, a skin disease.

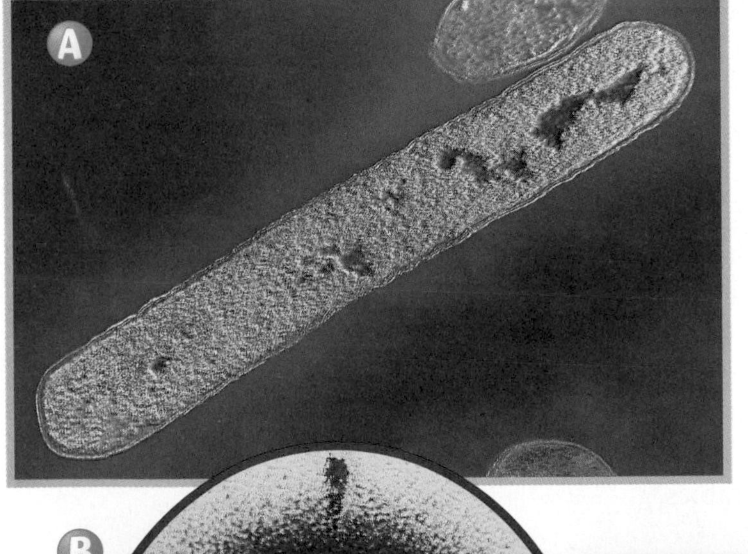

Viruses Viruses are tiny particles, much smaller than bacteria and other pathogens. Viruses cannot reproduce unless they are inside living cells. The cells are damaged or destroyed in the process, releasing new viruses to infect other cells. Both colds and influenza—or flu—are caused by viruses that invade cells in the respiratory system. In fact, there are over 200 different kinds of cold viruses, and each of them can give you a sore throat and a runny nose! Chicken pox and AIDS are also caused by viruses. You will learn more about AIDS later in the chapter.

Fungi and Protists Fungi, which include molds, yeasts, and other organisms, cause some infectious diseases, including athlete's foot. Malaria, an infection of the blood that is common in tropical areas, is one disease caused by protists.

☑ ***Checkpoint*** *What are two ways in which bacteria cause disease?*

How Diseases Are Spread

Pathogens are something like ants at a picnic. They aren't trying to harm you. However, like the ants, pathogens need food. They also need a place to live and reproduce. Unfortunately, your body may be just the right place for a pathogen to meet those needs.

You can become infected by a pathogen in one of several ways. **Sources of pathogens include another person, a contaminated object, an animal bite, and the environment.**

Person-to-Person Transfer Many pathogens are transferred from one person to another person. Pathogens often pass from one person to another through direct physical contact, such as kissing, hugging, and shaking hands. For example, if you kiss someone who has a cold sore, cold-sore viruses can then get into your body.

Diseases are also spread through indirect contact with an infected person. For example, if a person with pneumonia sneezes, pathogens shoot into the air. Pathogens from a sneeze can travel most of the way across a small room! Other people may catch pneumonia if they inhale these pathogens. Colds, flu, and tuberculosis can be spread through coughing and sneezing.

Posing Questions

ACTIVITY

Cholera is a deadly disease that is spread through food or water contaminated with cholera bacteria. In 1854, cholera spread through London, England. Dr. John Snow analyzed where most of the cholera victims lived, as well as the locations of the water pumps in the area. The map in Figure 4 shows Dr. Snow's findings. Dr. Snow hypothesized that the disease was spread by water that came from one of the pumps. Which pump was probably the source of the contaminated water?

Suppose that Dr. Snow just learned that two additional people had died of cholera. What questions would Dr. Snow most likely ask about the additional cholera cases?

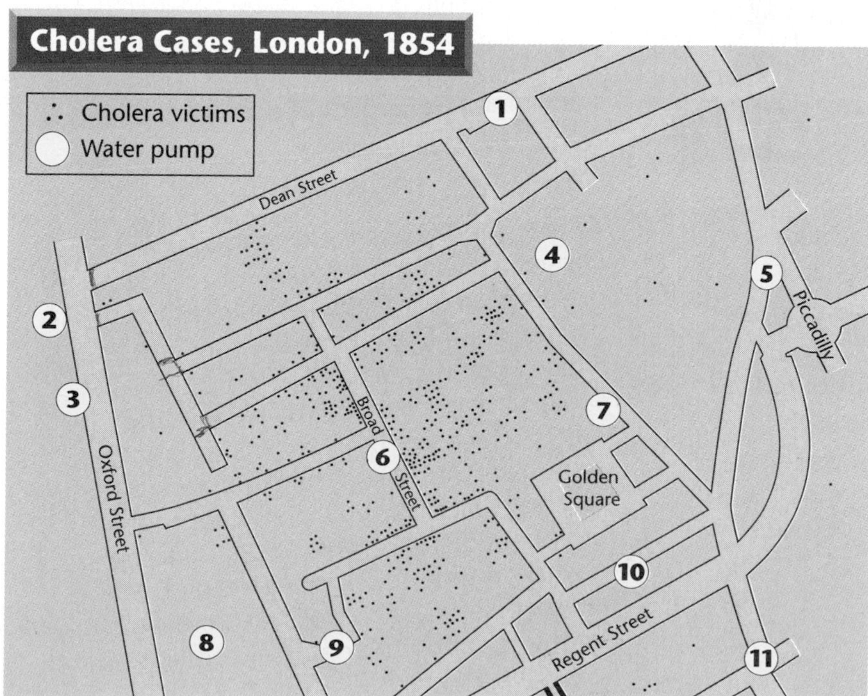

Figure 4 The map shows the location of cholera cases in the 1854 epidemic in London, England.

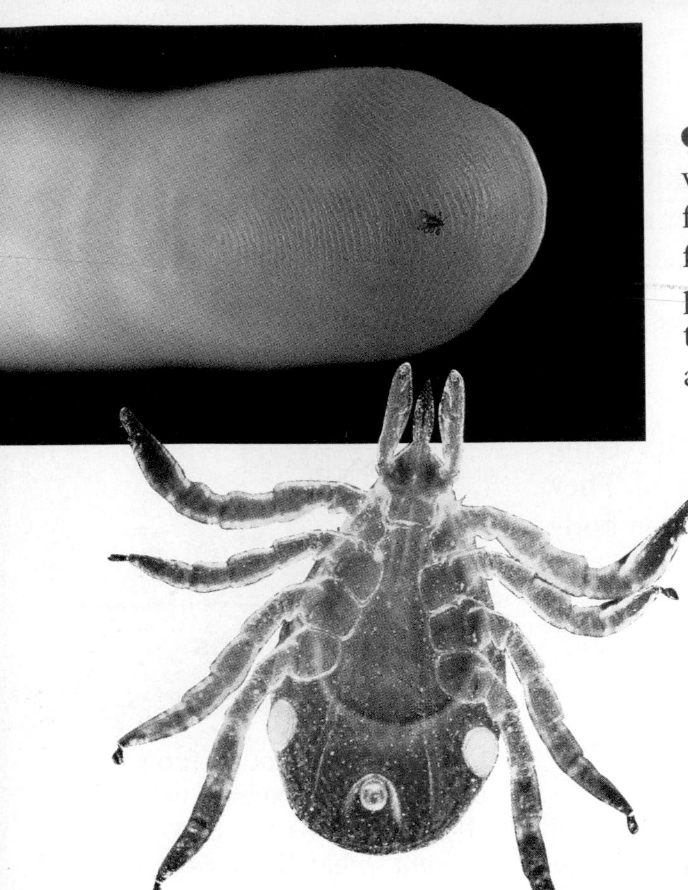

Figure 5 The tiny deer tick may carry the bacteria that cause Lyme disease, a serious condition that can damage the joints. If a deer tick that is carrying Lyme disease bacteria bites a person, the person may get Lyme disease. ***Problem Solving*** *How might people reduce their risk of catching Lyme disease?*

Contaminated Objects Some pathogens can survive for a time outside a person's body. Water and food can become contaminated. If people then eat the food or drink the water, they may become sick. Some pathogens that cause severe diarrhea are spread through contaminated food and water. People can also pick up pathogens by using objects, such as towels or silverware, that have been handled by an infected person. Colds and flu can be spread in this way. Tetanus bacteria can enter the body if a person steps on a contaminated nail.

Animal Bites If an animal is infected with certain pathogens and then bites a person, it can pass the pathogens to the person. People can get rabies, a serious disease that affects the nervous system, from the bite of an infected animal, such as a dog or a raccoon. Lyme disease and Rocky Mountain spotted fever are both spread by tick bites. The protist that causes malaria is transferred by the bites of mosquitoes that live in tropical regions.

Pathogens from the Environment Some pathogens occur naturally in the environment. The bacteria that cause tetanus live in soil or water. The bacteria that cause botulism, an especially severe form of food poisoning, also live in soil. Botulism bacteria can produce a toxin in foods that have been improperly canned. The toxin is extremely powerful.

Section 1 Review

1. Name four kinds of pathogens that cause disease in humans.
2. Describe four ways that pathogens can infect humans.
3. Explain how Pasteur and Koch contributed to the understanding of infectious disease.
4. **Thinking Critically Applying Concepts** If you have a cold, what steps can you take to keep from spreading it to other people? Explain.

CHAPTER PROJECT 6

Check Your Progress

At this stage, you should have chosen a specific infectious disease to research. You should also decide whether to do newspaper articles, radio programs, or a television series. Begin to plan how you will explain the way in which the body is invaded by pathogens. Also begin thinking about how you will make your show appropriate for your audience. (*Hint:* To get ideas on how to present news stories, read newspapers or watch or listen to real news programs about international conflicts.)

SECTION 2 The Body's Defenses

DISCOVER ACTIVITY

Which Pieces Fit Together?

1. Your teacher will give you a piece of paper with one jagged edge.
2. One student in the class has a piece of paper whose edges match your paper edge, like two pieces of a jigsaw puzzle.
3. Find the student whose paper matches yours and fit the two edges together.

Think It Over

Inferring Imagine that one of each pair of matching pieces is a pathogen. The other is a cell in your body that defends your body against the invading pathogen. How many kinds of invaders can each defender cell recognize?

GUIDE FOR READING

- **What is the body's first line of defense against pathogens?**
- **What happens during the inflammatory response?**
- **How does the immune system respond to pathogens?**

Reading Tip **Before you read, preview *Exploring the Immune Response* on page 165. List any unfamiliar terms. As you read, write definitions of those terms in your own words.**

Your eyes are glued to the screen. The situation in the video game is desperate. Enemy troops have gotten through an opening in the wall. Your soldiers have managed to hold back most of the invaders. However, some enemy soldiers are breaking through the defense lines. You need your backup defenders. They can zap the invaders with their powerful weapons. If your soldiers can fight off the enemy until the backup team arrives, you can save your fortress.

Video games create fantasy wars, but in your body, real battles happen all the time. In your body, the "enemies" are invading pathogens. You are hardly ever aware of these battles. The body's disease-fighting system is so effective that most people get sick only occasionally. By eliminating pathogens that can destroy your cells, your body maintains homeostasis.

Figure 6 The pathogens that invade your body are something like the enemy soldiers in a video game. Your body has to defend itself against the pathogens.

Barriers That Keep Pathogens Out

Your body has three lines of defense against pathogens. The first line consists of barriers that keep pathogens from getting into the body. You do not wear a sign that says "Pathogens Keep Out," but that doesn't matter. **Barriers such as the skin, breathing passages, mouth, and stomach trap and kill most pathogens with which you come into contact.**

Figure 7 Skin is covered with bacteria. The dots in the photo are colonies of bacteria living on a person's hand.
Relating Cause and Effect *How can a cut in the skin lead to an infection?*

The Skin When pathogens land on the skin, they are exposed to destructive chemicals in oil and sweat. Even if these chemicals don't kill them, the pathogens may fall off with dead skin cells. If the pathogens manage to stay on the skin, they must get through the tightly packed dead cells that form a barrier on top of living skin cells. Most pathogens get through the skin only when it is cut. Scabs form over cuts so rapidly that the period in which pathogens can enter the body in this way is very short.

The Breathing Passages As you know, you can inhale pathogens when you breathe in. The nose, pharynx, trachea, and bronchi, however, contain mucus and cilia. Together, the mucus and cilia trap and remove most of the pathogens that enter the respiratory system. In addition, irritation by pathogens may make you sneeze or cough. Both actions force the pathogens out of your body.

The Mouth and Stomach Some pathogens are found in foods, even if the foods are handled safely. The saliva in your mouth contains destructive chemicals and your stomach produces acid. Most pathogens that you swallow are destroyed by saliva or stomach acid.

General Defenses

In spite of barriers, pathogens sometimes get into your body and begin to damage cells. When body cells are damaged, they release chemicals that trigger the **inflammatory response,** which is the second line of defense. **In the inflammatory response, fluid and certain types of white blood cells leak from blood vessels into nearby tissues. The white blood cells then fight the pathogens.** Because the inflammatory response is the same no matter what the pathogen, it is sometimes called the body's general defense.

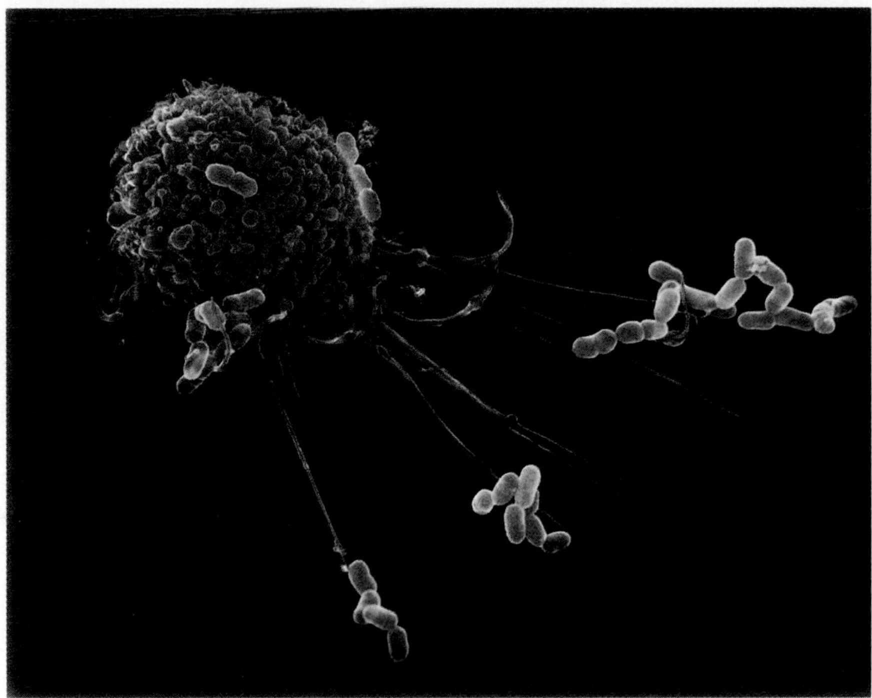

Figure 8 Caught! The bacteria, shown in green, don't stand a chance against the phagocyte, shown in red. Phagocytes are white blood cells that engulf and destroy bacteria.

All white blood cells are disease fighters, but there are different types, each with its own particular function. The kinds involved in the inflammatory response are called phagocytes. A **phagocyte** (FAG uh syt) is a white blood cell that engulfs pathogens and destroys them by breaking them down.

During the inflammatory response, blood vessels widen in the area affected by the pathogens. This enlargement increases the flow of blood to the area. The enlarged blood vessels—and the fluid that leaks out of them—make the affected area red and swollen. If you touch the swollen area, it will feel slightly warmer than normal. In fact, the term *inflammation* comes from a Latin word meaning "to set on fire."

In some cases, chemicals produced during the inflammatory response cause a fever, raising your body temperature above its normal temperature of 37° Celsius. Although fever makes you feel bad, it actually may help your body fight the infection. Some pathogens may not grow and reproduce well at higher temperatures.

Checkpoint *What role do white blood cells play in the inflammatory response?*

Social Studies CONNECTION

Today the Panama Canal is an important shipping route that links the Atlantic and Pacific oceans. But because of two diseases that cause high fever—malaria and yellow fever—the Panama Canal almost didn't get built. Much of the canal, which links the Atlantic and Pacific oceans, passes through the mosquito-filled rain forests of Panama. Mosquitoes carry the pathogens that cause malaria and yellow fever.

In 1889 an attempt at digging a canal was abandoned, partly because so many workers became sick. In 1904, an American physician, Colonel William C. Gorgas, began a project in which swamps in the work area were drained. In addition, brush and grass were cut down. Gorgas's project destroyed the places where mosquitoes lived and reproduced. This action greatly reduced the mosquito population. The Panama Canal was completed in 1914.

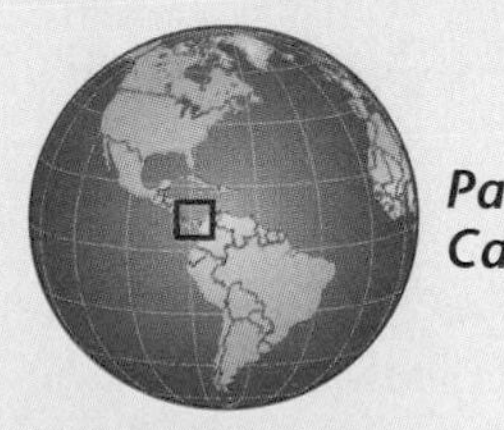

In Your Journal

Write a newspaper article about the construction of the Panama Canal. The article should focus on the problem of disease and the contribution of Colonel Gorgas.

The Immune System

If a pathogen infection is severe enough to cause a fever, it also triggers the third line of defense—the **immune response.** The immune response is controlled by the immune system, your body's disease fighting system. **The cells of the immune system can distinguish between different kinds of pathogens. The immune-system cells react to each kind of pathogen with a defense targeted specifically at that pathogen.** The white blood cells that do this are called **lymphocytes** (LIM fuh syts). There are two major kinds of lymphocytes—T lymphocytes and B lymphocytes, which are also called T cells and B cells. In *Exploring the Immune Response* , you can see how T cells and B cells work together to destroy flu viruses.

T Cells A major function of **T cells** is to identify pathogens and *INTEGRATING CHEMISTRY* distinguish one kind of pathogen from another. You have tens of millions of T cells circulating in your blood. Each kind of T cell recognizes a different kind of pathogen. What T cells actually recognize are marker molecules, called antigens, found on each pathogen. **Antigens** are molecules on cells that the immune system recognizes either as part of your body or as coming from outside your body. All cells have antigens, and each person's antigens are different from those of all other people.

You can think of antigens as something like the uniforms that athletes wear. When you watch a track meet, you can look at the runners' uniforms to tell which school each runner comes from. Like athletes from different schools, each different pathogen has its own kind of antigen. Antigens differ from one another because each kind of antigen has a different chemical structure.

Figure 9 By looking at the runners' uniforms, you can tell that they come from different schools. Similarly, the immune system recognizes a pathogen by its antigens—marker molecules on the pathogen. ***Applying Concepts*** *What is the name of the cell that distinguishes one pathogen from another?*

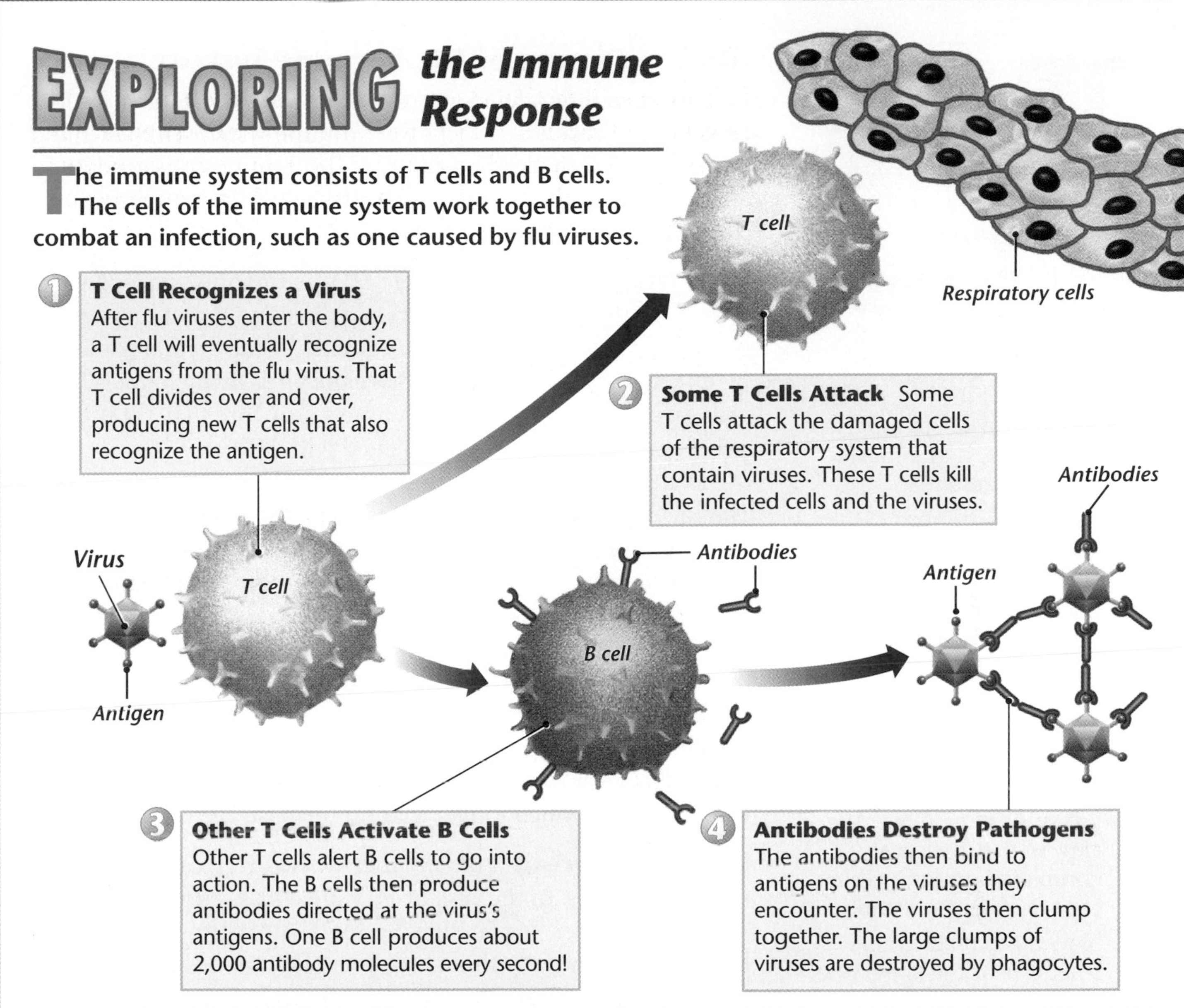

B Cells The lymphocytes called **B cells** produce chemicals that help destroy each kind of pathogen. These chemicals are called **antibodies.** Antibodies lock onto antigens. Each kind of B cell produces only one kind of antibody. Each kind of antibody has a different structure. Antigen and antibody molecules fit together, like pieces of a puzzle. An antigen on a flu virus will only bind to one kind of antibody—the antibody that acts against that flu virus.

INTEGRATING CHEMISTRY

When antibodies bind to the antigens on a pathogen, they mark the pathogen for destruction. Some antibodies make pathogens clump together. Others keep pathogens from attaching to the body cells that they might damage. Still other antibodies make it easier for phagocytes to destroy the pathogens.

☑ *Checkpoint* *What is the function of an antibody?*

Stuck Together

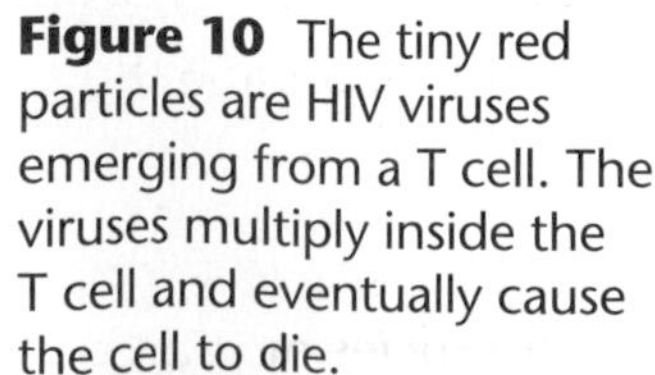

In this activity, you will model one way in which an antibody prevents a pathogen from infecting a body cell.

1. Use a large ball to represent a body cell, and a smaller ball to represent a pathogen.
2. Press a lump of modeling clay onto the small ball. Then use the clay to stick the two balls together. This models how a pathogen attaches itself to a body cell.
3. Pull the two balls apart, keeping the clay on the small ball (the pathogen).
4. Put strips of tape over the clay, so that the clay is completely covered. The tape represents an antibody.
5. Now try to reattach the small ball to the larger one.

Making Models Use the model to explain how antibodies prevent pathogens from attaching to body cells.

AIDS, a Disease of the Immune System

Acquired immunodeficiency syndrome, or **AIDS,** is a disease caused by a virus that attacks the immune system. In the United States, AIDS is the leading cause of death in persons aged 25 to 44. The virus that causes AIDS is called human immunodeficiency virus, or HIV.

How HIV Affects the Body HIV is the only kind of virus known to attack the immune system directly. Once it invades the body, HIV enters T cells and reproduces inside them. People can be infected with HIV—that is, have the virus living in their body cells—for years before they become sick. More than 30 million people in the world may be infected with HIV.

Eventually HIV begins to destroy the T cells it has infected. Damage to the immune system is usually slow. But as the viruses destroy T cells, the body loses its ability to fight disease. Most persons infected with HIV eventually develop the disease AIDS.

Because their immune systems no longer function properly, people with AIDS become sick with diseases not normally found in people with healthy immune systems. Many people survive attack after attack of such diseases. But eventually their immune systems fail, ending in death. At this time, there is no cure for AIDS. However, new drug treatments allow people with the disease to survive much longer than in the past.

How HIV Is Spread Like all other viruses, HIV can only reproduce inside cells. In the case of HIV, the virus reproduces inside T cells. However, it can survive for a short time outside the human body in body fluids, such as blood and the fluids produced by the male and female reproductive systems.

HIV can spread from one person to another only if body fluids from an infected person come in contact with those of an uninfected person. Sexual contact is one way in which this can happen. HIV may also pass from an infected woman to her baby

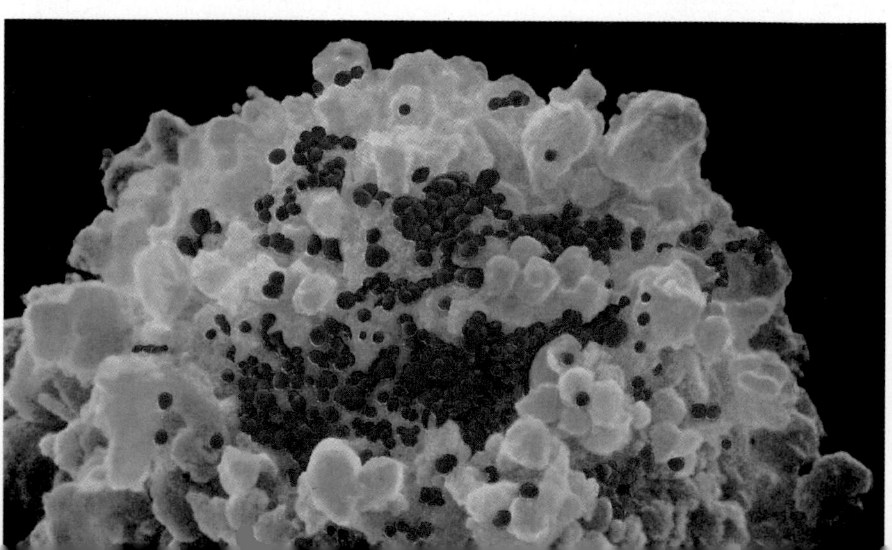

Figure 10 The tiny red particles are HIV viruses emerging from a T cell. The viruses multiply inside the T cell and eventually cause the cell to die.
Relating Cause and Effect *Why does the death of T cells interfere with the body's ability to fight disease?*

Figure 11 You cannot get HIV, the virus that causes AIDS, by hugging someone infected with the virus.

during pregnancy or childbirth or through breast milk. In addition, when drug users share needles, some infected blood may get into the needle and then infect the next person who uses it. A person can also get HIV through a transfusion of blood that contains the virus. But since 1985, all donated blood in the United States has been tested for signs of HIV, and infected blood is not used in transfusions.

It is important to know the many ways in which HIV is *not* spread. HIV does not live on skin, so you cannot be infected by hugging or shaking hands with an infected person. You can't get infected by using a toilet seat after it has been used by someone with HIV. And HIV is not spread when you bump into someone while playing sports.

Section 2 Review

1. Name four barriers that prevent pathogens from getting into the body. Explain how each barrier prevents infection.
2. Describe the inflammatory response.
3. What is the function of the immune system?
4. How is HIV different from other virus pathogens?
5. **Thinking Critically Applying Concepts** Explain why you can't contract HIV by touching a doorknob that someone infected with the virus has touched.

CHAPTER PROJECT 6

Check Your Progress

At this point you should begin writing the newspaper articles or scripts for each of your broadcasts. Before you begin writing, outline the main ideas that you want to communicate. Work to make your descriptions sound like real news. (*Hint:* Make sure that your articles or scripts include information about each of the body's three lines of defense).

Real-World Lab

How It Works

The Skin as a Barrier

Bacteria are all around you. Many of those bacteria can cause disease, yet you usually remain free of disease. In this lab, you will investigate how the skin protects you from infectious disease.

Problem

How does skin act as a barrier to pathogens?

Skills Focus

making models, controlling variables, drawing conclusions

Materials

sealable plastic bags, 4
fresh apples, 4
rotting apple
cotton swabs
marking pen
paper towels
toothpick
rubbing alcohol

Procedure   

1. Read over the entire procedure to see how you will treat each of four fresh apples. Write a prediction in your notebook about the change(s) you expect to see in each apple. Then copy the data table into your notebook.
2. Label four plastic bags *1, 2, 3,* and *4.*
3. Gently wash four fresh apples with water, then dry them carefully with paper towels. Place one apple in plastic bag 1, and seal the bag.
4. Insert a toothpick tip into a rotting apple and withdraw it. Lightly draw the tip of the toothpick down the side of the second apple without breaking the skin. Repeat these actions three more times, touching the toothpick to different parts of the apple without breaking the skin. Insert the apple in plastic bag 2, and seal the bag.
5. Insert the toothpick tip into the rotting apple and withdraw it. Use the tip to make a long, thin scratch down the side of the third apple. Be sure to pierce the apple's skin. Repeat these actions three more times, making additional scratches on different parts of the apple. Insert the apple into plastic bag 3, and seal the bag.
6. Repeat Step 5 to make four scratches in the fourth apple. However, before you place the apple in the bag, dip a cotton swab in rubbing alcohol, and swab the scratches. Then place the apple in plastic bag 4, and seal the bag. **CAUTION:** *Alcohol and its vapors are flammable. Work where there are no sparks, exposed flames, or other heat sources.*
7. Store the four bags in a warm, dark place. Wash your hands thoroughly with soap and water.
8. Every day for one week, remove the apples from their storage place, and observe them without opening the bags. Record your observations, then return the bags to their storage location. At the end of the activity, dispose of the unopened bags as directed by your teacher.

Analyze and Conclude

1. How did the appearance of the four apples compare? Explain your results.
2. In this activity, what condition in the human body is each of the four fresh apples supposed to model?
3. What is the control in this experiment?
4. What is the role of the rotting apple in this activity?
5. **Apply** How does this investigation show why routine cuts and scrapes should be cleaned and bandaged?

Design an Experiment

Using apples as you did in this activity, design an experiment to model how washing hands can prevent the spread of disease. Obtain your teacher's permission before carrying out your investigation.

DATA TABLE

Date	*Apple 1* *(no contact with decay)*	*Apple 2* *(contact with decay, unbroken skin)*	*Apple 3* *(contact with decay, scratched, untreated)*	*Apple 4* *(contact with decay, scratched, treated with alcohol)*

SECTION 3

Preventing Infectious Disease

DISCOVER ACTIVITY

What Substances Can Kill Pathogens?

1. Your teacher will give you a variety of products, such as disinfectant soaps and mouthwashes, that claim to kill pathogens. Read the labels to learn the pathogens that each product is supposed to destroy.
2. Also note the ingredients in each product that act against pathogens. These are labeled "active ingredients."

Think It Over

Designing Experiments How could you determine which of two different soaps is more effective at killing bacteria? Design an experiment to find out. Do not perform the experiment without obtaining your teacher's approval.

GUIDE FOR READING

- **What is active immunity?**
- **What is passive immunity?**

Reading Tip **Before you read, rewrite the headings in the section as questions that begin with *how, why,* or *what.* As you read, write short answers to those questions.**

Itch, itch, itch. That's probably what you remember about chicken pox, if you ever had it. But once you got better, you could be pretty sure that you would never get that disease again. As people recover from some diseases, they develop immunity to the diseases. **Immunity** is the body's ability to destroy pathogens before they can cause disease. There are two basic types of immunity—active and passive.

Active Immunity

If you've been sick with chicken pox, your body was invaded by chicken pox viruses. Your immune system responded to the virus antigens by producing antibodies against them. The next time that chicken pox viruses invade your body, your immune system will probably produce antibodies so quickly that you won't become sick. You now have **active immunity** to chicken pox, because your own body has produced the antibodies that fight the chicken pox pathogens. **Active immunity occurs when a person's own immune system produces antibodies in response to the presence of a pathogen.**

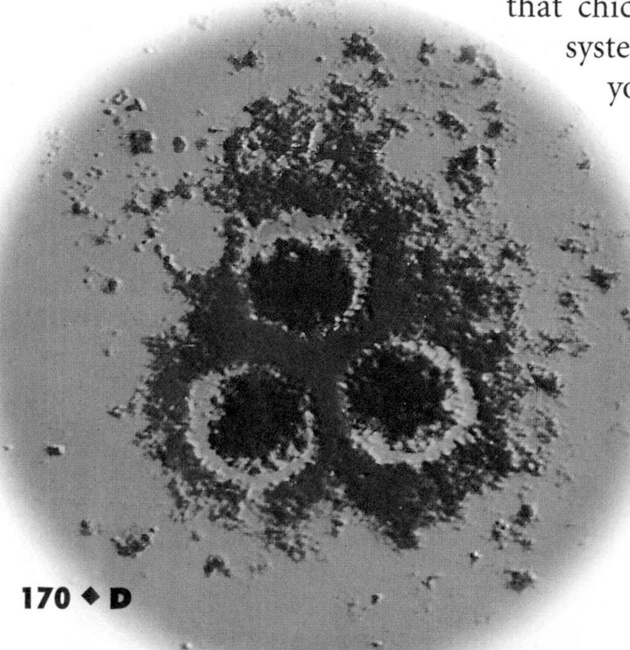

Figure 12 These virus particles cause chicken pox. Once you have had chicken pox you will probably never get that disease again.

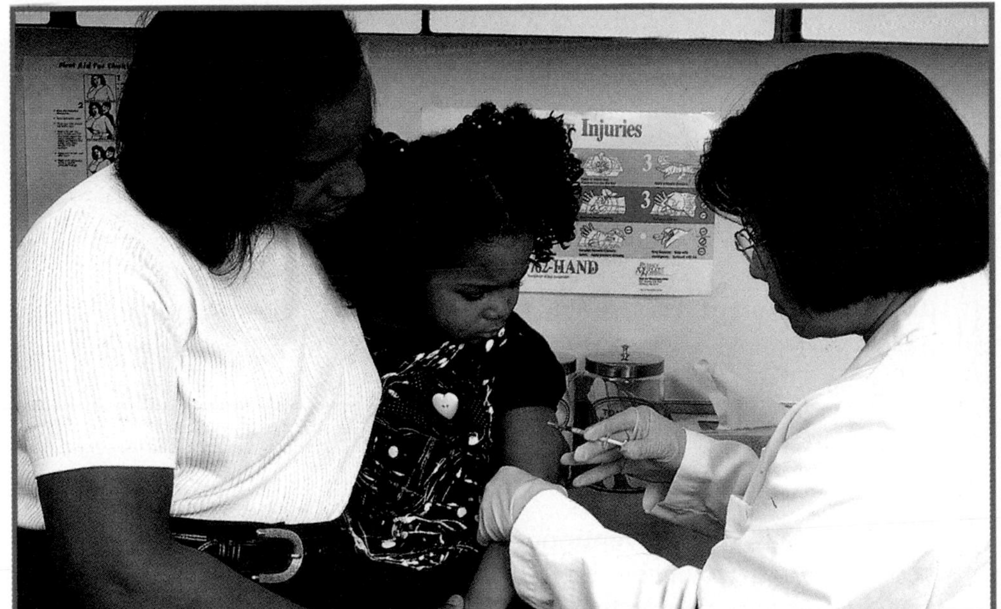

Figure 13 Ouch! The injection may sting a bit, but it is a vaccination that will protect the little girl against disease. Vaccinations consist of dead or weakened pathogens that do not make you sick. ***Classifying*** *Why does a vaccination produce active immunity to a disease?*

How Active Immunity Is Produced Active immunity is produced by the cells of a person's immune system as part of the immune response. Remember that during the immune response, T cells and B cells help destroy the disease-causing pathogens. After the person recovers, some of the T cells and B cells keep the "memory" of the pathogen's antigen. If that kind of pathogen enters the body again, these memory cells recognize the pathogen's antigen. The memory cells start the immune response so quickly that the person usually doesn't get sick. Active immunity usually lasts for many years, and sometimes it lasts for life.

Vaccination One way in which you can gain active immunity is by coming down with the disease. Another way is by being vaccinated against the disease. **Vaccination** (vac suh NAY shun), or immunization, is the process by which harmless antigens are deliberately introduced into a person's body to produce active immunity. Vaccinations are given by injection or by mouth. Vaccinations can prevent polio, chicken pox, and other diseases.

The substance that is used in a vaccination is called a vaccine. A **vaccine** (vak SEEN) usually consists of pathogens that have been weakened or killed but can still trigger the immune system to go into action. The T cells and B cells still recognize and respond to the antigens of the weakened or dead pathogen. When you receive a vaccination, the weakened pathogens usually do not make you sick. However, your immune system responds by producing memory cells and active immunity to the disease.

Checkpoint *What are two ways in which a person can gain active immunity?*

Passive Immunity

Some diseases, such as rabies, are so uncommon that people rarely receive vaccinations against them. If a person is bitten by an animal that might have rabies, however, the person is usually given injections that contain antibodies to the rabies antigen. The protection that the person acquires this way is an example of passive immunity. This type of immunity is called **passive immunity** because the antibodies are given to the person—the person's own immune system did not make them.

Fighting Infectious Disease

From ancient times, people have practiced methods for preventing disease and caring for sick people. Ancient peoples, however, did not know what caused disease. About 200 years ago, people began to learn much more about the causes of infectious diseases and how to protect against them.

1854

Florence Nightingale

As an English nurse caring for British soldiers during the Crimean War, Florence Nightingale insisted that army hospitals be kept clean. By doing this, she saved many soldiers' lives. She is considered to be the founder of the modern nursing profession.

1800 | 1825 | 1850

1796

Edward Jenner

Edward Jenner, a country doctor in England, successfully vaccinated a child against smallpox, a deadly viral disease. Jenner used material from a sore of a person with cowpox, a mild but similar disorder. Although Jenner's procedure was successful, he did not understand why it worked.

1860s

Joseph Lister

Joseph Lister, an English surgeon, used carbolic acid to prevent infections in surgical patients. Because of Lister's techniques, far more people recovered from surgery than before.

Passive immunity occurs when the antibodies that fight the pathogen come from another source rather than from the person's own body. Unlike active immunity, which is long-lasting, passive immunity usually lasts no more than a few months.

A baby acquires passive immunity to some diseases before birth. This happens because antibodies from the mother's body pass into the baby's body. After birth, these antibodies protect the baby for a few months. After that time, the baby's own immune system has begun to function.

In Your Journal

Learn more about the work of one of these people. Then imagine that a new hospital is going to be dedicated to that person, and that you have been chosen to deliver the dedication speech. Write a speech that praises the person's contributions to fighting disease.

1882

Robert Koch

In Germany, Robert Koch identified one kind of microorganism in many samples of tissue taken from people with tuberculosis. Because he always found the same microorganism, Koch hypothesized that each infectious disease is caused by one specific pathogen.

1875 | **1900** | **1925**

1868

Louis Pasteur

In France, Louis Pasteur showed that microorganisms were the cause of a disease in silkworms. Pasteur reasoned that he could control the spread of disease by killing microorganisms. He also proposed that infectious diseases in humans are caused by microorganisms.

1928

Alexander Fleming

In Britain, Alexander Fleming observed that bacteria growing on laboratory plates were killed when some kinds of fungi grew on the same plate. He discovered that one fungus produced a substance—penicillin—that killed bacteria. Penicillin became the first antibiotic.

Preventing Infectious Diseases

- ◆ Don't share items that might carry pathogens, such as toothbrushes, drinking straws, or silverware.
- ◆ Keep clean. Wash your hands before eating and after using the bathroom.
- ◆ Cover your mouth when sneezing or coughing.
- ◆ Get eight hours of sleep every night.
- ◆ Eat a well-balanced diet.
- ◆ Get regular exercise.

Figure 14 Your actions can help prevent the spread of infectious diseases. ***Applying Concepts*** *How does keeping clean prevent the spread of disease?*

Staying Healthy

INTEGRATING HEALTH You almost certainly have immunity to some diseases, either because you have had the diseases or because you have been vaccinated against them. However, no one is immune to all diseases. But there are several steps you can take to decrease your risk of getting and spreading infectious diseases. Figure 14 summarizes these steps.

Unfortunately, you will probably become sick from time to time. When that happens, there are ways in which you can help yourself recover. Get plenty of rest. In addition, unless your stomach is upset, you should eat well-balanced meals. Drink plenty of fluids. These actions are all that you need to recover from most mild illnesses.

Sometimes when you are sick, medications can help you get better. If you have a disease that is caused by bacteria, you may be given an antibiotic. An **antibiotic** (an tih by AHT ik) is a chemical that kills bacteria or slows their growth without harming body cells. Unfortunately, there are no medications that cure viral illnesses, including the common cold. The best way to deal with most viral diseases is to get plenty of rest.

Some medicines don't kill pathogens but may help you feel more comfortable while you get better. Many of these are over-the-counter medications—drugs that can be purchased without a doctor's prescription. Such medications may reduce fever, clear your nose so you can breathe more easily, or stop a cough. Be sure you understand and follow the instructions for all types of medications. And if you don't start to feel better in a short time, you should see a doctor.

Section 3 Review

1. What is active immunity? How is it produced?
2. How is passive immunity produced? How does passive immunity differ from active immunity?
3. Identify four things that you can do that will help you avoid catching an infectious disease.
4. **Thinking Critically Applying Concepts** After receiving a vaccination, you may develop mild symptoms of the disease. Explain why.

Science at Home

With a family member, make a list of the vaccinations you have received. For each, note when you received the vaccination. Then, with your family member, learn about one of the diseases for which you were vaccinated. What kind of pathogen causes the disease? What are the symptoms of the disease? Is the disease still common in the United States?

Noninfectious Disease

DISCOVER

What Happens When Airflow Is Restricted?

1. Asthma is a disorder in which breathing passages become narrower than normal. This activity will help you understand how this condition affects breathing. Begin by breathing normally, first through your nose and then through your mouth. Observe how deeply you breathe.
2. Put one end of a drinking straw in your mouth. Then gently pinch your nostrils shut so that you cannot breathe through your nose.
3. With your nostrils pinched closed, breathe by inhaling air through the straw. Continue breathing this way for thirty seconds.

Think It Over

Observing Compare your normal breathing pattern to that when breathing through the straw. Which way were you able to take deeper breaths? Did you ever feel short of breath?

GUIDE FOR READING

- **What is an allergy?**
- **How does diabetes affect the body?**
- **What is cancer?**

Reading Tip **As you read, create a table in which you record the characteristics of each noninfectious disease.**

Americans are living longer today than ever before. A person who was born in 1990 can expect to live about 75 years. In contrast, a person born in 1950 could expect to live only about 68 years.

Progress against infectious disease is one reason why life spans have increased. However, as infectious diseases have become less common, noninfectious diseases have grown more prevalent. **Noninfectious diseases** are diseases that are not spread from person to person. Unlike infectious diseases, noninfectious diseases are not caused by microorganisms. A noninfectious disease, cardiovascular disease, is the leading cause of death in America. Allergies, diabetes, and cancer are other noninfectious diseases.

Allergies

Spring has arrived. Flowers are in bloom, and the songs of birds fill the air. Unfortunately for some people, sneezing is another sound that fills the air. People who sneeze and cough in the spring may not have colds. Instead, they may be suffering from an **allergy** to plant pollen in the air. **An allergy is a disorder in which the immune system is overly sensitive to a foreign substance—something not normally found in the body.**

▼ Plant pollen

Sharpen your Skills

Drawing Conclusions

ACTIVITY

Two weeks ago, after you ate strawberry shortcake with whipped cream, you broke out in an itchy rash. Besides strawberries, the ingredients in the dessert were sugar, flour, butter, eggs, vanilla, baking powder, salt, and cream. Then last night, you ate a strawberry custard tart with whipped cream and again broke out in a rash. The tart's ingredients were strawberries, sugar, cornstarch, milk, eggs, flour, shortening, salt, and vanilla.

You think that you may be allergic to strawberries. Do you have enough evidence to support this conclusion? If so, why? If not, what additional evidence do you need?

Allergens An **allergen** is any substance that causes an allergy. In addition to different kinds of pollen, people may be allergic to dust, molds, some foods, and even some medicines. If you are lucky, you have no allergies at all. However, many people are allergic to one or more substances.

Reaction to Allergens Allergens may get into your body when you inhale them, eat them in food, or touch them with your skin. When lymphocytes encounter the allergen, they produce antibodies. These antibodies, unlike the ones made during the immune response, signal cells in the body to release a chemical called histamine. **Histamine** (HIS tuh meen) is a chemical that is responsible for the symptoms of an allergy, such as sneezing and watery eyes. Drugs that interfere with the action of histamine, called antihistamines, may lessen this reaction. However, if you have an allergy, the best strategy is to try to avoid the substance to which you are allergic.

Asthma If some people inhale a substance to which they are allergic, they may develop a condition called asthma. **Asthma** (AZ muh) is a disorder in which the respiratory passages narrow significantly. This narrowing causes the person to wheeze and become short of breath. Asthma attacks may be brought on by factors other than allergies, such as stress and exercise. People who have severe asthma attacks may require emergency care. If you have asthma, avoid the substances or activities that trigger asthma attacks and learn how to treat an attack.

☑ *Checkpoint* *What is the effect of histamine on the body?*

Figure 15 Some people have allergic reactions to cats (left) or dust mites, tiny animals found in dust (below).

Diabetes

The pancreas produces a chemical called insulin. **Insulin** (IN suh lin) enables body cells to take in glucose from the blood and use it for energy. In the condition known as **diabetes** (dy uh BEE tis), either the pancreas fails to produce enough insulin or the body's cells can't use it properly. **As a result, a person with diabetes has high levels of glucose in the blood and excretes glucose in the urine. The person's body cells, however, do not have enough glucose.**

Figure 16 Many people with diabetes must test their blood frequently to determine the level of glucose in their blood. ***Relating Cause and Effect*** *What accounts for the high level of glucose in the blood of people with diabetes?*

Effects of Diabetes People with diabetes may lose weight, feel weak, and be hungry all the time. These symptoms occur because the cells are unable to take in the glucose they need to function efficiently. In addition, these people may urinate frequently and feel thirsty as the kidneys work to eliminate the excess glucose from the body.

Diabetes is a serious condition that, if not treated properly, can result in death. Even with proper treatment, diabetes can have serious long-term effects. These effects can include blindness, kidney failure, and heart disease.

Forms of Diabetes There are two main forms of diabetes. Type I diabetes, the more serious form, usually begins in childhood or early adulthood. In Type I diabetes, the pancreas produces little or no insulin. People with this condition must get insulin injections.

Type II diabetes usually develops during adulthood. In this condition, either the pancreas doesn't make enough insulin or body cells do not respond normally to insulin. People with Type II diabetes may not need to take insulin. Instead, they may be able to control the symptoms of diabetes through proper diet, weight control, and exercise.

☑ *Checkpoint What are some symptoms of diabetes?*

Cancer

Under normal conditions, the body produces new cells at about the same rate that other cells die. In a condition known as cancer, however, the situation is quite different. **Cancer is a disease in which cells multiply uncontrollably, over and over, destroying healthy tissue in the process.** The word *cancer* is the Latin word for crab. Cancerous growths act something like a crab, pinching healthy tissues as they grow.

Tumor Formation As cancerous cells divide over and over, they often form abnormal tissue masses called **tumors.** Cancerous tumors invade the healthy tissue around them and destroy the tissue. Cancer cells can break away from a tumor and invade blood or lymph vessels. The blood or lymph then carries the cancer cells to other parts of the body, where they may begin to divide and form new tumors. Unless stopped by treatment, cancer progresses through the body.

Causes of Cancer Different factors may work together to determine what makes cells become cancerous. One such factor is the characteristics that people inherit from their parents. Because of their inherited characteristics, some people are more likely than others to develop certain kinds of cancer. For example, women whose mothers had breast cancer have a higher risk of developing breast cancer than do women with no family history of the disease.

Figure 17 The large orange mass in the X-ray is a cancerous tumor in the lung. The graph shows leading types of cancer that affect men and women in the United States. ***Interpreting Graphs*** *Do more women or men develop lung cancer each year?*

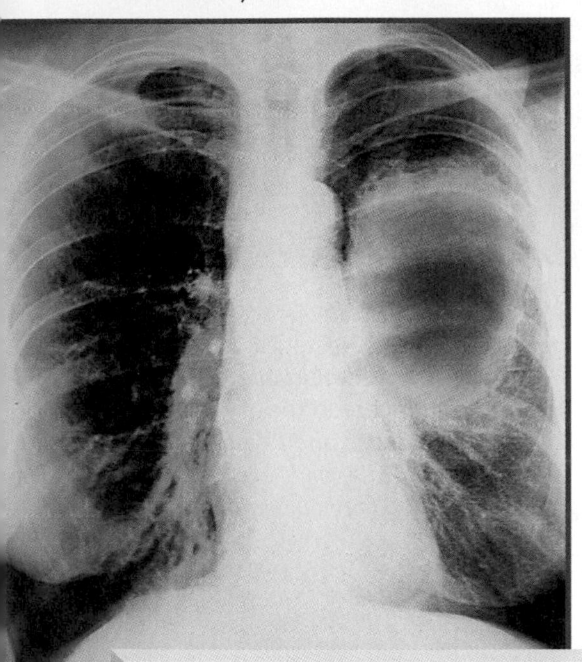

Some substances or factors in the environment, called **carcinogens** (kahr SIN uh junz), can cause cancer. The tar in cigarette smoke is a carcinogen. Ultraviolet light, which is part of sunlight, can also be a carcinogen.

Cancer Treatment Surgery, drugs, and radiation are all used to treat cancer. If cancer is detected before it has spread, doctors remove the cancerous tumors through surgery. Sometimes, however, a surgeon can't remove all of the cancer. In some cases, drugs or radiation may be used to kill the cancer cells or slow their spread.

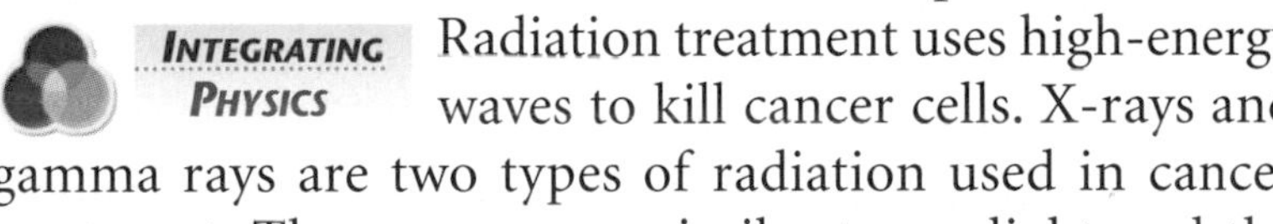

Radiation treatment uses high-energy waves to kill cancer cells. X-rays and gamma rays are two types of radiation used in cancer treatment. These waves are similar to sunlight and the

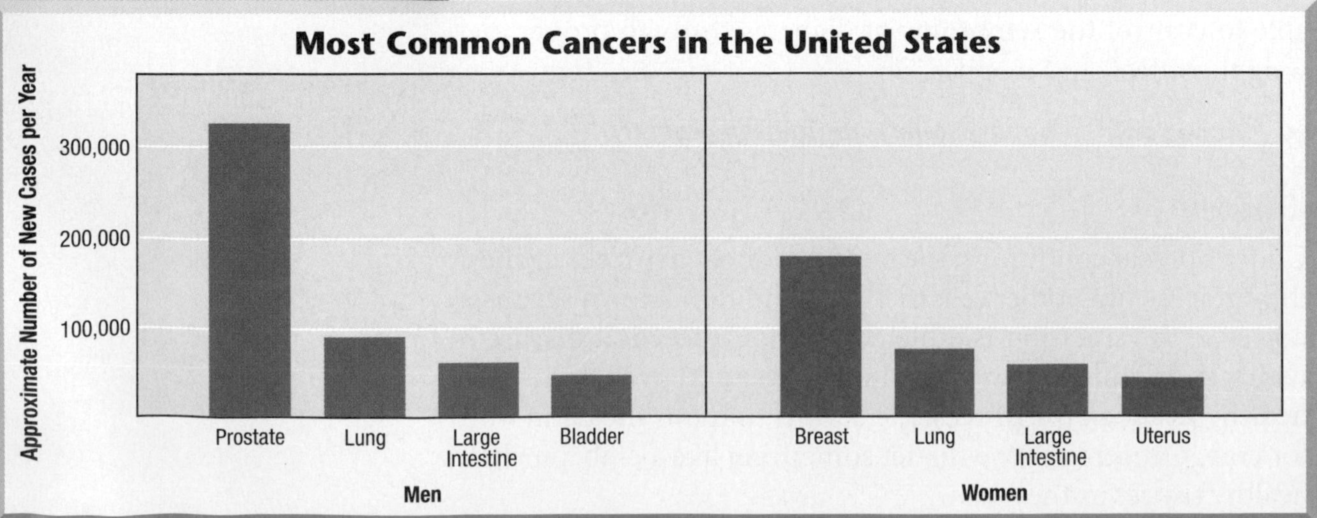

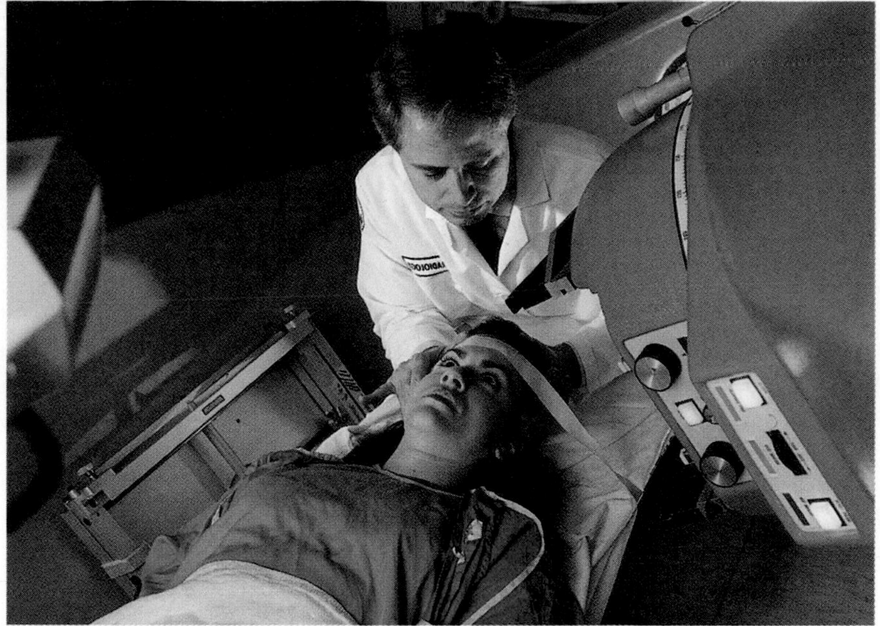

Figure 18 Radiation is one method that is used to treat cancer. The machine beams high-energy radiation at the tumor. This radiation kills cancer cells.

waves that make radios and microwave ovens work. However, X-rays and gamma rays have far more energy than sunlight, radio waves, or microwaves. When X-rays and gamma rays are aimed at tumors, they blast the cancer cells and kill them.

Cancer Prevention People can take steps to reduce their risk of developing cancer. For instance, they can avoid any form of tobacco, since tobacco and tobacco smoke contain carcinogens. Chewing tobacco and snuff contain carcinogens as well—they can cause cancers in the mouth. To prevent skin cancer, people can protect their skin from exposure to too much sunlight. A diet that is low in fat and includes plenty of fruits and vegetables can help people avoid some kinds of cancer, such as certain cancers of the digestive system.

Regular medical checkups are also important. Physicians or nurses may notice signs of cancer during a checkup. The earlier cancer is detected, the more likely it can be treated successfully.

Section 4 Review

1. What is an allergy? Describe how the body reacts to the presence of an allergen.
2. How does diabetes affect the level of glucose in the blood?
3. Describe how cancer cells harm the body.
4. **Thinking Critically Inferring** Doctors sometimes recommend that people with diabetes eat several small meals rather than three large ones. Why do you think doctors give this advice?

Science at Home

Explain to your family what allergies are and how allergens affect the body. Make a list of any substances your family members are allergic to. Use this list to determine whether certain allergies occur frequently in your family.

Skills Lab

Interpreting Data

Causes of DEATH, Then and Now

In this lab you'll compare data on the leading causes of death in 1900 and today.

Problem

How do the leading causes of death today compare with those of a hundred years ago?

Materials

colored pencils
calculator (optional)
compass
ruler
protractor

Procedure 

1. The data table on the next page shows the leading causes of death in the United States during two different years. Examine the data and note that two causes of death—accidents and suicides—are not diseases. The other causes are labeled either "I," indicating an infectious disease, or "NI," indicating a noninfectious disease.

Part 1 Comparing Specific Causes of Death

2. Look at the following causes of death in the data table: **(a)** pneumonia and influenza, **(b)** heart disease, **(c)** accidents, and **(d)** cancer. Construct a bar graph that compares the numbers of deaths from each of those causes in 1900 and today. Label the horizontal axis "Causes of Death." Label the vertical axis "Deaths per 100,000 People." Draw two bars side by side for each cause of death. Use a key to show which bars refer to 1900 and which refer to today.

Part 2 Comparing Infectious and Noninfectious Causes of Death

3. In this part of the lab, you will make two circle graphs showing three categories: infectious diseases, noninfectious diseases, and "other." You may want to review the information on creating circle graphs on page 272 of the Skills Handbook.

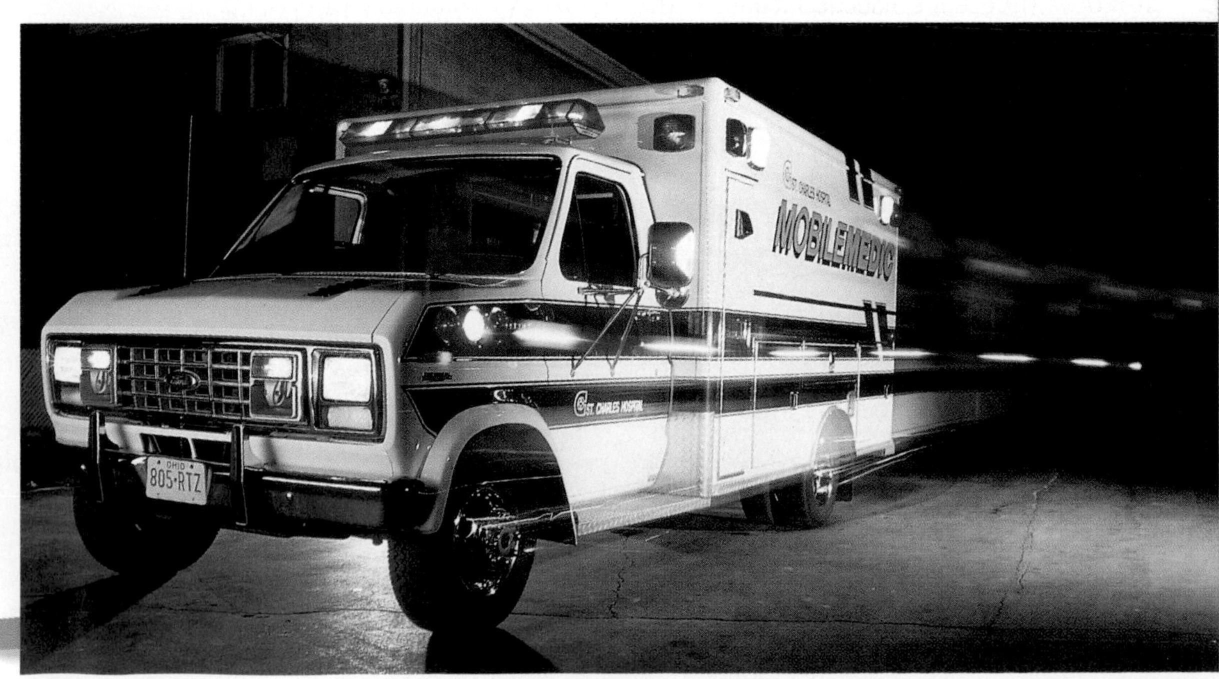

Ten Leading Causes of Death in the United States, 1900 and Today			
1900		**Today**	
Cause of Death	**Deaths per 100,000**	**Cause of Death**	**Deaths per 100,000**
Pneumonia, influenza (I)*	215	Heart disease (NI)	281
Tuberculosis (I)	185	Cancer (NI)	205
Diarrhea (I)	140	Stroke (NI)	59
Heart disease (NI)	130	Lung disease (NI)	39
Stroke (NI)	110	Accidents	35
Kidney disease (NI)	85	Pneumonia (I)	31
Accidents	75	Diabetes (NI)	22
Cancer (NI)	65	HIV Infection (I)	16
Senility (NI)	55	Suicide	12
Diphtheria (I)	40	Liver disease (NI)	10
Total	**1,100**	**Total**	**710**

*"I" indicates an infectious disease. "NI" indicates a noninfectious disease.

4. Start by grouping the data from 1900 into the three categories—infectious diseases, noninfectious diseases, and other causes. Find the total number of deaths for each category. Then find the size of the "pie slice" (the number of degrees) for each category, and construct your circle graph. To find the size of the infectious disease slice for 1900, for example, use the following formula:

$$\frac{\text{number of deaths from infectious diseases}}{\text{1,100 deaths total}} = \frac{x}{360°}$$

5. Calculate the percentage represented by each category using this formula:

$$\frac{\text{number of degrees in a slice}}{360°} \times 100 = \underline{\ ?\ }\ \%$$

6. Repeat Steps 4 and 5 using the data from today to make the second circle graph. What part of the formula in Step 4 do you need to change?

Analyze and Conclude

1. What kind of information did you learn just from examining the data table in Step 1?
2. According to your bar graph, which cause of death showed the greatest increase between 1900 and today? The greatest decrease?
3. In your circle graphs, which category decreased the most from 1900 to today? Which increased the most?
4. Suggest an explanation for the change in the number of deaths due to infectious diseases from 1900 to today.
5. **Think About It** How do graphs help you identify patterns and other information in data that you might otherwise overlook?

More to Explore

Write a question related to the data table that you have not yet answered. Then create a graph or work with the data in other ways to answer your question.

INTEGRATING ENVIRONMENTAL SCIENCE 

SECTION 5 Cancer and the Environment

DISCOVER

ACTIVITY

What Does Sunlight Do to the Beads?

1. Your teacher will give you beads that change color under certain conditions. Thread five beads on a pipe cleaner. Observe what the beads look like. Record your observations.
2. Wrap the pipe cleaner around your wrist. Go outdoors for one minute. Observe what happens to the beads.

Think It Over

Developing Hypotheses The ultraviolet light in sunlight causes the reaction you observed. Form a hypothesis about how you might prevent the beads from reacting as they did. How can you test your hypothesis?

GUIDE FOR READING

- **How can people's environments affect their chances of developing cancer?**

Reading Tip **As you read, write short summaries of the information under each heading.**

You are trapped in a place that is dark, tight, and so warm that it is hard to breathe. You climb upwards, carefully feeling for footholds as you inch along. The surfaces are so warm that your knees begin to feel hot as they scrape against the walls. Grimy dirt falls on your face, and you blink to keep it out of your eyes. This story sounds like a nightmare. But it was real life for the boys who worked as chimney sweeps.

Chimney Sweeps and Skin Cancer

In 1775, about one million people lived in London, England. Their homes were heated by coal fires. Because burning coal produces lots of grimy black soot, the soot had to be cleaned out of the chimneys regularly. Chimney sweeps did this job by crawling into the chimneys and scraping the soot off the walls.

Because chimney sweeps had to be small and thin enough to fit inside a chimney, most were boys rather than men. Since the work was dangerous, only boys who badly needed a job were willing to do it. Therefore, chimney sweeps were usually poor. Their homes did not have a water supply, and bathing was difficult. At the end of a hard day, chimney sweeps were covered with soot, but few washed it off.

A Link Between Soot and Cancer Percivall Pott, a London doctor, saw many chimney sweeps at his medical clinic. Pott noticed that the chimney sweeps often had soot ground deeply into their skin. He also observed that an alarmingly high number of chimney sweeps developed skin cancer. Pott hypothesized that something in soot caused the cancer. He recommended frequent bathing to reduce the risk of skin cancer. Many years later, scientists identified the carcinogens in soot. They are the same substances that make up the tar in cigarette smoke.

Carcinogens in the Environment Percivall Pott was one of the first scientists to understand that the environment can affect people's health. Cancer is one disease that can be caused by harmful environmental factors. **People's environments may contain carcinogens. To reduce the risk of cancer, the carcinogens need to be removed or people need to be protected from them.**

Pott's work led to present-day efforts to control environmental carcinogens. In the United States, the Environmental Protection Agency (EPA) is in charge of enforcing environmental laws. The EPA identifies environmental carcinogens and develops strategies for protecting people from them.

☑ ***Checkpoint*** *What did Pott recommend that chimney sweeps do in order to reduce their risk of skin cancer?*

Figure 19 Percivall Pott followed scientific procedure as he figured out the cause of skin cancer in chimney sweeps.

1770s—Observations
Percivall Pott notices that chimney sweeps have a high rate of cancer.

1775—Formation of hypothesis
Pott hypothesizes that something in soot causes skin cancer.

1775—Testing of hypothesis
Pott recommends that chimney sweeps bathe frequently, thus removing the cancer-causing soot.

1892—Result of testing
Evidence shows that chimney sweeps who bathe regularly develop skin cancer at a lower rate than sweeps who rarely bathe.

Early 1900s—Confirmation of hypothesis
Certain substances in soot are found to cause skin cancer in laboratory animals.

Figure 20 These asbestos ceiling panels were installed before people knew that asbestos can cause cancer. To protect the people who use the building, a worker is removing the panels.

Environmental Carcinogens Today

Scientists have identified many carcinogens found in the environment. Two important environmental carcinogens are asbestos and ultraviolet light.

Asbestos The mineral asbestos, which occurs in the form of fibers, is strong and does not burn. Because of these characteristics, asbestos was once widely used in materials such as roof shingles, brake linings, and insulation. However, scientists have since discovered that asbestos fibers can sometimes cause lung cancer when people inhale them repeatedly. Because of the dangers of asbestos, in 1989 the United States banned the manufacture and use of most asbestos products.

Ultraviolet Light As you learned in Chapter 2, skin cancer can result from overexposure to sunlight. Ultraviolet light is the part of sunlight that causes cancer. Fortunately, as sunlight travels from the sun to Earth, much of its ultraviolet light is absorbed high in the atmosphere, before it can reach Earth's surface. The gas ozone is the substance that absorbs most of the ultraviolet light.

In the 1970s and 1980s, scientists noticed that ozone levels in the upper atmosphere were decreasing. This decrease in ozone means that more ultraviolet light is reaching Earth's surface. At the same time, cases of skin cancer have been increasing. While the causes of the increase in skin cancer are complicated, some scientists believe that it is linked to the loss of ozone in the atmosphere.

Section 5 Review

1. How can the environment increase a person's risk for getting cancer?
2. What did Percivall Pott observe about the relationship between skin cancer and soot?
3. Why is asbestos dangerous?
4. **Thinking Critically Predicting** If ozone levels in the atmosphere decrease, what will probably happen to the number of skin cancers that develop each year? Explain.

Check Your Progress

CHAPTER PROJECT 6

Before your presentation, make your final revisions. If you are doing broadcasts, practice reading your scripts aloud. Experiment with different ways of bringing your series to a dramatic ending. Try to include answers to questions that might occur to your audience. For instance, are people around the patient at risk of invasion? If so, how can they defend themselves?

STUDY GUIDE

CHAPTER 6 REVIEW

Section 1 Infectious Diseases

Key Ideas

- Infectious diseases are caused by pathogens: bacteria, viruses, fungi, and protists.
- Pathogens that infect humans can come from another person, a contaminated object, an animal bite, or the environment.

Key Terms

pathogen infectious disease toxin

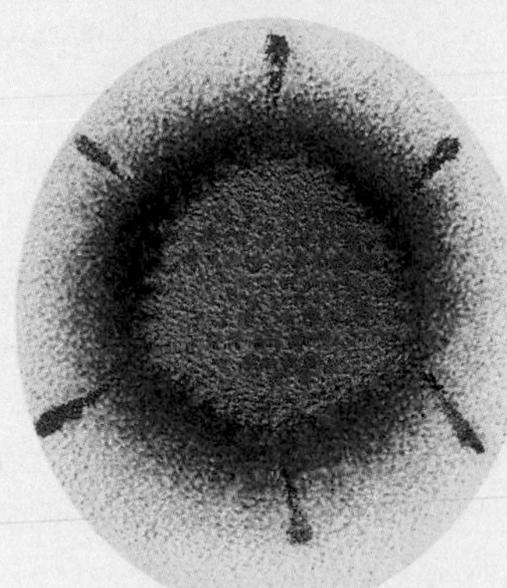

Section 2 The Body's Defenses

Key Ideas

- The body has three lines of defense against pathogens. The first consists of barriers such as the skin that keep pathogens out. The second line of defense consists of the inflammatory response.
- The immune system, which is the third line of defense, targets specific pathogens. T lymphocytes, or T cells, identify pathogens and distinguish one kind from another. B lymphocytes, or B cells, produce antibodies that destroy pathogens.
- AIDS is a disease of the immune system. HIV, the virus that causes AIDS, infects and destroys T cells, and therefore destroys the body's ability to fight disease.

Key Terms

inflammatory response
phagocyte
immune response
lymphocyte
T cell
antigen
B cell
antibody
AIDS

Section 3 Preventing Infectious Disease

Key Ideas

- In active immunity, a person's own immune system produces antibodies. A person can acquire active immunity by having the disease or by being vaccinated.
- In passive immunity, the antibodies come from a source other than the person's body.

Key Terms

immunity
active immunity
vaccination
vaccine
passive immunity
antibiotic

Section 4 Noninfectious Disease

Key Ideas

- An allergy is a disorder in which the immune system is overly sensitive to a foreign substance, called an allergen.
- In diabetes, the body does not produce enough insulin or can't use it properly.
- In cancer, cells multiply uncontrollably, destroying healthy tissues.

Key Terms

noninfectious disease
allergy
allergen
histamine
asthma
insulin
diabetes
tumor
carcinogen

Section 5 Cancer and the Environment

INTEGRATING ENVIRONMENTAL SCIENCE

Key Ideas

- In 1775, Percivall Pott hypothesized that soot caused cancer in chimney sweeps.
- Asbestos, which can cause lung cancer, and ultraviolet light, which can cause skin cancer, are environmental carcinogens.

ACTIVITY

USING THE INTERNET

www.science-explorer.phschool.com

CHAPTER 6 REVIEW

Reviewing Content

For more review of key concepts, see the Interactive Student Tutorial CD-ROM.

Multiple Choice

Choose the letter of the best answer.

1. Some pathogenic bacteria produce poisons called
   a. histamines.
   b. toxins.
   c. phagocytes.
   d. pathogens.
2. Antibodies are produced by
   a. phagocytes.
   b. B cells.
   c. T cells.
   d. pathogens.
3. Which disease is caused by HIV?
   a. diabetes
   b. flu
   c. AIDS
   d. tetanus
4. A carcinogen causes
   a. cancer.
   b. colds.
   c. allergies.
   d. food poisoning.
5. Ozone in the atmosphere absorbs
   a. allergens.
   b. T cells.
   c. soot.
   d. ultraviolet light.

True or False

If a statement is true, write true. If it is false, change the underlined word or words to make the statement true.

6. People can get Lyme disease from <u>animal bites</u>.
7. A <u>T cell</u> engulfs pathogens and destroys them.
8. Vaccination produces <u>active immunity</u>.
9. A <u>tumor</u> is a mass of cancer cells.
10. Percivall Pott linked soot to <u>stomach</u> cancer.

Checking Concepts

11. Explain why it is difficult for pathogens to get to a part of the body in which they can cause disease.
12. Why is it important not to share a drinking straw with someone else?
13. What is the relationship between antigens and antibodies?
14. How does diabetes harm the body?
15. Identify two factors that can make a person likely to develop cancer.
16. What evidence led Percivall Pott to hypothesize that something in soot causes cancer?
17. **Writing to Learn** A patient of Joseph Lister is angry because Lister has covered her surgery wound with a bandage dipped in carbolic acid. The acid stings and the bandage is uncomfortable. Write a conversation between Lister and the patient in which Lister explains why she shouldn't take the bandage off.

Thinking Visually

18. **Flowchart** Complete the flowchart, which shows what happens after tuberculosis bacteria begin to multiply in the lungs. (For more information on flowcharts, see the Skills Handbook.)

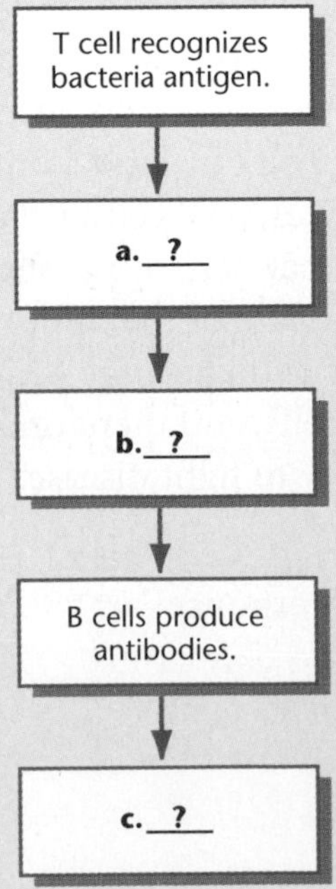

Applying Skills

A person had an illness caused by bacteria. The table shows how the person's temperature and antibody level changed over the course of the disease. Use the table to answer Questions 19–21.

Week	Body Temperature (°C)	Antibody Level
0	37	low
1	39.8	low
2	39	medium
3	37	high
4	37	medium
5	37	low

19. **Graphing** Make a line graph of the temperature data. Label the horizontal axis "Week Number" and the vertical axis "Body Temperature."
20. **Interpreting Data** During what week did the person's temperature return to normal?
21. **Drawing Conclusions** When do antibody levels start to rise? What effect do antibodies have on the illness? Explain.

Thinking Critically

22. **Applying Concepts** Can you catch a cold by sitting in a chilly draft? Explain.
23. **Comparing and Contrasting** Compare the functions of T cells and B cells.
24. **Relating Cause and Effect** Why can the immune system successfully fight most pathogens, but not HIV?
25. **Inferring** Why did Pott think that frequent bathing would reduce chimney sweeps' risk of developing cancer?

CHAPTER 6 REVIEW

Performance Assessment

CHAPTER PROJECT 6

Wrap Up

Present Your Project Now you can share your news series and enjoy those prepared by your classmates. Before your presentation, make sure any sound effects and props support the story.

Reflect and Record In your notebook, reflect on what you learned by using your imagination to explore a science topic. Did it help you to better understand how the body fights disease? What new information did you learn from presentations made by other groups? If you had your project to do over, what would you do differently?

Getting Involved

In Your School Ask the school nurse to describe the signs of a serious allergic reaction. Find out what you should do if someone appears to be having such a reaction. Also ask what provisions the school makes for helping students who know that they have severe allergic reactions—for example, to bee stings. Then prepare a booklet on dealing with serious allergies. Have the nurse check your rough draft for accuracy. Put the finished booklet in the school library or nurse's office.

CHAPTER 7

The Nervous System

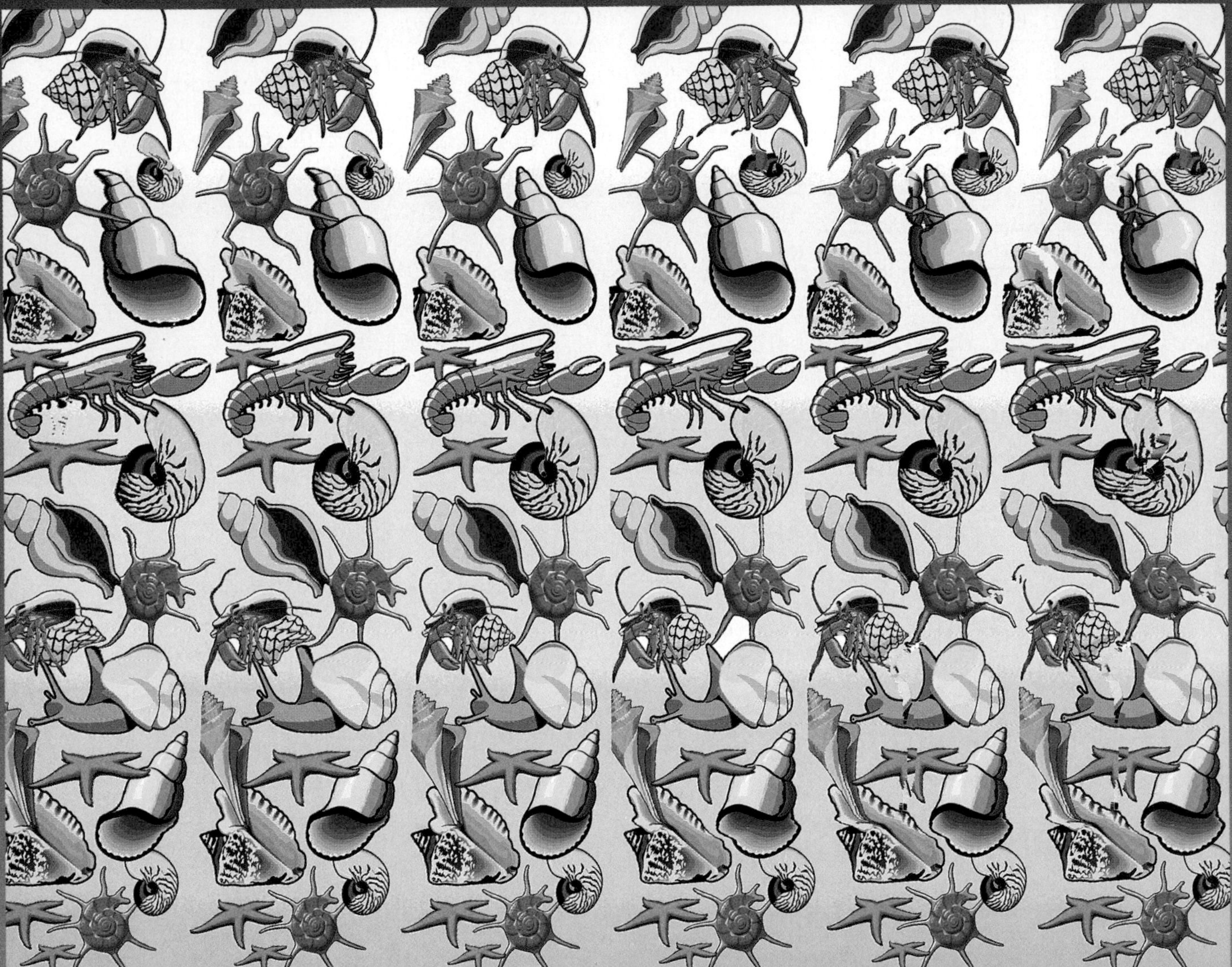

WHAT'S AHEAD

Section 1 How the Nervous System Works

Discover **How Simple Is a Simple Task?**
Skills Lab **Ready or Not!**

Section 2 Divisions of the Nervous System

Discover **How Does Your Knee React?**
Sharpen Your Skills **Controlling Variables**

Section 3 The Senses

Discover **What's in the Bag?**
Try This **Why Do You Need Two Eyes?**
Try This **Tick, Tick, Tick**
Sharpen Your Skills **Designing Experiments**

PROJECT 7

Tricks and Illusions

Can you be sure of what you see, hear, smell, taste, or touch? In this chapter, you'll learn how you experience your environment through your senses. You'll see how the senses send information to your nervous system and how your brain interprets the messages.

But things aren't always what they seem. For example, an optical illusion is a picture or other visual effect that tricks you into seeing something incorrectly. In this project, you'll investigate how your senses can sometimes be fooled by illusions.

Your Goal To set up a science fair booth to demonstrate how different people respond to one or more illusions.

To complete this project, you must

- try out a variety of illusions, including some that involve the senses of hearing or touch as well as sight
- select one or more illusions, and set up an experiment to monitor people's responses to the illusions
- learn why the illusions fool the senses
- follow the safety guidelines in Appendix A

Get Started In a small group, discuss optical illusions or other illusions that you know about. Look in books to learn about others. Try them out. Which illusions would make an interesting experiment? How could you set up such an experiment at a science fair?

Check Your Progress You'll be working on this project as you study this chapter. To keep your project on track, look for Check Your Progress boxes at the following points.

Section 2 Review, page 202: Plan the experiment you will perform.
Section 3 Review, page 211: Carry out your experiment.
Section 4 Review, page 220: Explain why the illusions trick the senses.

Wrap Up At the end of the chapter (page 223), be prepared to share your findings with your classmates. Then explain how your illusions work.

Now you see it. Now you don't. Sometimes your eyes can play tricks on you. The picture shows rows of seashells and sea animals. Or does it?

Stare at the picture for several seconds, as if it were far away. The picture should look slightly out of focus. After a while, does anything seem to pop out from the picture?

SECTION 4

Integrating Health

Alcohol and Other Drugs

Discover **How Can You Best Say No?**
Sharpen Your Skills **Communicating**
Real-World Lab **With Caffeine or Without?**

How the Nervous System Works

DISCOVER ACTIVITY

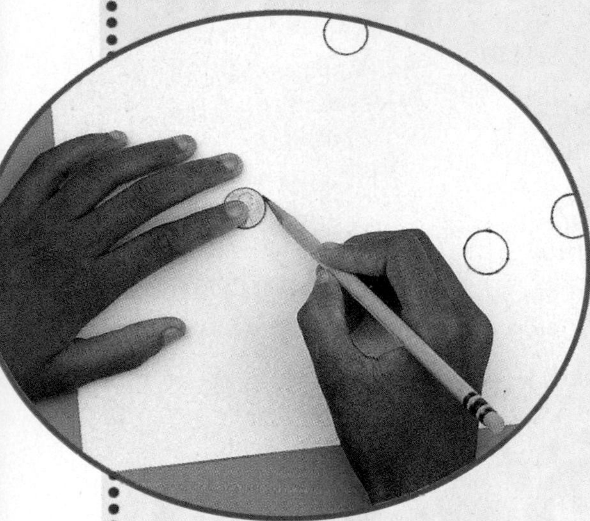

How Simple Is a Simple Task?

1. Trace the outline of a penny in twelve different places on a piece of paper.
2. Number the circles from 1 through 12. Write the numbers randomly, in no particular order.
3. Now pick up the penny again. Put it in each circle, one after another, in numerical order, beginning with 1 and ending with 12.

Think it Over

Inferring Make a list of all the sense organs, muscle movements, and thought processes in this activity. Compare your list with your classmates' lists. What organ system coordinated all the different processes involved in this task?

GUIDE FOR READING

- **What are the functions of the nervous system?**
- **What are the three types of neurons and how do they interact?**

Reading Tip **Before you read, preview *Exploring the Path of a Nerve Impulse* on page 193. List any unfamiliar terms. Then, as you read, write a definition for each term.**

The drums roll, and the crowd suddenly becomes silent. The people in the audience hold their breaths as the tightrope walker begins his long and dangerous journey across the wire. High above the circus floor, he inches along, slowly but steadily. One wrong movement could mean disaster.

To keep from slipping, tightrope performers need excellent coordination and a keen sense of balance. In addition, they must remember what they have learned from years of practice.

Even though you aren't a tightrope walker, you too need coordination, a sense of balance, memory, and the ability to learn. Your nervous system carries out all those functions. The nervous system consists of the brain, spinal cord, and nerves that run throughout the body. It also includes sense organs such as the eyes and ears.

Jobs of the Nervous System

Figure 1 The sparkling water is a stimulus. This toddler responds by thrusting her hands into the water and splashing.

The Internet lets people gather information from anywhere in the world with the click of a button. Like the Internet, your nervous system is a communications network. Your nervous system is much more efficient, however.

The nervous system receives information about what is happening both inside and outside your body. It also directs the way in which your body responds to this information. In addition, your nervous system helps maintain homeostasis. Without your nervous system, you could not move, think, feel pain, or taste a spicy taco.

Receiving Information Because of your nervous system, you are aware of what is happening in the environment around you. For example, you know that a soccer ball is zooming toward you, that the wind is blowing, or that a friend is telling a funny joke. Your nervous system also checks conditions inside your body, such as the level of glucose in your blood.

Responding to Information Any change or signal in the environment that can make an organism react is a **stimulus** (STIM yoo lus)(plural *stimuli*). A zooming soccer ball is a stimulus. After your nervous system analyzes the stimulus, it causes a response. A **response** is what your body does in reaction to a stimulus—you kick the ball toward the goal.

Some nervous system responses, such as kicking a ball, are voluntary, or under your control. However, many processes necessary for life, such as heartbeat rate, are controlled by involuntary actions of the nervous system.

Maintaining Homeostasis The nervous system helps maintain homeostasis by directing the body to respond appropriately to the information it receives. For example, when you are hungry, your nervous system directs you to eat. This action maintains homeostasis by supplying your body with nutrients and energy it needs.

☑ *Checkpoint* *What is a stimulus?*

The Neuron—A Message-Carrying Cell

The cells that carry information through your nervous system are called **neurons** (NOO rahnz), or nerve cells. The message that a neuron carries is called a **nerve impulse.** The structure of a neuron enables it to carry nerve impulses.

The Structure of a Neuron A neuron has a large cell body that contains the nucleus. The cell body has threadlike extensions. One kind of extension, a **dendrite,** carries impulses toward the cell body. An **axon** carries impulses away from the cell body. Nerve impulses begin in a dendrite, move toward the cell body, and then move down the axon. A neuron can have many dendrites, but it has only one axon. An axon, however, can have more than one tip, so the impulse can go to more than one other cell.

Axons and dendrites are sometimes called nerve fibers. Nerve fibers are often arranged in parallel bundles covered with connective tissue, something like a package of uncooked spaghetti wrapped in cellophane. A bundle of nerve fibers is called a **nerve.**

Kinds of Neurons Different kinds of neurons perform different functions. **Three kinds of neurons are found in the body—sensory neurons, interneurons, and motor neurons. Together they make up a chain of nerve cells that carry an impulse through the nervous system.** *Exploring the Path of a Nerve Impulse* shows how these three kinds of neurons work together.

A **sensory neuron** picks up stimuli from the internal or external environment and converts each stimulus into a nerve impulse. The impulse travels along the sensory neuron until it reaches an interneuron, usually in the brain or spinal cord. An **interneuron** is a neuron that carries nerve impulses from one neuron to another. Some interneurons pass impulses from sensory neurons to motor neurons. A **motor neuron** sends an impulse to a muscle, and the muscle contracts in response.

☑ *Checkpoint* *What is the function of an axon?*

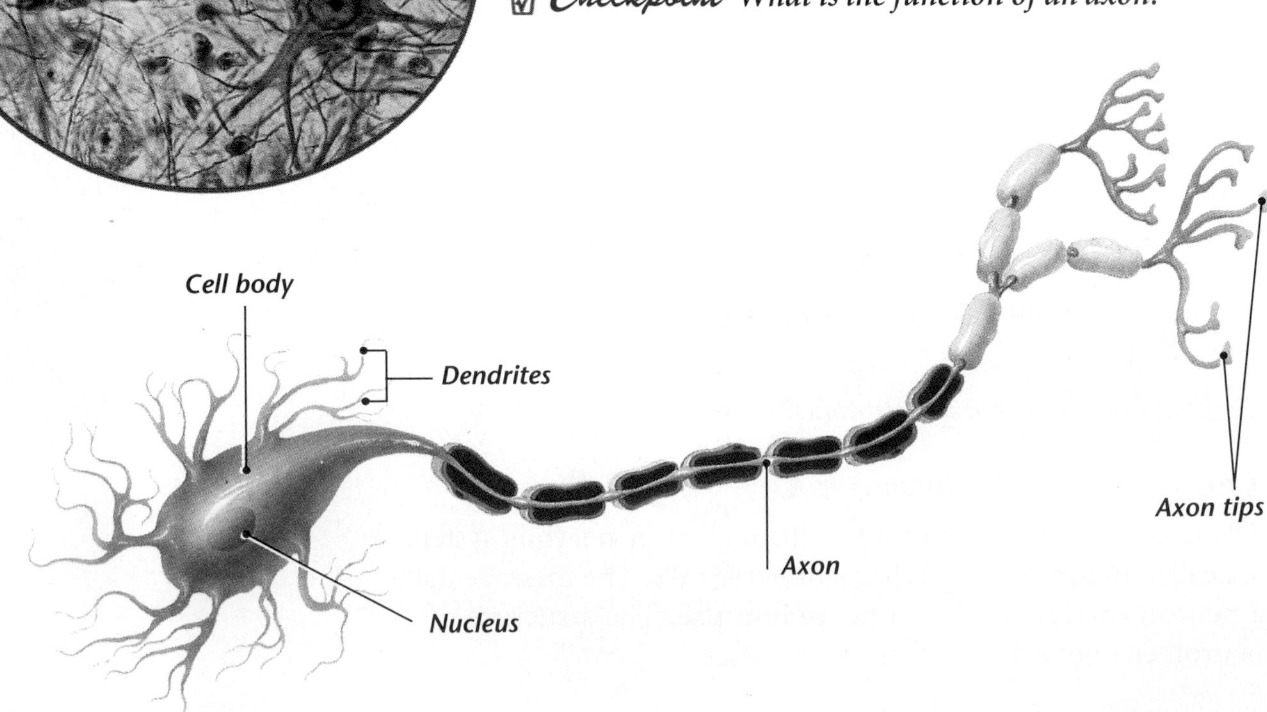

Figure 2 A neuron, or nerve cell, has one axon and many dendrites that extend from the cell body. The dendrites carry a nerve message toward the cell body, and the axon carries the message away from the cell body. ***Applying Concepts*** *How many axons can a neuron have?*

EXPLORING *the Path of a Nerve Impulse*

When you hear the phone ring, you pick it up to answer it. Many sensory neurons, interneurons, and motor neurons are involved in this action.

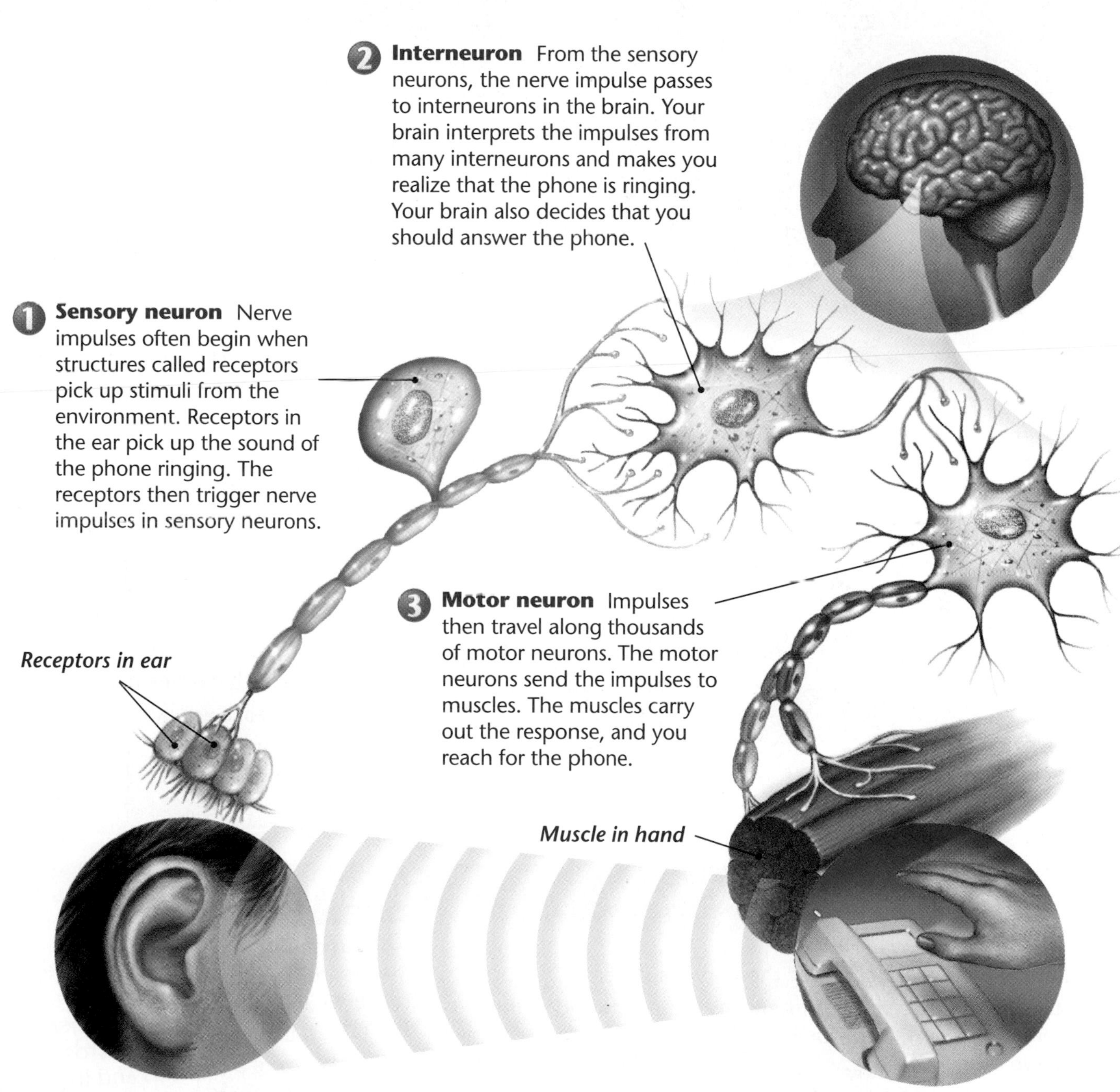

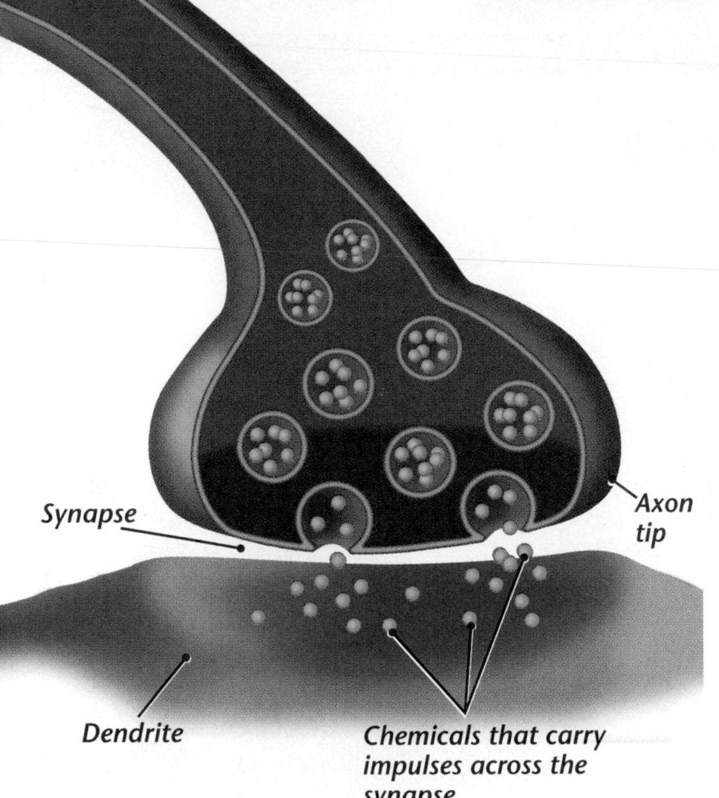

Figure 3 A synapse is the tiny space between the axon of one neuron and the dendrite of another neuron. When a nerve impulse reaches the end of an axon, chemicals are released into the synapse. These chemicals enable the nerve impulse to cross the synapse.

How a Nerve Impulse Travels

Every day of your life, millions of nerve impulses travel through your nervous system. Each of those nerve impulses begins in the dendrites of a neuron. The impulse moves rapidly toward the neuron's cell body and then down the axon until it reaches the axon tip. A nerve impulse travels along the neuron in the form of electrical and chemical signals. Nerve impulses can travel as fast as 120 meters per second!

There is a tiny space called a **synapse** (SIN aps) between each axon tip and the next structure. Sometimes this next structure is a dendrite of another neuron. Other times the next structure can be a muscle or a cell in another organ, such as a sweat gland. Figure 3 illustrates a synapse between the axon of one neuron and a dendrite of another neuron.

In order for a nerve impulse to be carried along, it must cross the gap between the axon and the next structure. The axon tips release chemicals that enable the impulse to cross the synapse. If that didn't happen, the impulse would stop at the end of the axon. The impulse would not be passed from sensory neuron, to interneuron, to motor neuron. Nerve impulses would never reach your brain or make your muscles contract.

You can think of a synapse as a river, and an axon as a road that leads up to the riverbank. The nerve impulse is like a car traveling on the road. To get to the other side, the car has to cross the river. The car gets on a ferry boat, which carries it across the river. The chemicals that the axon tips release are like a ferry that carries the nerve impulse across the synapse.

Section 1 Review

1. Describe three functions of the nervous system.
2. Identify the three kinds of neurons that are found in the nervous system. Describe how they interact to carry nerve impulses.
3. How does a nerve impulse cross a synapse?
4. **Thinking Critically Predicting** What would happen to a nerve impulse carried by an interneuron if the tips of the interneuron's axon were damaged? Explain.

Science at Home

During dinner, ask a family member to pass the salt and pepper to you. Observe what your family member then does. Explain that the words you spoke were a stimulus and that the family member's reaction was a response. Discuss other examples of stimuli and responses with your family.

Designing Experiments

Ready or Not

Do people carry out tasks better at certain times of day? In this lab, you will design an experiment to answer this question.

Problem

Do people's reaction times vary at different times of day?

Materials

meter stick

Design a Plan

Part 1 Observing a Response to a Stimulus

1. Have your partner hold a meter stick with the zero end about 50 cm above a table.
2. Get ready to catch the meter stick by positioning the top of your thumb and forefinger just at the zero position as shown in the photograph.
3. Your partner should drop the meter stick without any warning. Using your thumb and forefinger only (no other part of your hand), catch the meter stick as soon as you can. Record the distance in centimeters that the meter stick fell. This distance is a measure of your reaction time.

Part 2 Design Your Experiment

4. With your partner, discuss how you can use the activity from Part 1 to find out whether people's reaction times vary at different times of day. Be sure to consider the questions below. Then write up your experimental plan.
   - What hypothesis will you test?
   - What variables do you need to control?
   - How many people will you test? How many times will you test each person?
5. Submit your plan for your teacher's review. Make any changes your teacher recommends. Create a data table to record your results. Then perform your experiment.

Analyze and Conclude

1. In this lab, what is the stimulus? What is the response? Is this response voluntary or involuntary? Explain.
2. Why can you use the distance on the meter stick as a measure of reaction time?
3. Based on your results, do people's reaction times vary at different times of day? Explain.
4. **Think About It** In Part 2, why is it important to control all variables except the time of day?

More to Explore

Do you think people can do arithmetic problems more quickly and accurately at certain times of the day? Design an experiment to investigate this question. Obtain your teacher's permission before trying your experiment.

Skills Lab

Divisions of the Nervous System

Discover Activity

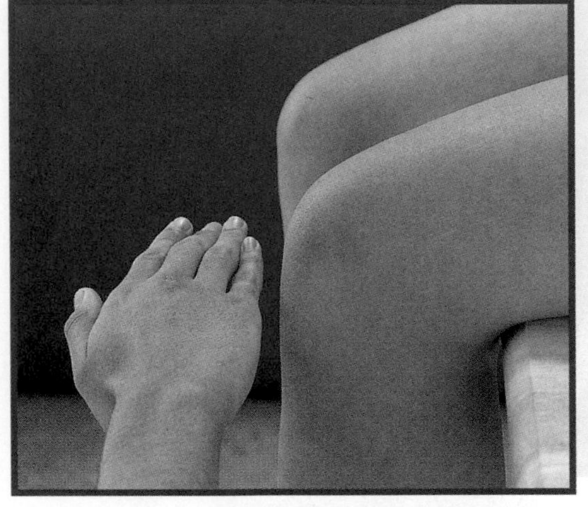

How Does Your Knee React?

1. Sit on a table or counter so that your legs dangle freely. Your feet should not touch the floor.
2. Have your partner use the side of his or her hand to *gently* tap one of your knees just below the kneecap. Observe what happens to your leg. Note whether you have any control over your reaction.
3. Change places with your partner. Repeat Steps 1 and 2.

Think It Over

Inferring When might it be an advantage for your body to react very quickly and without your conscious control?

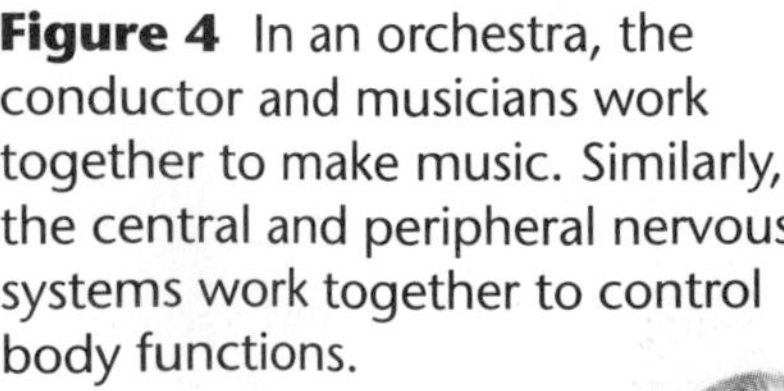

GUIDE FOR READING

- **What is the function of the central nervous system?**
- **What functions does the peripheral nervous system perform?**
- **What is a reflex?**

Reading Tip **As you read, make a list of main ideas and supporting details about the central and peripheral nervous systems.**

A concert is about to begin. The conductor gives the signal, and the musicians begin to play. The sound of music, beautiful and stirring, fills the air.

To play music in harmony, an orchestra needs both musicians and a conductor. The musicians play the music, and the conductor directs the musicians and coordinates their playing.

Similarly, your nervous system has two divisions that work together—the central nervous system and the peripheral nervous system. The **central nervous system** consists of the brain and spinal cord. The **peripheral nervous system** consists of all the nerves located outside of the central nervous system. The central nervous system is like a conductor. The nerves of the peripheral nervous system are like the musicians.

Figure 4 In an orchestra, the conductor and musicians work together to make music. Similarly, the central and peripheral nervous systems work together to control body functions.

The Central Nervous System

You can see the central and peripheral nervous systems in Figure 5. **The central nervous system is the control center of the body.** All information about what is happening in the world inside or outside your body is brought to the central nervous system. The **brain,** located in the skull, is the part of the central nervous system that controls most functions in the body. The **spinal cord** is the thick column of nerve tissue that links the brain to most of the nerves in the peripheral nervous system.

Most impulses from the peripheral nervous system travel through the spinal cord to get to the brain. Your brain then directs a response. The response usually travels from the brain, through the spinal cord, and then to the peripheral nervous system.

For example, here is what happens when you reach under the sofa to find a lost quarter. Your fingers move over the floor, searching for the quarter. When your fingers finally touch the quarter, the stimulus of the touch triggers nerve impulses in sensory neurons in your fingers. These impulses travel through nerves of the peripheral nervous system to your spinal cord. Then the impulses race up to your brain. Your brain interprets the impulses, telling you that you've found the quarter. Your brain starts nerve impulses that move down the spinal cord. From the spinal cord, the impulses travel through motor nerves in your arm and hand. The impulses in the motor neurons cause your fingers to grasp the quarter.

☑ ***Checkpoint*** *What does the spinal cord do?*

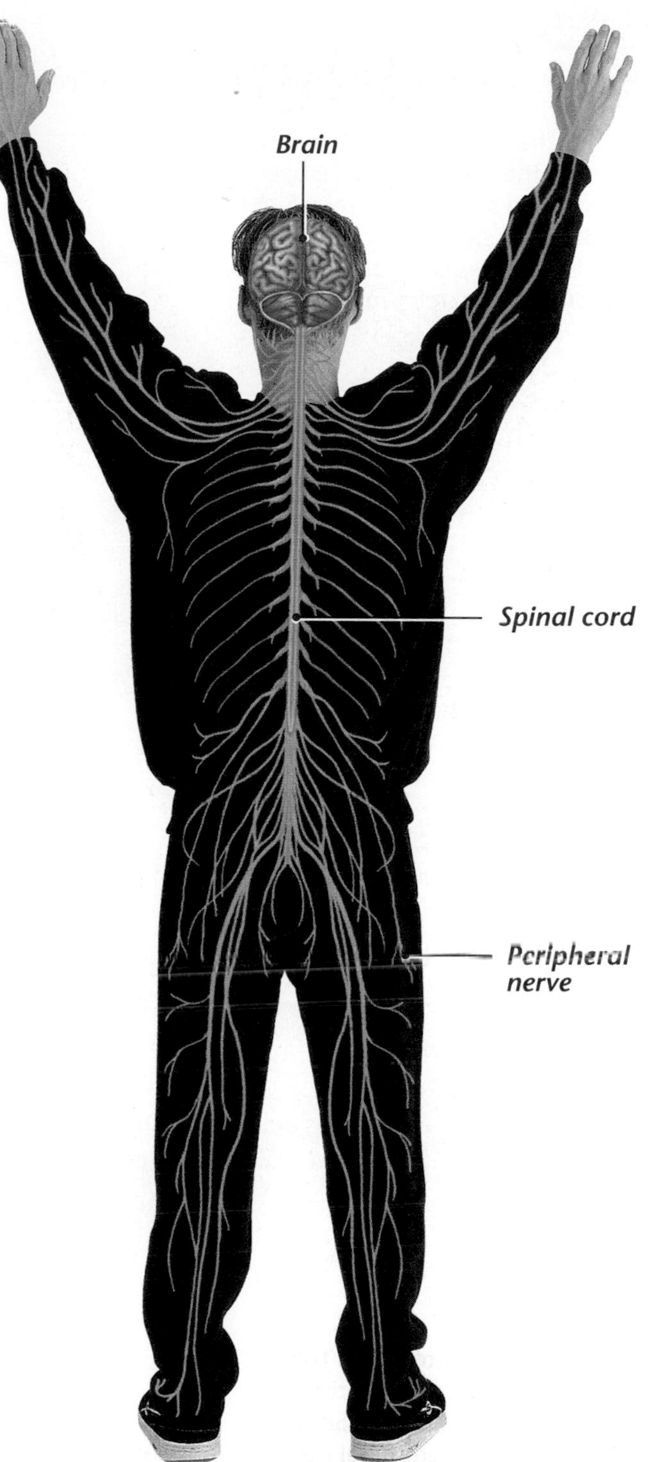

Figure 5 The central nervous system consists of the brain and spinal cord. The peripheral nervous system contains all the nerves that branch out from the brain and spinal cord.

The Brain

Your brain contains about 100 billion neurons, all of which are interneurons. Each of those neurons may receive messages from up to 10,000 other neurons and may send messages to about 1,000 more! Three layers of connective tissue cover the brain. The space between the outermost layer and the middle layer is filled with a watery fluid. The skull, layers of connective tissue, and fluid all help protect the brain from injury.

Figure 6 The cerebrum, cerebellum, and brainstem are the three main parts of the human brain. The two halves of the cerebrum have been separated to show the cerebellum and the brainstem.
Applying Concepts *What are three functions of the cerebrum?*

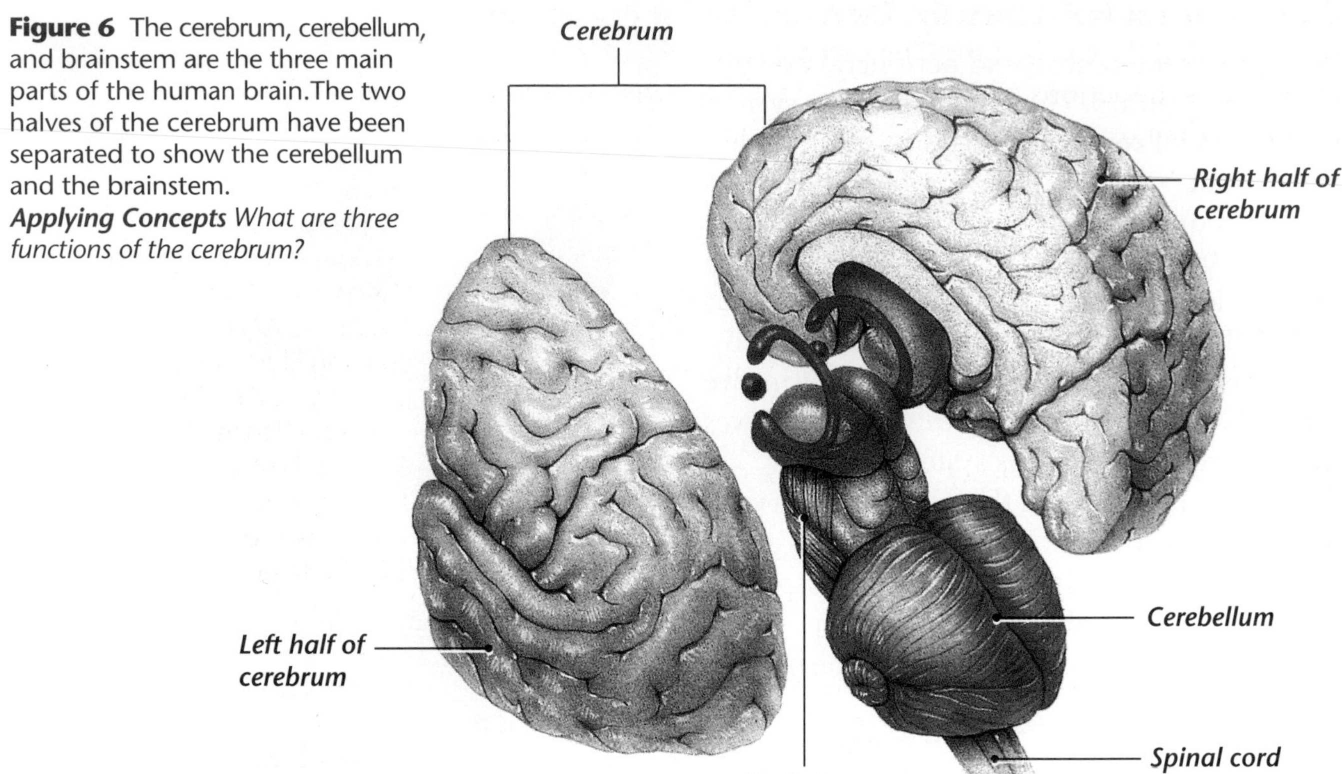

Controlling Variables

ACTIVITY

Are people better able to memorize a list of words in a quiet room or in a room where soft music is playing? First write a hypothesis. Then design an experiment to test your hypothesis. Make sure that all variables are controlled except the one you are testing—music versus quiet. Check your procedure with your teacher. Then perform your experiment. Analyze your results to see whether they support your hypothesis.

Cerebrum There are three main regions of the brain. These are the cerebrum, the cerebellum, and the brainstem. Find each in Figure 6. The largest part of the brain is called the cerebrum. The **cerebrum** (suh REE brum) interprets input from the senses, controls the movement of skeletal muscles, and carries out complex mental processes such as learning, remembering, and making judgments. Because of your cerebrum, you can find the comics in a newspaper and locate your favorite comic strip on the page. Your cerebrum also enables you to read the comic strip and laugh at its funny characters.

Notice in Figure 6 that the cerebrum is divided into a right and a left half. The two halves have somewhat different functions. The right half of the cerebrum contains the neurons that send impulses to the skeletal muscles on the left side of the body. In contrast, the left half of the cerebrum controls the right side of the body. When you reach with your right hand for a pencil, the messages that tell you to do so come from the left half of your cerebrum.

In addition, each half of the cerebrum controls slightly different kinds of mental activity. The right half of the cerebrum is usually associated with creativity and artistic ability. The left half, in contrast, is associated with mathematical skills, speech, writing, and logical thinking.

Cerebellum and Brainstem The second largest part of your brain is called the cerebellum. The **cerebellum** (sehr uh BEL um) coordinates the actions of your muscles and helps you keep your balance. When you put one foot in front of the other as you walk, the motor neuron impulses that tell your feet to move start in your cerebrum. However, your cerebellum gives you the muscular coordination and sense of balance that keep you from falling down.

The **brainstem,** which lies between the cerebellum and spinal cord, controls your body's involuntary actions—those that occur automatically. For example, the brainstem regulates your breathing and helps control your heartbeat.

☑ *Checkpoint* *What part of your brain coordinates the contractions of your muscles?*

The Spinal Cord

Run your fingers down the center of your back to feel the bones of the vertebral column. The vertebral column surrounds and protects the spinal cord. The spinal cord is the link between your brain and the peripheral nervous system. The layers of connective tissue that surround and protect the brain also cover the spinal cord. In addition, like the brain, the spinal cord is further protected by a watery fluid.

Visual Arts CONNECTION

Some artists deliberately create works of art that can be interpreted by the brain in more than one way. The Dutch artist M. C. Escher (1898–1972) delighted in creating illustrations that played visual tricks on his viewers. Glance quickly at Escher's illustration in Figure 7. Then look at it again. Do you see the two different scenes in this single picture?

In Your Journal

Which scene did you see when you first looked at Figure 7? Did your brain interpret the picture differently the second time? Write a description of the visual trick that Escher has played in this illustration.

Figure 7 This illustration, by the Dutch artist M. C. Escher, is called "Day and Night." Escher created this picture in 1938.

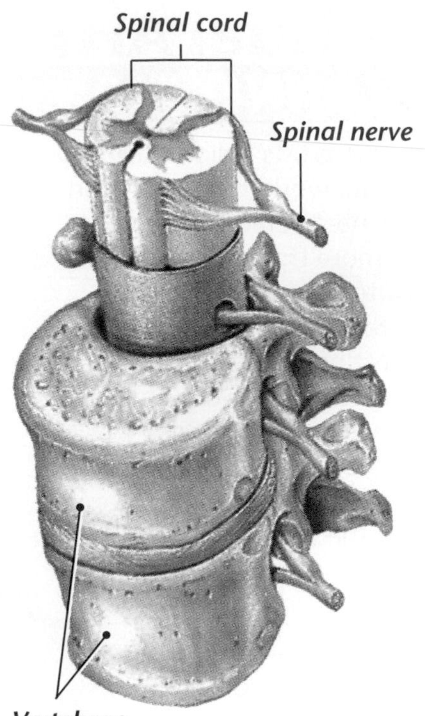

Figure 8 The spinal nerves, which connect to the spinal cord, emerge from spaces between the vertebrae. Each spinal nerve consists of both sensory and motor neurons.

The Peripheral Nervous System

The second division of the nervous system is the peripheral nervous system. **The peripheral nervous system consists of a network of nerves that branch out from the central nervous system and connect it to the rest of your body.** A total of 43 pairs of nerves make up the peripheral nervous system. Twelve pairs originate in the brain. The other 31 pairs—the spinal nerves—begin in the spinal cord. One nerve in each pair goes to the left side of the body, and the other goes to the right. As you can see in Figure 8, spinal nerves leave the spinal cord through spaces between the vertebrae.

Two-Way Traffic A spinal nerve is a little bit like a two-lane highway. Impulses travel on a spinal nerve in two directions—both to and from the central nervous system. Each spinal nerve contains axons of both sensory and motor neurons. The sensory neurons carry impulses from the body to the central nervous system. The motor neurons carry impulses in the opposite direction—from the central nervous system to the body.

Somatic and Autonomic Systems The nerves of the peripheral nervous system can be divided into two groups, called the somatic (soh MAT ik) and autonomic (awt uh NAHM ik) nervous systems. The nerves of the **somatic nervous system** control voluntary actions such as using a fork or tying your shoelaces. In contrast, nerves of the **autonomic nervous system** control involuntary actions. For example, the autonomic nervous system regulates the contractions of the smooth muscles that adjust the diameter of blood vessels.

Figure 9 The somatic nervous system controls voluntary actions. The girl's somatic nervous system is at work as she shapes the pot with her hands. ***Classifying*** *What part of the peripheral nervous system helps regulate the girl's heartbeat?*

Reflexes

Imagine that you are watching an adventure movie. The movie is so thrilling that you don't notice a fly circling above your head. When the fly zooms right in front of your eyes, however, your eyelids immediately blink shut. You didn't decide to close your eyes. The blink, which is an example of a **reflex,** happened automatically. **A reflex is an automatic response that occurs very rapidly and without conscious control.** If you did the Discover activity, you saw another example of a reflex.

As you have learned, the contraction of skeletal muscles is usually controlled by the brain. However, in some reflex actions, skeletal muscles contract with the involvement of the spinal cord only—not the brain. Figure 10 shows the reflex action that occurs when you touch a sharp object, such as a cactus thorn. When your finger touches the object, sensory neurons send impulses to the spinal cord. The impulses then pass to interneurons in the spinal cord. From there the impulses pass directly to motor neurons in your arm and hand. The muscles then contract, and your hand jerks up and away from the sharp object. By removing your hand quickly, this reflex protects you from getting badly cut.

At the same time that some nerve impulses make your arm muscles contract, other nerve impulses travel up your spinal cord and to your brain. When these impulses reach your brain, your brain interprets them. You then feel a sharp pain in your finger.

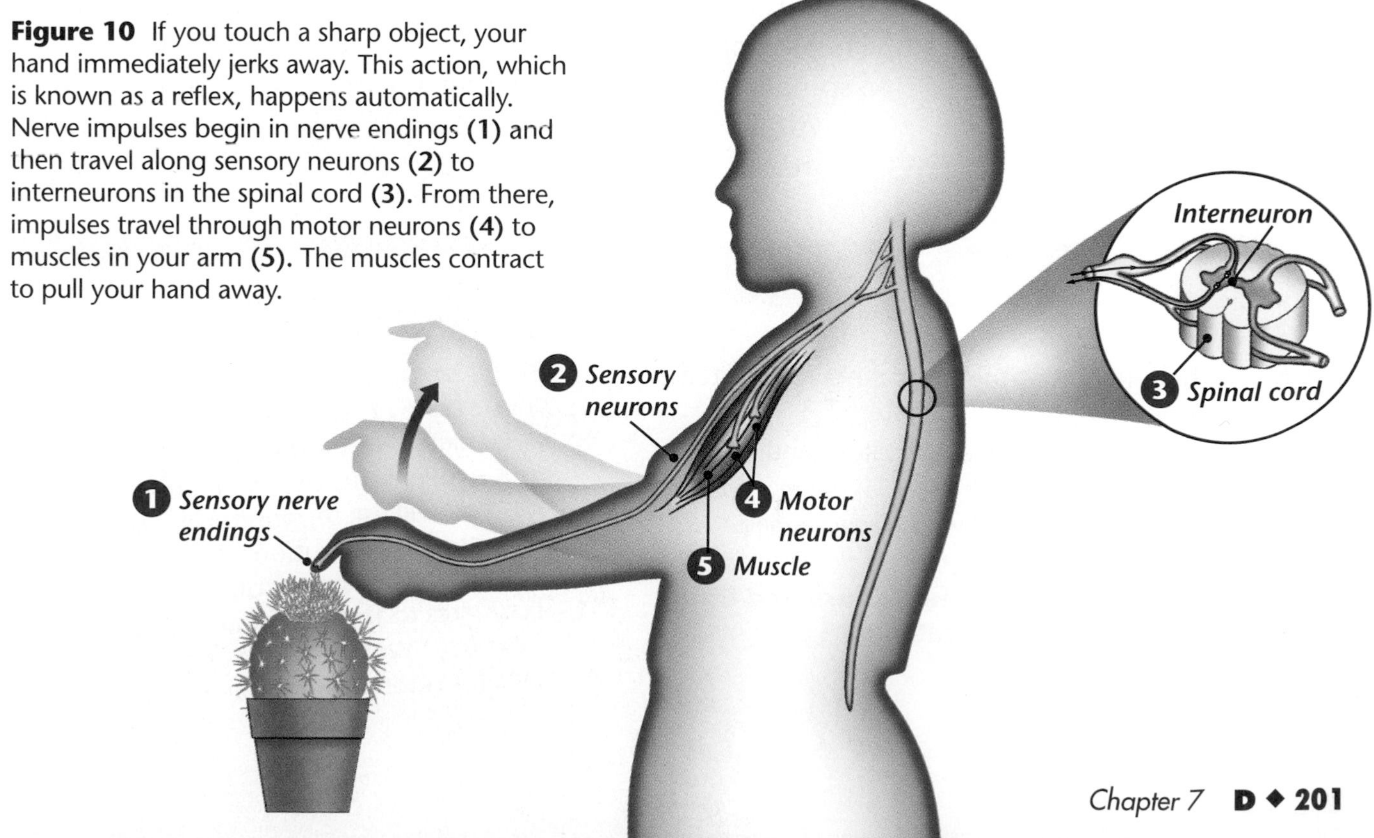

Figure 10 If you touch a sharp object, your hand immediately jerks away. This action, which is known as a reflex, happens automatically. Nerve impulses begin in nerve endings **(1)** and then travel along sensory neurons **(2)** to interneurons in the spinal cord **(3)**. From there, impulses travel through motor neurons **(4)** to muscles in your arm **(5)**. The muscles contract to pull your hand away.

Figure 11 By wearing a helmet, this skateboarder is helping to prevent injury to his brain.

It takes longer for the pain impulses to get to the brain and be interpreted than it does for the reflex action to occur. By the time you feel the pain, you have already moved your hand away from the sharp object.

Safety and the Nervous System

INTEGRATING HEALTH Like other parts of the body, the nervous system can suffer injuries that interfere with its functioning. Concussions and spinal cord injuries are two ways in which the nervous system can be damaged.

A **concussion** is a bruiselike injury of the brain. A concussion occurs when soft tissue of the cerebrum bumps against the skull. Concussions can happen during a hard fall, an automobile accident, or contact sports such as football. With most concussions, you may have a headache for a short time, but the injured tissue heals by itself. However, if you black out, experience confusion, or feel drowsy after the injury, you should be checked by a doctor. To decrease your chances of getting a brain injury, wear a helmet when bicycling, skating, or performing other activities in which you risk bumping your head.

Spinal cord injuries occur when the spinal cord is cut or crushed. When the spinal cord is cut, all the nerve axons in that region are split, so impulses cannot pass through them. This type of injury results in paralysis, which is the loss of movement in some part of the body. Car crashes are the most common cause of spinal cord injuries. You can help protect yourself from a spinal cord injury by wearing a seatbelt when you travel in a car. Also, when you swim, make sure the water is deep enough before you dive in.

Section 2 Review

1. What is the function of the central nervous system? Which organs are part of this system?
2. What is the peripheral nervous system and what are its functions?
3. Explain what a reflex is. How do reflexes help protect the body from injury?
4. **Thinking Critically Relating Cause and Effect** What symptoms might indicate that a person's cerebellum has been injured?

CHAPTER PROJECT 7

Check Your Progress

At this point, you should have chosen one or more illusions to investigate. Now write up the plan for your experiment. List some questions that you will ask to monitor people's responses to the illusions. (*Hint:* Try out your illusions and your questions on classmates to find out what responses to expect.) With your classmates, make plans for setting up the science fair.

Should People Be Required to Wear Bicycle Helmets?

Bicycle riding is an enjoyable activity. But unfortunately, many bicycle riders become injured while riding. Each year about 150,000 children alone are treated in hospitals for head injuries that occur while bicycling. Head injuries can affect everything your brain does—thinking, remembering, seeing, and being able to move. Experts estimate that as many as 85 percent of bicycle-related head injuries could be prevented if all bicyclists wore helmets. But only about 18 percent of bicyclists wear helmets. What is the best way to get bicycle riders to protect themselves from head injury?

The Issues

Should Laws Require the Use of Bicycle Helmets? About 15 states have passed laws requiring bicycle riders to wear helmets. Nearly all of these laws, however, apply only to children. Some supporters of bicycle laws want to see the laws extended to all bicycle riders. Supporters point out that laws increase helmet use by 47 percent. In contrast, educational programs without laws to back them up increase bicycle helmet use by only 18 percent.

What Are the Drawbacks of Helmet Laws? Opponents of helmet laws believe it is up to the individual, not the government, to decide whether or not to wear a helmet. They say it is not the role of the government to stop people from taking risks. Rather than making people who don't wear helmets pay fines, governments should educate people about the benefits of helmets. Car drivers should also be educated about safe driving procedures near bicycles.

Are There Alternatives to Helmet Laws? Instead of laws requiring people to wear helmets, some communities and organizations have set up educational programs that teach about the advantages of helmets. Effective programs teach about the dangers of head injuries and how helmets protect riders. In addition, they point out that safe helmets can be lightweight and comfortable. Effective education programs, though, can be expensive. They also need to reach a wide audience, including children, teens, and adults.

You Decide

1. **Identify the Problem**
   In your own words, explain the issues concerning laws requiring people to wear bicycle helmets.
2. **Analyze the Options**
   List two different plans for increasing helmet use by bicycle riders. List at least one advantage and one drawback of each plan.
3. **Find a Solution**
   You are a member of the city government hoping to increase helmet use. Write a speech outlining your position for either a helmet law or an alternative plan. Support your position.

SECTION 3

The Senses

Discover

What's in the Bag?

1. Your teacher will give you a paper bag that contains several objects. Your challenge is to use only your sense of touch to identify each object. You will not look inside the bag.
2. Put your hand in the bag and carefully touch each object. Observe the shape of each object. Note whether its surface is rough or smooth. Also note other characteristics, such as its size, what it seems to be made of, and whether it can be bent.
3. After you have finished touching each object, write your observations on a sheet of paper. Then write your inference about what each object is.

Think It Over

Observing What could you determine about each object without looking at it? What could you not determine?

GUIDE FOR READING

- **What overall function do the senses perform?**
- **How do your eyes enable you to see?**
- **How do you hear?**

Reading Tip **As you read, write an outline of this section. Use the headings in the section as the main topics in the outline.**

You waited in line to get on the ride, and now it's about to begin. You grip the bars as the ride suddenly starts to move. Before you know it, you are lifted high above the ground and you feel the air whipping by. All you see is a dizzy blur.

You can thrill to the speed of amusement park rides because of your senses. **Each of your major senses—vision, hearing, balance, smell, taste, and touch—picks up a specific type of information about your environment. The sense organs change that information into nerve impulses and send the impulses to your brain.** Your brain then interprets the information. Because of the way in which your senses and brain work together, you learn a great deal about your environment.

Figure 12 Riders and bright lights whizzing by—that's what you see when you watch this amusement park ride.

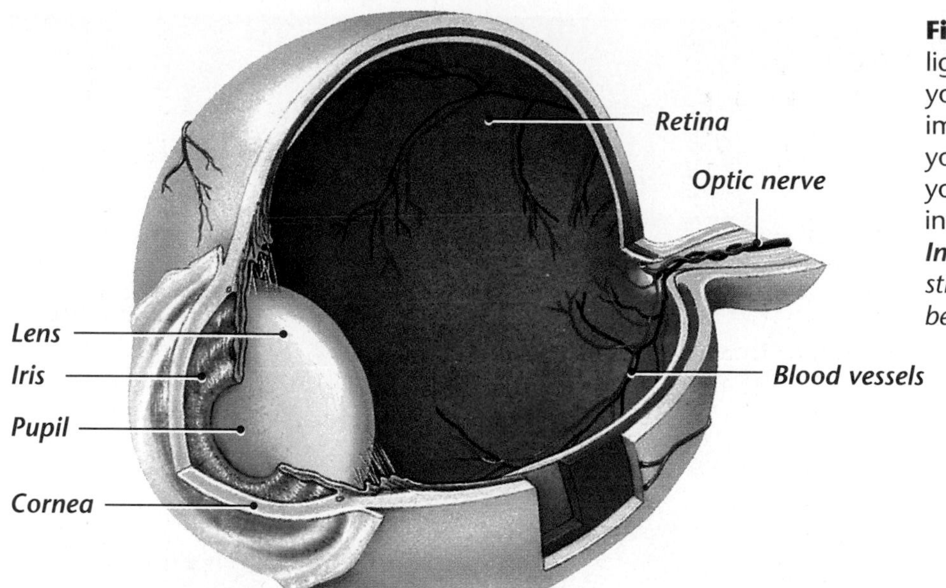

Figure 13 You see an object when light coming from the object enters your eye. The light produces an image on your retina. Receptors in your retina then send impulses to your cerebrum, and your cerebrum interprets these impulses. ***Interpreting Diagrams*** *What structures must light pass through before it reaches your retina?*

Vision

Your eyes are the sense organs that enable you to see the objects in your environment. They let you see this book in front of you, the window across the room, and the world outside the window. **Your eyes respond to the stimulus of light. They convert that stimulus into impulses that your brain interprets, enabling you to see.**

How Light Enters Your Eye When rays of light strike the eye, they pass through the structures shown in Figure 13. First, the light strikes the **cornea** (KAWR nee uh), the clear tissue that covers the front of the eye. The light then passes through a fluid-filled chamber behind the cornea and reaches the pupil. The **pupil** is the opening through which light enters the eye.

You may have noticed that people's pupils change size when they go from a dark room into bright sunshine. In bright light, the pupil becomes smaller. In dim light, the pupil becomes larger. The size of the pupil is adjusted by muscles in the iris. The **iris** is a circular structure that surrounds the pupil and regulates the amount of light entering the eye. The iris also gives the eye its color. If you have brown eyes, your irises are brown.

How Light Is Focused Light that passes through the pupil strikes the lens. The **lens** is a flexible structure that focuses light. The lens of your eye functions something like the lens of a camera, which focuses light on photographic film. Because of the way in which the lens of the eye bends the light rays, the image it produces is upside down and reversed. Muscles that attach to the lens adjust its shape. This adjustment produces an image that is clear and in focus.

Why Do You Need Two Eyes?

ACTIVITY

In this activity, you will investigate how your two eyes work together to allow you to see.

1. With your arms fully extended, hold a plastic drinking straw in one hand and a pipe cleaner in the other.
2. With both eyes open, try to insert the pipe cleaner into the straw.
3. Now close your right eye. Try to insert the pipe cleaner into the straw.
4. Repeat Step 3, but this time close your left eye instead of your right eye.

Inferring How does closing one eye affect your ability to judge distances?

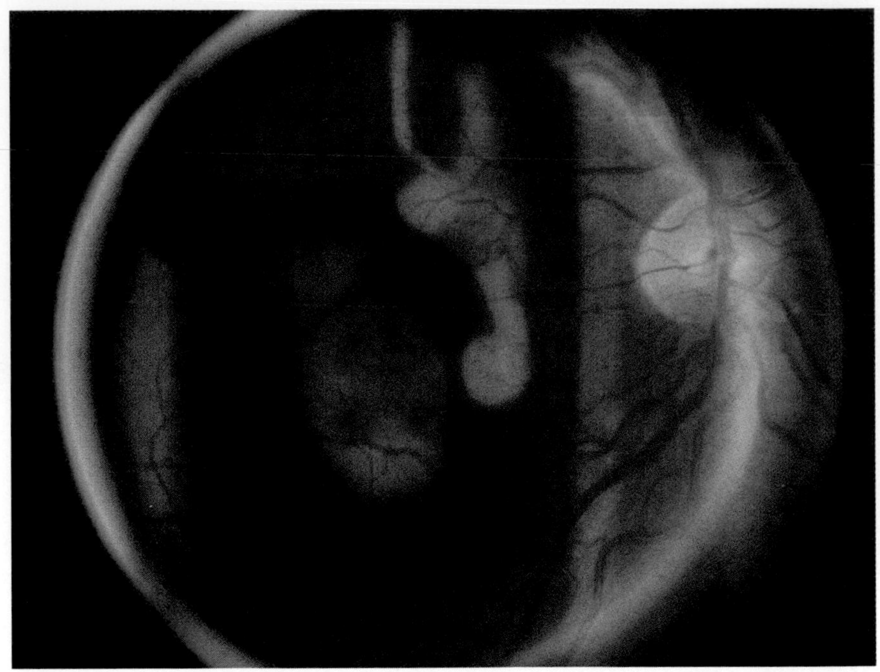

Figure 14 An upside-down image is focused on the retina. ***Applying Concepts*** *When you see an object, why does it appear right-side up?*

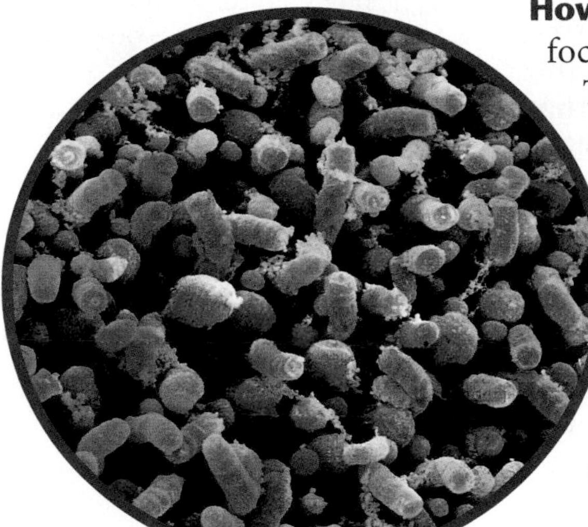

Figure 15 The retina of the eye contains light-sensitive cells. In this photograph, the rods have been colored pink, and the cones have been colored blue.

How You See an Image After passing through the lens, the focused light rays pass through a transparent, jellylike fluid. Then the light rays strike the **retina** (RET 'n uh), the layer of receptor cells that lines the back of the eye. The retina contains about 130 million receptor cells that respond to light. There are two types of receptors, rods and cones. Rod cells work best in dim light and enable you to see black, white, and shades of gray. In contrast, cone cells only work well in bright light and enable you to see colors. This difference between rods and cones explains why you see colors best in bright light, but you see only shadowy gray images in dim light.

When light strikes the rods and cones, nerve impulses begin. These nerve impulses travel to the cerebrum through the optic nerves. One optic nerve comes from the left eye and the other one comes from the right. In the cerebrum, two things happen. The brain turns the reversed image right-side up. In addition, the brain combines the images from each eye to produce a single image.

Correcting Vision Problems

INTEGRATING PHYSICS A lens—whether it is in your eye, in a camera, or in eyeglasses—is a curved, transparent object that bends light rays as they pass through it. If the lens of the eye does not focus light properly on the retina, vision problems result. The glass or plastic lenses in eyeglasses can help correct such vision problems.

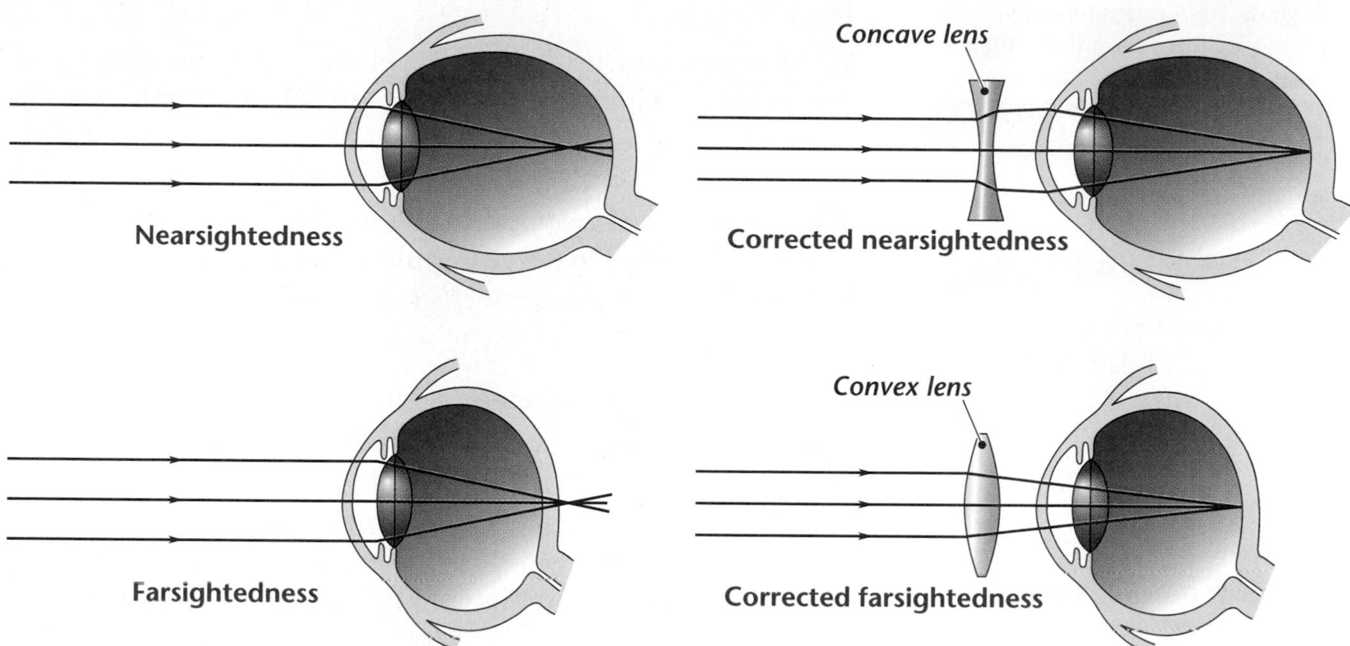

Figure 16 Nearsightedness and farsightedness are conditions in which images do not focus properly on the retina. The diagrams on the left show where the images are focused in both of these conditions. The diagrams on the right show how lenses in eyeglasses can help correct these conditions.

Nearsightedness People with **nearsightedness** can see nearby objects clearly. However, they have trouble seeing objects that are far away. Nearsightedness is caused by an eyeball that is too long. Because of the extra length that light must travel to reach the retina, distant objects do not focus sharply on the retina. Instead, the lens of the eye makes the image come into focus at a point in front of the retina, as shown in Figure 16.

To correct nearsightedness, a person needs to wear eyeglasses with concave lenses. A concave lens is a lens that is thicker at the edges than it is in the center. When light rays pass through a concave lens, they are bent away from the center of the lens. The concave lenses in glasses make light rays spread out before they reach the lens of the eye. Then, when these rays pass through the lens of the eye, they focus on the retina rather than in front of it.

Farsightedness People with **farsightedness** can see distant objects clearly. Nearby objects, however, look blurry. The eyeballs of people with farsightedness are too short. Because of this, the lens of the eye bends light from nearby objects so that the image does not focus properly on the retina. If light could pass through the retina, the image would come into sharp focus at a point behind the retina, as shown in Figure 16.

Convex lenses are used to help correct farsightedness. A convex lens is thicker in the middle than the edges. The convex lens makes the light rays bend toward each other before they reach the eye. Then the lens of the eye bends the rays even more. This bending makes the image focus exactly on the retina.

☑ ***Checkpoint*** *What type of lens is used to correct nearsightedness?*

Tick! Tick! Tick!

In this activity, you will determine whether one of a person's ears hears better than the other one.

1. Work in teams of three. Hold a ticking watch next to the right ear of one team member.
2. Slowly move the watch away from the ear. Stop moving it at the point where the student can no longer hear the ticking.
3. At that point, have the third team member measure the distance between the watch and the student's right ear.
4. Repeat Steps 1 through 3 to test the student's left ear.

Measuring How did the two distances compare? Do you think this is an accurate way to evaluate someone's hearing? Why or why not?

Hearing

What wakes you up in the morning? Maybe an alarm clock buzzes, or perhaps your parent calls you. On a summer morning, you might hear birds singing. Whatever wakes you up, there's a good chance that it's a sound of some sort. **Your ears are the sense organs that respond to the stimulus of sound. The ears convert the sound to nerve impulses that your brain interprets.** So when you hear an alarm clock or other morning sound, your brain tells you that it's time to wake up.

How Sound Is Produced Sound is produced by vibrations.

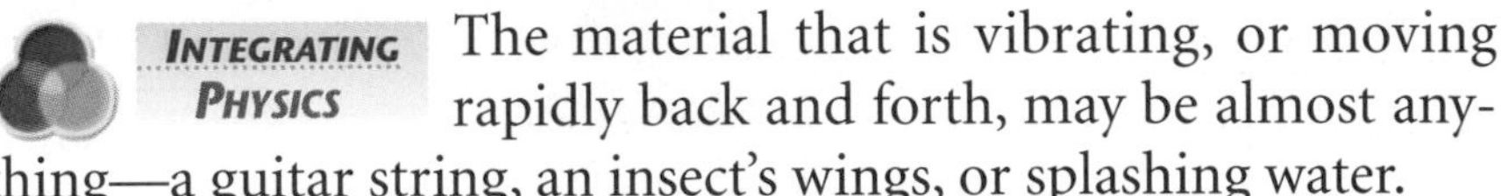

The material that is vibrating, or moving rapidly back and forth, may be almost anything—a guitar string, an insect's wings, or splashing water.

The vibrations create waves. The waves move outward from the source of the sound, something like ripples moving out from a stone dropped in water. The waves consist of moving particles, such as the molecules that make up air. When you hear a friend's voice, for example, sound waves have traveled from your friend's larynx to your ears. In addition to being able to travel through gases such as air, sound waves can also travel through liquids such as water and solids such as wood.

Sound Vibrations and the Ear The ear is structured to receive sound vibrations. As you can see in Figure 18, the ear consists of three parts—the outer ear, middle ear, and inner ear. The outer ear includes the part of the ear that you see. The visible part of the outer ear is shaped like a funnel.

Figure 17 When a wolf howls, its vocal cords vibrate. The vibrating vocal cords produce sound waves. When the sound waves reach a person's ear, the person hears the wolf.

This funnel-like shape enables the outer ear to gather sound waves. The sound waves then travel down the ear canal, which is also part of the outer ear.

At the end of the ear canal, sound waves reach the eardrum. The **eardrum,** which separates the outer ear from the middle ear, is a membrane that vibrates when sound waves strike it. Your eardrum vibrates in much the same way that the surface of a drum vibrates when it is struck. Vibrations from the eardrum pass to the middle ear, which contains the three smallest bones in the body—the hammer, anvil, and stirrup. The names of these bones are based on their shapes. The vibrating eardrum makes the hammer vibrate. The hammer passes the vibrations to the anvil, and the anvil passes them to the stirrup.

How You Hear The stirrup vibrates against a thin membrane that covers the opening of the inner ear. The membrane channels the vibrations into the fluid in the cochlea. The **cochlea** (KAHK le uh) is a snail-shaped tube that is lined with receptors that respond to sound. When the fluid in the cochlea vibrates, it stimulates these receptors. Sensory neurons then send nerve impulses to the cerebrum through the auditory nerve. These impulses are interpreted as sounds that you hear.

☑ *Checkpoint* *Where in the ear is the cochlea located?*

Your Sense of Balance

Your ear also controls your sense of balance. Above the cochlea in your inner ear are the **semicircular canals,** which are the structures in the ear that are responsible for your sense of balance.

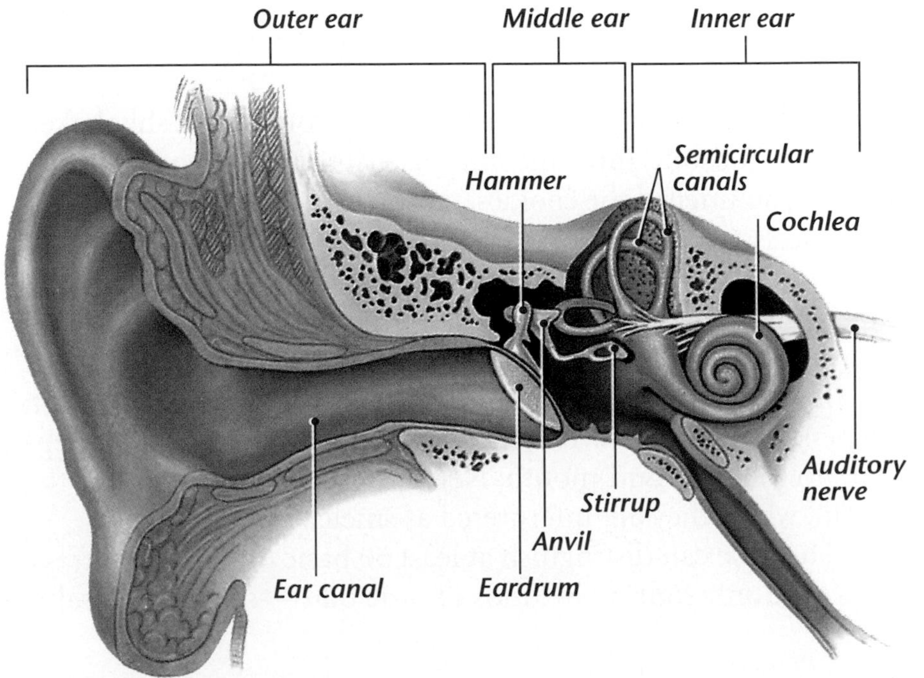

Figure 18 The ear has three regions—the outer ear, the middle ear, and the inner ear. Sound waves enter the outer ear and make structures in the middle ear vibrate. When the vibrations reach the inner ear, nerve impulses travel to the cerebrum through the auditory nerve. ***Predicting*** *What would happen if the bones of the middle ear were stuck together and could not move?*

Figure 19 The semicircular canals of the inner ear enable people to keep their balance—even in very tricky situations!

You can see how these structures got their name if you look at Figure 19. These canals, as well as two tiny sacs located behind them, are full of fluid. The canals and sacs are also lined with tiny cells that have hairlike extensions.

When your head moves, the fluid in the semicircular canals is set in motion. The moving fluid makes the cells' hairlike extensions bend. This bending produces nerve impulses in sensory neurons. The impulses travel to the cerebellum. The cerebellum then analyzes the impulses to determine the way your head is moving and the position of your body. If the cerebellum senses that you are losing your balance, it sends impulses to muscles that help you restore your balance.

Designing Experiments

ACTIVITY

Can people tell one food from another if they can taste the foods but not smell them? Design an experiment to find out. Use these foods: a peeled pear, a peeled apple, and a peeled raw potato. Be sure to control all variables except the one you are testing. Write your hypothesis and a description of your procedure. Show these to your teacher. Do not perform your experiment until your teacher approves your procedure.

Smell and Taste

You walk into the house and smell the aroma of freshly baked cookies. You bite into one and taste its rich chocolate flavor. When you smelled the cookies, receptors in your nose reacted to chemicals carried by the air from the cookies to your nose. When you took a bite of a cookie, taste buds on your tongue responded to chemicals in the food. These food chemicals were dissolved in saliva, which came in contact with your taste buds.

The senses of smell and taste work closely together, and both depend on chemicals. The chemicals trigger responses in receptors in the nose and mouth. Nerve impulses then travel to the brain, where they are interpreted as smells or tastes.

The nose can distinguish at least 50 basic odors. In contrast, there are only four main kinds of taste buds—sweet, sour, salty, and bitter. When you eat, however, you experience a much wider variety of tastes. The flavor of food is determined by both the the senses of smell and taste. When you have a cold, your favorite foods may not taste as good as they usually do. That is because a stuffy nose can decrease your ability to smell food.

Figure 20 Blind people use their sense of touch to read. To do this, they run their fingers over words written in Braille. Braille uses raised dots to represent letters and numbers. Here a teacher shows a blind child how to read Braille.

Touch

Unlike vision, hearing, balance, smell, and taste, the sense of touch is not found in one specific place. Instead, the sense of touch is found in all areas of your skin. Your skin is your largest sense organ!

Your skin contains different kinds of touch receptors. Some of these receptors respond to light touch and others to heavy pressure. Still other receptors pick up sensations of pain and temperature change.

The receptors that respond to light touch are in the upper part of the dermis. They tell you when something brushes against your skin. These receptors also let you feel the textures of objects, such as smooth glass and rough sandpaper. Receptors deeper in the dermis pick up the feeling of pressure. Press down hard on the top of your desk, for example, and you will feel pressure in your fingers.

The dermis also contains receptors that respond to temperature and pain. Pain is unpleasant, but it can be one of the body's most important feelings, because it alerts the body to possible danger. Have you ever stepped into a bathtub of very hot water and then immediately pulled your foot out? If so, you can appreciate how pain can trigger an important response in your body.

Section 3 Review

1. What overall role do the senses perform in the body?
2. Describe the process by which your eyes produce an image of your surroundings. Begin at the point at which light is focused by the lens.
3. How do sound vibrations affect structures in the ear to produce the sensation of hearing?
4. How are the senses of taste and smell similar? How are they different?
5. **Thinking Critically Relating Cause and Effect** Infections of the inner ear sometimes make people more likely to lose their balance and fall. Explain why this is so.

CHAPTER PROJECT 7

Check Your Progress

By now, you should have submitted your plans for your experiment to your teacher. Make any necessary changes in the plan. Prepare all the materials for the fair, including the illusions and questionnaire. Have a data table ready so you can record all responses. (*Hint:* Be sure the people you test cannot see or hear each other's responses. Also, test a large enough number of individuals.)

INTEGRATING HEALTH 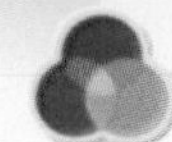

Section 4 Alcohol and Other Drugs

DISCOVER — ACTIVITY

How Can You Best Say No?

1. In this activity, you will use candy to represent drugs. Your teacher will divide the class into groups of three students. In each group, your teacher will appoint two students to try to convince the other person to take the "drugs."
2. Depending on your role, you should think of arguments to get the person to accept the candy or arguments against accepting it. After everyone has had a chance to think of arguments, begin the discussion.
3. After a while, students in each group should exchange roles.

Think It Over

Inferring What role does peer pressure play in whether or not a person decides to abuse drugs?

GUIDE FOR READING

- **How do commonly abused drugs affect the body?**
- **How does alcohol abuse harm the body?**

Reading Tip **Before you read, preview the table on page 215. List some ways in which drugs affect the central nervous system.**

Drugs! You probably hear and see that word in a lot of places. Drugstores sell drugs to relieve headaches, soothe upset stomachs, and stop coughs. Radio and television programs and magazine articles explore drug-related problems. Your school probably has a program to educate students about drugs. When people talk about drugs, what do they mean? To a scientist, a **drug** is any chemical that causes changes in a person's body or behavior. Many drugs affect the functioning of the nervous system.

Medicines

Medicines are legal drugs that help the body fight disease and injury. Aspirin, for example, is a medicine that can relieve pain. To purchase some medicines, you need a doctor's prescription. Other medicines, however, can be bought in drugstores or supermarkets without a prescription. If medicines are used properly, they can help you stay healthy or speed your recovery from sickness. Whenever you take medicines of any kind, it is important to follow the directions for their proper use.

◀ **Medicines in a drugstore**

Drug Abuse

The deliberate misuse of drugs for purposes other than medical ones is called **drug abuse.** Medicines can be abused drugs if they are used in a way for which they were not intended. Many abused drugs, however, such as cocaine and heroin, are illegal under any circumstances. The use of these drugs is against the law because their effects on the body are almost always very dangerous.

Immediate Effects of Abused Drugs Abused drugs start to affect the body very shortly after they are taken. Different drugs have different effects. Some drugs cause nausea and a fast, irregular heartbeat. Others can cause sleepiness. Drug abusers may also experience headaches, dizziness, and trembling.

Most commonly abused drugs, such as marijuana, alcohol, and cocaine, are especially dangerous because they act on the brain and other parts of the nervous system. For example, alcohol can cause confusion, poor muscle coordination, and blurred vision. These effects are especially dangerous in situations in which an alert mind is essential, such as driving a car.

Most abused drugs can alter, or change, a person's mood and feelings. Because of this effect, these drugs are often called mood-altering drugs. For example, the mood of a person under the influence of marijuana may change from calm to anxious. Alcohol can sometimes make a person angry and even violent. Mood-altering drugs also affect patterns of thinking and the way in which the brain interprets information from the senses.

Tolerance If a person takes a drug regularly, the body may develop a tolerance to the drug. **Tolerance** is a state in which a drug user needs larger and larger amounts of the drug to produce the same effect on the body. Tolerance can cause people to take a very large amount of a drug, or an overdose. People who take an overdose may become unconscious or even die.

Figure 21 Abused drugs such as these can cause serious physical and emotional problems.
Applying Concepts *List three ways in which drugs can affect the body.*

Communicating

ACTIVITY

Plan a 30-second television commercial aimed at teenagers to help them avoid the pressure to try drugs. Your commercial should reveal some harmful effects of drugs and give strategies for avoiding drugs. Create several storyboards to show what the commercial will look like. Then write a script for your commercial.

Addiction For many commonly abused drugs, repeated use can result in addiction. The body becomes physically dependent on the drug. If a drug addict misses a few doses of the drug, the body reacts to the lack of the drug. The person may experience headaches, fever, vomiting, body aches, and muscle cramps. The person is experiencing **withdrawal,** a period of adjustment that occurs when a person stops taking a drug.

Some drugs may also cause a person to become emotionally dependent on them. The person becomes accustomed to the feelings and moods produced by the drug. Therefore, the person has a strong desire to continue using the drug.

☑ *Checkpoint* *What is meant by a tolerance to a drug?*

Other Effects of Drug Abuse

Drugs can also affect a person's health indirectly. Drug users sometimes share needles. When a person uses a needle to inject a drug, some of the person's blood remains in the needle after it is withdrawn. If the person has HIV or another pathogen in the blood, the next person to use the needle may become infected with the pathogen.

The abuse of drugs also has serious legal and social effects. A person who is caught using or selling an illegal drug may have to pay a fine or go to jail. Drug abuse can also make a person unable to get along with others. Drug abusers often have a hard time doing well in school or holding a job.

Kinds of Drugs

Figure 22 lists and describes the characteristics of some commonly abused drugs. Notice in the chart that some drugs are classified as depressants. **Depressants** are drugs that slow down the activity of the central nervous system. When people take depressants, their muscles relax and they may become sleepy. They may take longer than normal to respond to stimuli. For example, depressants may prevent people from reacting quickly to the danger of a car rushing toward them. Alcohol and narcotics, such as heroin, are depressants.

Stimulants, in contrast, speed up body processes. They make the heart beat faster and make the breathing rate increase. Cocaine and nicotine are stimulants, as are amphetamines. Amphetamines (am FET uh meenz) are prescription drugs that are sometimes sold illegally.

Some Effects of Commonly Abused Drugs

Drug Type	Short-Term Effects	Long-Term Effects	Addiction?	Emotional Dependence?
marijuana (including hashish)	anxiety, panic, excitement, sleepiness	difficulty with concentration and memory, respiratory disease and lung cancer	probably not	yes
nicotine (in cigarettes, cigars, chewing tobacco)	stimulant; nausea, loss of appetite, headache	heart and lung disease, difficulty breathing, heavy coughing	yes, strongly so	yes
alcohol	depressant; decreased alertness, poor reflexes, nausea, emotional depression	liver and brain damage, inadequate nutrition	yes	yes
inhalants (glue, nail polish remover, paint thinner)	sleepiness, nausea, headaches, emotional depression	damage to liver, kidneys, and brain; hallucinations	no	yes
cocaine (including crack)	stimulant; nervousness, disturbed sleep, loss of appetite	mental illness, damage to lining of nose, irregular heartbeat, heart or breathing failure, liver damage	yes	yes, strongly so
amphetamines	stimulant; restlessness, rapid speech, dizziness	restlessness, irritability, irregular heartbeat, liver damage	possible	yes
hallucinogens (LSD, mescaline, PCP)	hallucinations, anxiety, panic; thoughts and actions not connected to reality	mental illness; fearfulness; behavioral changes, including violence	no	yes
barbiturates (Phenobarbital, Nembutal, Seconal)	depressant; decreased alertness, slowed thought processes, poor muscle coordination	sleepiness, irritability, confusion	yes	yes
tranquilizers (Valium, Xanax)	depressant; blurred vision, sleepiness, unclear speech, headache, skin rash	blood and liver disease	yes	yes
narcotics (opium, codeine, morphine, heroin)	depressant; sleepiness, nausea, hallucinations	convulsion, coma, death	yes, very rapid development	yes, strongly so
anabolic steroids	mood swings	heart, liver, and kidney damage; hypertension; overgrowth of skull and facial bones	no	yes

Figure 22 Abused drugs can have many serious effects on the body. ***Interpreting Charts*** *What are the long-term effects of using inhalants?*

Some substances, called inhalants, produce mood-altering effects when they are inhaled, or breathed in. Inhalants include paint thinner, nail polish remover, and some kinds of cleaning fluids. Hallucinogens, such as LSD and mescaline, can make people see or hear things that do not really exist.

Some athletes try to improve their performance by taking drugs known as steroids. **Anabolic steroids** (an uh BAH lik steer oydz) are synthetic chemicals that are similar to hormones produced in the body. You will learn more about hormones in Chapter 8.

Anabolic steroids may increase muscle size and strength. However, steroids can cause mood changes that lead to violence.

Real-World Lab

You, the Consumer

With Caffeine or Without?

Caffeine is a stimulant found in some beverages and foods, such as coffee and cola drinks. In this lab, you'll observe the effect that caffeine has on a nonhuman organism to help understand how caffeine may affect your own body.

Problem

What body changes does caffeine produce in water fleas (*Daphnia*)?

Skills Focus

developing hypotheses, designing experiments

Materials

drinking straw
scissors
metric ruler
toothpick
petroleum jelly
microscope slide
Daphnia culture
microscope
plastic dropper
adrenaline solution (about 0.01%)
clock or watch with second hand
beverages with and without caffeine

Procedure

Part 1 Observing Effects of a Known Stimulant

1. Cut off the tip of a drinking straw to form a tiny ring about 1 mm deep. With a toothpick, spread some petroleum jelly along the top rim of the ring.
2. Place the ring, jelly side down, on a microscope slide. This ring will be a chamber for your water fleas.
3. Using a plastic dropper, add a drop of *Daphnia* culture to the chamber. Then use the dropper to draw back most of the water. Leave the *Daphnia* and a small amount of water on the slide.
4. Use the low-power lens of a microscope to locate a water flea. Observe the heart, which you can see in the diagram.
5. Use a watch or clock with a second hand to count the number of heartbeats you observe in 1 minute. Record the heartbeat count in your notebook.

In addition, steroid abuse can cause serious health problems, such as heart damage, liver damage, and increased blood pressure. Steroid use is especially dangerous for teenagers, whose growing bodies can be permanently damaged.

Alcohol

Alcohol is a drug found in many beverages, including beer, wine, cocktails, and hard liquor. Alcohol is a powerful depressant. In the United States, it is illegal for people under the age of 21 to buy or possess alcohol. In spite of this fact, alcohol is the most commonly abused drug in people aged 12 to 17.

6. Remove the slide from the microscope. Use a plastic dropper to add 1 drop of adrenaline solution to the water flea chamber. (Adrenaline is a substance that is produced by the human body that acts in a manner similar to a stimulant.)
7. Place the slide on the microscope. Using low power, locate a water flea. Count and record the number of heartbeats in a minute.

Part 2 Testing the Effects of Caffeine

8. Using the procedures you followed in Part 1, design an experiment that tests the effect of caffeine on *Daphnia's* heartbeat. You can use beverages with and without caffeine in your investigation. Be sure to write a hypothesis and control all necessary variables.
9. Submit your experimental plan to your teacher for review. After making any necessary changes, carry out your experiment.

Analyze and Conclude

1. What effect does a stimulant have on the body?

▼ Daphnia

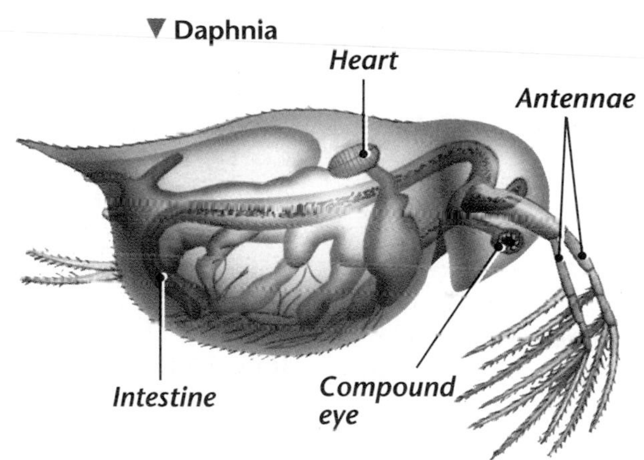

2. In Part 1, how did you know that adrenaline acted as a stimulant?
3. In Part 2, did caffeine act as a stimulant?
4. **Apply** Based on your work in Part 2, how do you think your body would react to drinks with caffeine? To drinks without caffeine?

Design an Experiment

Do you think that "decaffeinated" products will act as a stimulant in *Daphnia?* Design a controlled experiment to find out. Obtain your teacher's approval before performing this experiment.

How Alcohol Affects the Body Alcohol is absorbed by the digestive system quickly. If a person drinks alcohol on an empty stomach, the alcohol enters the blood and gets to the brain and other organs almost immediately. If alcohol is drunk with a meal, it takes longer to get into the blood.

To understand what alcohol does to the body, look at *Exploring the Effects of Alcohol.* The more alcohol in the blood, the more serious the effects. The amount of alcohol in the blood is usually expressed as blood alcohol concentration, or BAC. A BAC value of 0.1 percent means that one tenth of one percent of the fluid in the blood is alcohol. In some states, if car drivers have a BAC of 0.08 percent or more, they are legally drunk. In other states, drivers with a BAC of 0.1 are considered drunk.

Alcohol produces serious effects, including loss of normal judgment, at a BAC of less than 0.08 percent. This loss of judgment can have serious consequences. For example, people who have been drinking may not realize that they cannot drive a car safely. In the United States, alcohol is involved in about 40 percent of traffic-related deaths. About every two minutes, a person in the United States is injured in a car crash related to alcohol.

Long-Term Alcohol Abuse Many adults drink occasionally, and in moderation, without serious safety or health problems. However, heavy drinking, especially over a long period, can result in significant health problems. **The abuse of alcohol can cause the destruction of cells in the brain and liver, and it can also lead to addiction and emotional dependence.** Damage to the brain can cause mental disturbances, such as hallucinations and

Figure 23 Alcohol is involved in many car crashes. Alcohol decreases a driver's ability to react quickly to traffic and road conditions.

loss of consciousness. The liver, which breaks down alcohol for elimination from the body, can become so scarred that it does not function properly. In addition, long-term alcohol abuse can increase the risk of getting certain kinds of cancer.

Abuse of alcohol can result in **alcoholism,** a disease in which a person is both physically addicted to and emotionally dependent on alcohol. To give up alcohol, alcoholics must go through withdrawal, as with any addictive drug. To give up drinking,

EXPLORING *the Effects of Alcohol*

Alcohol is a drug that affects every system of the body. It also impacts a person's thought processes and judgment.

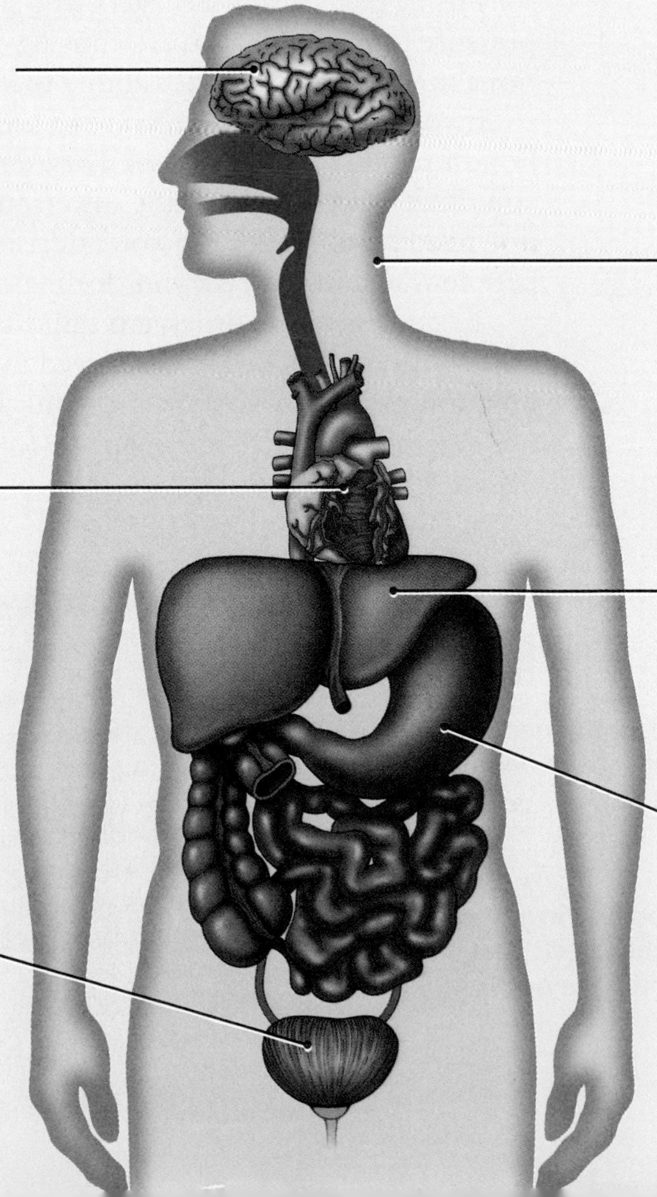

Nervous system Vision becomes blurred. Speech becomes unclear. Control of behavior is reduced. Judgment becomes poor.

Skin Blood flow to the skin increases, causing rapid loss of body heat.

Cardiovascular system At first, heartbeat rate and blood pressure increase. Later, with large amounts of alcohol, the heartbeat rate and blood pressure may decrease.

Liver The liver breaks down alcohol. Over many years, liver damage can result.

Digestive system Alcohol is absorbed directly from the stomach and small intestine. The alcohol passes into the bloodstream quickly.

Excretory system Alcohol causes the kidneys to produce more urine. As a result, the drinker loses more water than usual.

Figure 24 The message is clear: drugs are dangerous, and you have the right to refuse to take them.

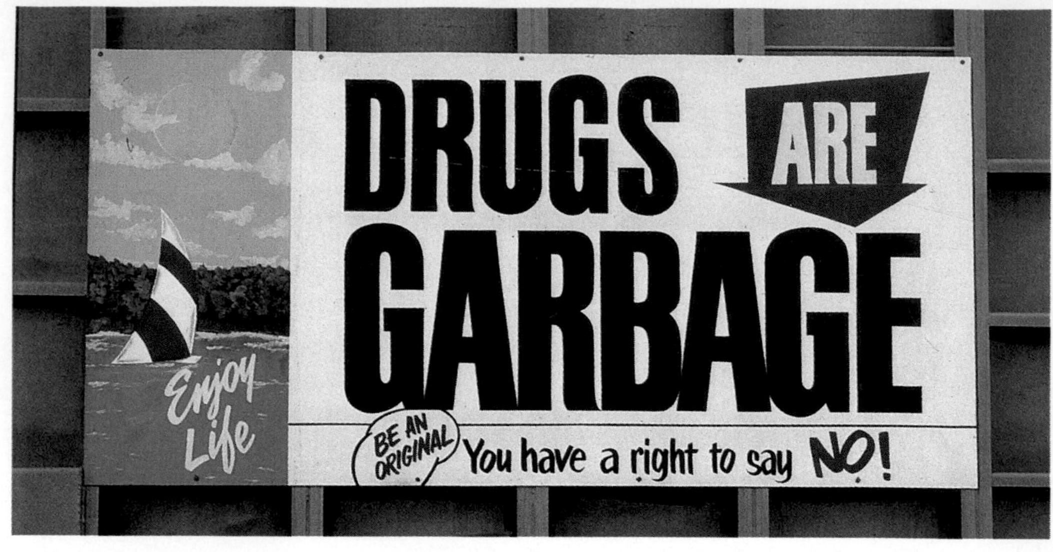

alcoholics need both medical and emotional help. Medical professionals and organizations such as Alcoholics Anonymous can help a person stop drinking.

Avoiding Drugs and Alcohol

The best way to avoid depending on drugs and alcohol is not to start using them. Many teenagers who start do so because of peer pressure from people who are abusing drugs. Try to avoid situations in which there is a possibility that drugs may be used.

If you are faced with pressure to use drugs, give a simple but honest reason for your refusal. For example, you might say that you don't want to risk getting into trouble with the law. You do not need to apologize for your decision. And remember that people who don't respect your feelings aren't very good friends.

To stay away from drugs, it is important to find healthy things to do with friends. Become involved in sports and other school or community activities in which you and your friends can have fun together. Such activities help you feel good about yourself. By deciding not to use drugs, you are protecting your health.

Section 4 Review

1. How do abused drugs affect the nervous system? Why can these effects be dangerous?
2. What are the effects of long-term alcohol abuse?
3. What is alcoholism?
4. **Thinking Critically Comparing and Contrasting** Contrast the effects that stimulants and depressants have on the body.

CHAPTER PROJECT 7

Check Your Progress

By now you should have finished collecting your data and recording your observations. Now begin preparing a report about your findings. Think about the best way to communicate the procedures you followed and the results you obtained. Your report should explain how you think the illusions you chose trick the senses. Decide how to use graphs and other visuals in your report.

SECTION 1 How the Nervous System Works

Key Ideas

- The nervous system receives information about the external and internal environment, responds to this information, and helps maintain homeostasis.
- Neurons are the cells that carry nerve impulses. Sensory neurons pick up stimuli from the environment. Interneurons pass messages between neurons. Motor neurons send impulses that cause a response.
- To pass from the axon of a neuron to another structure, a nerve impulse must cross a space called a synapse.

Key Terms

stimulus	dendrite	interneuron
response	axon	motor neuron
neuron	nerve	synapse
nerve impulse	sensory neuron	

SECTION 2 Divisions of the Nervous System

Key Ideas

- The central nervous system, which consists of the brain and spinal cord, is the control center of the body.
- The cerebrum in the brain receives input from the senses, controls voluntary muscles, and controls complex mental processes. The cerebellum coordinates muscle action and balance. The brainstem controls involuntary actions necessary for life.
- The peripheral nervous system links the central nervous system to the rest of the body.

Key Terms

central nervous system	cerebellum
peripheral nervous system	brainstem
brain	somatic nervous system
spinal cord	autonomic nervous system
cerebrum	reflex
	concussion

SECTION 3 The Senses

Key Ideas

- The senses change information about the environment to nerve impulses.
- After light enters the eye, it passes through the lens, which focuses it on the retina. Impulses then travel to the brain.
- Sound waves start vibrations in structures in the ear. When the vibrations reach the cochlea, impulses are sent to the brain.
- The senses of smell and taste both respond to chemical stimuli.

Key Terms

cornea
pupil
iris
lens
retina
nearsightedness
farsightedness
eardrum
cochlea
semicircular canals

SECTION 4 Alcohol and Other Drugs

INTEGRATING HEALTH

Key Ideas

- Abused drugs act on the nervous system. Depressants slow down the central nervous system. Stimulants speed up body processes. Marijuana, alcohol, amphetamines, and anabolic steroids are commonly abused drugs.
- The long-term abuse of alcohol can damage the liver and brain and lead to alcoholism.

Key Terms

drug	withdrawal	anabolic steroid
drug abuse	depressant	alcoholism
tolerance	stimulant	

CHAPTER 7 REVIEW

Reviewing Content

For more review of key concepts, see the Interactive Student Tutorial CD-ROM.

Multiple Choice

Choose the letter of the best answer.

1. A change or signal in the environment that makes the nervous system react is called a
   a. stimulus. b. response.
   c. receptor. d. synapse.
2. The structures that carry messages toward a neuron's cell body are
   a. axons.
   b. dendrites.
   c. nerves.
   d. impulses.
3. Which structure links the brain and the peripheral nervous system?
   a. the cerebrum
   b. the cerebellum
   c. the cochlea
   d. the spinal cord
4. Which structure adjusts the size of the pupil?
   a. the cornea
   b. the retina
   c. the lens
   d. the iris
5. Physical dependence on a drug is called
   a. withdrawal.
   b. response.
   c. addiction.
   d. tolerance.

True or False

If the statement is true, write true. If it is false, change the underlined word or words to make the statement true.

6. A nerve message is also called a <u>nerve impulse</u>.
7. The <u>brainstem</u> is the part of the brain that controls involuntary actions.
8. In <u>nearsightedness</u>, a person cannot see nearby objects clearly.
9. The hammer, anvil, and <u>wrench</u> are the three bones in the middle ear.
10. Alcohol is a <u>depressant</u>.

Checking Concepts

11. Compare the functions of axons and dendrites.
12. What is the function of the autonomic nervous system?
13. How do the cerebrum and cerebellum work together when you ride a bicycle?
14. What are some steps you can take to protect your central nervous system from injury?
15. Describe how lenses in eyeglasses correct nearsightedness and farsightedness.
16. List all the structures in your ear that must vibrate before you hear a sound. List them in the order in which they vibrate.
17. What are the effects of anabolic steroids on the body?
18. **Writing to Learn** Imagine that Earth has been invaded by space aliens who are exactly like humans except for the fact that they have no sense of touch. These aliens plan to take over Earth. Write a plan for fighting the aliens that makes use of the fact that they lack a sense of touch.

Thinking Visually

19. **Concept Map** Complete the following concept map about nerve cells and their functions. (For more on concept maps, see the Skills Handbook.)

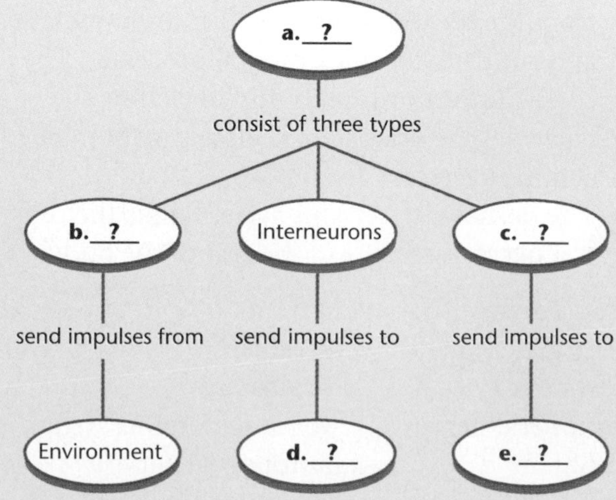

Applying Skills

A person with normal vision stood at different distances from an eye chart and tried to identify the letters on the chart. The table gives the results. Use the table to answer Questions 20–22.

Distance from Eye Chart	Percent of Letters Identified Correctly
2 meters	100
4 meters	92
6 meters	80
8 meters	71
10 meters	60

20. **Graphing** Make a line graph of the data. Plot the distance from the chart on the horizontal axis. On the vertical axis, plot the percent of letters identified correctly.
21. **Controlling Variables** What was the manipulated variable in this experiment? What was the responding variable?
22. **Predicting** How would you expect the results to differ for a farsighted person? Explain.

Thinking Critically

23. **Relating Cause and Effect** When a person has a stroke, blood flow to part of the brain is reduced, and severe brain damage can result. Suppose that after a stroke, a woman is unable to move her right arm and right leg. In which side of her brain did the stroke occur? Explain.
24. **Applying Concepts** As a man walks barefoot along a beach, he steps on a sharp shell. His foot automatically jerks upward, even before he feels pain. What process is this an example of? How does it help protect the man?
25. **Making Judgments** If someone tried to convince you to take drugs, what arguments would you use as a way of refusing? Why do you think these arguments would be effective?

Performance Assessment

CHAPTER PROJECT 7 Wrap Up

Present Your Project Your report should include an explanation of how you did your research, what you were trying to find out, and how your results compared with your expected results. Also include information on how the nervous system was involved in your illusions. If you can, try to explain why the illusions work.

Reflect and Record In your journal, summarize what you learned from doing this project. Did the project go as you expected, or were you surprised by some results? If you had a chance to continue your investigations, what would you do next? Why?

Getting Involved

In Your School Find out what programs exist in your school to discourage students from abusing alcohol and drugs. Talk to the school nurse, the guidance counselor, or the principal about these programs. Ask them why they chose each approach. Use what you have learned to write an article about the school's anti-drug abuse program for the school newspaper.

CHAPTER

8 The Endocrine System and Reproduction

"Breakfast now!" A baby may need care at any moment of the day or night.

Section 1 The Endocrine System

Discover **What's the Signal?**

Section 2 The Male and Female Reproductive Systems

Discover **What's the Big Difference?**
Sharpen Your Skills **Graphing**

Section 3 Pregnancy, Birth, and Childhood

Discover **How Many Ways Does a Child Grow?**
Try This **Way to Grow!**
Sharpen Your Skills **Designing Experiments**

PROJECT 8

A Precious Bundle

With the arrival of their first baby, most new parents discover that their lives are totally changed. Their usual schedules are disrupted, and they suddenly need a new set of skills. Parents must begin to learn how to keep the infant comfortable and happy.

As you learn about reproduction and development, you'll experience what it's like to care for a "baby." Although your baby will be only a physical model, you'll have a chance to learn about the responsibilities of parenthood.

Your Goal To develop and follow a plan to care for a "baby" for three days and nights.

To complete this project, you must

- ◆ list all the essential tasks involved in caring for a young infant, and prepare a 24-hour schedule of those tasks
- ◆ make a model "baby" from a bag of flour, and care for the baby according to your schedule
- ◆ keep a journal of your thoughts and feelings as you care for your "baby," making entries at least twice a day

Get Started With classmates write down all the things that parents must do when caring for infants. Prepare a plan describing how to carry out those activities with your "baby." List the materials you'll need. If you require more information, write down your questions, then consult adult caregivers, day care facilities, or other resources.

Check Your Progress You'll be working on this project as you study this chapter. To keep your project on track, look for Check Your Progress boxes at the following points.

Section 1 Review, page 230: Present your child-care plan to your teacher for review.

Section 2 Review, page 236: Care for your "baby," and record your experiences in your journal.

Section 4 Review, page 249: Summarize your experiences.

Wrap Up At the end of the chapter (page 253), you'll share what you learned about parenthood.

Integrating Health

SECTION 4 Adolescence—A Time of Change

Discover **How Do Ads Portray Teenagers?**

Skills Lab **Growing Up**

SECTION 1 The Endocrine System

DISCOVER

What's the Signal?

1. Stand up and move around the room until your teacher says "Freeze!" Then stop moving immediately. Stay perfectly still until your teacher says "Start!" Then begin moving again.
2. Anyone who moves between the "Freeze!" command and the "Start!" command has to leave the game.
3. Play until only one person is left in the game. That person is the winner.

Think It Over

Inferring Why is it important for players in this game to respond to signals? What types of signals does the human body use?

GUIDE FOR READING

- **What is the function of the endocrine system?**
- **How does negative feedback control hormone levels?**

Reading Tip **Before you read, preview *Exploring the Endocrine System* on pages 228–229. List the terms in the diagram that are new to you. Look for their meanings as you read.**

You're playing softball on a hot afternoon. Without warning, thick, dark clouds form. Suddenly, there's a flash of lightning. Thunder cracks overhead. Someone screams, you jump, and everyone runs for cover. Your heart is pounding, your palms are sweaty, and your muscles are tight.

Your body's reaction to the sudden storm was caused mainly by your body's endocrine system. In this section, you will learn about the role of the endocrine system in many body processes—from the quick response to a thunder clap, to the slower body changes that turn a child into an adult.

The Role of the Endocrine System

The human body has two systems that regulate its activities. You learned about one, the nervous system, in Chapter 7. The endocrine system is the other regulating system. **The endocrine system controls many of the body's daily activities as well as long-term changes such as development.**

The endocrine system is made up of glands. Glands are organs that produce chemicals. You already know about some glands, such as those that produce saliva or sweat. Those glands release their chemicals into tiny tubes. The tubes deliver the chemicals to a specific location within the body or to the skin's surface.

The endocrine system does not have delivery tubes. **Endocrine glands** (EN duh krin) produce and release their chemical products directly into the bloodstream. The blood then carries those chemicals throughout the body.

Figure 1 The endocrine system controls the body's response to an exciting situation (left) as well as the changes that occur as a child grows (right).
Applying Concepts *What substances produced by endocrine glands control these body processes?*

Hormones

The chemical product of an endocrine gland is called a **hormone.** Hormones turn on, turn off, speed up, or slow down the activities of different organs and tissues. You can think of a hormone as a chemical messenger. Because hormones are carried by blood, they can regulate activities in tissues and organs far from the glands that produced them.

Hormone Production What causes the release of hormones? In situations such as a sudden storm, nerve impulses from the senses travel to the brain. There, information, such as the sound of thunder, is interpreted. The brain then sends a nerve impulse to a specific endocrine gland. That gland, in turn, releases the hormone adrenaline into the bloodstream. As you read in Chapter 1, adrenaline causes your heart rate to increase, makes you breathe faster and deeper, and releases sugars that power your muscles.

In contrast to the body's response to a nerve impulse, hormones cause a slower, but longer-lasting, response. For example, the brain sends a quick signal to an endocrine gland to release adrenaline into the bloodstream. When the adrenaline reaches the heart, it makes the heart beat more rapidly. The heart continues to race until the amount of adrenaline in the blood drops to a normal level.

Target Cells When a hormone enters the bloodstream, why does it affect some organs but not others? The answer lies in its chemical structure. A hormone interacts only with certain **target cells,** cells that recognize the hormone's chemical structure. A hormone and its target cell fit together the way a key fits into a lock. Hormones not meant for a particular organ will travel through the bloodstream until they find the "lock" that they fit.

INTEGRATING CHEMISTRY

Each endocrine gland releases different hormones and thus controls different processes. *Exploring the Endocrine System* shows the locations of the endocrine glands and describes some activities they control.

The Hypothalamus

The nervous system and the endocrine system work together. The **hypothalamus** (hy poh THAL uh mus), a tiny part of the brain near the middle of your head, is the link between the two systems. Nerve messages controlling sleep, hunger, and other conditions come from the hypothalamus. The hypothalamus also produces hormones that control other endocrine glands and organs. Through its nerve impulses and hormones, the hypothalamus plays a major role in maintaining homeostasis.

EXPLORING *the Endocrine System*

Each of the endocrine glands has an important regulatory role in the body. Note the location of each gland and the functions of the hormones it produces.

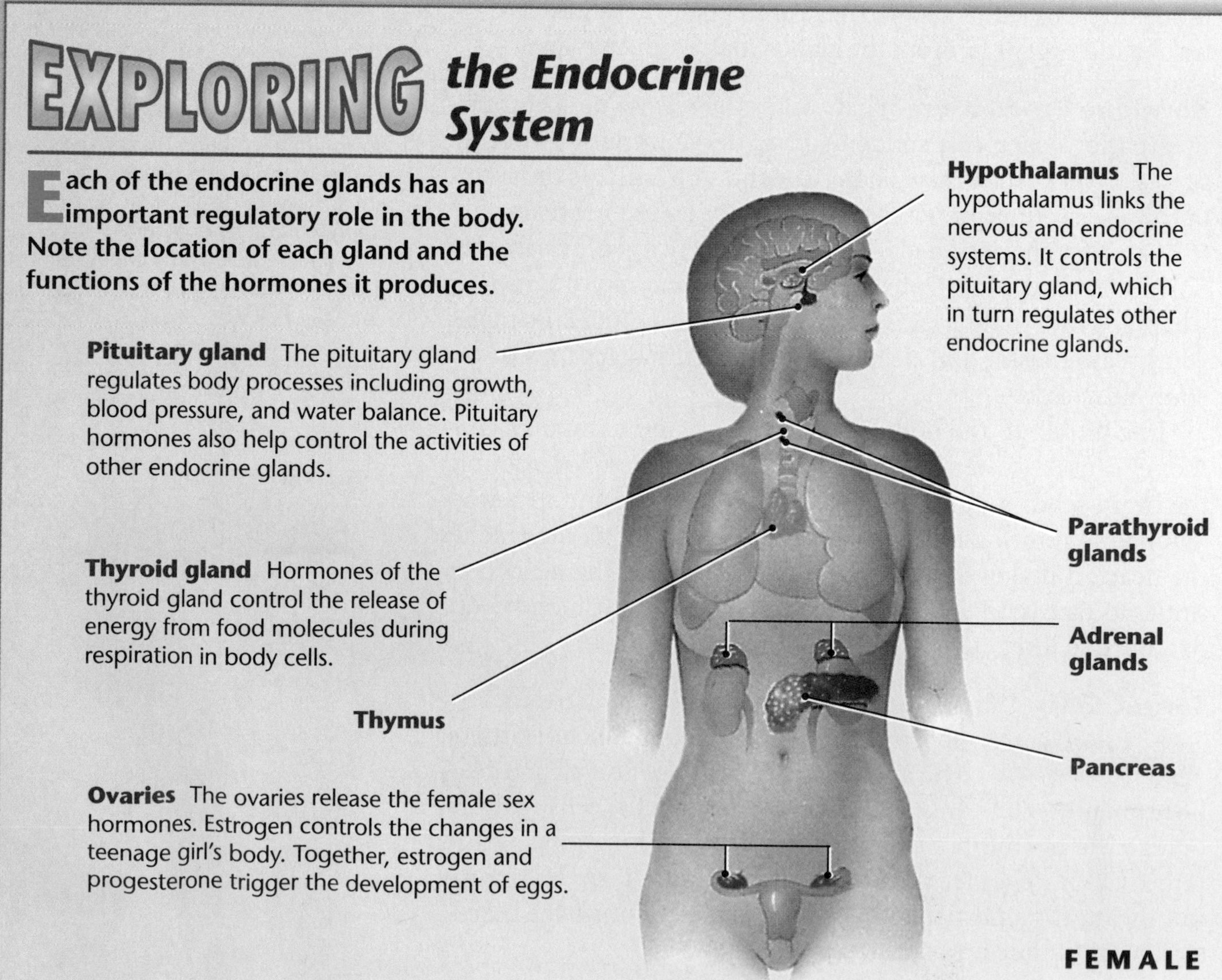

The Pituitary Gland

Just below the hypothalamus is an endocrine gland about the size of a pea. The **pituitary gland** (pih TOO ih tehr ee) communicates with the hypothalamus to control many body activities. In response to nerve impulses or hormone signals from the hypothalamus, the pituitary gland releases its hormones. Some of those hormones act as an "on" switch for other endocrine glands. For example, one pituitary hormone signals the thyroid gland to produce hormones. Other pituitary hormones control body activities directly. Growth hormone regulates growth from infancy to adulthood. Another pituitary hormone directs the kidneys to regulate the amount of water in the blood.

☑ ***Checkpoint*** *What causes the pituitary gland to release hormones?*

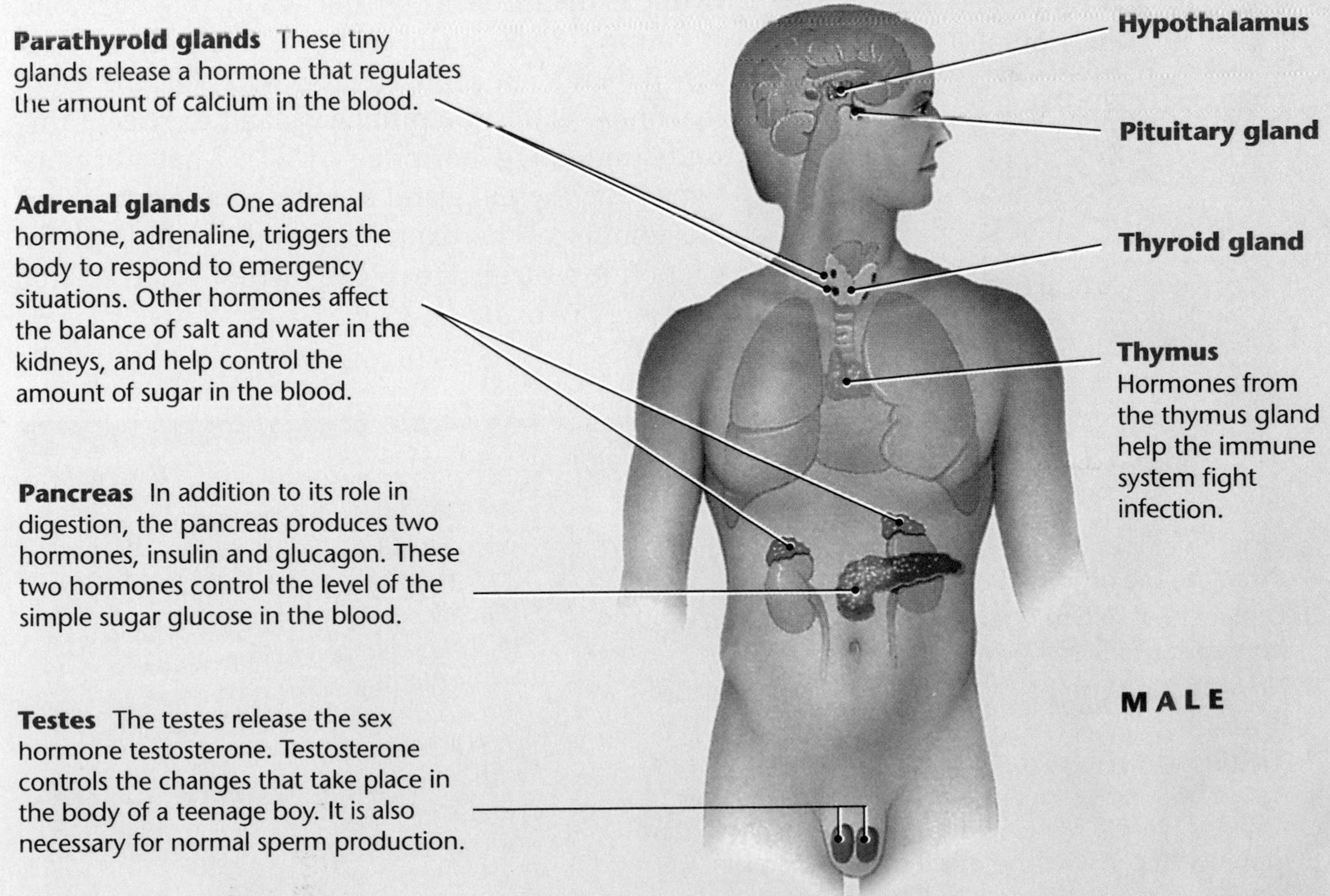

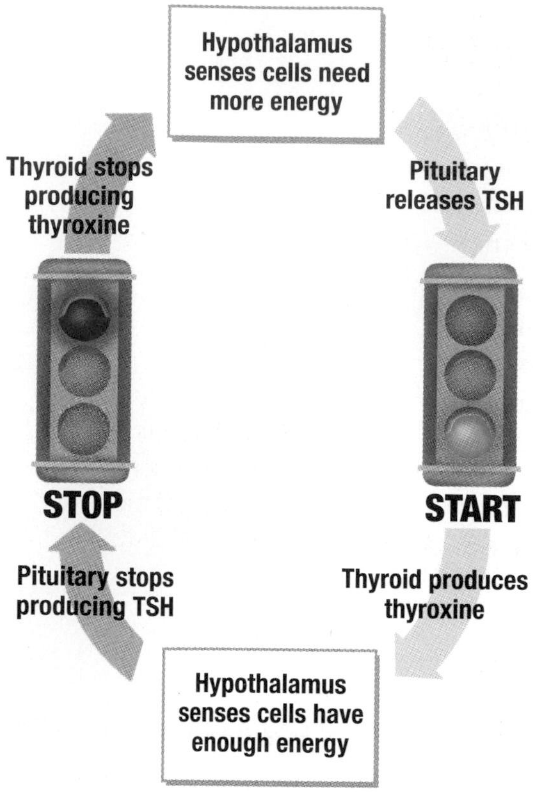

Hypothalamus senses cells need more energy

Pituitary releases TSH

START

Thyroid produces thyroxine

Hypothalamus senses cells have enough energy

Pituitary stops producing TSH

STOP

Thyroid stops producing thyroxine

Figure 2 The release of the hormone thyroxine is controlled through negative feedback. When enough thyroxine is present, the system signals the thyroid gland to stop releasing the hormone. ***Predicting*** *What happens when the amount of thyroxine becomes too low?*

Negative Feedback

One way that the endocrine system maintains homeostasis may remind you of the way a heating system works. Suppose you set a thermostat at 20°C. If the temperature falls below 20°, the thermostat signals the furnace to turn on. When the furnace heats the area to the proper temperature, information about the warm conditions "feeds back" to the thermostat. The thermostat then gives the furnace a negative signal that means "no more heat." That signal turns the furnace off.

The type of signal used in a heating system is called **negative feedback** because the system is turned off by the condition it produces. The endocrine system often works in this way. Through negative feedback, when the amount of a particular hormone in the blood reaches a certain level, the endocrine system sends signals that stop the release of that hormone. **Negative feedback is an important way that the body maintains homeostasis.**

You can see an example of negative feedback in Figure 2. Like a thermostat in a cool room, the endocrine system senses when there's not enough thyroxine in the blood. Thyroxine is a thyroid hormone. It controls how much energy is available to cells. When there's not enough energy available, the hypothalamus signals the pituitary gland to release thyroid-stimulating hormone (TSH). That hormone signals the thyroid gland to release thyroxine. When the amount of thyroxine reaches the right level, the endocrine system signals the thyroid gland to stop releasing thyroxine.

Section 1 Review

1. What role does the endocrine system play in the body? What are the organs of the endocrine system called?
2. Explain how negative feedback helps to maintain homeostasis in the body.
3. How do the hypothalamus and the pituitary gland interact?
4. **Thinking Critically Making Judgments** Years ago, one of the endocrine glands was called the "master gland." Which part of the endocrine system would you consider the master gland? Explain.

Check Your Progress

CHAPTER PROJECT 8

You should now be ready to turn in your plan for your teacher's review. Your plan should include your daily schedule and a list of the materials you'll need. Be sure to describe the kind of journal you plan to keep. (*Hint:* Discuss with your teacher any problems you foresee in caring for the "baby" for three full days and nights.)

The Male and Female Reproductive Systems

DISCOVER

What's the Big Difference?

1. Your teacher will provide prepared slides of eggs and sperm.
2. Examine each slide under the microscope, first under low power, then under high power. Be sure you view at least one sample of egg and sperm from the same species.
3. Sketch and label each sample.

Think It Over

Observing What differences did you observe between sperm cells and egg cells? What general statement can you make about eggs and sperm?

Many differences between an adult animal and its young are controlled by the endocrine system. In humans, two endocrine glands—the ovaries in girls and the testes in boys—control many of the changes that occur as a child matures. These glands release hormones that cause the body to develop as a person grows older.

GUIDE FOR READING

- **What are the organs of the male and female reproductive systems?**
- **What events occur during the menstrual cycle?**

Reading Tip **As you read, create a table comparing the male and female reproductive systems. Include the type of sex cells and primary reproductive organs of each.**

Sex Cells

You may find it hard to believe that you began life as a single cell. That single cell was produced by the joining of two other cells, an egg and a sperm. An **egg** is the female sex cell. A **sperm** is the male sex cell.

The joining of a sperm and an egg is called **fertilization.** Fertilization is an important part of **reproduction,** the process by which living things produce new individuals of the same type. When fertilization occurs, a fertilized egg, or **zygote,** is produced. Every one of the trillions of cells in your body is descended from the single cell that formed during fertilization.

Figure 3 This gosling began its life as a single cell. When it is fully grown, it will be made up of millions of cells.

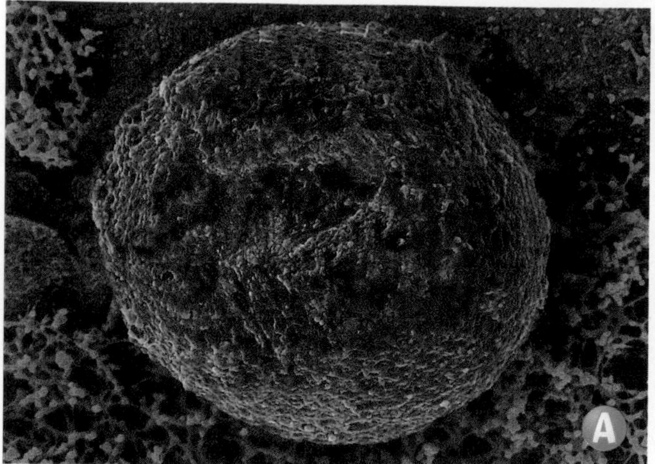

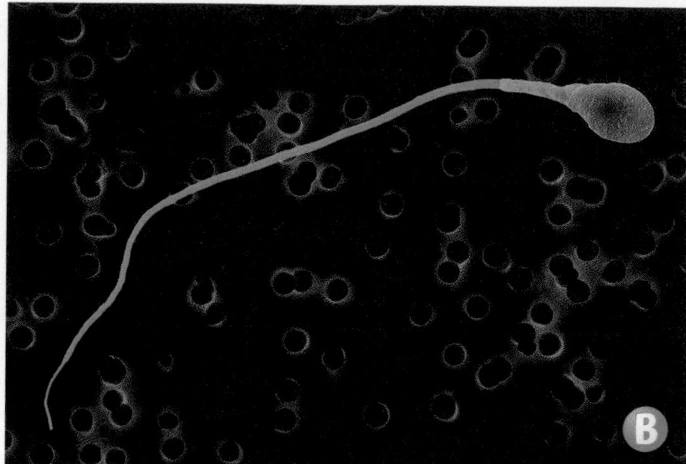

Figure 4 The human reproductive system produces either eggs or sperm. **A.** An egg is one of the largest cells in the body. **B.** A sperm, which is much smaller than an egg, has a tail that allows it to move.

Like other cells in the body, sex cells contain rod-shaped structures called chromosomes. **Chromosomes** (KROH muh sohmz) carry the information that controls inherited characteristics, such as eye color and blood type. Every cell in the human body, except the sex cells, contains 46 chromosomes. Each sex cell contains half that number, or 23 chromosomes. During fertilization, the 23 chromosomes in a sperm join the 23 chromosomes in an egg. The result is a zygote with 46 chromosomes. The zygote contains all of the information needed to produce a new human being.

☑ ***Checkpoint*** ***What happens to the number of chromosomes when a male sex cell and a female sex cell join?***

The Male Reproductive System

The male reproductive system is shown in Figure 5. **The male reproductive system is specialized to produce sperm and the hormone testosterone.**

The Testes The oval-shaped **testes** (tes teez) (singular *testis*), are the organs of the male reproductive system in which sperm are produced. The testes are actually clusters of hundreds of tiny coiled tubes. Sperm are formed inside the tubes.

The testes also produce the hormone **testosterone** (tes TAHS tuh rohn). Testosterone controls the development of physical characteristics in men. Some of those characteristics include facial hair, a deep voice, broad shoulders, and the ability to produce sperm.

Notice in Figure 5 that the testes are located in an external pouch of skin called the **scrotum** (SKROH tum). That external location keeps the testes about 2° to 3°C below the usual body temperature of 37°C. That temperature difference is important. Sperm need the slightly cooler conditions to develop normally.

Sperm Production The production of sperm cells begins in males at some point during the teenage years. Each sperm is composed of a head that contains chromosomes and a long, whiplike tail. Basically, a sperm cell is a tiny package of chromosomes that can swim.

The Path of Sperm Cells Once sperm cells form in the testes, they travel through other structures in the male reproductive system. During this passage, sperm mix with fluids produced by nearby glands. This mix of sperm cells and fluids is called **semen** (SEE mun). Semen contains a huge number of sperm—about 5 to 10 million per drop! The fluids in semen provide an environment in which sperm can swim. Semen also contains nutrients that the moving sperm use as a source of energy.

Semen leaves the body through an organ called the **penis.** The male urethra runs through the penis. The urethra is the tube through which the semen travels as it leaves the body.

Urine also leaves the body through the urethra, as you learned in Chapter 5. When semen passes through the urethra, however, muscles near the bladder contract. Those muscles prevent urine and semen from mixing.

☑ ***Checkpoint*** *What is a sperm composed of?*

Figure 5 In the male reproductive system, the testes produce sperm and the hormone testosterone. ***Interpreting Diagrams*** *What pathway do sperm follow to reach the urethra?*

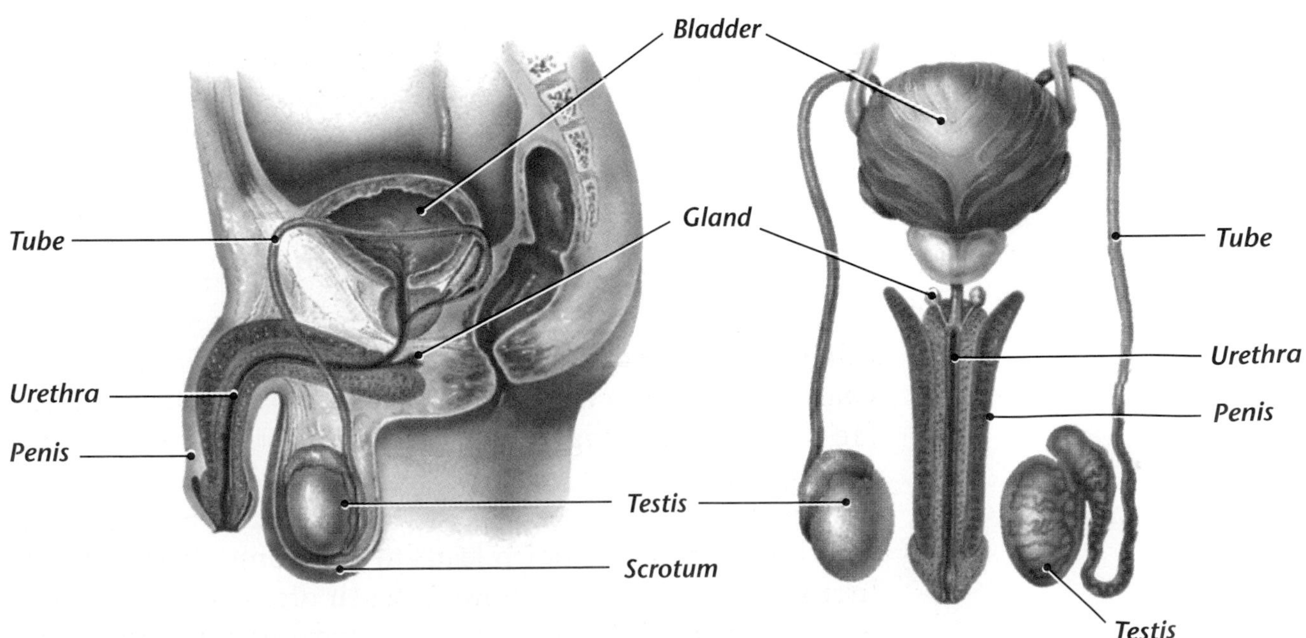

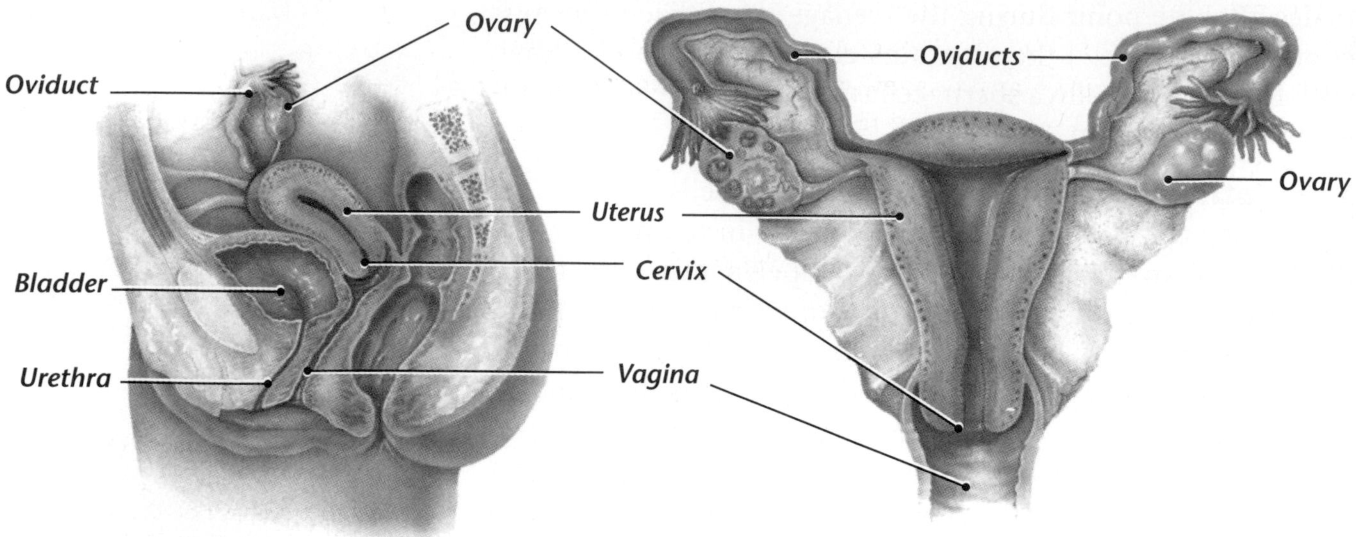

Figure 6 In the female reproductive system, the two ovaries produce eggs and hormones such as estrogen. From an ovary, an egg travels through an oviduct to the uterus. ***Interpreting Diagrams*** *Through what opening does an unfertilized egg pass when leaving the uterus?*

The Female Reproductive System

Unlike the male reproductive system, almost all of the female reproductive system is inside the body. **The role of the female reproductive system is to produce eggs and, if an egg is fertilized, to nourish a developing baby until birth.** The organs of the female reproductive system are shown in Figure 6.

The Ovaries Find the two ovaries in Figure 6. The **ovaries** (OH vuh reez) are located slightly below the waist, one on each side of the body. The name for these organs comes from the word *ova,* meaning "eggs." One major role of the ovaries is to produce egg cells.

Like the testes in males, the ovaries also are endocrine glands that produce hormones. One hormone, **estrogen** (ES truh jun), triggers the development of some adult female characteristics. For example, estrogen causes the hips to widen and the breasts to develop. Estrogen also plays a role in the process by which egg cells develop.

The Path of the Egg Cell As you can see in Figure 6, each ovary is located near an **oviduct** (OH vih duct). The two oviducts are passageways for eggs. They are also the places where fertilization usually occurs. Each month, one of the ovaries releases a mature egg, which enters the nearest oviduct. The egg moves through the oviduct, which leads to the uterus, or womb. The **uterus** (YOO tur us) is a hollow muscular organ about the size of a pear. If the egg has been fertilized, it remains in the uterus and begins to develop.

An egg that has not been fertilized starts to break down as it enters the uterus. It leaves the uterus through an opening at its base called the cervix. The egg then enters the vagina. The **vagina** (vuh JY nuh) is a muscular passageway leading to the outside of the body. The vagina is also called the birth canal. It is the passageway through which a baby leaves the mother's body during the birth process.

☑ *Checkpoint* *What is one of the roles of the ovaries?*

The Menstrual Cycle

When the female reproductive system becomes mature during the teenage years, there are about 400,000 undeveloped eggs in a woman's ovaries. However, only about 500 of those eggs will actually leave the ovaries and reach the uterus. An egg is released about once a month in a mature female's body. The monthly cycle of changes that occurs in the female reproductive system is called the **menstrual cycle** (MEN stroo ul).

During the menstrual cycle, an egg develops in an ovary. At the same time, the uterus prepares for the arrival of a fertilized egg. In this way, the menstrual cycle prepares the female's body for pregnancy, the condition that begins after fertilization has taken place.

Stages of the Cycle The menstrual cycle begins when an egg starts to mature in one of the ovaries. At the same time, the lining of the uterus begins to thicken. About halfway through a typical cycle, the mature egg is released from the ovary into an oviduct. This process is called **ovulation** (OH vyuh lay shun).

Graphing ACTIVITY

A woman's hormone levels change throughout the menstrual cycle. The table below shows the levels of one female hormone, known as LH, during the menstrual cycle.

Day	Level of LH
1	12
5	14
9	14
13	70
17	12
21	12
25	8

Construct a line graph using the information in the table. Label the horizontal axis *Day.* Label the vertical axis *Hormone Level.* What event takes place about the same time that LH reaches its highest level?

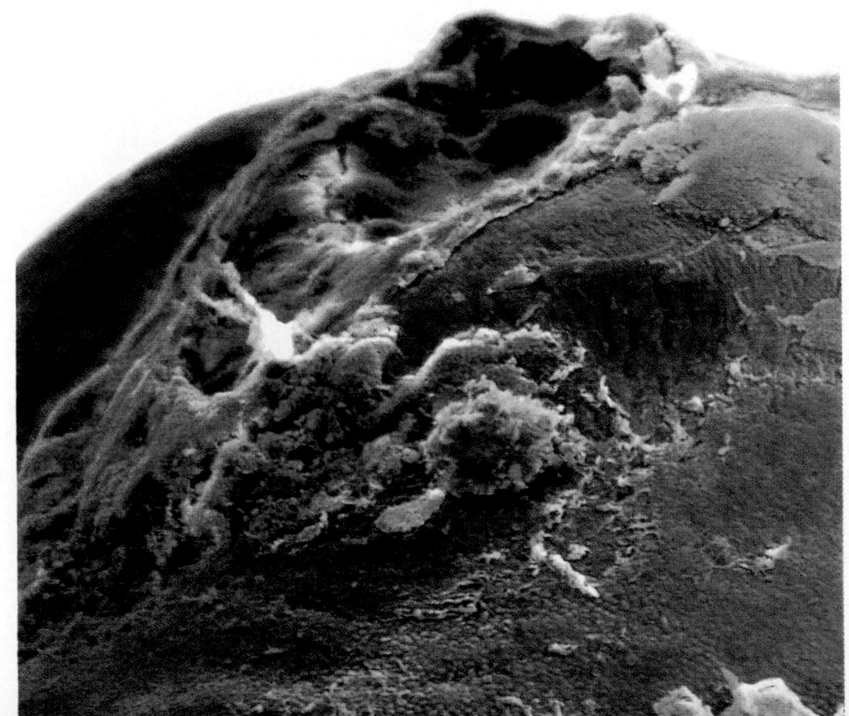

Figure 7 During ovulation an egg bursts from the side of an ovary. In this photograph, the egg is the round red structure on the right.

Once the egg is released, it can be fertilized for the next few days if sperm are present in the oviduct. If the egg is not fertilized, it begins to break down. The lining of the uterus also breaks down. The extra blood and tissue of the thickened lining pass out of the body through the vagina. This process is called **menstruation** (men stroo AY shun). On average, menstruation lasts about 4 to 6 days. At the same time that menstruation occurs, a new egg begins to mature in the ovary, and the cycle continues. You can follow the main steps in the cycle in Figure 8.

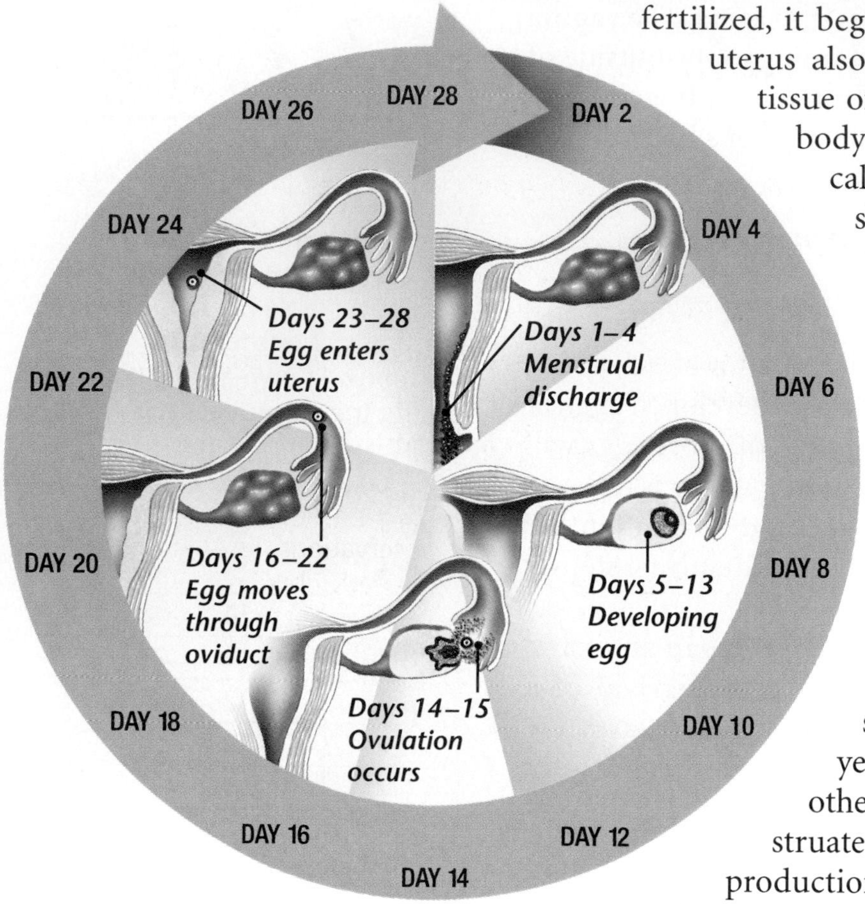

Endocrine Control The menstrual cycle is controlled by hormones of the endocrine system. Hormones also trigger a girl's first menstruation. Many girls begin menstruation between the ages of 10 and 14 years. Some girls start earlier, while others start later. Women continue to menstruate until about age 50. At around that age, production of sex hormones drops. As a result, the ovaries stop releasing mature egg cells.

DAY 28
DAY 2
DAY 4
DAY 6
DAY 8
DAY 10
DAY 12
DAY 14
DAY 16
DAY 18
DAY 20
DAY 22
DAY 24
DAY 26

Days 1–4 Menstrual discharge

Days 5–13 Developing egg

Days 14–15 Ovulation occurs

Days 16–22 Egg moves through oviduct

Days 23–28 Egg enters uterus

Figure 8 During the menstrual cycle, the lining of the uterus builds up with extra blood and tissue. About halfway through a typical cycle, ovulation takes place. If the egg is not fertilized, menstruation occurs.

Section 2 Review

1. What specialized cells are produced in the male and female reproductive systems?
2. How does the uterus change during the menstrual cycle?
3. How does a sperm's structure help it function?
4. What is ovulation? How often does it occur?
5. **Thinking Critically Comparing and Contrasting** In what ways are the functions of the ovaries and the testes similar? How do their functions differ?

Check Your Progress

CHAPTER PROJECT 8

You should now be caring for your "baby," taking it with you everywhere or arranging for a responsible person to care for it. You or your substitute must continue to perform all the child-care tasks, such as feeding the baby, changing diapers, and playing with the baby. Whenever you travel, you must have a safe method for transporting the baby. Don't forget to make at least two journal entries each day.

SECTION 3

Pregnancy, Birth, and Childhood

DISCOVER

How Many Ways Does a Child Grow?

1. Compare the two photographs at the left. One shows a baby girl. The other shows the same girl at the age of five.
2. Make two lists—one of the similarities and the other of the differences you see.
3. Compare your lists with those of your classmates.

Think It Over

Observing Based on your observations, list three physical changes that occur in early childhood.

GUIDE FOR READING

- **What are the stages of human development that occur before birth?**
- **What happens during childbirth?**

Reading Tip **As you read, use the headings to outline the events that occur during pregnancy, birth, and childhood.**

An egg can be fertilized during the first few days after ovulation. If fertilization occurs, the amazing process of human development begins.

A fertilized egg, or zygote, is no larger than the period at the end of this sentence. Yet after fertilization, the zygote undergoes changes that result in the formation of a new human. **The zygote develops first into an embryo and then into a fetus.** About nine months after fertilization, a baby is born.

The Zygote

After an egg cell and sperm cell join, the zygote moves down the oviduct toward the uterus. During this trip, which takes about four days, the zygote begins to divide. The original cell divides to make two cells, these two cells divide to make four, and so on. Eventually, the growing mass of hundreds of cells forms a hollow ball. The ball attaches to the lining of the uterus. For the next eight weeks or so, the developing human is called an **embryo** (EM bree oh).

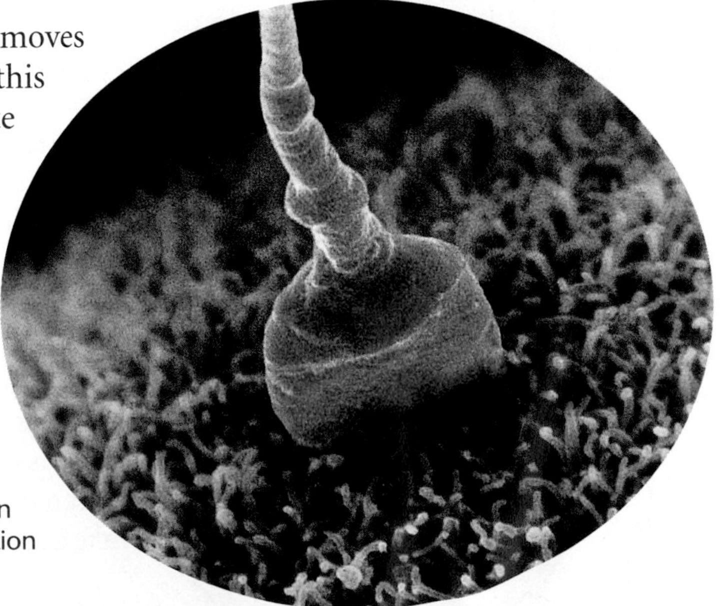

Figure 9 Only one sperm can fertilize an egg. Once fertilization occurs, the process of human development begins.

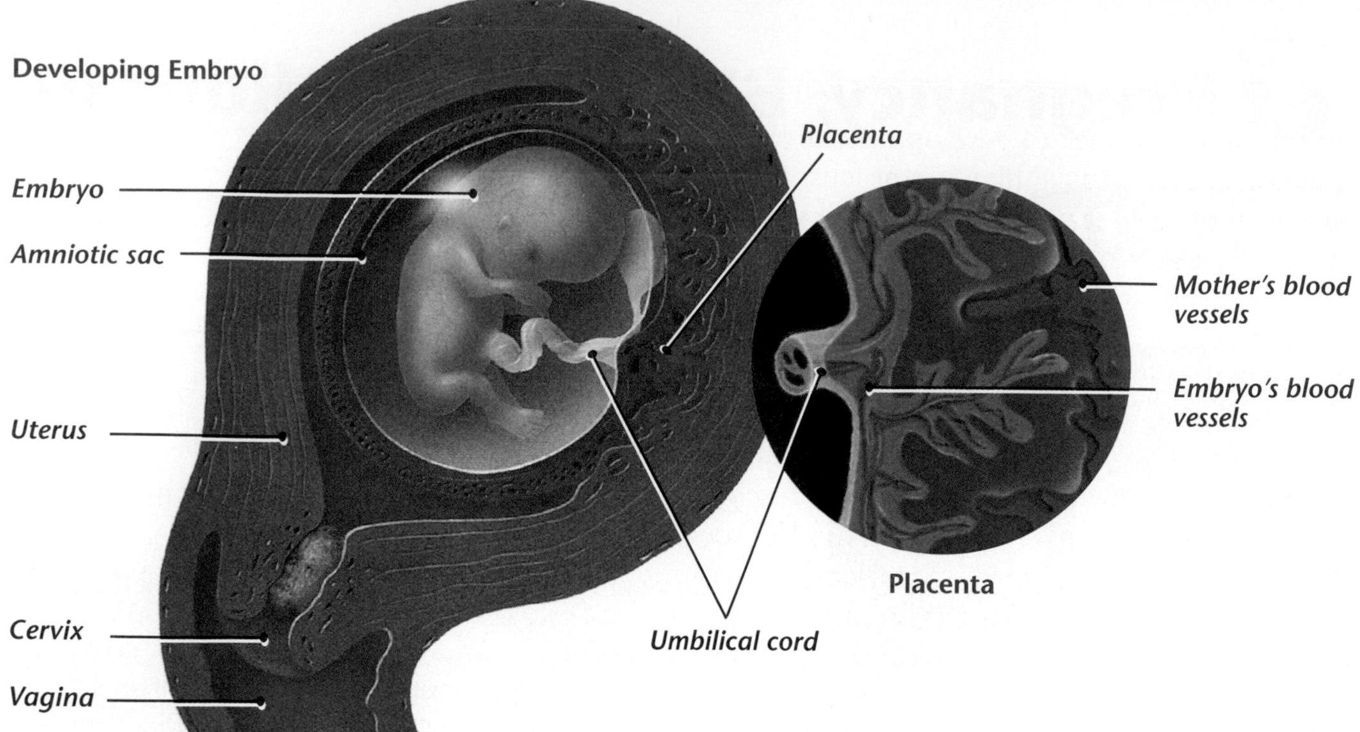

Figure 10 The placenta connects the mother and the developing embryo. But the mother's and the embryo's blood vessels remain separate, as you can see in the closeup of the placenta. ***Interpreting Diagrams*** *What structure carries nutrients and oxygen from the placenta to the embryo?*

The Development of the Embryo

Soon after the embryo attaches to the uterus, many changes take place. The hollow ball of cells grows inward. New membranes form. One membrane surrounds the embryo and develops into a fluid-filled sac called the **amniotic sac** (am nee AHT ik). Locate the amniotic sac in Figure 10. The fluid in the amniotic sac cushions and protects the developing baby.

Another membrane that forms is the **placenta** (pluh SEN tuh). The placenta becomes the link between the developing embryo and the mother. In the placenta, the embryo's blood vessels are located next to the mother's blood vessels. Blood from the two systems does not mix, but many substances are exchanged. The embryo receives nutrients, oxygen, and other substances from the mother. It gives off carbon dioxide and other wastes.

The embryo soon moves a short distance from the placenta. A ropelike structure called the **umbilical cord** forms between the embryo and the placenta. It contains blood vessels that link the embryo to the mother, but the two circulatory systems remain separated by a thin barrier.

INTEGRATING HEALTH The barrier that separates the embryo's and mother's blood prevents some diseases from spreading from the mother to the embryo. However, substances such as chemicals in tobacco smoke, alcohol, and some other drugs can pass through the barrier to the embryo. For this reason, pregnant women should not smoke tobacco, drink alcohol, or take any drug without a doctor's approval.

Checkpoint *How does an embryo obtain oxygen?*

The Development of the Fetus

From the ninth week of development until birth, the embryo is called a **fetus** (FEE tus). Although the fetus starts out about as small as a walnut shell, it now looks more like a baby. Many internal organs have developed. The head is about half the body's total size. The fetus's brain is developing rapidly. It also has dark eye patches, fingers, and toes. By the end of the third month, the fetus is about 9 centimeters long and has a mass of about 26 grams.

Between the fourth and sixth months, the tissues of the fetus continue to develop into more recognizable shapes. Bones become distinct. A heartbeat can be heard with a stethoscope. A layer of soft hair grows over the skin. The arms and legs develop more completely. The fetus begins to move and kick, a sign that its muscles are growing. At the end of the sixth month, the mass of the fetus is approaching 700 grams. Its body is about 20 centimeters long.

The final 3 months prepare the fetus to survive outside the mother's body. The brain surface develops grooves and ridges. The lungs become developed enough to carry out the exchange of oxygen and carbon dioxide. The eyelids can open. Eyelashes and eyebrows grow. The fetus doubles in length. Its mass may reach 3 kilograms or more.

Way to Grow!

ACTIVITY

The table lists the average mass of a developing baby at different months of pregnancy.

Month of Pregnancy	Mass (grams)
1	0.02
2	2.0
3	26
4	150
5	460
6	640
7	1,500
8	2,300
9	3,200

1. Use a balance to identify an everyday object with a mass equal to each mass listed in the table. You may need to use different balances to cover the range of masses listed.
2. Arrange the objects in order by month.

Making Models What did you learn by gathering these physical models?

Figure 11 At the beginning of the fourth month of development, a fetus has developed internal organs, dark eye patches, fingers, and toes. Later, its eyes will open, and fingernails and toenails will form.

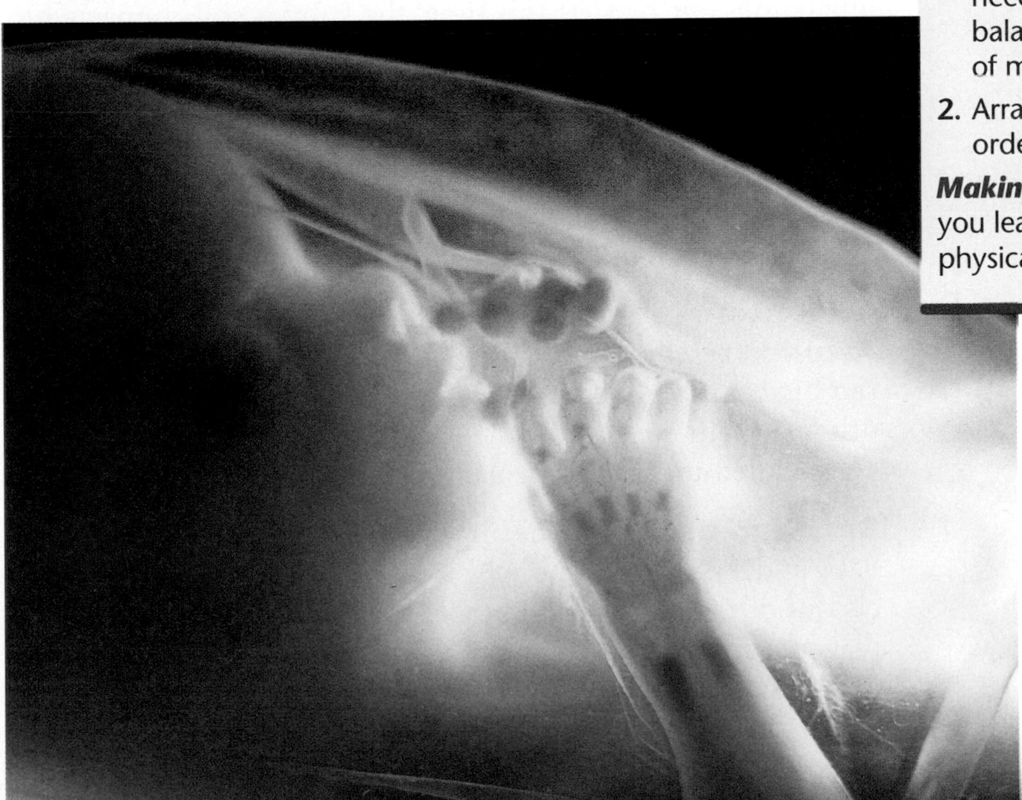

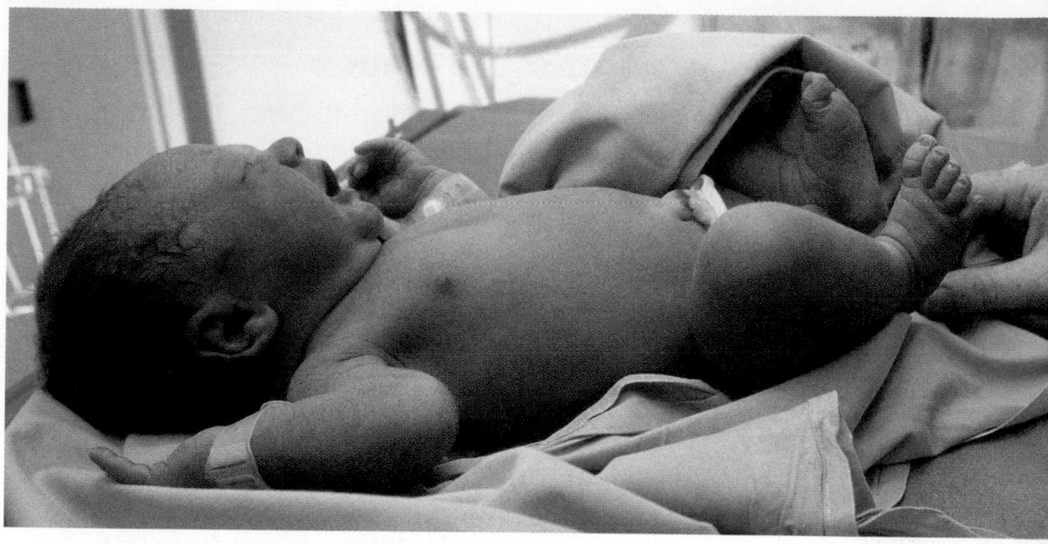

Figure 12 After about 9 months of growth and development inside the uterus, a baby is born. You can see where the umbilical cord of this newborn was clamped and cut.

Birth

After about 9 months of development inside the uterus, the baby is ready to be born. **The birth of a baby takes place in three stages—labor, delivery, and afterbirth.**

Labor During the first stage of birth, strong muscular contractions of the uterus begin. These contractions are called labor. The contractions cause the cervix to enlarge, eventually allowing the baby to fit through the opening. As labor progresses, the contractions become stronger and more frequent. Labor may last from about 2 hours to more than 20 hours.

Delivery The second stage of birth is called delivery. During delivery, the baby is pushed completely out of the uterus, through the vagina, and out of the mother's body. The head usually comes out first. At this time, the baby is still connected to the placenta by the umbilical cord. Delivery usually takes less time than labor does—from several minutes to a few hours.

Shortly after delivery, the umbilical cord is clamped, then cut about five centimeters from the baby's abdomen. Cutting the umbilical cord does not cause the baby any pain. Within 7 to 10 days, the remainder of the umbilical cord dries up and falls off, leaving a scar called the navel, or belly button.

Afterbirth About 15 minutes after delivery, the third stage of the birth process begins. Contractions push the placenta and other membranes out of the uterus through the vagina. This stage, called afterbirth, is usually completed in less than an hour.

Birth and the Baby The birth process is stressful for both the baby and the mother. The baby is pushed and squeezed as it travels out of the mother's body. Contractions put pressure on the placenta and umbilical cord, briefly cutting off the baby's supply of oxygen.

In response to the changes, the baby's endocrine system releases adrenaline. The baby's heart rate increases. Within a few seconds of delivery, a baby may cry or cough. This action helps rid the lungs of fluid and fills them with air. The newborn's heart rate then slows to a steady pace. Blood travels to the lungs and picks up oxygen from the air that the baby breathes in. The newborn's cry helps it adjust to the changes in its surroundings.

Checkpoint *What events occur during labor?*

Multiple Births

The delivery of more than one baby from a single pregnancy is called a multiple birth. In the United States, a set of twins is born in about one out of every 90 births. Triplets are born in about one out of every 7,000 births.

There are two types of twins: identical twins and fraternal twins. Identical twins develop from a single fertilized egg, or zygote: Early in development, the embryo splits into two identical embryos. The two embryos have identical inherited traits and are the same sex. Fraternal twins develop when two eggs are released from the ovary and are fertilized by two different sperm. Fraternal twins are no more alike than any other brothers or sisters. Fraternal twins may or may not be the same sex.

Triplets and other multiple births can occur when three or more eggs are produced and fertilized by different sperm. Such births can also occur when an embryo splits into three or more identical embryos.

Designing Experiments

ACTIVITY

How does the frequency of twins in your school compare to the frequency given in the text? Develop a plan to find out. With your teacher's permission, carry out your plan. Then collect and analyze your data. Of the total number of students, how many are twins? Are your results close to 1 out of 90?

Figure 13 Identical twins (left) develop from the same zygote; they share identical characteristics. Fraternal twins (right) develop from two different fertilized eggs. ***Applying Concepts*** *Why can fraternal twins be different sexes while identical twins cannot?*

Figure 14 During infancy, many physical and mental skills develop. Babies can usually crawl by about seven months of age (left). By the age of two (right), most babies are coordinated enough to feed themselves. ***Making Generalizations*** *What other skills develop during infancy?*

Infancy

What can a newborn baby do? You might say "Not much!" A newborn can perform only simple actions, such as crying, sucking, yawning, and blinking. But during infancy—the first two years of life—babies undergo many changes and learn to do many things.

Physical Changes A baby's shape and size change greatly during infancy. When a baby is born, its head makes up about one fourth of its body length. As the infant develops, its head grows more slowly, and its body, legs, and arms begin to catch up. Its nervous and muscular systems become better coordinated. The baby then starts to develop new physical skills.

The exact ages at which physical skills develop vary from baby to baby. A newborn cannot lift its head. But after about 3 months, it can hold its head up and reach for objects. Within the next 2 months or so, the infant can grasp objects. At about 7 months, most infants can move around by crawling. Somewhere between 10 and 16 months, most infants begin to walk by themselves.

Other Changes How does an infant communicate? You may think that babies display feelings mostly by crying. But young infants can show pleasure by smiling and laughing. They can turn their heads or spit out food they don't like. Babies also begin to make babbling sounds. Sometime between the ages of one and three years, many children speak their first word. By the end of infancy, children can do many things for themselves, such as understand simple directions, feed themselves, and play with toys. However, infants are too young to know when something can hurt them. They must be watched carefully at all times.

Childhood

Infancy ends and childhood begins at about two years of age. Childhood continues until about the age of 13 years. Children gradually become more active and independent, and experience many physical and mental changes.

Physical Changes Throughout childhood, children continue to grow. They become taller and heavier as their bones and muscles increase in size. They become more coordinated as they practice skills such as walking, holding a fork, using a pencil, and playing games. Over a period of several years, baby teeth fall out and are replaced by permanent teeth. Toward the end of childhood, the bones, especially the legs, begin to grow faster. An increased appetite signals that the body needs more nutrients for its next stage of growth and development.

Other Changes As they develop, children show a growing curiosity and increasing mental abilities. Their curiosity helps them learn about their surroundings. With the help of family members and teachers, children learn to read and to solve problems. Language skills improve rapidly. For example, most four-year-olds can express themselves clearly and can carry on conversations.

Over time, children learn to make friends, care about others, and behave responsibly. Between the ages of 3 and 6, they learn to share and play with others. As children think about and care more for others, friends become more important. About the age of 10, children develop a strong wish to fit in with others of their age group. As their independence increases, children take on more responsibilities at home and school.

Figure 15 During childhood, children learn to get along with others. Their physical activities and games help them become stronger and more coordinated.

Section 3 Review

1. What three stages of development does a fertilized egg go through before birth?
2. Briefly describe what happens during each of the three stages of birth.
3. What is the function of the amniotic sac? What is the function of the placenta?
4. List two physical changes that occur during infancy.
5. **Thinking Critically Relating Cause and Effect** Why is it dangerous for a pregnant woman to drink alcohol or to smoke?

Science at Home

Discuss with a family member some of the physical and other changes that take place during infancy and childhood. If possible, find out about some of your own milestones—when you first smiled, walked, or talked, for example. Discuss how these milestones relate to the physical changes that occur at each stage.

SECTION 4 Adolescence—A Time of Change

DISCOVER ACTIVITY

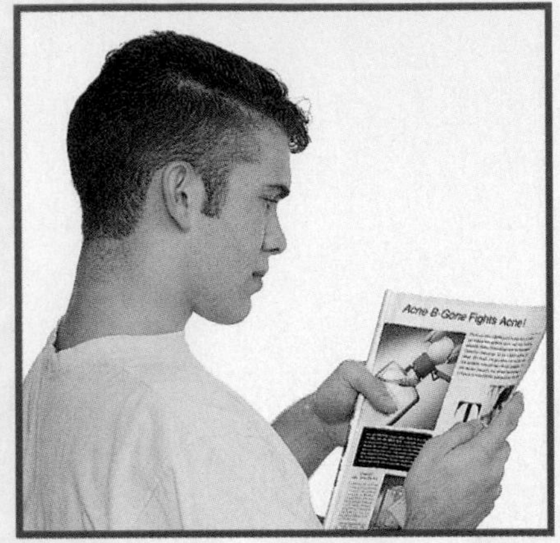

How Do Ads Portray Teenagers?

1. Carefully examine an advertisement taken from a teen magazine. The ad should show one or more teenagers. Be sure to read the text and examine the picture.
2. Think about how the ad portrays the teenagers. How do they look and act? Do you think they are typical teens? How accurate is this "picture" of teenagers? Write down your thoughts.

Think It Over

Drawing Conclusions How does the ad use teenagers to try to influence people your age? Explain your opinion. Do you think the ad is effective?

GUIDE FOR READING

- **What is the difference between adolescence and puberty?**
- **What mental and social changes are associated with adolescence?**

Reading Tip **As you read, make a list of the changes that take place during adolescence.**

If you compared a current photo of yourself with one taken three years ago, you would notice many changes. Starting at about the age of 12, you gradually begin to change from a child to an adult. Although many changes happen during infancy and childhood, some of the most significant changes occur during adolescence. **Adolescence** (ad ul ES uns) is the stage of development when children become adults physically and mentally.

By the end of adolescence, you will be able to do things you could not do during childhood. You will become eligible for privileges such as a driver's license and the right to vote. Along

Figure 16 During adolescence, teens mature both physically and mentally. It's a time when many teens try new experiences and take on more responsibilities. Working in the community is one way that teens can explore their interests while helping others.

with these privileges, you will be expected to take on adult responsibilities, such as driving safely. Adolescence is the time to work to become the healthy adult you want to be.

Physical Changes

Adolescence is a time of rapid physical growth. A person grows taller and heavier, and begins to look like an adult. However, some of the most important physical changes take place inside the body. These physical changes are controlled by the hormones of the endocrine system.

Puberty Sometime between the ages of about 9 and 14 years, a child enters puberty. **Puberty** (PYOO bur tee) is the period of sexual development in which the body becomes able to reproduce. Some people think that the term *puberty* is another word for adolescence, but that is not correct. **Adolescence includes more than just the physical changes of puberty. Many important mental and social changes take place as well.**

In girls, hormones produced by the pituitary gland and the ovaries control the physical changes of puberty. The sex organs develop. Ovulation and menstruation begin. The breasts begin to enlarge, and the hips start to widen. The skin begins to produce more oils, and body odor increases.

In boys, hormones from the testes and the pituitary gland govern the changes. The sex organs develop, and sperm production begins. The voice deepens. Hair appears on the face and sometimes on the chest. As with girls, more skin oils are produced, and body odor increases.

Figure 17 Despite their different sizes, each of these teens is developing normally. ***Relating Cause and Effect*** *What body system controls the rate at which changes occur during puberty?*

Bone and Muscle Growth Just as infants and children experience growth spurts, or periods of rapid growth, so do adolescents. Girls tend to experience their growth spurt slightly younger than boys do. Thus, during early adolescence girls tend to be taller than boys. Later in adolescence boys display rapid growth. Overall, boys tend to reach taller adult heights than girls.

Have you ever heard the phrase "growing pains"? Some adolescents grow so rapidly that they experience aches in their arms and legs. A sudden change in height or weight can cause a teen to feel clumsy or awkward at times. It takes time to adjust to a new body size and shape. Regular exercise can help a teen adjust more quickly. Teens should not over-exercise, however, as growing bones and muscles can be injured if overworked.

Another effect rapid growth can produce is hunger. It's normal for teens to go through periods when they eat huge amounts of food. The extra food provides the raw materials and energy required by the growing body. Nutritious meals and snacks can supply the body with the nutrients it needs.

When Puberty Begins As adolescents mature, they may compare their physical development with that of their peers. Teens of the same age can be at different stages of growth. This is because the age at which puberty begins varies from person to person.

These different rates of physical development may lead to misunderstandings. Adolescents whose bodies mature at a younger age may be expected to have adult judgment and take on more responsibilities than other teens. Those whose bodies develop later may face different challenges. They may be treated like children because of their young appearance.

☑ ***Checkpoint*** *What is a growth spurt?*

Mental and Social Changes

Adolescents may notice changes in the way they think, feel, and get along with others. Many teenagers have mixed feelings about the changes they are experiencing. They may feel excited and happy about them one day, and shy and confused the next day. **Adolescents undergo many mental and social changes as they become more mature.**

Mental Changes Between about the ages of 13 and 15, a teenager gradually becomes able to think and reason like an adult. Teens can think in ways that they could not as children. For example, young children think of hunger only when their stomachs are empty, or of pain only when they are hurt. They don't think beyond what's happening at the moment. Teenagers' thoughts are no longer limited to their immediate experiences. They begin to consider the consequences of their actions and make thoughtful judgments. Memory and problem-solving skills also improve. These and other mental abilities are often developed at school or through interests such as music or theater.

Adolescence is a time when individuals begin to question things that they accepted as children. Adolescents may wonder about the opinions and actions of friends and family members. They may also begin to ask themselves questions such as "Who am I?" and "What will I do with my life?" Often teens find answers by talking with parents, religious leaders, and other adults. Other times teens try out new experiences—from new hairstyles and clothes to volunteering their time to help others.

Social Studies CONNECTION

In many cultures, adolescence is seen as a passage from childhood to adulthood. In the Apache culture, girls who have entered puberty and begun their menstrual cycles undergo the Changing Woman ceremony. Often the whole community enjoys the feasting, dancing, and performances that are part of the ceremony. The girl dresses in a decorated buckskin dress and is sprinkled with cattail pollen. Other parts of the ceremony include fasting followed by special meals and prayer. After the ceremony, the girl is considered a woman by tribal members.

In Your Journal

Imagine you have just witnessed the Changing Woman ceremony. Write a short letter to a friend describing the event. Include information about the significance of the ceremony. Relate the experience to events with which you are familiar.

Figure 18 In the ceremony being celebrated here, tribal members help this 14-year-old Apache girl mark her passage to adulthood.

Figure 19 During the adolescent years, teens place a high value on friendships. ***Making Judgments*** *How can friends help each other develop skills that will be important throughout life?*

Social Changes It is common for adolescents to experience changes in their relationships with others. As they become more independent, teens spend more time with their friends. Because friends' opinions are very important, teens may worry whether friends approve of their clothing, looks, personality, and interests. Some teens may also become interested in members of the opposite sex.

As you learned in Chapter 1, peer pressure may influence the decisions and actions of teenagers. Peer pressure can produce both negative and positive results. Negative peer pressure can lead teens to do things that go against their values. The support of friends, on the other hand, can encourage teens to work toward their goals or develop new interests and skills.

☑ *Checkpoint* *What social changes occur during adolescence?*

Life as an Adult

At what point does adolescence end and adulthood begin? On a certain birthday? When people are physically mature? When people start to live on their own? If you look up the word *adult* in the dictionary, it is defined as being grown up, or mature. Legally, Americans are considered to be adults at the age of 16 or 18 for some activities and at the age of 21 for others. From a physical and mental standpoint, however, it is difficult to say when adulthood begins.

Physical changes continue to occur throughout adulthood. After about the age of 30, a process known as aging begins. Aging becomes more noticeable between the ages of 40 and 65. The skin starts to become wrinkled, the eyes lose their ability to focus on close objects, the hair may lose its coloring, and muscle strength decreases. During this period, females stop menstruating and ovulating. Males usually continue to produce sperm throughout their lives, although the number of sperm they produce decreases with age.

After age 65, aging intensifies, often leading to less efficient heart and lung action. But the effects of aging can be slowed if people follow sensible diets and good exercise plans. With the help of such healthy behaviors, more and more adults remain active throughout their lives.

Figure 20 Adulthood is a time when opportunities and choices expand. Adults can also share their knowledge and experience with younger people.

Responsibilities—as well as opportunities, rights, and privileges—arrive with adulthood. During adolescence you learn to take care of yourself. Eventually, no one will tell you how to spend your money or what to eat. As an adult, you may need to make decisions that affect not just yourself, but your spouse and your children as well. You will need know what values are important to you, and make decisions that match those values.

Section 4 Review

1. What is the difference between puberty and adolescence? Describe three physical changes that occur in boys and girls during puberty.
2. Name two mental changes and one social change that adolescents experience.
3. Why do adolescents sometimes feel clumsy or awkward?
4. What behaviors can adults practice to slow down the effects of aging?
5. **Thinking Critically Making Judgments** "Developing a sense of who you are is the most important part of adolescence." What does this statement mean? Do you agree with it? Explain.

CHAPTER PROJECT 8

Check Your Progress

By now, you should be preparing a summary of what you learned about being a parent. What skills do parents need? What are some of the rewards of parenthood? What are some of the challenges? How would you feel if you had to continue caring for the "baby" past the project deadline? Write answers to these questions as your final journal entry.

Skills Lab

Interpreting Data

Growing Up

Problem

How do the proportions of the human body change during development?

Procedure

1. Examine the diagram below. Notice that the figures are drawn against a graph showing percents. You can use this diagram to determine how the lengths of major body parts compare to each figure's height. Make a data table in which to record information about each figure's head size and leg length.
2. Look at Figure D. You can use the graph to estimate that the head is about 15% of the figure's full height. Record that number in your data table.
3. Examine Figures A through C. Determine the percent of the total height that the head makes up. Record your results. (*Hint:* Figure A shows the legs folded. You will need to estimate the data for that figure.)
4. Now compare the length of the legs to the total body height for Figures A through D. Record your results.

Analyze and Conclude

1. How do the percents for head size and leg length change from infancy to adulthood?
2. What can you infer about the rate at which different parts of the body grow? Explain.
3. **Think About It** If you made a line graph using the data in the diagram, what would be on the horizontal axis? On the vertical axis? What additional information could you gain from this line graph?

Design an Experiment

Make a prediction about the relationship between the circumference of the head compared to body height. Then design an experiment to test your prediction, using people for test subjects. Obtain your teacher's permission before carrying out the experiment.

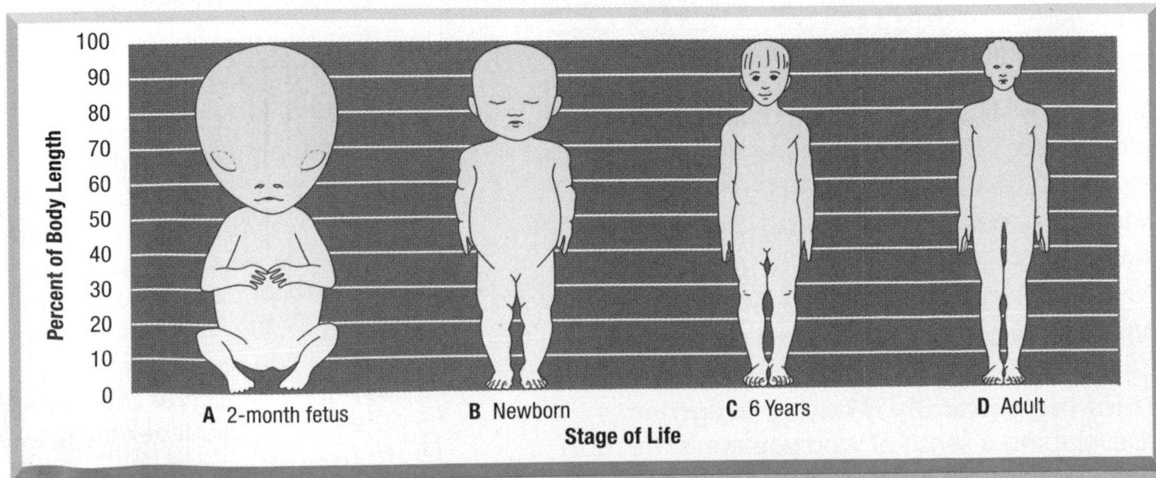

Section 1 The Endocrine System

Key Ideas

- The endocrine system controls many of the body's daily activities, as well as the body's overall development.
- The endocrine system releases chemical messages called hormones. Hormones travel through the bloodstream to their target organs.
- Homeostasis in the body is maintained partly through negative feedback: the right amount of a particular hormone signals the body to stop producing that hormone.

Key Terms

endocrine gland
hormone
target cell
hypothalamus
pituitary gland
negative feedback

Section 2 The Male and Female Reproductive Systems

Key Ideas

- The male reproductive system is specialized to produce sperm and the hormone testosterone.
- The role of the female reproductive system is to produce eggs and to nourish a developing baby until birth.
- Eggs are produced in the ovaries of the female. During the menstrual cycle, an egg develops, and the uterus prepares for the arrival of a fertilized egg.

Key Terms

egg
sperm
fertilization
reproduction
zygote
chromosome
testis
testosterone
scrotum
semen
penis
ovary
estrogen
oviduct
uterus
vagina
menstrual cycle
ovulation
menstruation

Section 3 Pregnancy, Birth, and Childhood

Key Ideas

- If an egg is fertilized, pregnancy begins. The zygote develops into an embryo and then a fetus.
- A baby develops inside the mother's uterus for about 9 months before it is born. Birth takes place in three stages—labor, delivery, and afterbirth.
- Infancy is a time of rapid physical growth and mastery of basic skills. During childhood, children become more independent.

Key Terms

embryo
amniotic sac
placenta
umbilical cord
fetus

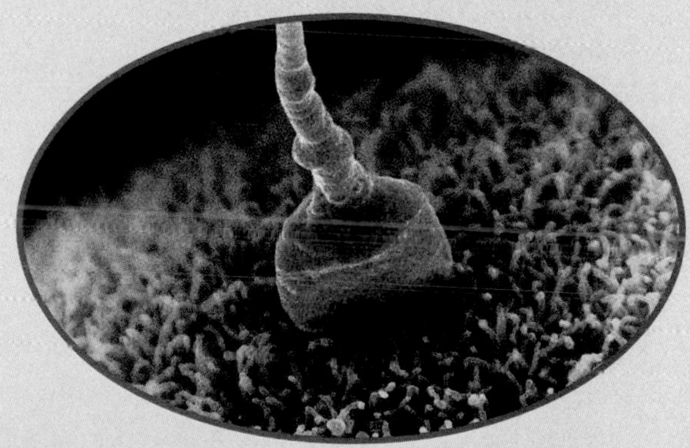

Section 4 Adolescence— A Time of Change

INTEGRATING HEALTH

Key Ideas

- Adolescence includes the physical changes of puberty as well as mental and social changes.
- Puberty is the period of sexual development in which the body becomes able to reproduce. Males and females develop the physical characteristics of adult men and women.

Key Terms

adolescence
puberty

www.science-explorer.phschool.com

CHAPTER 8 REVIEW

Reviewing Content

For more review of key concepts, see the Interactive Student Tutorial CD-ROM.

Multiple Choice

Choose the letter of the best answer.

1. Which structure links the nervous system and the endocrine system?
- **a.** pituitary gland
- **b.** adrenal gland
- **c.** parathyroid gland
- **d.** hypothalamus

2. What is the male sex cell called?
- **a.** testis
- **b.** sperm
- **c.** egg
- **d.** ovary

3. The release of an egg from an ovary is known as
- **a.** ovulation.
- **b.** fertilization
- **c.** menstruation.
- **d.** afterbirth.

4. Two individuals that develop from the same zygote are called
- **a.** embryos.
- **b.** fraternal twins.
- **c.** identical twins.
- **d.** triplets.

5. Sex organs develop rapidly during
- **a.** infancy.
- **b.** childhood.
- **c.** puberty.
- **d.** adulthood.

True or False

If the statement is true, write true. If it is false, change the underlined word or words to make the statement true.

6. The pituitary gland produces adrenaline.

7. The female reproductive glands are the ovaries.

8. The joining of a sperm and an egg is called fertilization.

9. An oviduct is the passageway through which an egg travels from the ovary to the uterus.

10. The physical changes of adolescence are controlled by the nervous system.

Checking Concepts

11. What is the function of the hypothalamus?

12. When enough thyroxine has been released into the blood, what signal is sent to the thyroid gland? How is that signal sent?

13. What changes occur in the uterus during the menstrual cycle?

14. How does a zygote form? What happens to the zygote about four days after it forms?

15. Describe how a fetus receives food and oxygen and gets rid of wastes.

16. Summarize the physical changes that take place during infancy.

17. List six changes a ten-year-old boy should expect to occur in the next five years. Include physical, mental, and social changes.

18. Writing to Learn Imagine you're a skeleton in the body of a sixteen-year-old person. Write about the changes you've experienced since infancy.

Thinking Visually

19. Flowchart Copy this flowchart and fill in the main stages that occur between fertilization and birth. (For more on flowcharts, see the Skills Handbook.)

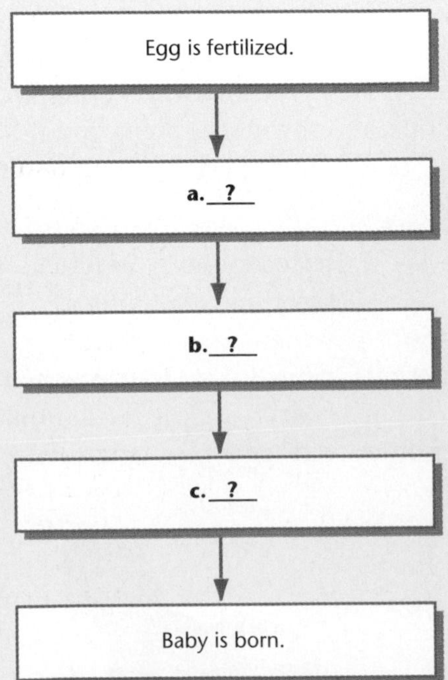

Applying Skills

The data table below shows how the length of a developing baby changes during pregnancy. Use the table to answer Questions 20–22.

Week of Pregnancy	Average Length (mm)	Week of Pregnancy	Average Length (mm)
4	7	24	300
8	30	28	350
12	75	32	410
16	180	36	450
20	250	38	500

20. **Measuring** Use a metric ruler to mark each length on a piece of paper. During which four-week period did the greatest increase in length occur?
21. **Graphing** Graph the data by plotting time on the horizontal axis and length on the vertical axis.
22. **Interpreting Data** At the twelfth week, a developing baby measures about 75 mm. By which week has the fetus grown to four times that length? Six times that length?

Thinking Critically

23. **Applying Concepts** The pancreas produces insulin, a hormone that lowers the level of sugar in the blood. Glucagon, another hormone of the pancreas, increases the level of sugar in the blood. Suggest how these two hormones might work together to maintain homeostasis in the body.
24. **Relating Cause and Effect** How can playing games help children develop important skills?
25. **Comparing and Contrasting** In what way is development during adolescence similar to development before birth? How are the two stages different?

Performance Assessment

CHAPTER PROJECT 8

Wrap Up

Present Your Project You now have the chance to discuss what you learned as you cared for your "baby." What do you now know about parenting that you didn't know before? Consider reading passages from your journal to the class, including the summary you wrote.

Reflect and Record In your journal, describe how well you carried out this project. Did you care for the baby for three complete days? Did you do each task as carefully as you would have for a real infant? How do you think this project was similar to caring for a real baby? How was it different?

Getting Involved

In Your Community Find out from your teachers or from your school nurse whether baby-sitting courses are offered in your community. With your classmates, discuss what skills and information a baby-sitting course should teach. If possible, contact the organization that offers baby-sitting courses. Does your description match what the course offers?

The Olympic flame is a symbol of the spirit of the Olympic Games.

THE OLYMPIC GAMES

WHAT EVENT —

- *began in the spirit of competition and fair play?*
- *has the motto "faster, higher, stronger"?*
- *supports amateur sports?*
- *is the dream of young athletes around the world?*

The Olympic Games began more than 2,500 years ago in Olympia, Greece. For one day every four years, the best athletes in Greece gathered to compete. The games honored the Greek god Zeus. The ancient Greeks valued both physical and intellectual achievement. A winning athlete at the Olympic Games was rewarded with a lifetime of honor and fame.

For more than a thousand years, the Greeks held the games at Olympia every four years. This four-year period was called an Olympiad. The games were discontinued in A.D. 394, when the Romans ruled Greece.

Centuries later, in the 1880s, Pierre de Coubertin, a Frenchman, convinced the United States and other nations to bring back the Olympic games. Coubertin hoped that the modern Olympics would promote world peace by bringing together athletes from all nations. The modern Olympics began in Athens in 1896.

Today the Summer and Winter Olympics alternate every two years. For several weeks, athletes from all around the world experience the excitement of competing. Only a few know the joy of winning. But all who participate learn about fair play, striving toward a goal, and becoming a little bit faster and stronger through training.

This ancient marble statue is called *Discobolus,* ancient Greek for "discus thrower." The statue is a Roman copy of a statue made in Greece about 2,500 years ago.

Sports in Ancient Greece

The ancient Greeks valued physical fitness as much as an educated mind. Men and boys exercised regularly by wrestling, sprinting, throwing the discus, and tossing the javelin. Greek philosophy taught that a sound mind and body created a well-balanced person. Greek art glorified the muscles and movement of the human body in magnificent sculptures and paintings.

The first recorded Olympic Games were held in 776 B.C. That year a cook named Coroebus from Elis, Greece, won the only event in the games—a sprint of about 192 meters. The prize was a wreath of olive leaves. In ancient Greece an olive wreath was the highest mark of honor.

Over the next 130 years, other events were added to the games, including longer running events, wrestling, chariot racing, boxing, and the pentathlon. *Pent-* comes from the Greek word meaning "five." A pentathlon included five competitions: long jump, javelin toss, discus throw, foot race, and wrestling. Early records indicate that women were not allowed to compete in the games.

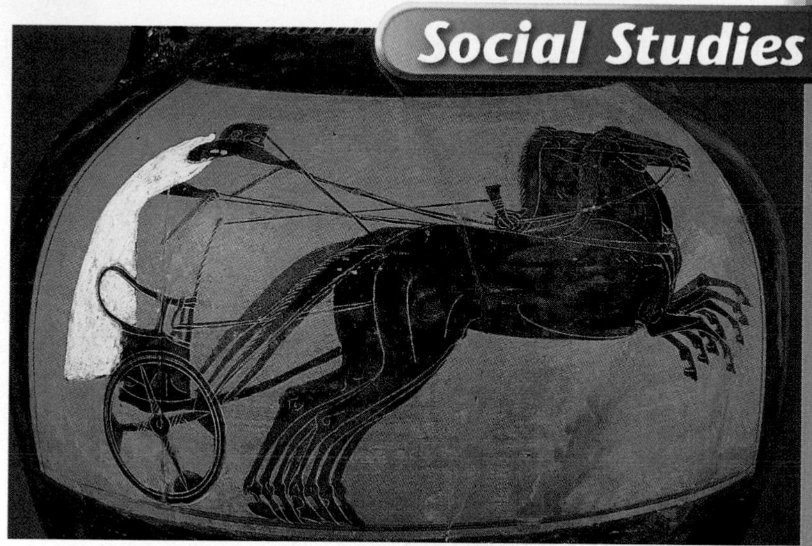

Chariot racing became a popular sport in the ancient Olympics. This scene is painted on a Greek amphora, a pottery jar for olive oil or wine.

Ancient Greece was a land of many rival city-states, such as Athens and Sparta. Each city-state sent its best athletes to the games at Olympia.

Social Studies Activity

The Olympics encourage peaceful competition among athletes from many nations. But political conflicts sometimes have disrupted or canceled the games. For example, the 1916 games were canceled because of World War I. Other Olympics are remembered for the achievements of certain athletes, such as Babe Didrikson in 1932. Find out what political events affected particular Olympics during the twentieth century. Or find out who were the outstanding athletes at different games. Report your findings to the class.

Language Arts

Modern Olympic Games

At the 1988 Olympic games in Seoul, South Korea, Jackie Joyner-Kersee was one of the star athletes. She won two gold medals there. In total, between 1984 and 1996, she won six Olympic medals (three of them gold), making her one of the world's greatest athletes.

Jackie grew up in East St. Louis, Illinois, where she started running and jumping at age ten. Although she was a natural at the long jump, she wasn't a fast runner. But her coach, Mr. Fennoy, encouraged her. After her final Olympics, Jackie wrote an autobiography—a story of her life. Here is an excerpt from her book *A Kind of Grace.*

Jackie Joyner-Kersee throws the javelin, one of seven events in the Olympic heptathlon. She won the heptathlon twice, in 1988 and 1992.

After school the boys' and girls' teams jogged to Lincoln Park's irregular-shaped track and makeshift long-jump pit. The track was a 36-inch-wide strip of black cinders sprinkled amid the rest of the dirt and grass. We called it the bridle path because that's what it looked like. We ran over, around and through the potholes, rocks, glass and tree limbs that littered the track. . . . After practice, we jogged another two or three miles around the neighborhood to complete our workout.

In winter, when it was too cold to practice outside, we trained inside the Lincoln High building. Every afternoon after school and at 9:00 every Saturday morning, the team of twenty-five girls split into groups on the two floors and ran along the brown concrete corridors. When it was time for hurdling drills, Mr. Fennoy set up hurdles in the center of the hallway on the second floor, and put us through our paces. We sprinted and leaped past the doors to the math and science classrooms. We ran to the end of the hall, turned around and repeated the drill in the opposite direction. . . .

The running drills, exhausting as they were, eventually paid off. In 1977, between the ninth and tenth grade, I developed booster rockets and cut an astonishing four seconds off my 440 time. I surged to the front of the pack in practice heats. By the time we entered Lincoln High as tenth-graders, I was the fastest 440 runner on the team. The last was—at long last—first.

Language Arts Activity

What does Jackie mean by "the last was—at long last—first"? How did she get to be first? Some people say that Jackie was just a natural athlete. Jackie herself says, "I think it was my reward for all those hours of work on the bridle path, the neighborhood sidewalks and the schoolhouse corridors."

Think about a period in your life when you had to prepare for a math competition, a recital, a performance, a sports event, or other event. Write a short autobiographical sketch describing how you worked to improve your performance.

Olympic Records

To prepare for the Olympic Games, top athletes train for years. Sometimes they even move to climates that will help them prepare to compete in their sports. Skiers, for example, might move to a mountain region where they can train year-round. Athletes also use the most advanced equipment available in their sport. This scientific approach to training has helped athletes set new records for speed, height, and distance. In addition, measurement tools such as timing clocks have become more precise. Sprinters and other athletes can now break records by just a few hundredths of a second.

The table and graph below show how the winning height in the women's high jump has changed over many Olympic Games. Notice that the high jump measures height in inches.

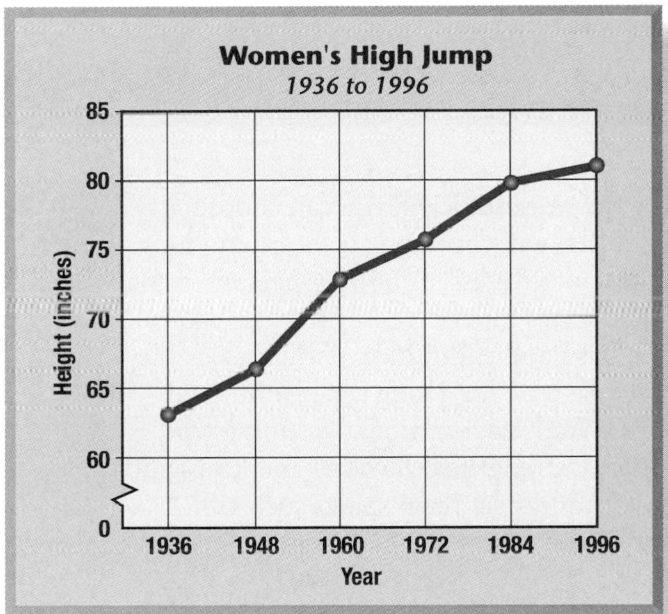

Women's High Jump (height in inches)	
1936	63
1948	$66\frac{1}{8}$
1960	$72\frac{3}{4}$
1972	$75\frac{1}{2}$
1984	$79\frac{1}{2}$
1996	$80\frac{3}{4}$

Stefka Kostadinova of Bulgaria won the women's high jump at the 1996 Olympics in Atlanta, Georgia. How much higher did she jump than the 1936 winner?

Men's 400-Meter Run (time in seconds)	
1936	46.5
1948	46.2
1960	44.9
1972	44.66
1984	44.27
1996	43.49

Math Activity

The line graph above shows how the heights in the Olympic women's high jump have changed since 1936. Use the table showing times for the men's 400-meter run to create your own line graph.

How did the winning performance in the men's 400-meter run change over time? How does your graph differ from that of the women's high jump? Why do the graphs differ?

Science

Getting Fit, Staying Fit

If you could be an Olympic athlete, would you be a runner, an ice skater, a gymnast, or some other athlete? Whatever their sport, Olympic athletes need to be physically fit to compete at their best. Physical fitness is the ability of the heart, blood vessels, lungs, and muscles to work together to meet the body's needs. Most people never compete in the Olympics. But if you are physically fit, you can reach your personal best.

The best way to boost your fitness is to exercise regularly. When you exercise, your heart, lungs, and muscles benefit. Team sports are good exercise, but so are activities such as walking, riding a bicycle, skating, swimming, and dancing. For the most benefit, people should exercise at least three times a week. Before you start an exercise program, have a physical examination to make sure that you do not have any health problems that rule out vigorous exercise.

A good exercise routine consists of stages, as shown in the flowchart below. Begin by warming up for five to ten minutes. To warm up, do your workout activity, but at a slower pace. If you plan to run, you can warm up by walking. You also should do exercises that gently stretch the muscles that you will use in your workout.

For the workout itself, you can choose exercises that will develop your heart and lungs, your muscular fitness, or both. A person whose heart and lungs function easily during vigorous exercise has good endurance. Endurance is the ability to exercise for a long time without getting tired. Walking, running, swimming, and bicycling all strengthen the heart and lungs and increase endurance. Team sports such as basketball and soccer also build endurance.

Stages in a Fitness Workout

Warm-up	Stretch	Workout	Cool-down	Stretch
Slowly move muscles to be used in workout.	Stretch muscles to be used in workout.	Do an activity such as walking, running, swimming, gymnastics, or riding a bicycle.	Move muscles used in workout at a reduced pace.	Stretch muscles used in workout.
5–10 minutes	5–10 minutes	20–45 minutes	5–10 minutes	5–10 minutes

These cross-country runners are about to test their physical fitness.

To improve muscular fitness, activities such as gymnastics and weight training are good choices. But many activities that are good for your heart and lungs contribute to muscular fitness too.

After you exercise vigorously, you should cool down by doing a gentler exercise. Stretching is also important for cooling down.

Science Activity

Your target heart rate is the approximate heart rate you need to maintain during a workout in order to increase your endurance. Target heart rate is usually expressed as a range—for example, 145 to 170 beats per minute.

1. To calculate your target heart rate, first take your pulse when you are at rest. Refer to page 112 for instructions on taking your pulse. Determine the number of times that your heart beats in one minute. This number is called your resting heart rate.
2. Subtract your resting heart rate from 210, which is about the maximum number of times your heart can beat in a minute.
3. To find the lower limit of your target heart rate, multiply the number you obtained in Step 2 by 0.6. Then add this number to your resting heart rate.
4. To get the upper limit of your target heart rate, multiply the number you obtained in Step 2 by 0.8. Then add this number to your resting heart rate.

Tie It Together

Plan an Olympic Day!

Design a competition that can be held at your school. Decide the time, place, and kind of contests to hold. Remember that the ancient Greeks honored intellect as well as athletics. So you could include games that test the mind as well as the body.

Research the decathlon, pentathlon, heptathlon, and marathon in the ancient and modern Olympics. You could design your own pentathlon that includes athletic and nonathletic events.

To organize the Olympic Day, you should:

- Set up the sports contests by measuring and marking the ground for each event.
- Find stopwatches, meter sticks, tape measures, and any necessary equipment.
- Locate or make prizes for first, second, and third place in each event.
- Enlist volunteers to compete in the events.
- Assign someone to take notes and to write a newspaper story on your Olympic Day.

Think Like a Scientist

Although you may not know it, you think like a scientist every day. Whenever you ask a question and explore possible answers, you use many of the same skills that scientists do. Some of these skills are described on this page.

Observing

When you use one or more of your five senses to gather information about the world, you are **observing.** Hearing a dog bark, counting twelve green seeds, and smelling smoke are all observations. To increase the power of their senses, scientists sometimes use microscopes, telescopes, or other instruments that help them make more detailed observations.

An observation must be factual and accurate—an exact report of what your senses detect. It is important to keep careful records of your observations in science class by writing or drawing in a notebook. The information collected through observations is called evidence, or data.

Inferring

When you explain or interpret an observation, you are **inferring,** or making an inference. For example, if you hear your dog barking, you may infer that someone is at your front door. To make this inference, you combine the evidence—the barking dog—and your experience or knowledge—you know that your dog barks when strangers approach—to reach a logical conclusion.

Notice that an inference is not a fact; it is only one of many possible explanations for an observation. For example, your dog may be barking because it wants to go for a walk. An inference may turn out to be incorrect even if it is based on accurate observations and logical reasoning. The only way to find out if an inference is correct is to investigate further.

Predicting

When you listen to the weather forecast, you hear many predictions about the next day's weather—what the temperature will be, whether it will rain, and how windy it will be. Weather forecasters use observations and knowledge of weather patterns to predict the weather. The skill of **predicting** involves making an inference about a future event based on current evidence or past experience.

Because a prediction is an inference, it may prove to be false. In science class, you can test some of your predictions by doing experiments. For example, suppose you predict that larger paper airplanes can fly farther than smaller airplanes. How could you test your prediction?

Use the photograph to answer the questions below.

Observing Look closely at the photograph. List at least three observations.

Inferring Use your observations to make an inference about what has happened. What experience or knowledge did you use to make the inference?

Predicting Predict what will happen next. On what evidence or experience do you base your prediction?

Classifying

Could you imagine searching for a book in the library if the books were shelved in no particular order? Your trip to the library would be an all-day event! Luckily, librarians group together books on similar topics or by the same author. Grouping together items that are alike in some way is called **classifying.** You can classify items in many ways: by size, by shape, by use, and by other important characteristics.

Like librarians, scientists use the skill of classifying to organize information and objects. When things are sorted into groups, the relationships among them become easier to understand.

ACTIVITY Classify the objects in the photograph into two groups based on any characteristic you choose. Then use another characteristic to classify the objects into three groups.

ACTIVITY This student is using a model to demonstrate what causes day and night on Earth. What do the flashlight and the tennis ball in the model represent?

Making Models

Have you ever drawn a picture to help someone understand what you were saying? Such a drawing is one type of model. A model is a picture, diagram, computer image, or other representation of a complex object or process. **Making models** helps people understand things that they cannot observe directly.

Scientists often use models to represent things that are either very large or very small, such as the planets in the solar system, or the parts of a cell. Such models are physical models—drawings or three-dimensional structures that look like the real thing. Other models are mental models—mathematical equations or words that describe how something works.

Communicating

Whenever you talk on the phone, write a letter, or listen to your teacher at school, you are communicating. **Communicating** is the process of sharing ideas and information with other people. Communicating effectively requires many skills, including writing, reading, speaking, listening, and making models.

Scientists communicate to share results, information, and opinions. Scientists often communicate about their work in journals, over the telephone, in letters, and on the Internet. They also attend scientific meetings where they share their ideas with one another in person.

ACTIVITY On a sheet of paper, write out clear, detailed directions for tying your shoe. Then exchange directions with a partner. Follow your partner's directions exactly. How successful were you at tying your shoe? How could your partner have communicated more clearly?

Making Measurements

When scientists make observations, it is not sufficient to say that something is "big" or "heavy." Instead, scientists use instruments to measure just how big or heavy an object is. By measuring, scientists can express their observations more precisely and communicate more information about what they observe.

Measuring in SI

The standard system of measurement used by scientists around the world is known as the International System of Units, which is abbreviated as SI (in French, *Système International d'Unités*). SI units are easy to use because they are based on multiples of 10. Each unit is ten times larger than the next smallest unit and one tenth the size of the next largest unit. The table lists the prefixes used to name the most common SI units.

Common SI Prefixes

Prefix	Symbol	Meaning
kilo-	k	1,000
hecto-	h	100
deka-	da	10
deci-	d	0.1 (one tenth)
centi-	c	0.01 (one hundredth)
milli-	m	0.001 (one thousandth)

Length To measure length, or the distance between two points, the unit of measure is the **meter (m).** One meter is the approximate distance from the floor to a doorknob. Long distances, such as the distance between two cities, are measured in kilometers (km). Small lengths are measured in centimeters (cm) or millimeters (mm). Scientists use metric rulers and meter sticks to measure length.

Common Conversions

1 km = 1,000 m
1 m = 100 cm
1 m = 1,000 mm
1 cm = 10 mm

ACTIVITY

The larger lines on the metric ruler in the picture show centimeter divisions, while the smaller, unnumbered lines show millimeter divisions. How many centimeters long is the shell? How many millimeters long is it?

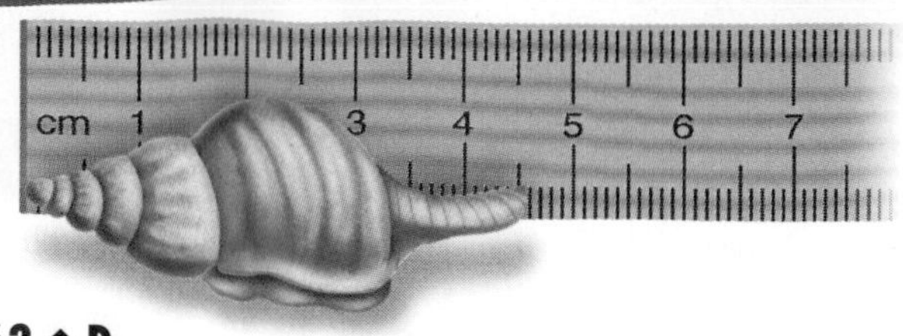

Liquid Volume To measure the volume of a liquid, or the amount of space it takes up, you will use a unit of measure known as the **liter (L).** One liter is the approximate volume of a medium-sized carton of milk. Smaller volumes are measured in milliliters (mL). Scientists use graduated cylinders to measure liquid volume.

Common Conversion

1 L = 1,000 mL

ACTIVITY

The graduated cylinder in the picture is marked in milliliter divisions. Notice that the water in the cylinder has a curved surface. This curved surface is called the *meniscus*. To measure the volume, you must read the level at the lowest point of the meniscus. What is the volume of water in this graduated cylinder?

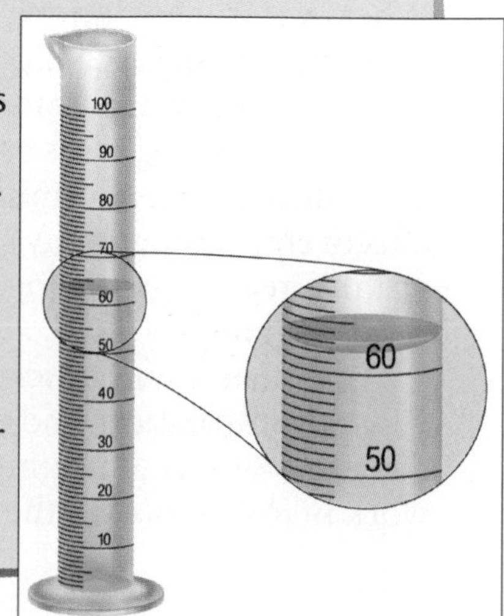

Mass To measure mass, or the amount of matter in an object, you will use a unit of measure known as the **gram (g)**. One gram is approximately the mass of a paper clip. Larger masses are measured in kilograms (kg). Scientists use a balance to find the mass of an object.

Common Conversion

1 kg = 1,000 g

ACTIVITY The electronic balance displays the mass of an apple in kilograms. What is the mass of the apple? Suppose a recipe for applesauce called for one kilogram of apples. About how many apples would you need?

Temperature
To measure the temperature of a substance, you will use the **Celsius scale.** Temperature is measured in degrees Celsius (°C) using a Celsius thermometer. Water freezes at 0°C and boils at 100°C.

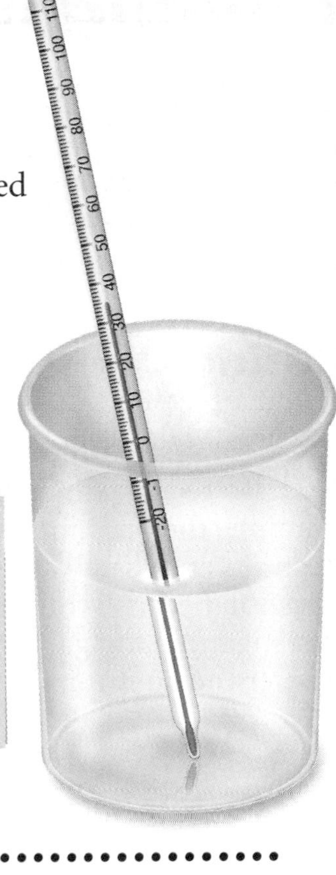

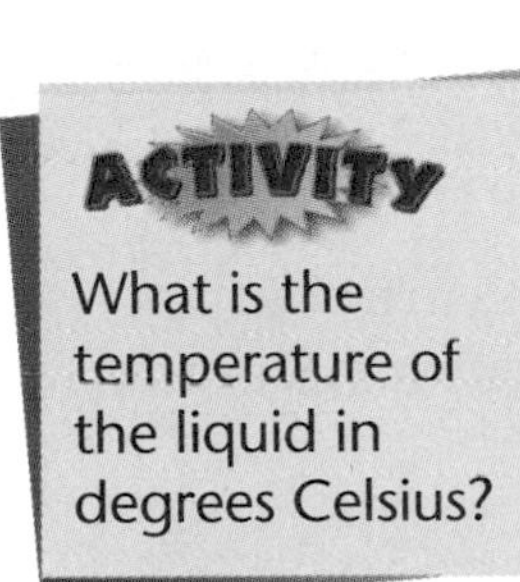

What is the temperature of the liquid in degrees Celsius?

Converting SI Units

To use the SI system, you must know how to convert between units. Converting from one unit to another involves the skill of **calculating**, or using mathematical operations. Converting between SI units is similar to converting between dollars and dimes because both systems are based on multiples of ten.

Suppose you want to convert a length of 80 centimeters to meters. Follow these steps to convert between units.

1. Begin by writing down the measurement you want to convert—in this example, 80 centimeters.
2. Write a conversion factor that represents the relationship between the two units you are converting. In this example, the relationship is *1 meter = 100 centimeters.* Write this conversion factor as a fraction, making sure to place the units you are converting from (centimeters, in this example) in the denominator.
3. Multiply the measurement you want to convert by the fraction. When you do this, the units in the first measurement will cancel out with the units in the denominator. Your answer will be in the units you are converting to (meters, in this example).

Example

80 centimeters = ___?___ meters

$$80 \text{ centimeters} \times \frac{1 \text{ meter}}{100 \text{ centimeters}} = \frac{80 \text{ meters}}{100}$$

$$= 0.8 \text{ meters}$$

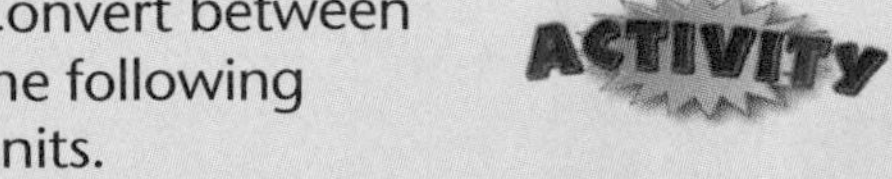

ACTIVITY Convert between the following units.

1. 600 millimeters = __?__ meters
2. 0.35 liters = __?__ milliliters
3. 1,050 grams = __?__ kilograms

Conducting a Scientific Investigation

In some ways, scientists are like detectives, piecing together clues to learn about a process or event. One way that scientists gather clues is by carrying out experiments. An experiment tests an idea in a careful, orderly manner. Although all experiments do not follow the same steps in the same order, many follow a pattern similar to the one described here.

Posing Questions

Experiments begin by asking a scientific question. A scientific question is one that can be answered by gathering evidence. For example, the question "Which freezes faster—fresh water or salt water?" is a scientific question because you can carry out an investigation and gather information to answer the question.

Developing a Hypothesis

The next step is to form a hypothesis. A **hypothesis** is a prediction about the outcome of the experiment. Like all predictions, hypotheses are based on your observations and previous knowledge or experience. But, unlike many predictions, a hypothesis must be something that can be tested. A properly worded hypothesis should take the form of an *If... then...* statement. For example, a hypothesis might be *"If I add salt to fresh water, then the water will take longer to freeze."* A hypothesis worded this way serves as a rough outline of the experiment you should perform.

Designing an Experiment

Next you need to plan a way to test your hypothesis. Your plan should be written out as a step-by-step procedure and should describe the observations or measurements you will make.

Two important steps involved in designing an experiment are controlling variables and forming operational definitions.

Controlling Variables In a well-designed experiment, you need to keep all variables the same except for one. A **variable** is any factor that can change in an experiment. The factor that you change is called the **manipulated variable.** In this experiment, the manipulated variable is the amount of salt added to the water. Other factors, such as the amount of water or the starting temperature, are kept constant.

The factor that changes as a result of the manipulated variable is called the responding variable. The **responding variable** is what you measure or observe to obtain your results. In this experiment, the responding variable is how long the water takes to freeze.

An experiment in which all factors except one are kept constant is a **controlled experiment.** Most controlled experiments include a test called the control. In this experiment, Container 3 is the control. Because no salt is added to Container 3, you can compare the results from the other containers to it. Any difference in results must be due to the addition of salt alone.

Forming Operational Definitions

Another important aspect of a well-designed experiment is having clear operational definitions. An **operational definition** is a statement that describes how a particular variable is to be measured or how a term is to be defined. For example, in this experiment, how will you determine if the water has frozen? You might decide to insert a stick in each container at the start of the experiment. Your operational definition of "frozen" would be the time at which the stick can no longer move.

EXPERIMENTAL PROCEDURE

1. *Fill 3 containers with 300 milliliters of cold tap water.*
2. *Add 10 grams of salt to Container 1; stir. Add 20 grams of salt to Container 2; stir. Add no salt to Container 3.*
3. *Place the 3 containers in a freezer.*
4. *Check the containers every 15 minutes. Record your observations.*

Interpreting Data

The observations and measurements you make in an experiment are called data. At the end of an experiment, you need to analyze the data to look for any patterns or trends. Patterns often become clear if you organize your data in a data table or graph. Then think through what the data reveal. Do they support your hypothesis? Do they point out a flaw in your experiment? Do you need to collect more data?

Drawing Conclusions

A conclusion is a statement that sums up what you have learned from an experiment. When you draw a conclusion, you need to decide whether the data you collected support your hypothesis or not. You may need to repeat an experiment several times before you can draw any conclusions from it. Conclusions often lead you to pose new questions and plan new experiments to answer them.

ACTIVITY

Is a ball's bounce affected by the height from which it is dropped? Using the steps just described, plan a controlled experiment to investigate this problem.

Thinking Critically

Has a friend ever asked for your advice about a problem? If so, you may have helped your friend think through the problem in a logical way. Without knowing it, you used critical-thinking skills to help your friend. Critical thinking involves the use of reasoning and logic to solve problems or make decisions. Some critical-thinking skills are described below.

Comparing and Contrasting

When you examine two objects for similarities and differences, you are using the skill of **comparing and contrasting.** Comparing involves identifying similarities, or common characteristics. Contrasting involves identifying differences. Analyzing objects in this way can help you discover details that you might otherwise overlook.

ACTIVITY

Compare and contrast the two animals in the photo. First list all the similarities that you see. Then list all the differences.

Applying Concepts

When you use your knowledge about one situation to make sense of a similar situation, you are using the skill of **applying concepts.** Being able to transfer your knowledge from one situation to another shows that you truly understand a concept. You may use this skill in answering test questions that present different problems from the ones you've reviewed in class.

ACTIVITY

You have just learned that water takes longer to freeze when other substances are mixed into it. Use this knowledge to explain why people need a substance called antifreeze in their car's radiator in the winter.

Interpreting Illustrations

Diagrams, photographs, and maps are included in textbooks to help clarify what you read. These illustrations show processes, places, and ideas in a visual manner. The skill called **interpreting illustrations** can help you learn from these visual elements. To understand an illustration, take the time to study the illustration along with all the written information that accompanies it. Captions identify the key concepts shown in the illustration. Labels point out the important parts of a diagram or map, while keys identify the symbols used in a map.

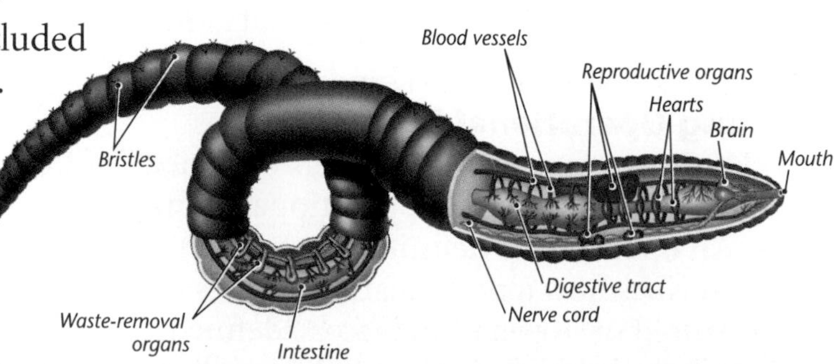

▲ **Internal anatomy of an earthworm**

Study the diagram above. Then write a short paragraph explaining what you have learned.

Relating Cause and Effect

If one event causes another event to occur, the two events are said to have a cause-and-effect relationship. When you determine that such a relationship exists between two events, you use a skill called **relating cause and effect.** For example, if you notice an itchy, red bump on your skin, you might infer that a mosquito bit you. The mosquito bite is the cause, and the bump is the effect.

It is important to note that two events do not necessarily have a cause-and-effect relationship just because they occur together. Scientists carry out experiments or use past experience to determine whether a cause-and-effect relationship exists.

ACTIVITY

You are on a camping trip and your flashlight has stopped working. List some possible causes for the flashlight malfunction. How could you determine which cause-and-effect relationship has left you in the dark?

Making Generalizations

When you draw a conclusion about an entire group based on information about only some of the group's members, you are using a skill called **making generalizations.** For a generalization to be valid, the sample you choose must be large enough and representative of the entire group. You might, for example, put this skill to work at a farm stand if you see a sign that says, "Sample some grapes before you buy." If you sample a few sweet grapes, you may conclude that all the grapes are sweet—and purchase a large bunch.

ACTIVITY

A team of scientists needs to determine whether the water in a large reservoir is safe to drink. How could they use the skill of making generalizations to help them? What should they do?

Making Judgments

When you evaluate something to decide whether it is good or bad, or right or wrong, you are using a skill called **making judgments.** For example, you make judgments when you decide to eat healthful foods or to pick up litter in a park. Before you make a judgment, you need to think through the pros and cons of a situation, and identify the values or standards that you hold.

ACTIVITY

Should children and teens be required to wear helmets when bicycling? Explain why you feel the way you do.

Problem Solving

When you use critical-thinking skills to resolve an issue or decide on a course of action, you are using a skill called **problem solving.** Some problems, such as how to convert a fraction into a decimal, are straightforward. Other problems, such as figuring out why your computer has stopped working, are complex. Some complex problems can be solved using the trial and error method—try out one solution first, and if that doesn't work, try another. Other useful problem-solving strategies include making models and brainstorming possible solutions with a partner.

Organizing Information

As you read this textbook, how can you make sense of all the information it contains? Some useful tools to help you organize information are shown on this page. These tools are called *graphic organizers* because they give you a visual picture of a topic, showing at a glance how key concepts are related.

Concept Maps

Concept maps are useful tools for organizing information on broad topics. A concept map begins with a general concept and shows how it can be broken down into more specific concepts. In that way, relationships between concepts become easier to understand.

A concept map is constructed by placing concept words (usually nouns) in ovals and connecting them with linking words. Often, the most general concept word is placed at the top, and the words become more specific as you move downward. Often the linking words, which are written on a line extending between two ovals, describe the relationship between the two concepts they connect. If you follow any string of concepts and linking words down the map, it should read like a sentence.

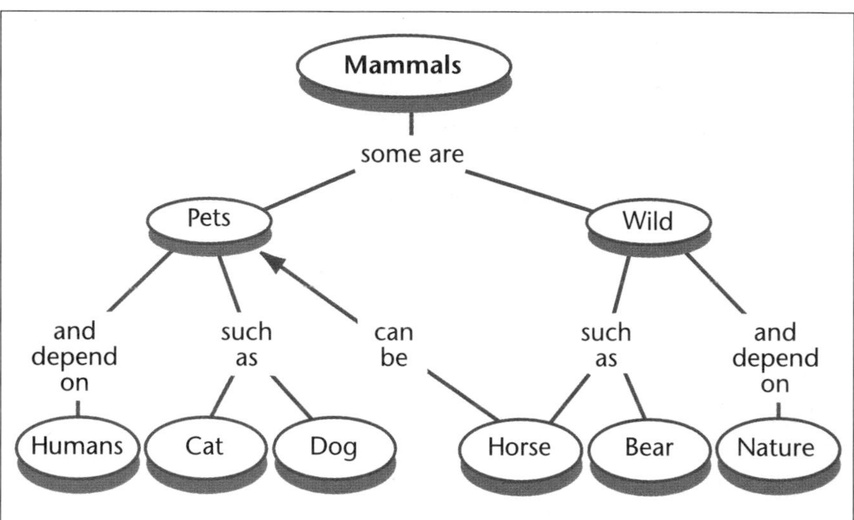

Some concept maps include linking words that connect a concept on one branch of the map to a concept on another branch. These linking words, called cross-linkages, show more complex interrelationships among concepts.

Compare/Contrast Tables

Compare/contrast tables are useful tools for sorting out the similarities and differences between two or more items. A table provides an organized framework in which to compare items based on specific characteristics that you identify.

To create a compare/contrast table, list the items to be compared across the top of a table. Then list the characteristics that will form the basis of your comparison in the left-hand column. Complete the table by filling in information about each characteristic, first for one item and then for the other.

Characteristic	Baseball	Basketball
Number of Players	9	5
Playing Field	Baseball diamond	Basketball court
Equipment	Bat, baseball, mitts	Basket, basketball

Venn Diagrams

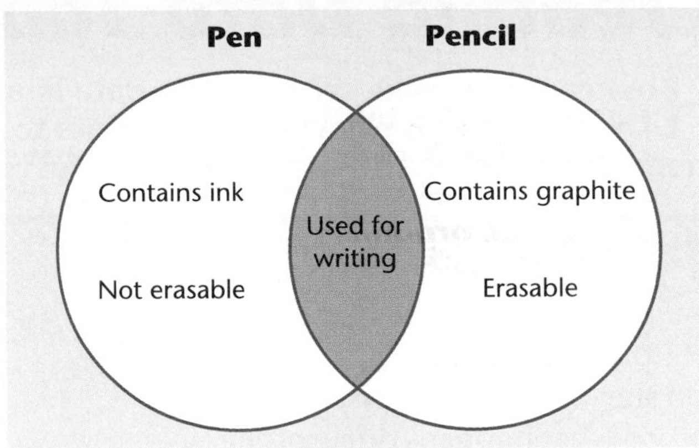

Another way to show similarities and differences between items is with a Venn diagram. A Venn diagram consists of two or more circles that partially overlap. Each circle represents a particular concept or idea. Common characteristics, or similarities, are written within the area of overlap between the two circles. Unique characteristics, or differences, are written in the parts of the circles outside the area of overlap.

To create a Venn diagram, draw two overlapping circles. Label the circles with the names of the items being compared. Write the unique characteristics in each circle outside the area of overlap. Then write the shared characteristics within the area of overlap.

Flowcharts

A flowchart can help you understand the order in which certain events have occurred or should occur. Flowcharts are useful for outlining the stages in a process or the steps in a procedure.

To make a flowchart, write a brief description of each event in a box. Place the first event at the top of the page, followed by the second event, the third event, and so on. Then draw an arrow to connect each event to the one that occurs next.

Preparing Pasta

Boil water → Cook pasta → Drain water → Add sauce

Cycle Diagrams

A cycle diagram can be used to show a sequence of events that is continuous, or cyclical. A continuous sequence does not have an end because, when the final event is over, the first event begins again. Like a flowchart, a cycle diagram can help you understand the order of events.

To create a cycle diagram, write a brief description of each event in a box. Place one event at the top of the page in the center. Then, moving in a clockwise direction around an imaginary circle, write each event in its proper sequence. Draw arrows that connect each event to the one that occurs next, forming a continuous circle.

Steps in a Science Experiment

Pose a question → Develop a hypothesis → Design an experiment → Interpret data → Draw conclusions → Pose a question

Creating Data Tables and Graphs

How can you make sense of the data in a science experiment? The first step is to organize the data to help you understand them. Data tables and graphs are helpful tools for organizing data.

Data Tables

You have gathered your materials and set up your experiment. But before you start, you need to plan a way to record what happens during the experiment. By creating a data table, you can record your observations and measurements in an orderly way.

Suppose, for example, that a scientist conducted an experiment to find out how many Calories people of different body masses burn while doing various activities. The data table shows the results.

CALORIES BURNED IN 30 MINUTES OF ACTIVITY

Body Mass	Experiment 1 Bicycling	Experiment 2 Playing Basketball	Experiment 3 Watching Television
30 kg	60 Calories	120 Calories	21 Calories
40 kg	77 Calories	164 Calories	27 Calories
50 kg	95 Calories	206 Calories	33 Calories
60 kg	114 Calories	248 Calories	38 Calories

Notice in this data table that the manipulated variable (body mass) is the heading of one column. The responding variable (for Experiment 1, the number of Calories burned while bicycling) is the heading of the next column. Additional columns were added for related experiments.

Bar Graphs

To compare how many Calories a person burns doing various activities, you could create a bar graph. A bar graph is used to display data in a number of separate, or distinct, categories. In this example, bicycling, playing basketball, and watching television are three separate categories.

To create a bar graph, follow these steps.

1. On graph paper, draw a horizontal, or *x*-, axis and a vertical, or *y*-, axis.
2. Write the names of the categories to be graphed along the horizontal axis. Include an overall label for the axis as well.
3. Label the vertical axis with the name of the responding variable. Include units of measurement. Then create a scale along the axis by marking off equally spaced numbers that cover the range of the data collected.
4. For each category, draw a solid bar using the scale on the vertical axis to determine the appropriate height. For example, for bicycling, draw the bar as high as the 60 mark on the vertical axis. Make all the bars the same width and leave equal spaces between them.
5. Add a title that describes the graph.

Calories Burned by a 30-kilogram Person in Various Activities

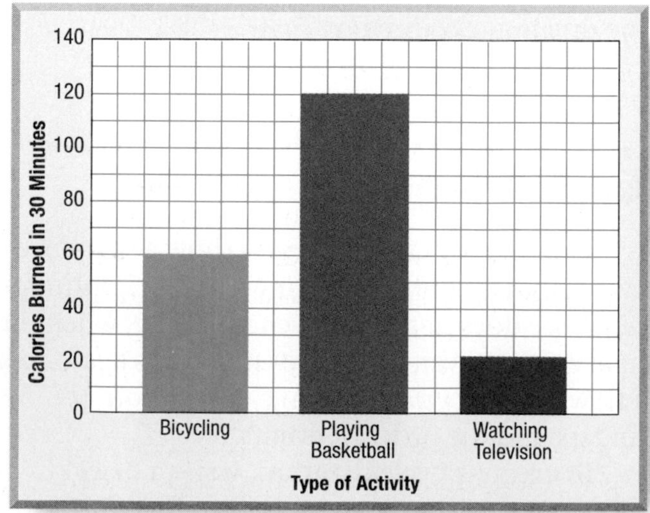

Line Graphs

To see whether a relationship exists between body mass and the number of Calories burned while bicycling, you could create a line graph. A line graph is used to display data that show how one variable (the responding variable) changes in response to another variable (the manipulated variable). You can use a line graph when your manipulated variable is *continuous*, that is, when there are other points between the ones that you tested. In this example, body mass is a continuous variable because there are other body masses between 30 and 40 kilograms (for example, 31 kilograms). Time is another example of a continuous variable.

Line graphs are powerful tools because they allow you to estimate values for conditions that you did not test in the experiment. For example, you can use the line graph to estimate that a 35-kilogram person would burn 68 Calories while bicycling.

To create a line graph, follow these steps.

1. On graph paper, draw a horizontal, or *x*-, axis and a vertical, or *y*-, axis.
2. Label the horizontal axis with the name of the manipulated variable. Label the vertical axis with the name of the responding variable. Include units of measurement.
3. Create a scale on each axis by marking off equally spaced numbers that cover the range of the data collected.
4. Plot a point on the graph for each piece of data. In the line graph above, the dotted lines show how to plot the first data point (30 kilograms and 60 Calories). Draw an imaginary vertical line extending up from the horizontal axis at the 30-kilogram mark. Then draw an imaginary horizontal line extending across from the vertical axis at the 60-Calorie mark. Plot the point where the two lines intersect.

Effect of Body Mass on Calories Burned While Bicycling

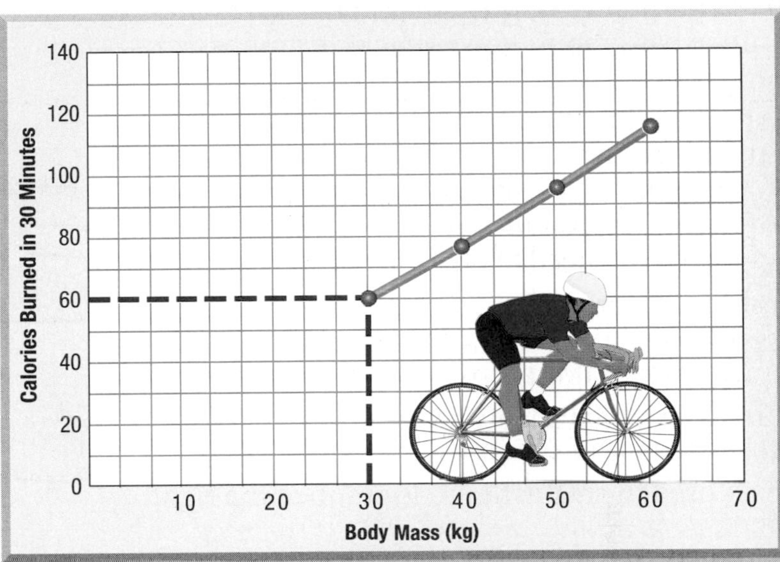

5. Connect the plotted points with a solid line. (In some cases, it may be more appropriate to draw a line that shows the general trend of the plotted points. In those cases, some of the points may fall above or below the line.)
6. Add a title that identifies the variables or relationship in the graph.

ACTIVITY

Create line graphs to display the data from Experiment 2 and Experiment 3 in the data table.

ACTIVITY

You read in the newspaper that a total of 4 centimeters of rain fell in your area in June, 2.5 centimeters fell in July, and 1.5 centimeters fell in August. What type of graph would you use to display these data? Use graph paper to create the graph.

Circle Graphs

Like bar graphs, circle graphs can be used to display data in a number of separate categories. Unlike bar graphs, however, circle graphs can only be used when you have data for *all* the categories that make up a given topic. A circle graph is sometimes called a pie chart because it resembles a pie cut into slices. The pie represents the entire topic, while the slices represent the individual categories. The size of a slice indicates what percentage of the whole a particular category makes up.

The data table below shows the results of a survey in which 24 teenagers were asked to identify their favorite sport. The data were then used to create the circle graph at the right.

FAVORITE SPORTS

Sport	Number of Students
Soccer	8
Basketball	6
Bicycling	6
Swimming	4

To create a circle graph, follow these steps.

1. Use a compass to draw a circle. Mark the center of the circle with a point. Then draw a line from the center point to the top of the circle.
2. Determine the size of each "slice" by setting up a proportion where x equals the number of degrees in a slice. (NOTE: A circle contains 360 degrees.) For example, to find the number of degrees in the "soccer" slice, set up the following proportion:

$$\frac{\text{students who prefer soccer}}{\text{total number of students}} = \frac{x}{\text{total number of degrees in a circle}}$$

$$\frac{8}{24} = \frac{x}{360}$$

Cross-multiply and solve for x.

$$24x = 8 \times 360$$
$$x = 120$$

The "soccer" slice should contain 120 degrees.

Sports That Teens Prefer

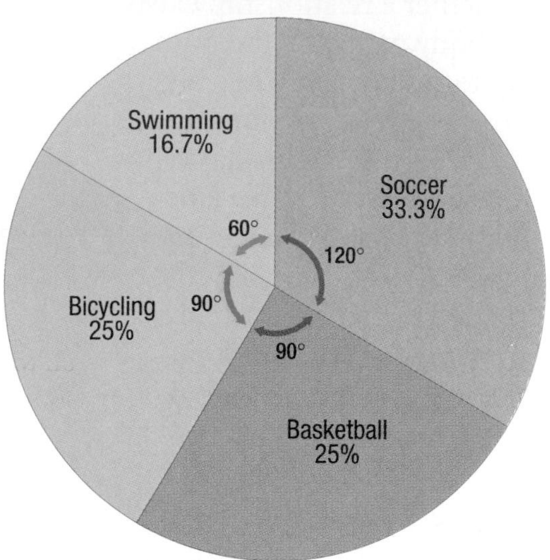

3. Use a protractor to measure the angle of the first slice, using the line you drew to the top of the circle as the 0° line. Draw a line from the center of the circle to the edge for the angle you measured.
4. Continue around the circle by measuring the size of each slice with the protractor. Start measuring from the edge of the previous slice so the wedges do not overlap. When you are done, the entire circle should be filled in.
5. Determine the percentage of the whole circle that each slice represents. To do this, divide the number of degrees in a slice by the total number of degrees in a circle (360), and multiply by 100%. For the "soccer" slice, you can find the percentage as follows:

$$\frac{120}{360} \times 100\% = 33.3\%$$

6. Use a different color to shade in each slice. Label each slice with the name of the category and with the percentage of the whole it represents.
7. Add a title to the circle graph.

ACTIVITY

In a class of 28 students, 12 students take the bus to school, 10 students walk, and 6 students ride their bicycles. Create a circle graph to display these data.

Laboratory Safety

Safety Symbols

These symbols alert you to possible dangers in the laboratory and remind you to work carefully.

Safety Goggles Always wear safety goggles to protect your eyes in any activity involving chemicals, flames or heating, or the possibility of broken glassware.

Lab Apron Wear a laboratory apron to protect your skin and clothing from damage.

Breakage You are working with materials that may be breakable, such as glass containers, glass tubing, thermometers, or funnels. Handle breakable materials with care. Do not touch broken glassware.

Heat-resistant Gloves Use an oven mitt or other hand protection when handling hot materials. Hot plates, hot glassware, or hot water can cause burns. Do not touch hot objects with your bare hands.

Heating Use a clamp or tongs to pick up hot glassware. Do not touch hot objects with your bare hands.

Sharp Object Pointed-tip scissors, scalpels, knives, needles, pins, or tacks are sharp. They can cut or puncture your skin. Always direct a sharp edge or point away from yourself and others. Use sharp instruments only as instructed.

Electric Shock Avoid the possibility of electric shock. Never use electrical equipment around water, or when the equipment is wet or your hands are wet. Be sure cords are untangled and cannot trip anyone. Disconnect the equipment when it is not in use.

Corrosive Chemical You are working with an acid or another corrosive chemical. Avoid getting it on your skin or clothing, or in your eyes. Do not inhale the vapors. Wash your hands when you are finished with the activity.

Poison Do not let any poisonous chemical come in contact with your skin, and do not inhale its vapors. Wash your hands when you are finished with the activity.

Physical Safety When an experiment involves physical activity, take precautions to avoid injuring yourself or others. Follow instructions from your teacher. Alert your teacher if there is any reason you should not participate in the activity.

Animal Safety Treat live animals with care to avoid harming the animals or yourself. Working with animal parts or preserved animals also may require caution. Wash your hands when you are finished with the activity.

Plant Safety Handle plants in the laboratory or during field work only as directed by your teacher. If you are allergic to certain plants, tell your teacher before doing an activity in which those plants are used. Avoid touching harmful plants such as poison ivy, poison oak, or poison sumac, or plants with thorns. Wash your hands when you are finished with the activity.

Flames You may be working with flames from a lab burner, candle, or matches. Tie back loose hair and clothing. Follow instructions from your teacher about lighting and extinguishing flames.

No Flames Flammable materials may be present. Make sure there are no flames, sparks, or other exposed heat sources present.

Fumes When poisonous or unpleasant vapors may be involved, work in a ventilated area. Avoid inhaling vapors directly. Only test an odor when directed to do so by your teacher, and use a wafting motion to direct the vapor toward your nose.

Disposal Chemicals and other laboratory materials used in the activity must be disposed of safely. Follow the instructions from your teacher.

Hand Washing Wash your hands thoroughly when finished with the activity. Use antibacterial soap and warm water. Lather both sides of your hands and between your fingers. Rinse well.

General Safety Awareness You may see this symbol when none of the symbols described earlier appears. In this case, follow the specific instructions provided. You may also see this symbol when you are asked to develop your own procedure in a lab. Have your teacher approve your plan before you go further.

Science Safety Rules

To prepare yourself to work safely in the laboratory, read over the following safety rules. Then read them a second time. Make sure you understand and follow each rule. Ask your teacher to explain any rules you do not understand.

Dress Code

1. To protect yourself from injuring your eyes, wear safety goggles whenever you work with chemicals, burners, glassware, or any substance that might get into your eyes. If you wear contact lenses, notify your teacher.
2. Wear a lab apron or coat whenever you work with corrosive chemicals or substances that can stain.
3. Tie back long hair to keep it away from any chemicals, flames, or equipment.
4. Remove or tie back any article of clothing or jewelry that can hang down and touch chemicals, flames, or equipment. Roll up or secure long sleeves.
5. Never wear open shoes or sandals.

General Precautions

6. Read all directions for an experiment several times before beginning the activity. Carefully follow all written and oral instructions. If you are in doubt about any part of the experiment, ask your teacher for assistance.
7. Never perform activities that are not assigned or authorized by your teacher. Obtain permission before "experimenting" on your own. Never handle any equipment unless you have specific permission.
8. Never perform lab activities without direct supervision.
9. Never eat or drink in the laboratory.
10. Keep work areas clean and tidy at all times. Bring only notebooks and lab manuals or written lab procedures to the work area. All other items, such as purses and backpacks, should be left in a designated area.
11. Do not engage in horseplay.

First Aid

12. Always report all accidents or injuries to your teacher, no matter how minor. Notify your teacher immediately about any fires.
13. Learn what to do in case of specific accidents, such as getting acid in your eyes or on your skin. (Rinse acids from your body with lots of water.)
14. Be aware of the location of the first-aid kit, but do not use it unless instructed by your teacher. In case of injury, your teacher should administer first aid. Your teacher may also send you to the school nurse or call a physician.
15. Know the location of emergency equipment, such as the fire extinguisher and fire blanket, and know how to use it.
16. Know the location of the nearest telephone and whom to contact in an emergency.

Heating and Fire Safety

17. Never use a heat source, such as a candle, burner, or hot plate, without wearing safety goggles.
18. Never heat anything unless instructed to do so. A chemical that is harmless when cool may be dangerous when heated.
19. Keep all combustible materials away from flames. Never use a flame or spark near a combustible chemical.
20. Never reach across a flame.
21. Before using a laboratory burner, make sure you know proper procedures for lighting and adjusting the burner, as demonstrated by your teacher. Do not touch the burner. It may be hot. And never leave a lighted burner unattended!
22. Chemicals can splash or boil out of a heated test tube. When heating a substance in a test tube, make sure that the mouth of the tube is not pointed at you or anyone else.
23. Never heat a liquid in a closed container. The expanding gases produced may blow the container apart.
24. Before picking up a container that has been heated, hold the back of your hand near it. If you can feel heat on the back of your hand, the container is too hot to handle. Use an oven mitt to pick up a container that has been heated.

Using Chemicals Safely

25. Never mix chemicals "for the fun of it." You might produce a dangerous, possibly explosive substance.
26. Never put your face near the mouth of a container that holds chemicals. Never touch, taste, or smell a chemical unless you are instructed by your teacher to do so. Many chemicals are poisonous.
27. Use only those chemicals needed in the activity. Read and double-check labels on supply bottles before removing any chemicals. Take only as much as you need. Keep all containers closed when chemicals are not being used.
28. Dispose of all chemicals as instructed by your teacher. To avoid contamination, never return chemicals to their original containers. Never simply pour chemicals or other substances into the sink or trash containers.
29. Be extra careful when working with acids or bases. Pour all chemicals over the sink or a container, not over your work surface.
30. If you are instructed to test for odors, use a wafting motion to direct the odors to your nose. Do not inhale the fumes directly from the container.
31. When mixing an acid and water, always pour the water into the container first and then add the acid to the water. Never pour water into an acid.
32. Take extreme care not to spill any material in the laboratory. Wash chemical spills and splashes immediately with plenty of water. Immediately begin rinsing with water any acids that get on your skin or clothing, and notify your teacher of any acid spill at the same time.

Using Glassware Safely

33. Never force glass tubing or thermometers into a rubber stopper or rubber tubing. Have your teacher insert the glass tubing or thermometer if required for an activity.
34. If you are using a laboratory burner, use a wire screen to protect glassware from any flame. Never heat glassware that is not thoroughly dry on the outside.
35. Keep in mind that hot glassware looks cool. Never pick up glassware without first checking to see if it is hot. Use an oven mitt. See rule 24.
36. Never use broken or chipped glassware. If glassware breaks, notify your teacher and dispose of the glassware in the proper broken-glassware container. Never handle broken glass with your bare hands.
37. Never eat or drink from lab glassware.
38. Thoroughly clean glassware before putting it away.

Using Sharp Instruments

39. Handle scalpels or other sharp instruments with extreme care. Never cut material toward you; cut away from you.
40. Immediately notify your teacher if you cut your skin when working in the laboratory.

Animal and Plant Safety

41. Never perform experiments that cause pain, discomfort, or harm to mammals, birds, reptiles, fishes, or amphibians. This rule applies at home as well as in the classroom.
42. Animals should be handled only if absolutely necessary. Your teacher will instruct you as to how to handle each animal species brought into the classroom.
43. If you know that you are allergic to certain plants, molds, or animals, tell your teacher before doing an activity in which these are used.
44. During field work, protect your skin by wearing long pants, long sleeves, socks, and closed shoes. Know how to recognize the poisonous plants and fungi in your area, as well as plants with thorns, and avoid contact with them.
45. Never eat any part of an unidentified plant or fungus.
46. Wash your hands thoroughly after handling animals or the cage containing animals. Wash your hands when you are finished with any activity involving animal parts, plants, or soil.

End-of-Experiment Rules

47. After an experiment has been completed, clean up your work area and return all equipment to its proper place.
48. Dispose of waste materials as instructed by your teacher.
49. Wash your hands after every experiment.
50. Always turn off all burners or hot plates when they are not in use. Unplug hot plates and other electrical equipment. If you used a burner, check that the gas-line valve to the burner is off as well.

Glossary

A

absorption The process by which nutrient molecules pass through the wall of the digestive system into the blood. (p. 83)

acne A bacterial infection of the skin in which the oil glands become blocked and swollen. (p. 62)

active immunity Immunity that occurs when a person's own immune system produces antibodies in response to the presence of a pathogen. (p. 170)

addiction A physical dependence on a substance; an intense need by the body for a substance. (p. 141)

adolescence The stage of development between childhood and adulthood when children become adults physically and mentally. (p. 244)

adrenaline A chemical that gives a burst of energy and causes changes in the body to prepare a person for quick action. (p. 26)

AIDS (acquired immunodeficiency syndrome) A disease caused by a virus that attacks the immune system. (p. 166)

alcoholism A disease in which a person is both physically addicted to and emotionally dependent on alcohol. (p. 219)

allergen A substance that causes an allergy. (p. 176)

allergy A disorder in which the immune system is overly sensitive to a foreign substance. (p. 175)

alveoli Tiny sacs of lung tissue specialized for the movement of gases between the air and the blood. (p. 134)

amino acids Small units that are linked together chemically to form large protein molecules. (p. 72)

amniotic sac A fluid-filled sac that cushions and protects a developing fetus in the uterus. (p. 238)

anabolic steroids Synthetic chemicals that are similar to hormones produced in the body and that may increase muscle size and cause mood swings. (p. 216)

antibiotic A chemical that kills bacteria or slows their growth without harming the body cells of humans. (p. 174)

antibody A chemical produced by a B cell of the immune system that destroys a specific kind of pathogen. (p.165)

antigen A molecule on a cell that the immune system can recognize either as part of the body or as coming from outside the body. (p. 164)

anus A muscular opening at the end of the rectum through which digestive waste material is eliminated from the body. (p. 93)

aorta The largest artery in the body. (p. 106)

artery A blood vessel that carries blood away from the heart. (p. 104)

asthma A disorder in which the respiratory passages narrow significantly. (p. 176)

atherosclerosis A condition in which an artery wall thickens as a result of the buildup of fatty materials. (p. 121)

atrium Each of the two upper chambers of the heart that receives blood that comes into the heart. (p. 102)

autonomic nervous system The group of nerves that controls involuntary actions. (p. 200)

axon A threadlike extension of a neuron that carries nerve impulses away from the cell body. (p. 192)

B cell A lymphocyte that produces chemicals that help destroy a specific kind of pathogen. (p. 165)

bile A substance produced by the liver that breaks up fat particles. (p. 91)

blood pressure The pressure that is exerted by the blood against the walls of blood vessels. (p. 111)

blood transfusion The transference of blood from one person to another. (p. 116)

brain The part of the central nervous system that is located in the skull and controls most functions in the body. (p. 197)

brainstem The part of the brain that controls many body functions that occur automatically. (p. 199)

bronchi The passages that branch from the trachea and direct air into the lungs. (p. 134)

bronchitis An irritation of the breathing passages in which the small passages become narrower than normal and may be clogged with mucus. (p. 142)

calorie The amount of energy needed to raise the temperature of one gram of water by one Celsius degree. (p. 69)

cancer A disease in which some body cells divide uncontrollably. (p. 61)

capillary A tiny blood vessel where substances are exchanged between the blood and the body cells. (p. 104)

carbohydrates Nutrients composed of carbon, oxygen, and hydrogen that are a major source of energy and provide the raw materials to make parts of cells. (p. 69)

carbon monoxide A colorless, odorless gas produced when substances—including tobacco—are burned. (p. 141)

carcinogen A substance or a factor in the environment that can cause cancer. (p. 178)

cardiac muscle Muscle tissue found only in the heart. (p. 53)

cardiovascular system The body system that consists of the heart, blood vessels, and blood, and that carries needed substances to cells and carries waste products away from cells. (p. 100)

cartilage A connective tissue that is more flexible than bone and that gives support to some parts of the body. (p. 42)

cell membrane The outside boundary of a cell. (p. 18)

cell The basic unit of structure and function in a living thing. (p. 18)

central nervous system The brain and spinal cord; the control center of the body. (p. 196)

cerebellum The part of the brain that coordinates the actions of the muscles and helps maintain balance. (p. 199)

cerebrum The part of the brain that interprets input from the senses, controls the movement of skeletal muscles, and carries out complex mental processes. (p. 198)

cholesterol A waxy, fatlike substance, found only in animal products, that is an important part of your body's cells; can build up on artery walls. (p. 71)

chromosomes Rod-shaped structures in cells that carry the information that controls inherited characteristics such as eye color and blood type. (p. 231)

cilia Tiny hairlike extensions of cells that can move together like whips. (p. 132)

cochlea A snail-shaped tube in the inner ear lined with sound receptors; nerve impulses are sent from the cochlea to the brain. (p. 209)

concussion A bruiselike injury of the brain that occurs when the soft tissue of the cerebrum bumps against the skull. (p. 202)

connective tissue A body tissue that provides support for the body and connects all of its parts. (p. 19)

continuum A gradual progression through many stages between one extreme and another, as in the illness-wellness continuum. (p. 30)

controlled experiment An experiment in which all factors are identical except one. (p. 265)

cornea The clear tissue that covers the front of the eye. (p. 205)

coronary artery An artery that supplies blood to the heart itself. (p. 107)

cytoplasm The area in a cell between the cell membrane and the nucleus; contains a clear, jellylike substance in which cell structures are found. (p. 18)

delivery The second stage of birth, in which the baby is pushed completely out of the uterus, through the vagina, and out of the mother's body. (p. 240)

dendrite A threadlike extension of a neuron that carries nerve impulses toward the cell body. (p. 192)

depressant A drug that slows down the activity of the central nervous system. (p. 214)

dermis The lower layer of the skin. (p. 59)

diabetes A condition in which either the pancreas fails to produce enough insulin, or the body's cells can't use it properly. (p. 177)

diaphragm A large, dome-shaped muscle that plays an important role in breathing. (p. 136)

diffusion The process by which molecules move from an area in which they are highly concentrated to an area in which they are less concentrated. (p. 109)

digestion The process by which the body breaks down food into small nutrient molecules. (p. 82)

dislocation An injury in which a bone comes out of its joint. (p. 46)

drug abuse The deliberate misuse of drugs for purposes other than appropriate medical ones. (p. 213)

drug Any chemical that causes changes in a person's body or behavior. (p. 212)

eardrum The membrane that separates the outer ear from the middle ear, and that vibrates when sound waves strike it. (p. 209)

egg A female sex cell. (p. 231)

embryo A developing human during the first eight weeks after fertilization has occurred. (p. 237)

emphysema A serious disease that destroys lung tissue and causes difficulty in breathing. (p. 142)

endocrine gland An organ of the endocrine system which produces and releases its chemical products directly into the bloodstream. (p. 226)

enzyme A protein that speeds up chemical reactions in the body. (p. 84)

epidermis The outermost layer of the skin. (p. 58)

epiglottis A flap of tissue that seals off the windpipe and prevents food from entering. (p. 85)

epithelial tissue A body tissue that covers the surfaces of the body, inside and out. (p. 19)

esophagus A muscular tube that connects the mouth to the stomach. (p. 85)

estrogen A hormone produced by the ovaries that controls the development of adult female characteristics. (p. 234)
excretion The process by which wastes are removed from the body. (p. 145)

F

farsightedness The condition in which distant objects can be seen clearly but nearby objects look blurry. (p. 207)
fats High-energy nutrients that are composed of carbon, oxygen, and hydrogen and contain more than twice as much energy as an equal amount of carbohydrates. (p. 71)
fertilization The joining of a sperm and an egg. (p. 231)
fetus A developing human from the ninth week of development until birth. (p. 239)
fiber A complex carbohydrate, found in plant foods, that cannot be broken down into sugar molecules by the body. (p. 70)
fibrin A chemical that is important in blood clotting because it forms a fiber net that traps red blood cells. (p. 116)
follicle Structure in the dermis of the skin from which a strand of hair grows. (p. 59)
Food Guide Pyramid A chart that classifies foods into six groups to help people plan a healthy diet. (p. 78)
force A push or a pull. (p.106)
fracture A break in a bone. (p. 46)

G

gallbladder The organ that stores bile after it is produced by the liver. (p. 91)
glucose A sugar that is the major source of energy for the body's cells. (p. 70)

heart A hollow, muscular organ that pumps blood throughout the body. (p. 102)
heart attack A condition in which blood flow to a part of the heart muscle is blocked, which causes heart cells to die. (p. 121)
hemoglobin An iron-containing protein that binds chemically to oxygen molecules and makes up most of red blood cells. (p. 114)
histamine A chemical that is responsible for the symptoms of an allergy. (p. 176)
homeostasis The process by which an organism's internal environment is kept stable in spite of changes in the external environment. (p. 24)
hormone The chemical product of an endocrine gland that speeds up or slows down the activities of an organ or tissue. (p. 227)
hypertension A disorder in which a person's blood pressure is consistently higher than normal. (p. 121)
hypothalamus A tiny part of the brain that links the nervous system and the endocrine system. (p. 228)
hypothesis A prediction about the outcome of an experiment. (p. 264)

immune response Part of the body's defense against pathogens in which cells of the immune system react to each kind of pathogen with a defense targeted specifically at that pathogen. (p. 164)
immunity The ability of the immune system to destroy pathogens before they can cause disease. (p. 170)
infectious disease A disease that can pass from one organism to another. (p. 157)
inflammatory response Part of the body's defense against pathogens, in which fluid and white blood cells leak from blood vessels into tissues; the white blood cells destroy pathogens by breaking them down. (p. 162)
insulin A chemical produced in the pancreas that enables the body's cells to take in glucose from the blood and use it for energy. (p. 177)
interneuron A neuron that carries nerve impulses from one neuron to another. (p. 192)
involuntary muscle A muscle that is not under conscious control. (p. 50)
iris The circular structure that surrounds the pupil and regulates the amount of light entering the eye. (p. 205)

joint A place where two bones come together. (p. 42)

kidney A major organ of the excretory system; eliminates urea, excess water, and other waste materials from the body. (p. 145)

labor The first stage of birth, in which strong muscular contractions of the uterus occur. (p. 240)
large intestine The last section of the digestive system, where water is absorbed from food and the remaining material is eliminated from the body. (p. 93)
larynx The voice box, located in the top part of the trachea, underneath the epiglottis. (p. 137)
lens The flexible structure that focuses light that has entered the eye. (p. 205)
ligament Strong connective tissue that holds together the bones in a movable joint. (p.44)
liver The largest and heaviest organ inside the body; it breaks down substances and eliminates nitrogen from the body. (p. 91)

lungs The main organs of the respiratory system. (p. 134)
lymph node A small knob of tissue in the lymphatic system that filters lymph. (p. 118)
lymph The fluid that the lymphatic system collects and returns to the bloodstream. (p. 118)
lymphatic system A network of veinlike vessels that returns the fluid that leaks out of blood vessels to the bloodstream. (p. 118)
lymphocyte White blood cell that reacts to each kind of pathogen with a defense targeted specifically at that pathogen. (p. 164)

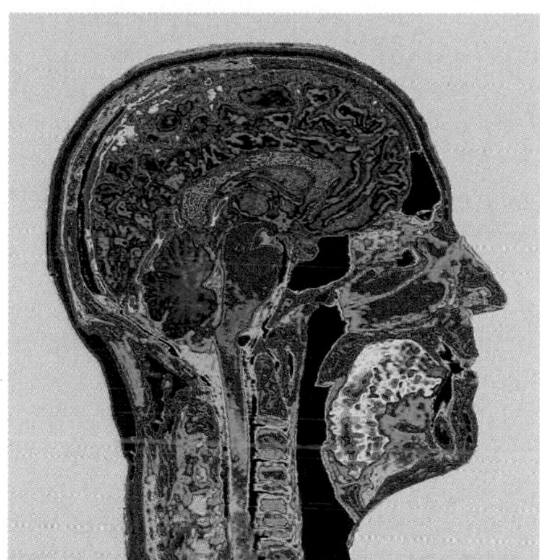

M

magnetic resonance imaging A method for taking clear images of both the bones and soft tissues of the body. (p. 47)
manipulated variable The one factor that a scientist changes during an experiment. (p. 265)
marrow The soft tissue that fills the internal spaces in bone. (p. 42)
melanin A pigment that gives the skin its color (p. 59)
menstrual cycle The monthly cycle of changes that occurs in the female reproductive system, during which an egg develops and the uterus prepares for the arrival of a fertilized egg. (p. 235)
menstruation The process that occurs if fertilization does not take place, in which the thickened lining of the uterus breaks down and blood and tissue then pass out of the female body through the vagina. (p. 236)
mental health A component of wellness that involves a person's feelings, or emotions. (p. 29)
minerals Nutrients that are needed by the body in small amounts and are not made by living things. (p. 74)
motor neuron A neuron that sends an impulse to a muscle, causing the muscle to contract. (p. 192)
mucus A thick, slippery substance produced by the body. (p. 85)
muscle tissue A body tissue that contracts or shortens, making body parts move. (p. 18)

N

nearsightedness The condition in which nearby objects can be seen clearly but distant objects look blurry. (p. 207)
negative feedback A process in which a system is turned off by the condition it produces; examples of negative feedback systems include regulation of temperature by a thermostat and the regulation of the levels of many hormones in the blood. (p. 230)
nephron One of a million tiny, filtering structures found in the kidneys that removes wastes from blood and produces urine. (p. 146)
nerve A bundle of nerve fibers. (p. 192)
nerve impulse The message carried by a neuron. (p. 191)
nerve tissue A body tissue that carries messages back and forth between the brain and every other part of the body. (p. 19)
neuron A cell that carries messages through the nervous system. (p. 191)
nicotine A drug in tobacco that speeds up the activities of the nervous system, heart, and other organs. (p. 141)
noninfectious disease A disease that is not spread from person to person. (p. 175)
nucleus The control center of a cell that directs the cell's activities and contains information that determines the cell's characteristics. (p. 18)
nutrients Substances in food that provide the raw materials and energy the body needs to carry out all the essential life processes. (p. 68)

O

operational definition A statement that describes how a particular variable is to be measured or a term is to be defined. (p. 265)
organ A structure in the body that is composed of different kinds of tissue. (p. 20)
organ system A group of organs that work together to perform a major function in the body. (p. 20)
osteoporosis A condition in which the body's bones become weak and break easily. (p. 45)
ovary Organ of the female reproductive system in which eggs and estrogen are produced. (p. 234)
oviduct A passageway for eggs from an ovary to the uterus; the place where fertilization usually occurs. (p. 234)
ovulation The process in which a mature egg is released from the ovary into an oviduct; occurs about halfway through a typical menstrual cycle. (p. 235)

P

pacemaker A group of cells located in the right atrium that sends out signals that make the heart muscle contract and that regulates heartbeat rate. (p. 104)

pancreas A triangular organ that produces enzymes that flow into the small intestine. (p. 92)

passive immunity Immunity in which the antibodies that fight a pathogen come from another organism rather than from the person's own body. (p. 172)

passive smoking The involuntary inhalation of smoke from other people's cigarettes, cigars, or pipes. (p. 143)

pathogen An organism that causes disease. (p. 157)

peer pressure The pressure from friends and classmates to behave in certain ways. (p. 29)

penis The organ through which both semen and urine leave the male body. (p. 233)

Percent Daily Value An indication of how the nutritional content of a food fits into the diet of a person who consumes a total of 2,000 Calories a day. (p. 80)

peripheral nervous system All the nerves located outside the central nervous system; connects the central nervous system to all parts of the body. (p. 196)

peristalsis Involuntary waves of muscle contraction that keep food moving along in one direction through the digestive system. (p. 85)

phagocyte A white blood cell that destroys pathogens by engulfing them and breaking them down. (p. 163)

pharynx The throat; part of both the respiratory and digestive systems. (p. 132)

physical health A component of wellness that consists of how well the body functions. (p. 28)

pituitary gland An endocrine gland just below the hypothalamus that communicates with the hypothalamus to control many body activities. (p. 229)

placenta A membrane that becomes the link between the developing embryo or fetus and the mother. (p. 238)

plasma The liquid part of blood. (p. 113)

platelet A cell fragment that plays an important part in forming blood clots. (p. 116)

pore An opening through which sweat reaches the surface of the skin. (p. 59)

pressure The force that something exerts over a given area. (p. 110)

proteins Nutrients that contain nitrogen as well as carbon, hydrogen, and oxygen; they are needed for tissue growth and repair and play a part in chemical reactions within cells. (p. 72)

puberty The period of sexual development during the teenage years in which the body becomes able to reproduce. (p. 245)

pupil The opening through which light enters the eye. (p. 205)

R

rectum A short tube at the end of the large intestine where waste material is compressed into a solid form before being eliminated. (p. 93)

red blood cell A cell in the blood that takes up oxygen in the lungs and delivers it to cells elsewhere in the body. (p. 114)

reflex An automatic response that occurs very rapidly and without conscious control. (p. 201)

reproduction The process by which living things produce new individuals of the same type. (p. 231)

respiration The process in which oxygen and glucose undergo a complex series of chemical reactions inside cells. (p. 131)

response What the body does in reaction to a stimulus. (p. 191)

retina The layer of receptor cells at the back of the eye on which an image is focused; nerve impulses are sent from the retina to the brain. (p. 206)

S

saliva The fluid released when the mouth waters that plays an important role in both mechanical and chemical digestion. (p. 84)

saturated fats Fats, such as butter, that are usually solid at room temperature. (p. 71)

scrotum An external pouch of skin in which the testes are located. (p. 232)

semen A mixture of sperm cells and fluids. (p. 233)

semicircular canals Structures in the inner ear that are responsible for the sense of balance. (p. 209)

sensory neuron A neuron that picks up stimuli from the internal or external environment and converts each stimulus into a nerve impulse. (p. 192)

skeletal muscle A muscle that is attached to the bones of the skeleton. (p. 51)

small intestine The part of the digestive system in which most chemical digestion takes place. (p. 90)

smooth muscle Involuntary muscle found inside many internal organs of the body. (p. 52)

social health A component of wellness that consists of how well a person gets along with others. (p. 29)

somatic nervous system The group of nerves that controls voluntary actions. (p. 200)

sperm A male sex cell. (p. 231)

sphygmomanometer An instrument that measures blood pressure. (p. 111)

spinal cord The thick column of nerve tissue that is enclosed by the vertebrae and that links the brain to most of the nerves in the peripheral nervous system. (p. 197)

sprain An injury in which the ligaments holding bones together are stretched too far and tear. (p. 46)

stimulant A drug that speeds up body processes. (p. 214)

stimulus Any change or signal in the environment that can make an organism react in some way. (p. 191)

stomach A J-shaped, muscular pouch located in the abdomen that expands to hold all of the food that is swallowed. (p. 86)

stress The reaction of a person's body and mind to threatening, challenging, or disturbing events. (p. 25)

synapse The tiny space between the tip of an axon and the next structure (p. 194)

T

T cell A lymphocyte that identifies pathogens and distinguishes one pathogen from the other. (p. 164)

tar A dark, sticky substance produced when tobacco burns. (p. 140)

target cell A cell in the body that recognizes a hormone's chemical structure; a cell to which a hormone binds chemically. (p. 227)

tendon Strong connective tissue that attaches a muscle to a bone. (p. 52)

testis Organ of the male reproductive system in which sperm and testosterone are produced. (p. 232)

testosterone A hormone produced by the testes that controls the development of physical characteristics in men. (p. 232)

tissue A group of similar cells that perform the same function. (p. 18)

tolerance A state in which a drug user, after repeatedly taking a drug, needs larger and larger doses of the drug to produce the same effect. (p. 213)

toxin A poison that is produced by bacterial pathogens and that damages cells. (p. 158)

trachea The windpipe; a passage through which air moves in the respiratory system. (p. 133)

tumor An abnormal tissue mass that results from the rapid division of cancerous cells. (p. 178)

U

umbilical cord A ropelike structure that forms in the uterus between the embryo and the placenta. (p. 238)

unsaturated fats Fats, such as olive oil and canola oil, that are usually liquid at room temperature. (p. 71)

urea A chemical that comes from the breakdown of proteins and that is removed from the body by the kidneys. (p. 145)

ureter A narrow tube that carries urine from one of the kidneys to the urinary bladder. (p. 145)

urethra A small tube through which urine flows from the body. (p. 146)

urinary bladder A sacklike muscular organ that stores urine until it is eliminated from the body. (p. 146)

urine A watery fluid produced by the kidneys that contains urea and other waste materials. (p. 145)

uterus The hollow muscular organ of the female reproductive system in which a baby develops. (p. 234)

V

vaccination The process by which harmless antigens are deliberately introduced into a person's body to produce active immunity. (p. 171)

vaccine A substance used in a vaccination that consists of pathogens that have been weakened or killed but can still trigger the immune system into action. (p. 171)

vagina A muscular passageway through which a baby leaves the mother's body. (p. 235)

valve A flap of tissue in the heart or a vein that prevents blood from flowing backward. (p. 102)

variable Any factor that can change in an experiment. (p. 265)

vein A blood vessel that carries blood back to the heart. (p. 104)

ventricle Each of the two lower chambers of the heart that pumps blood out of the heart. (p. 102)

vertebrae The 26 small bones that make up the backbone. (p. 39)

villi Tiny finger-shaped structures that cover the inner surface of the small intestine and provide a large surface area through which digested food is absorbed. (p. 92)

vitamins Molecules that act as helpers in a variety of chemical reactions within the body. (p. 73)

vocal cords Folds of connective tissue that stretch across the opening of the larynx and produce a person's voice. (p. 137)

voluntary muscle A muscle that is under conscious control. (p. 50)

W

wellness The state of being at the best possible level of health—in the body, the mind, and relationships with others. (p. 28)

white blood cell A blood cell that fights disease. (p. 115)

withdrawal A period of adjustment that occurs when a drug-dependent person stops taking the drug. (p. 214)

X

X-ray A form of energy that travels in waves that can pass through some living tissue, but not through bone. (p. 47)

zygote A fertilized egg, produced by the joining of a sperm and an egg. (p. 231)

Index

Acknowledgments

Illustration

Carmella Clifford: 91, 205, 209
Bruce Day: 26
John Edwards and Associates: 40–41 **(Henry Hill)**, 193 **(Dave Fischer)**
Function thru Form: 79
GeoSystems Global Corporation: 255
Floyd E. Hosmer: 192
Keith Kasnot: 85, 87, 146–147, 228, 229, 238
Martucci Design: 35, 80, 127, 146, 159, 178
Matt Mayerchak: 34, 64, 96, 152, 186, 222
Fran Milner: 17, 53, 83, 92, 108–109, 114–115, 134–135, 233, 234
Morgan Cain & Associates: 18, 30, 58, 86, 102, 107, 113, 117, 138, 161, 165, 194, 200, 230
Pat Rossi: 43
Sandra Sevigny: 21, 39, 51, 101, 118, 197
Tim Spransy: 23
Walter Stuart: 103, 133
J/B Woolsey Associates: 84, 105, 131, 137, 201, 207, 217, 219, 236

Photography

Photo Research by - Paula Wehde
Cover image - David Job/TSI

Nature of Science
Page 10, Courtesy of Alex Martinez; **11t**, Lawrence Migdale/Stock Boston; **11b**, Josh Mitchell/TSI; **12t,mt,b**, PhotoDisc; **12m**, Russ Lappa; **12mb**, Steven Maus; **14**, Steven Mays.

Chapter 1
Pages 14–15, Jean Francois Causse/TSI; **16t**, Richard Haynes; **16b**, Russ Lappa; **19tl**, Robert Becker/Custom Medical Stock; **19bl**, Fred Hossler/Visuals Unlimited; **19m**, Clive Brunckill/Allsport; **19tr**, Biophoto Associates/Science Source/Photo Researchers; **19br**, John D. Cunningham/Visuals Unlimited; **20**, Wayne Hoy/The Picture Cube; **22**, **23**, Richard Haynes; **24**, Lori Adamski Peek/TSI; **25**, Paul J. Sutton/Duomo; **27**, Michael P. Manheim/ MidwestStock; **28–29**, Charles Gupton/TSI; **29tr**, Melanie Carr/Zephyr Pictures; **29br**, Bob Daemmrich/Stock Boston; **31**, Superstock; **32**, Betsy Fuchs/The Picture Cube; **33**, Charles Gupton/TSI.

Chapter 2
Pages 36–37, Globus, Holway & Lobel/The Stock Market; **38t**, Russ Lappa; **38b**, Cathy Cheney/Stock Boston; **39**, Richard Haynes; **41**, Andrew Syred/Science Photo Library/Photo Researchers; **42**, Salisbury District Hospital/Science Photo Library/Photo Researchers; **43**, William R. Sallaz/Duomo; **44**, The Granger Collection, NY; **45 both**, Superstock; **46**, John Meyer/Custom Medical Stock; **47l**, Michael Acliolo/International Stock; **47r**, Simon Fraser/Science Photo Library/Photo Researchers; **48**, Ted Horowitz/The Stock Market; **49**, Adamski–Peek/TSI; **50t**, Richard Haynes; **50b**, Superstock; **51tl**, Astrid & Hanns–Frieder Michler/Science Photo Library/Photo Researchers; **51bl**, Eric Grave/Photo Researchers; **51m**, Richard Haynes; **51r**, Ed Reschke/Peter Arnold; **52l**, Richard Haynes; **52r**, Jim Cummins/FPG International; **54**, Superstock; **55**, Richard Haynes; **56t**, Richard Haynes; **56b**, Jed Jacobson/Allsport; **57l**, David Young Wolff/TSI; **57r**, Lennart Nilsson/Behold Man; **59l**, Prof. P. Motta/Dept. of Anatomy/University "La Sapienza", Rome/Science Photo Library/Photo Researchers; **59r**, Russ Lappa; **60,61**, Richard Haynes; **62**, Bob Daemmrich/Stock Boston; **63l**, Superstock; **63r**, Ed Reschke/Peter Arnold.

Chapter 3
Pages 66–67, Superstock; **68**, Bob Daemmrich/Stock Boston; **69l**, Richard Haynes; **69r,70,71,72–73,73 all, 74 all**, Russ Lappa; **75**, Joan Baron/The Stock Market; **76**, **77t**, Richard Haynes; **77b**, David Young-Wolff/PhotoEdit; **78**, David Young Wolff/TSI; **81**, David Young-Wolff/PhotoEdit; **82**, The Granger Collection, NY; **83**, **84**, Richard Haynes; **87**, CNRI/Science Photo Library/Photo Researchers; **89**, **90t**, Richard Haynes; **90b**, Llewellyn/Uniphoto; **92**, Prof. P. Motta/Dept. of Anatomy/ University "La Sapienza", Rome/Science Photo Library/Photo Researchers; **93**, CNRI/Science Photo Library/Photo Researchers; **94**, Donna Day/TSI; **95**, Joan Baron/The Stock Market.

Chapter 4
Pages 98–99, National Cancer Institute/Science Photo Library/Photo Researchers; **100**, **101**, Richard Haynes; **102t**, Erich Lessing/Art Resource; **102b** Science Photo Library/Photo Researchers; **104–105**, Pete Saloutos/The Stock Market; **106**, Scott Weersing/Allsport; **107**, Richard Haynes; **109**, Prof. P. Motta/Dept. of Anatomy/University "La Sapienza", Rome/Science Photo Library/Photo Researchers; **110**, Cabisco/Visuals Unlimited; **111**, Matt Meadows/Peter Arnold; **112**, Richard Haynes; **113**, Andrew Syred/Science Photo Library/Photo Researchers; **114**, Bill Longcore/Science Source/Photo Researchers; **115t**, Andrew Syred/Science Photo Library/Photo Researchers; **115b**, National Cancer Institute/Science Photo Library/Photo Researchers; **116**, Oliver Meckes/Photo Researchers; **118**, Richard Haynes; **120t**, Daemmrich/Stock Boston; **120b**, Thom Duncan/Adventure Photo; **121 both**, Custom Medical Stock; **122t** AP/Wide World Photos; **122b**, The Granger Collection, NY; **123t**, Liaison International; **123b**, Brad Nelson/Custom Medical Stock; **124**, Nicole Katodo/TSI; **125**, Prof. P. Motta/Dept. of Anatomy/University "La Sapienza", Rome/Science Photo Library/Photo Researchers.

Chapter 5
Pages 128–129, Mark Gibson/The Stock Market; **130t**, Richard Haynes; **130b**, Dick Dickinson/Photo Network; **132l**, Richard Haynes; **132 inset**, Eddy Gray/Science Photo Library/Photo Researchers; **133**, Richard Haynes; **136**, Paul Harris/TSI; **138**, J. Sohm/The Image Works; **139**, Russ Lappa; **140**, Spencer Jones/FPG International; **141**, Ken Karp; **142**, Al Bello/TSI; **143l**, Clark Overton/Phototake; **143m**, SIV/Photo Researchers; **143r**, Martin Rotker/Phototake; **144**, Smoke Free Educational Services; **145**,**148**, Richard Haynes; **150**, Ken Karp; **151**, Eddy Gray/Science Photo Library/Photo Researchers.

Chapter 6
Pages 154–155, Microworks/Phototake; **156t**, Richard Haynes; **156b**, The Granger Collection, NY; **157**, Pete Saloutos/The Stock Market; **158t**, CNRI/Science Photo Library/Photo Researchers; **158m**, Biozentrum/Science Photo Library/Photo Researchers; **158b**, Gucho/CNRI/Science Photo Library/Photo Researchers; **160t**, Mike Peres/Custom Medical Stock Photo; **160b**, Scott Camazine/Photo Researchers; **161**, Russ Lappa; **162**, Science Pictures Ltd./Science Photo Library/Photo Researchers; **163**, Lennart Nilsson/Boehringer Ingelheim International GmbH; **164**, Lori Adamski Peek/TSI; **166**, NIBSC/Science Photo Library/Photo Researchers; **167**, Jon Riley/TSI; **168**, **169**, Richard Haynes; **170t**, Russ Lappa; **170b**, CNRI/Science Photo Library/Photo Researchers; **171**, Aaron Haupt/Photo Researchers; **172t**, Historical Picture Service/Custom Medical Stock; **172b**, The Granger Collection, NY; **173t**, Granger Collection, NY; **173b**, Giraudon/Art Resource; **175t**, Richard Haynes; **175b**, Richard Haynes; **176l**, Ron Kimball; **176r**, Andrew Syred/Science Photo Library/Photo Researchers; **177**, Therisa Stack/Tom Stack & Associates; **178**, Dept. of Clinical Radiology, Salisbury District Hospital/Science Photo Library/Photo Researchers; **179**, Yoav levy/Phototake; **180**, Stevie Grand/Science Photo Library/Photo Researchers; **182t**, Richard Haynes; **182bl,182–183**, The Granger Collection, NY; **184**, Phil Savoie/The Picture Cube; **185**, Biozentrum/Science Photo Library/Photo Researchers.

Chapter 7
Pages 188–189, 1998 Magic Eye Inc.; **190t**, Richard Haynes; **190b**, Lee Snider/The Image Works; **191**, Gordon R. Gainer/The Stock Market; **192**, Biophoto Associates/Photo Researchers; **195**, **196t**, Richard Haynes; **196b**, Milton Feinberg/ The Picture Cube; **197**, Richard Haynes; **199**, Art Resouce; **200**, Tom Stewart/The Stock Market; **202**, William Sallaz/Duomo; **203**, Robert E. Daemmrich/ TSI; **204**, Superstock; **206t**, Prof. P. Motta/Dept. of Anatomy/U. "La Sapienza," Rome/Science Photo Library/Photo Researchers; **206b**, Lennart Nilsson; **208**, Renee Lynn/TSI; **210l**, Spencer Grant/The Picture Cube; **210r**, Lennart Nilsson; **211**, Mugshots/The Stock Market; **212t**, Russ Lappa; **212b**, Uniphoto; **213**, Tom Croke/Liaison International; **214**, David Young-Wolff/PhotoEdit; **218**, Index Stock; **220**, Bob Daemmrich/Stock Boston; **221**, Spencer Grant/The Picture Cube.

Chapter 8
Pages 224–225, Uniphoto; **226**, Keith Kent/Photo Researchers; **227l**, Chad Slattery/TSI; **227r**, Nancy Sheehan/The Picture Cube; **231**, Mitsuaki Iwago/Minden Pictures; **232 both**, Dr. Dennis Kunkel/Phototake; **235**, Prof. P.M. Motta & J. Van Blerkom/Science Photo Library/ Photo Researchers; **237tl**, Stephen R. Swinburne/Stock Boston; **237tm**, Stephen R. Swinburne/Stock Boston; **237b**, David Phillips/Science Photo Library/ Photo Researchers; **239**, Lennart Nilsson; **240**, Index Stock; **241l**, Roy Morsch/The Stock Market; **241r**, Frauke/Mauritius/H. Armstrong Roberts; **242l**, Penny Gentieu; **242r**, Elizabeth Hathol/The Stock Market; **243**, Don Semtzer/TSI; **244t**, Ken Karp; **244b**, Roy Morso/The Stock Market; **245l**, James D. Wilson/Liaison International; **245r**, Robert E. Daemmrich/TSI; **246**, Mark Burnett/ Photo Researchers; **247**, Bruce Dale/National Geographic Society; **248**, David Young-Wolff/Photo Edit; **249**, David Young Wolff/TSI; **251t** David Phillips/Science Photo Library/ Photo Researchers; **251b**, Penny Gentieu.

Interdisciplinary Exploration
Page 254t, Duomo; **254b**, Scala/Art Resource; **255**, Louvre, Dpt. des Antiquités Grecques/Romaines, Paris, France. Photograph by Erich Lessing/Art Resource; **256**, Tony Duffy/Allsport USA; **257**, Pascal Rondeau/Allsport USA; **258–259**, Mark C. Burnett/Stock Boston/PNI;

Skills Handbook
Page 260, Mike Moreland/Photo Network; **261t**, Foodpix; **261m**, Richard Haynes; **261b**, Russ Lappa; **264**, Richard Haynes; **266**, Ron Kimball; **267**, Renee Lynn/Photo Researchers.